# APPLE GRAPHICS
## Activities Handbook

*Harold J. Bailey*      *J. Edward Kerlin*

Department of Mathematics & Computer Science
Bloomsburg University
Bloomsburg, PA

D1494113

**Robert J. Brady Co., Bowie, MD 20715**
**A Prentice-Hall Publishing and Communications Company**

Editor-in-Chief: David Culverwell
Acquisitions Editor: Gisele Asher
Production Editor/Text Design: Paula Huber
Art Director/Cover Design: Don Sellers
Assistant Art Director: Bernard Vervin

Typesetter: Creative Communications Corp., Baltimore, MD
Printer: R.R.Donnelley and Sons Co., Harrisonburg, VA
Typefaces: Caledonia (text), Bookman (display), Typewriter (programs)

---

### Note to Authors

Do you have a manuscript or a software program related to
personal computers? Do you have an idea for developing such
a project? If so, we would like to hear from you. The Brady
Co. produces a complete range of books and applications software for the personal computer market. We invite you to write
to David Culverwell, Editor-in-Chief, Robert J. Brady Co.,
Bowie, Maryland 20715.

---

Apple Graphics Activities Handbook

Library of Congress Cataloging in Publication Data

Bailey, Harold J., 1940–
    Apple graphics.
    Includes index.
    1. Computer graphics. 2. Apple II (Computer)—Programming. 3. Apple IIe (Computer—
Programming. 4. Franklin computer—Programming. I. Kerlin, J. Edward, 1944–    . II.
Title.
T385.B34    1983        001.64'43        83-21406

ISBN 0-89303-308-1

Prentice-Hall International, Inc., London
Prentice-Hall Canada, Inc., Scarborough, Ontario
Prentice-Hall of Australia, Pty., Ltd., Sydney
Prentice-Hall of India Private Limited, New Delhi
Prentice-Hall of Japan, Inc., Tokyo
Prentice-Hall of Southeast Asia Pte. Ltd., Singapore
Whitehall Books, Limited, Petone, New Zealand
Editora Prentice-Hall Do Brasil LTDA., Rio de Janeiro

Printed in the United States of America

84 85 86 87 89 90 91 92 93    10 9 8 7 6 5 4 3 2

# Contents

## 1  LOW RESOLUTION GRAPHICS

## 2  HIGH RESOLUTION GRAPHICS

## Optional Program Diskette

A diskette containing the COMPREHENSIVE EXAMPLES and answers to selected EXERCISES is available from the publisher. The principle advantage of owning this diskette is to eliminate the typing of lengthy programs. For a copy of the diskette, see the order form inserted in this book.

Copies will be on a 16-sector diskette and will execute on any 48K Apple II Plus®, Apple IIe®, or Franklin ACE 1000® or 1200 system.

Apple, Apple II, Apple II Plus, Apple IIe, and Applesoft are trademarks of Apple Computer Corp. Franklin ACE 1000 and Franklin ACE 1200 are trademarks of Franklin Computer Corp.

## Limits of Liability and Disclaimer of Warranty

The authors and publisher of this book have used their best efforts in preparing this book and the programs contained in it. These efforts include the development, research, and testing of the theories and programs to determine their effectiveness. The authors and publisher make no warranty of any kind, expressed or implied, with regard to these programs or the documentation contained in this book. The authors and publisher shall not be liable in any event for incidental or consequential damages in connection with, or arising out of, the furnishing, performance, or use of these programs.

# Preface

Since the beginning of our existence, we have attempted to graphically display our thoughts. The necessity of using images to communicate ideas is evidenced as far back as the cave drawings of the Stone Ages. In today's world, detailed artistic designs are developed with light pens on video screens, graphics systems, and the like.

The advent of the microcomputer offers another medium by which the cliche "a picture is worth a thousand words" can be demonstrated. While low cost microcomputer systems cannot compete with sophisticated graphics systems, some are quite capable of displaying images acceptable for many purposes. Unfortunately, each computer system with graphic capabilities also has a unique and often complex way of handling it.

This book deals with creating graphics on a 48K RAM Apple II Plus, Apple IIe, or Franklin 1000 or 1200 microcomputer system, using the Applesoft BASIC language. The graphics created in the book are most effectively displayed with a color monitor. The book assumes you have no familiarity with graphics, but are familiar with Applesoft.

The practical approach to learning graphics concepts and techniques, via "hands-on" activities, makes this book suitable for anyone, particularly the novice.

Chapter 1 presents a comprehensive coverage of low resolution graphics, a mode which is easy to use and understand. Low resolution graphics also has many useful applications when precision designs are not required. High resolution graphics, as covered in Chapter 2, demonstrates how more precise images can be displayed. Both Chapters 1 and 2 assume the reader is inexperienced; consequently, they are introductory in nature. Each begins with the simple display of primitive images, then extends to the more complex graphing techniques of animation and the effective use of color. While it is suggested the reader follow the book in its intended sequential pattern, low resolution graphics in Chapter 1 could be omitted without detracting from the continuity of the book.

Chapters 3, 4, and 5 should be studied in the presented order. Chapter 3 investigates the more involved aspects of graphics such as shapes and a high resolution character generator, and deals with making better use of allocated memory. Chapter 4 involves scaling, clipping, and plotting curves in two dimensions. Three-dimensional graphics is discussed in Chapter 5.

While no treatment of two- and three-dimensional graphics can be completely devoid of mathematics, considerable effort has been made to minimize the mathematical background necessary to develop the techniques covered in Chapters 4 and 5. As a result, more advanced three-dimensional applications, such as hidden line and surface techniques (which involve more sophisticated mathematics) are not included in this book.

Each chapter consists of a collection of instructional activities. These carefully sequenced activities help the reader progress in a deliberate manner, culminating in a comprehensive understanding of Applesoft graphics. The structure of each activity includes five sections:

LEARNING BY DISCOVERY
DISCUSSION

COMPREHENSIVE EXAMPLE
EXERCISE
CHALLENGE

The LEARNING BY DISCOVERY section begins with a statement of the activity objective, followed by a series of "hands-on" experiences. The reader enters Applesoft commands and then is asked to describe (or discover) the resulting displays. These exercises demonstrate both the proper usage and common errors associated with the activity objective. The reader is encouraged to write descriptions, notes, and observations in the book.

A narrative reinforcement of the activity experience occurs in the DISCUSSION section. The reader should first complete the activity to understand the discussion more readily.

The COMPREHENSIVE EXAMPLE provides another Applesoft program to reinforce the correct application of the activity objective. This section also demonstrates another imaginative graphics example, which is intended to spark enthusiasm and interest in the reader to develop innovative graphic designs.

The EXERCISE section permits the reader to demonstrate an understanding of the activity objective by writing an Applesoft program for a given situation.

Finally, the CHALLENGE section presents one more exercise for the reader, but at a more advanced level.

Many of the programs contain remarks (REM statements) to assist the reader in understanding the program logic. It is not necessary to type these remarks when entering program segments. Because of the progressive nature of each activity, the reader must not diverge from the line numbering used to sequence program statements.

# Acknowledgments

The writing of this book was motivated by students who were less than satisfied with studying graphics using traditional teaching methods and whose mathematical backgrounds did not permit learning from existing materials. The development of these "hands-on" activities resulted in an interactive and meaningful educational experience.

Much appreciation is expressed to our students for serving as a catalyst to the project and for reviewing the prepared materials. A special thanks must be given to colleague Julie Abell for her dedicated effort in proofreading and critiquing the manuscript.

Finally, we are particularly grateful to our wives, Linda and Kathy, for their typing and editorial comments, as well as their patience and understanding, during this entire project.

# DEDICATION

This book is dedicated to the two individuals who have been most influential in our professional development.

*The late Richard J. Kohlmeyer*

and

*Bernard R. Gelbaum*
Suny at Buffalo, New York

# Low Resolution Graphics

## MODULE 1A   Fundamental Low Resolution Commands

### ACTIVITY 1.1   Plotting Points on the Mixed Graphics Screen

**LEARNING BY DISCOVERY**   This activity introduces the drawing of the smallest possible diagram on the low resolution graphics mixed screen.

1.  Enter the following commands.

```
NEW
HOME
10  GR
30  PLOT 30, 5
RUN
```

Describe what happens. _____

2.  Add line 20 as follows:

```
TEXT : HOME
20  COLOR = 1
LIST
RUN
```

Observe the screen display.
What geometric object appears? _____
What color is the object? _____
Where is the object located? _____

1

3. Retype lines 20 and 30 and add line 40 as follows:

```
TEXT : HOME
20   COLOR = 9
30   PLOT 2, 25
40   PRINT "AN ORANGE BRICK"
LIST
RUN
```

Observe the screen display.

What color is the object? _____

Where is the object located? _____

Where does the message appear? _____

4. Retype line 30 as follows:

```
TEXT : HOME
30   PLOT 40, 5
LIST
RUN
```

Describe what happens. _____

5. Retype line 30 as follows:

```
TEXT : HOME
30 PLOT 5, 40
LIST
RUN
```

Describe what happens. _____

**NOTE:**   The typing of LIST before each RUN is suggested so the reader can observe the modified program as additions and deletions are made. For the sake of brevity, the LIST command will be omitted throughout the remainder of the book, but should be used when needed.

**DISCUSSION**   The GR command converts the screen to low resolution mixed graphics mode. Figure 1.1.1 displays the layout and boundary limits of the mixed graphics screen.

When GR is executed, the graphics portion of the screen is cleared to black and the cursor is moved to the bottom of the text window.

COLOR = sets the color for low resolution graphics. Numerals 0 through 15 are used to obtain the various hues. Table 1.1.1 defines the available color codes.

The PLOT command displays a rectangular "brick" of a specified color on the screen at a particular column and row. If the COLOR command is omitted, as in Section 1, the PLOT command results in an invisible "brick," since GR sets the color to black(0).

In Section 1, PLOT 30, 5 displays the brick at the intersection of column 30 and row 5. PLOT 40, 5 in Section 4 gives an error message, since 40 is beyond the allowable column limits of 0 through 39. PLOT 5, 40 in Section 5 gives no graphics display, since row 40 is outside the graphics area, in the text window area.

In Section 3, the PRINT command causes a message to appear at the bottom of the text window.

The TEXT command returns the screen to full screen text mode from graphics mode. The strange screen display caused by the TEXT command is the textual representation of the graphics mode, since both low resolution graphics and the text area share the same APPLE memory locations. By following the TEXT command with the HOME command, this distracting nonsense is cleared from the screen.

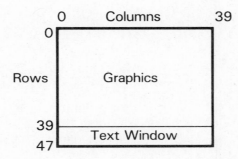

Figure 1.1.1

| COLOR | NUMERAL |
|---|---|
| Black | 0 |
| Magenta | 1 |
| Dark blue | 2 |
| Purple | 3 |
| Dark green | 4 |
| Gray 1 | 5 |
| Medium blue | 6 |
| Light blue | 7 |
| Brown | 8 |
| Orange | 9 |
| Gray 2 | 10 |
| Pink | 11 |
| Light green | 12 |
| Yellow | 13 |
| Aqua | 14 |
| White | 15 |

Table 1.1.1

**COMPREHENSIVE EXAMPLE**    Study the following APPLESOFT program to determine the screen display. Check your answer by entering the program into the computer. Note: INT (16 * RND (1)) randomly generates numbers 0 through 15.

```
TEXT : HOME : NEW
10   REM ******************************
11   REM *            CE1.1           *
12   REM ******************************
15   GR
20   FOR I = 0 TO 39
30   COLOR = INT (16 * RND (1))
40   PLOT I, I
50   NEXT
60   PRINT "SCOTTISH LACE"
65   GET Q$ : TEXT : HOME : REM USER PRESS ANY KEY TO
     COMPLETE PROGRAM
70   END
```

**Check Your Comprehension**

What lines control the number of "beads" in the lace? _____

What APPLESOFT commands provide for the different colored "bead?" _____

Describe the coordinates of each "bead." _____

**NOTE:**  It is good style to end all APPLESOFT programs with the commands listed on line 65. The GET Q$ command stops the execution of the program and awaits any keyboard response by the user. This technique permits the user to control the duration of the screen display. The TEXT and HOME commands return the computer to normal text mode with a clear screen.

**EXERCISE**  Write a program to place a brick, each of a different color, in the four corners of the low resolution screen with the message "FOUR BRICKS" appearing in the text window.

**CHALLENGE**  Write a program that randomly places twenty different randomly generated colored "bricks" on the screen.

## ACTIVITY 1.2   Drawing Lines on the Mixed Graphics Screen

**LEARNING BY DISCOVERY**  This activity introduces the drawing of horizontal and vertical lines on the low resolution mixed graphics screen.

1. Enter the following commands.

```
TEXT : HOME : NEW
20   GR
```

```
30   COLOR = 14
40   HLIN 5, 30 AT 10
50   PRINT "AN AQUA HORIZONTAL LINE"
RUN
```

Observe the screen display.

What is the result of an HLIN command? _____

Estimate the length of the line in terms of "bricks." _____

What is the purpose of the 10 in line 40? _____

2. Retype lines 30, 40, 50 and add line 10 as follows:

```
TEXT : HOME
10   HOME
30   COLOR = 11
40   VLIN 15, 35 AT 20
50   PRINT "A PINK VERTICAL LINE"
RUN
```

Observe the screen display.

What is the result of a VLIN command? _____

Estimate the length of the line in terms of "bricks."_____

What is the purpose of the 20 in line 40? _____

What is the purpose of the HOME command? _____

3. Enter the following commands.

```
TEXT : HOME : NEW
10   HOME
15   GR
20   COLOR = 4
25   HLIN 0, 39 AT 0
30   VLIN 0, 39 AT 39
35   HLIN 0, 39 AT 39
40   VLIN 0, 39 AT 0
RUN
```

Describe what happens. _____

4. Enter the following commands.

```
TEXT : HOME : NEW
10   HOME
15   GR
20   COLOR = 12
25   FOR I =  10 TO 30
30   HLIN 12, 33 AT I
35   NEXT
```

RUN

Describe what happens. _____

**DISCUSSION**    The HLIN and VLIN commands are used, respectively, to draw horizontal and vertical lines on the screen in low resolution graphics.

In Section 1, the command, HLIN 5, 30 AT 10 draws a horizontal line from column 5 to column 30 at row 10. The length of this line is 26 (or (30 − 5) + 1) "bricks." VLIN 15, 35 AT 20 in Section 2 draws a vertical line from row 15 to row 35 at column 20, giving a length of 21 (or (35 − 15) + 1) "bricks."

Both the VLIN and HLIN commands must be preceded by the GR command (to establish graphics mode) and the COLOR command (to specify the color of the line). Since GR establishes a mixed graphics screen, any PRINT statements cause the messages to appear in the text window.

The HOME command introduced in Section 2 clears the text window, removing the typing of the RUN command. It is good style to begin all programs with the HOME command.

In Section 3, a sequence of HLIN and VLIN commands is used to display a border on the screen. Section 4 demonstrates that shaded regions can be displayed by including an HLIN or VLIN command in a loop.

**COMPREHENSIVE EXAMPLE**    Study the following APPLESOFT program to determine the screen display. Check your answer by entering the program into the computer.

```
NEW
10    REM ********************************
11    REM *           CE1.2            *
12    REM ********************************
15    HOME
20    GR
25    COLOR = 2
30    FOR I = 0 TO 39
40    VLIN 0, 39 AT I
50    NEXT
60    COLOR = 15
70    HLIN 8, 10 AT 7
75    HLIN 7, 11 AT 8
80    HLIN 7, 12 AT 9
85    HLIN 8, 11 AT 10
90    HLIN 9, 10 AT 11
95    PRINT "A NEARLY PERFECT SKY"
97    GET Q$ : TEXT : HOME
99    END
```

**Check Your Comprehension**

What lines color the sky blue? _____

Describe the method used to color the sky._____

What lines draw the cloud? _____

**EXERCISE**   Write a program to place a graphics yellow "H" in the center of the screen with a height of 11 "bricks," a width of 6 "bricks," and with the message "CAPITAL H".

**CHALLENGE**   Write a program that uses PLOT, HLIN, and VLIN commands to draw a pink face with blue eyes, a black nose, magenta lips, and brown ears.

# ACTIVITY 1.3   Subsequent Drawing on the Mixed Graphics Screen

**LEARNING BY DISCOVERY**   This activity demonstrates how to effectively change the text window and graphics portion of the low resolution screen when drawing a sequence of graphics displays.

1. Enter the following commands.

```
NEW : HOME
10   HOME
15   GOTO 40
20   FOR I = 0 TO 10
25   HLIN 15 - I, 15 + I AT 15 + I
30   NEXT I
35   RETURN
40   GR : COLOR = 9
45   GOSUB 20
50   PRINT "AN ORANGE TRIANGLE"
55   GET Q$ : REM PRESS ANY KEY TO CONTINUE
RUN
```

   Observe the screen display.
   Describe the position of the message within the text window. _____
   Is a cursor or prompt visible on the screen? _____
   Now press any key and describe the position of the message and cursor within the text window. _____

2. Add lines 60 through 75 as follows:

```
TEXT : HOME
60   COLOR = 3
65   GOSUB 20
70   PRINT "A VIOLET TRIANGLE"
75   GET Q$
RUN
```

Observe the screen display.

How many lines appear in the text window? _____

Describe how the lines are positioned within this window. _____

3. Retype line 60 as follows:

```
TEXT : HOME
60  HOME : COLOR = 3
RUN
```

Observe the screen display.

How many lines appear in the text window? _____

Where is it positioned within the text window? _____

4. Add line 67 as follows:

```
TEXT : HOME
67  VTAB 24
RUN
```

Observe the screen display.

Where is the message positioned now? _____

5. Add lines 80 through 98 as follows:

```
TEXT : HOME
80  HOME : COLOR = 10
85  FOR I = 1 TO 3
90  VLIN 5, 25 AT 13 + I
95  NEXT I
97  VTAB 24
98  PRINT "A GRAY RECTANGLE"
RUN
```

Observe the screen displays.

How many different screen displays occur? _____

Describe the last screen display. _____

6. Add line 77 as follows:

```
TEXT : HOME
77  GR
RUN
```

Observe the screen displays.

Describe the last screen display. _____

**DISCUSSION**   When developing a sequence of graphic screen displays, there are three possible effects available when progressing from one frame to the next:

1. The graphics portion of the screen changes and the text window changes;

2. The graphics portion of the screen changes and the text window remains the same, or;

3. The graphics portion of the screen remains the same and the text window changes.

A thorough understanding of how the HOME and GR commands affect both the text window and the graphics portion of the screen will facilitate the use of these three modes.

The text window can display a maximum of four lines of messages, labelled lines 21, 22, 23, and 24. Following a GR command, and if a VTAB statement is not used, PRINT messages appear (or scroll) in sequence from the bottom of the text window to the top (in the order 24, 23, 22, 21). An attempt to display more than four lines of text will result in earlier PRINTed lines being scrolled above the text window.

In Section 1, the message "AN ORANGE TRIANGLE" first appears toward the bottom of the screen, but scrolls upward one line to make room for the cursor when you depress a key on the keyboard, as requested. The GET command causes execution of the program to stop until the user presses any key. It is a useful command for controlling the display of each successive frame, at a speed determined by the user.

When changing from one frame to another, the text window from the previous frame can be cleared by using the HOME command, as was illustrated in Section 3. Otherwise, an accumulative scrolling of the messages will occur, as in Section 2. Note that any HOME command following the GR command positions the message at the top of the text window(line 21) and may be otherwise positioned by an appropriate VTAB command, as is used in Section 4.

The reader should also note the use of a subroutine in lines 20 through 30. Rather than write the code for drawing the triangle twice, two frames are developed by changing colors prior to accessing the subroutine.

One can also continue the drawing of a previously created diagram, as is demonstrated in Section 5, or begin the drawing of a completely different diagram. In Section 5, however, it would have been more appropriate to clear the graphics from the previous frame before preparing the new frame, as is corrected in Section 6. If a completely new screen display is desired, both the HOME and GR commands are required prior to the commands creating the new frame. Make sure you remember to include a COLOR = statement after each GR command.

**COMPREHENSIVE EXAMPLE**   Study the following APPLESOFT program to determine the sequence of screen displays. Check your answer by entering the program into the computer.

```
TEXT : HOME : NEW
100  REM ****************************************
101  REM *              CE1.3                   *
102  REM ****************************************
105  HOME
110  GOTO 300
150  VLIN 16, 24 AT 15 : PLOT 16, 16 : PLOT 16, 24
160  RETURN
```

```
200   VLIN 16, 24 AT 25 : PLOT 24, 16 : PLOT 24, 24
210   RETURN
300   HOME : GR : COLOR = 7
310   GOSUB 150
320   VTAB 22 : PRINT "A LEFT BRACKET"
330   GET Q$
340   HOME : GR : COLOR = 7
350   GOSUB 200
360   VTAB 22 : PRINT "A RIGHT BRACKET"
370   GET Q$
380   HOME : GR : COLOR = 7
390   GOSUB 150 : GOSUB 200
400   VTAB 22 : PRINT "BOTH BRACKETS"
410   GET Q$ : TEXT : HOME
RUN
```

## Check Your Comprehension

What is the first graphics display? _____

What is the beginning line number of the subroutine that draws the right bracket? _____

What is the last message to appear within the text window? _____

_____

What is the purpose of the GET Q$ command in lines 330 and 370?

_____

**EXERCISE**   Write a program which displays the two frames illustrated in Exhibit 1.3.1 in the given order. Use subroutines to create the background colors and to create the triangle. Be sure to include the indicated messages on lines 22 and 23 of the text window.

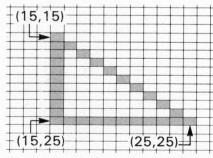

BLACK TRIANGLE ON
ORANGE BACKGROUND
FRAME 1

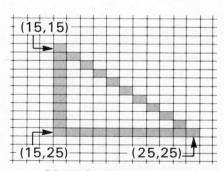

ORANGE TRIANGLE ON
BLACK BACKGROUND
FRAME 2

Exhibit 1.3.1

**CHALLENGE** Write a program which alternates the drawing of a red "X" and then an orange "T" ten times. On line 21 of the text window, include the printing of a corresponding message, either "A RED X" or "AN ORANGE T".

# ACTIVITY 1.4   Optimizing the View of the Text Window

**LEARNING BY DISCOVERY** This activity demonstrates how to enhance the capabilities of using the text window on the low resolution graphics screen.

1. Enter the following commands.

```
NEW : HOME
100   HOME : GOTO 300
150   VTAB 24
160   PRINT "PRESS THE SPACE BAR TO CONTINUE"
170   GET Q$
180   RETURN
300   GR : COLOR = 2
310   HLIN 13, 17 AT 15 : HLIN 13, 17 AT 20 : VLIN 15, 25 AT
      13 : VLIN 15, 25 AT 17
320   VTAB 22
330   PRINT "AN 'A'"
340   GOSUB 150
RUN
```

Describe the text window display. _____

2. Retype lines 150 and 320 as follows:

```
TEXT : HOME
150   VTAB 24 : HTAB 5
320   VTAB 22 : HTAB 17
RUN
```

Describe what change occurs in the text window display. _____

3. Retype line 320 as follows:

```
TEXT : HOME
320   VTAB 21 : HTAB 18
RUN
```

Describe what change occurs in the text window display. _____

4. Retype line 160 as follows:

```
TEXT : HOME
160   PRINT "HIT THE SPACE BAR TO CONTINUE";
RUN
```

Describe what change occurs in the text window display. _____

5. Add lines 350 through 410 as follows:

```
TEXT : HOME
350   COLOR = 13
360   HLIN 23, 27 AT 15 : VLIN 15, 25 AT 25
370   VTAB 22 : HTAB 13
380   PRINT "AND THEN A 'T'"
390   VTAB 23 : HTAB 15
400   PRINT "SPELLS 'AT'"
410   GOSUB 150
420   TEXT : HOME
RUN
```

Observe the screen display.

How many lines of text appear? _____

What is the position of the cursor? _____

6. Retype line 160 as follows:

```
160   PRINT "PRESS THE SPACE BAR TO CONTINUE"
RUN
```

Observe the screen display.

How many lines of text appear? _____

What is the position of the cursor? _____

**DISCUSSION**   In ACTIVITY 1.3, we stated it was possible to display four lines of messages within the text window. This is possible only if the PRINT statement, which includes the alphanumeric string to appear on line 24, is completed with a semicolon (;). The semicolon retains the cursor on the same line, and does not cause the message on line 21 to scroll above the text window. In this activity, the message "PRESS THE SPACE BAR TO CONTINUE" is to appear on line 24 of the text window. The various inclusions and omissions of the semicolon after the string throughout the various sections of the activity demonstrate both the desired and undesired forms of output.

The HTAB statement is useful for centering each message on the 40 character line. For example, the six character string "AN 'A' " is centered with HTAB 17 (i.e., 17 = (40 − 6) / 2). The COMPREHENSIVE EXAMPLE introduces a general subroutine which uses string manipulation to center any message without having to individually perform the arithmetic calculations described above.

**COMPREHENSIVE EXAMPLE**   Study the following APPLESOFT program to determine the screen display. Check your answer by entering the program in the computer. Lines 140 through 170 provide a subroutine which centers each message on a line within the text window.

```
NEW
100   REM ****************************************
101   REM *              CE1.4                   *
102   REM ****************************************
130   HOME : GOTO 300
140   REM CENTER MESSAGES SUBROUTINE
150   C = (40 - LEN (A$)) / 2
170   RETURN
200   VTAB 24 : HTAB 5
210   PRINT "PRESS THE SPACE BAR TO CONTINUE";
220   GET Q$ : TEXT : HOME
230   RETURN
300   GR : COLOR = 6
310   HLIN 0, 39 AT 0 : HLIN 0, 39 AT 39
320   VLIN 0, 39 AT 0 : VLIN 0, 39 AT 39
330   COLOR = 11
340   FOR I = 1 TO 38
350   PLOT I, I
360   PLOT 39 - I, I
370   NEXT I
380   A$ = "A PINK X"
390   GOSUB 150
400   VTAB 21 : HTAB C : PRINT A$
410   A$ = "CENTERED IN A"
420   GOSUB 150
430   VTAB 22 : HTAB C : PRINT A$
440   A$ = "MEDIUM BLUE FRAME"
450   GOSUB 150
460   VTAB 23 : HTAB C : PRINT A$
470   GOSUB 200
480   END
```

**Check Your Comprehension**

What line numbers are used to draw the "x?" _____

How many lines of messages appear within the text window? _____

What is the purpose of defining strings in lines 380, 410, and 440? _____

**EXERCISE**   Write a program which displays the diagram illustrated in Exhibit 1.4.1 shaded in green, with white boundaries at the given coordinates, and the four given lines of text centered within the text window.

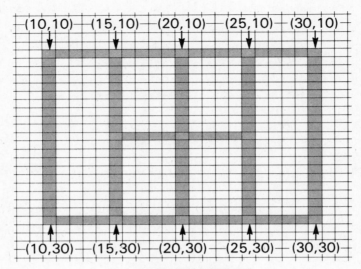

A TENNIS COURT
FOR
SINGLES' PLAY
HIT THE SPACE BAR TO CONTINUE

Exhibit 1.4.1

**CHALLENGE**   Write a program which displays the diagram illustrated in Exhibit 1.4.2. Color the poles brown, the sign yellow, and the word "END" green. Center the four messages within the text window.

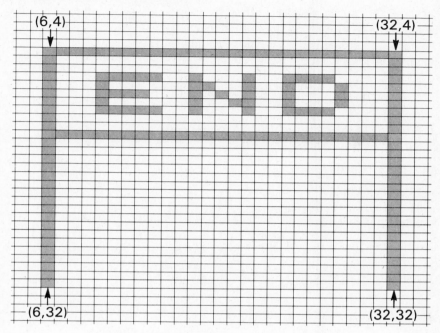

THE WINNER WILL BE FIRST
TO CROSS THE
FINISH LINE
PRESS THE SPACE BAR TO CONTINUE

Exhibit 1.4.2

# ACTIVITY 1.5   Obtaining Full Screen Low Resolution Graphics

**LEARNING BY DISCOVERY**   This activity demonstrates how the entire screen can be used for low resolution graphics, without having a text window.

1.  Enter the following commands.

```
NEW
10   HOME
20   GR
30   COLOR = 2
```

```
40   FOR I = 0 TO 39
50   HLIN 0, 39 AT I
60   NEXT
RUN
```

Describe the appearance of the text window. _____

2. Retype line 40 as follows:

```
TEXT : HOME
40   FOR I = 0 TO 47
RUN
```

Describe the appearance of the text window. _____

3. Add line 25 as follows:

```
TEXT : HOME
25   POKE −16302, 0
RUN
```

Describe the appearance of the text window. _____

4. Add line 70 as follows:

```
TEXT : HOME
70   GET Q$ : TEXT : HOME
RUN
```

Describe the appearance of the text window. _____

5. Retype line 40 as follows:

```
40   FOR I = 0 TO 39
RUN
```

Describe the appearance of the text window. _____

6. Retype line 25 as follows:

```
25   POKE −16302, 0 : CALL −1998
RUN
```

Describe the appearance of the text window. _____

7. Retype lines 40 and 70 and add line 80 as follows:

```
40   FOR I = 0 TO 47
70   FOR I = 1 TO 3000 : NEXT
80   TEXT : HOME
RUN
```

Describe the appearance of the text window. _____

**DISCUSSION**   The sequence of commands GR : POKE  −16302, 0 converts the screen display to full graphics mode. Figure 1.5.1 illustrates that the graphics screen is extended from 40 to 48 rows of graphics. While full screen graphics is particularly useful for exhibiting introductory titles for computer assisted lessons, pictures, and other interesting displays, there are several limitations which must be examined.

One difficulty in using the full graphics mode is determining an appropriate procedure by which to control the progression from one frame to the next, where the first frame uses full screen graphics. The approach used in Section 4 is to include the GET command to stop the execution of the program. Since there is no text window, no messages can be provided to inform the user to hit a key to continue. Also, the GET command creates the displeasing presence of a cursor on the bottom left corner of the screen.

An alternative procedure is to include an empty delay loop, as in Section 7, to permit the viewing of the screen for a designated period before automatically moving to the next frame. The concern here is the duration of the delay must be appropriate for all users.

A strange band of horizontal lines appears in the text window in Section 5, when the graphics screen is only partially filled but in full graphics mode. This problem is quickly corrected in Section 6 by including the CALL −1998 command. CALL −1998 clears the entire screen to black when in low resolution, full graphics mode.

It is recommended, for aesthetic and informative purposes, that the following conditions be included when using full screen low resolution graphics:

  1.  The sequence of commands, GR : POKE  −16302, 0 : CALL −1998;

  2.  A delay rather than a GET command to control the termination of a frame, and;

  3.  The sequence, TEXT : HOME,  to clear the screen for the next frame.

The mysterious POKE and CALL commands that appear throughout the APPLESOFT manual are quite puzzling to beginning programmers. The numbers −16302 and −1998 are artificial representations of memory locations in Apple RAM. For the time being, simply accept their described functions. A much more comprehensive coverage of POKEing and CALLing other important memory locations pertaining to graphics appears in CHAPTER 2.

Exhibit 1.5.1 provides a summary in flow chart form of the low resolution graphics commands covered thus far.

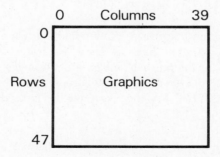

Figure 1.5.1

**COMPREHENSIVE EXAMPLE**   The following program introduces a technique by which a rectangular region is shaded in a specific color by providing the coordinates of the opposite corners of the rectangle as data. Study the program to determine the screen display. Check your answer by entering the program in the computer.

```
NEW
100   REM *****************************************
101   REM *              CE 1.5                   *
102   REM *****************************************
110   HOME : GOTO 300
120   REM DRAW A RECTANGULAR REGION
125   COLOR = C1
140   FOR I = Y2 TO Y1
150   HLIN X1, X2 AT I
160   NEXT
170   RETURN
300   GR : POKE -16302, 0 : CALL -1998
305   C1 = 3
310   FOR J = 1 TO 4
320   REM ENTER OPPOSITE COORDINATES
330   READ X1, Y1, X2, Y2
340   C1 = C1 + 2
350   GOSUB 125
360   NEXT
370   FOR J = 1 TO 3000 : NEXT
380   TEXT : HOME
500   DATA 0, 23, 19, 0 : REM UPPER LEFT RECT.
510   DATA 20, 23, 39, 0 : REM UPPER RIGHT RECT.
520   DATA 0, 47, 19, 24 : REM LOWER LEFT RECT.
530   DATA 20, 47, 39, 24 : REM LOWER RIGHT RECT.
540   END
```

## Check Your Comprehension

What do the commands in line 300 accomplish? _____

What is the purpose of line 370? _____

What line number controls the changing of colors? _____

**EXERCISE**   Write a program that draws a low resolution white frame in full graphics mode, with the upper interior half of the white frame shaded in dark blue (COLOR = 2) and the lower interior half shaded in light green (COLOR = 12). Use the method of defining coordinates for opposite corners as data demonstrated in the COMPREHENSIVE EXAMPLE. Use the recommended procedures for drawing on the full graphics screen.

**CHALLENGE**   Write a program that draws a quilted pattern in full graphics mode.

Divide the screen so the quilt consists of 64 randomly colored rectangles (8 rows by 8 columns).

## LOW RESOLUTION SCREEN DISPLAY

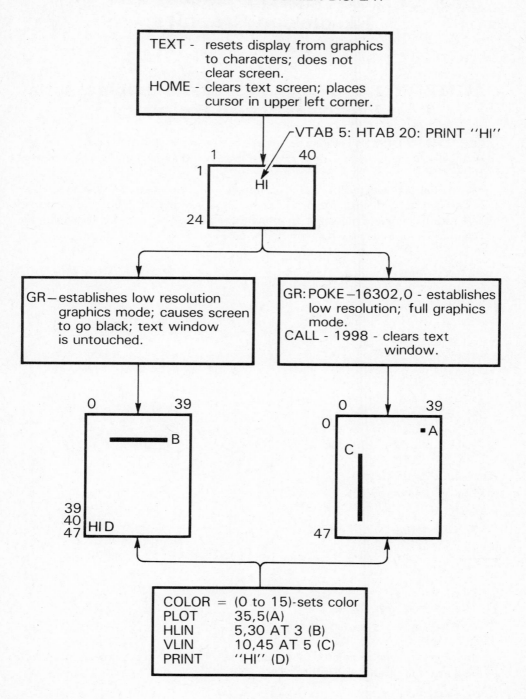

TEXT - resets display from graphics
to characters; does not
clear screen.
HOME - clears text screen; places
cursor in upper left corner.

VTAB 5: HTAB 20: PRINT "HI"

GR — establishes low resolution
graphics mode; causes screen
to go black; text window
is untouched.

GR: POKE —16302,0 - establishes
low resolution; full graphics
mode.
CALL - 1998 - clears text
window.

COLOR = (0 to 15)-sets color
PLOT     35,5(A)
HLIN     5,30 AT 3 (B)
VLIN     10,45 AT 5 (C)
PRINT    "HI" (D)

Exhibit 1.5.1

# MODULE 1B   Special Effects with Low Resolution Graphics

## ACTIVITY 1.6   Designing Artistic Graphics for a Particular Screen Position

**LEARNING BY DISCOVERY**    The purpose of this activity is to demonstrate a procedure by which the drawing of more involved low resolution diagrams can be achieved.

1. When the following APPLESOFT commands are executed, the debonair fellow illustrated (solid shaded region) in Exhibit 1.6.1 is displayed. Study the command for each line number in relation to its indicated location on the grid. Then enter the commands to display the diagram on the screen.

```
NEW
100  HOME : GR
110  COLOR = 11
120  HLIN 18, 22 AT 5
130  HLIN 18, 22 AT 6
140  HLIN 18, 22 AT 7
150  FOR I = 1 TO 4
160  HLIN 17, 23 AT I + 7
170  NEXT I
180  PLOT 20, 12
190  COLOR = 3
200  FOR I = 1 TO 4
205  HLIN 17, 23 AT I + 12
210  NEXT I
220  HLIN 18, 22 AT 17
230  COLOR = 7
240  VLIN 18, 22 AT 19
250  VLIN 18, 22 AT 21
260  COLOR = 15
270  HLIN 17, 19 AT 23
280  HLIN 21, 23 AT 23
RUN
```

Observe the screen display.

What figure is beginning to form? _____

2. Add the following commands to give our debonair fellow eyes, a nose, a smile, ears, and arms, illustrated in Exhibit 1.6.1 by X's.

```
TEXT : HOME
290  COLOR = 2 : REM EYES
```

```
300   PLOT 19, 6 : PLOT 21, 6
310   COLOR = 11 : REM CHEEKS
320   VLIN 9, 10 AT 16: VLIN 9, 10 AT 24
330   COLOR = 2 : REM SMILE AND NOSE
340   PLOT 20, 8
350   HLIN 19, 21 AT 10 : PLOT 18, 9 : PLOT 22, 9
360   COLOR = 14 : REM ARMS
370   HLIN 14, 16 AT 14 : PLOT 14, 13 : HLIN 24, 26 AT 14 :
      PLOT 26, 13
RUN
```

Compare the diagram on the screen display with that illustrated in Exhibit 1.6.1.

What is still missing on the screen display? _____

3. Now add the following commands to give our gentleman a hat as illustrated by the dots (. . .) in Exhibit 1.6.1.

```
TEXT : HOME
380   COLOR = 12 : REM HAT
390   FOR I = 1 TO 3
400   HLIN 18, 22 AT I
410   NEXT
420   HLIN 16, 24 AT 4
RUN
```

Observe the screen display.

Are you pleased with the final product? _____

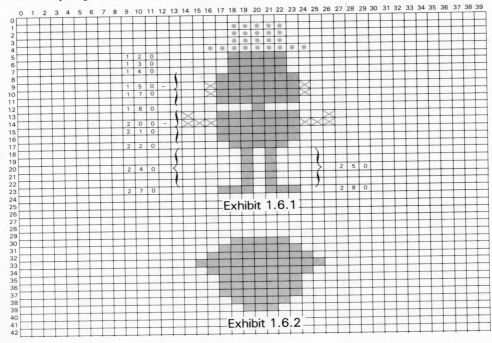

Exhibit 1.6.1

Exhibit 1.6.2

**DISCUSSION**   The simple use of HLIN, VLIN, PLOT, and COLOR commands offers an opportunity for creative and entertaining graphics. The provided graph paper represents an approximation of the low resolution screen for a 13 inch diagonal TV or monitor. Each rectangle represents a possible position for a low resolution PLOT in any of the 1920 cells in full graphics mode or 1600 cells in mixed graphics mode. Any diagram drawn on the graph paper can be displayed on the screen with the same approximate size, shape, and location by appropriately labelling the coordinates of the cells used in the diagram.

The changing of colors in combination with HLIN, VLIN, and PLOT commands provides the first step in creating our debonair fellow in Section 1. The coordinates for each of these commands are easily identified by reading the appropriate column and row numbers on the graph paper for the horizontal line, vertical line, or "brick" to be displayed. The use of FOR-NEXT loops (i.e., lines 150-170) facilitates the drawing of regions which are defined by repetitive common commands.

In Section 2, our figure is embellished by adding arms and cheeks, and was given an identity by redrawing parts of the face in different colors. Finally, a hat is drawn in Section 3.

**COMPREHENSIVE EXAMPLE**   The planning of one design can include the possibility for two or more different screen displays. The following program subroutine draws either a happy or sad face, depending upon a predetermined value for variable C provided in the main flow of the program. Study and enter the program and then compare the screen display with the picture illustrated in Exhibit 1.6.2.

```
TEXT : HOME : NEW
100    REM ****************************************
101    REM *           CE1.6                    *
102    REM ****************************************
105    HOME : GOTO 300
150    COLOR = 8 : REM HAIR
155    HLIN 18, 22 AT 30 : PLOT 17, 31 : PLOT 23, 31 : PLOT 16,
       32 : PLOT 24, 32 : PLOT 15, 33 : PLOT 25, 33
160    COLOR = 13 : REM FACE
165    HLIN 18, 22 AT 31 : HLIN 17, 23 AT 32 : HLIN 16, 24 AT
       33 : HLIN 16, 24 AT 34 : HLIN 17, 23 AT 35 : HLIN 17,
       23 AT 36 : HLIN 17, 23 AT 37 : HLIN 18, 22 AT 38 : HLIN
       19, 21 AT 39
170    COLOR = 6 : REM EYES
175    PLOT 18, 32 : PLOT 22, 32
180    COLOR = 1 : REM NOSE
185    PLOT 20, 34
190    COLOR = 15 : REM LIP CONFIGURATION
195    HLIN 19, 21 AT 36
200    ON C GOTO 215, 225
215    PLOT 18, 35 : PLOT 22, 35 : RETURN : REM HAPPY FACE
225    PLOT 18, 37 : PLOT 22, 37 : RETURN : REM SAD FACE
300    GR : C = 1 : GOSUB 150
305    VTAB 22 : HTAB 16 : PRINT "HAPPY FACE"
```

```
310  FOR J = 1 TO 3000 : NEXT
315  HOME : GR : C = 2 : GOSUB 150
320  VTAB 22 : HTAB 17 : PRINT "SAD FACE"
325  FOR J = 1 TO 3000 : NEXT
330  GET Q$ : TEXT : HOME
340  END
```

### Check Your Comprehension

What line number is used for drawing both a happy and a sad face? _____

What is the purpose of variable C in the program? _____

How many low resolution graphic lines are used to display the hair? _____

**EXERCISE**  Write a low resolution graphics program that draws the picture of the train illustrated in Exhibit 1.6.3. You should select different colors for the various parts of the train.

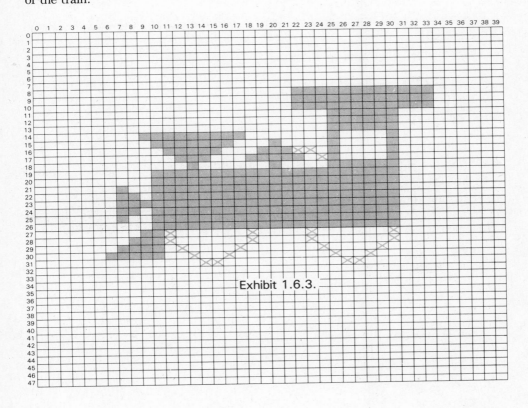

Exhibit 1.6.3.

**CHALLENGE**  Write a program that draws a low resolution picture of an object of your choice. Prepare your diagram by designing it first on graph paper.

# ACTIVITY 1.7   Designing Artistic Graphics for Any Position on the Screen

**LEARNING BY DISCOVERY**   This activity demonstrates how graphic commands can be written to display a picture anywhere on the screen.

1. Enter the following commands.

```
NEW
100   HOME : GOTO 300
150   VLIN 2, 5 AT 3 : VLIN 2, 7 AT 6 : HLIN 3, 7 AT 5
160   RETURN
300   GR : COLOR = 2
310   GOSUB 150
RUN
```

   Observe the screen display and compare it with the picture illustrated in Exhibit 1.7.1.

   Are the two approximately the same? _____

2. Retype line 150 as follows:

```
TEXT : HOME
150   VLIN 4, 7 AT 30 : VLIN 4, 9 AT 33 : HLIN 30, 34 AT 7
RUN
```

   Observe the screen display and compare it with the picture illustrated in Exhibit 1.7.2.

   Are the two approximately the same? _____

3. Retype line 150 as follows:

```
TEXT : HOME
150   VLIN Y — 3, Y AT X — 4 : VLIN Y — 3, Y + 2
      AT X — 1 : HLIN X — 4, X AT Y
RUN
```

   What message do you receive? _____

4. Add line 305 as follows:

```
TEXT : HOME
305   X = 30 : Y = 25
RUN
```

   Describe the position of the picture on the screen. _____

5. Retype line 305 as follows:

```
TEXT : HOME
```

```
305  X = 10 : Y = 5
RUN
```

Describe the position of the picture on the screen. _____

6. Retype line 150 as follows:

```
TEXT : HOME
150  VLIN Y, Y + 2 AT X : VLIN Y, Y + 4 AT X + 3 : HLIN X,
     X + 4 AT Y + 2
RUN
```

Describe the size and shape of the picture on the screen in comparison with that obtained in Section 5. _____

7. Retype line 305 as follows:

```
TEXT : HOME
305  X = 37 : Y = 15
RUN
```

Describe what happens. _____

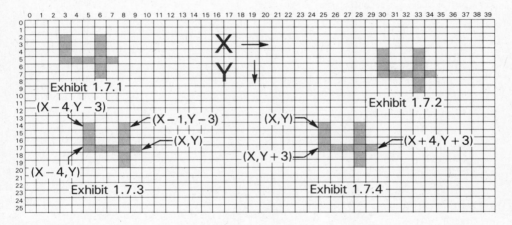

**DISCUSSION**  Fortunately, there is a better way to display a diagram in a variety of locations on the screen without having to continually change the graphics commands which display the diagram, as occurs in Sections 1 and 2. Rather than provide HLIN, VLIN, and PLOT commands with specific row and column numbers, we can generalize the graphics commands which define the diagram by using variables.

Exhibit 1.7.3 shows that the (X, Y) coordinate is located at the tail end of the horizontal line in the "4." The HLIN and VLIN commands are written in relation to that defining coordinate.

Exhibit 1.7.4, in conjunction with Section 6, demonstrates the selected position for the (X, Y) coordinate (upper left corner of the "4") is arbitrary, assuming the graphics commands are modified accordingly. The result in Section 3 is a reminder that the X and Y variables must receive values prior to accessing the subroutine which draws the diagram, while the result in Section 7 is a reminder that these values must be appropriate in magnitude to assure that the diagram remains within the screen boundaries.

**COMPREHENSIVE EXAMPLE**   The following APPLESOFT program positions an apple at several locations on the screen. Check that the (X, Y) coordinate illustrated in Exhibit 1.7.5 agrees with the description of the graphics commands in the subroutine which draws the apple. Enter and execute the program to observe the screen display.

```
TEXT : HOME : NEW
100  REM *****************************************
101  REM *            CE1.7                      *
102  REM *****************************************
120  HOME : GOTO 500
150  COLOR = 4
160  HLIN X, X + 1 AT Y
165  HLIN X, X + 1 AT Y + 1
170  PLOT X - 1, Y + 2
175  HLIN X - 2, X AT Y + 3 : HLIN X + 2, X + 3 AT Y + 3
180  COLOR = 13
185  HLIN X - 4, X + 5 AT Y + 4
190  HLIN X - 3, X + 6 AT Y + 5
200  COLOR = 1
205  HLIN X - 2, X + 7 AT Y + 6
210  HLIN X - 2, X + 7 AT Y + 7
215  COLOR = 9
220  HLIN X - 2, X + 8 AT Y + 8
225  HLIN X - 3, X + 8 AT Y + 9
230  COLOR = 3
235  HLIN X - 4, X + 7 AT Y + 10
240  HLIN X - 3, X + 6 AT Y + 11
245  COLOR = 2
250  HLIN X - 2, X + 5 AT Y + 12
255  HLIN X - 1, X + 4 AT Y + 13
260  FOR I = 1 TO 2000 : NEXT
265  RETURN
500  GR
510  X = 25 : Y = 25 : GOSUB 150
520  X = 5 : Y = 20 : GOSUB 150
530  X = 10 : Y = 4 : GOSUB 150
540  X = 30 : Y = 8 : GOSUB 150
550  VTAB 22 : HTAB 13
560  PRINT "APPLE ORCHARD"
570  VTAB 24 : HTAB 5
580  PRINT "PRESS THE SPACE BAR TO CONTINUE";
590  GET Q$ : TEXT : HOME
600  END
```

**Check Your Comprehension**

How many apples are in the orchard? _____

Where is the third apple located on the screen? _____

What lines draw the stem of the apple? _____

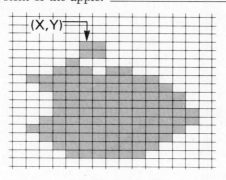

Exhibit 1.7.5

**EXERCISE**   Write a program that places the tennis player illustrated in Exhibit 1.7.6 at six different locations on the screen. Develop the subroutine that draws the tennis player so that his eyes, shorts, and shoes can change color by control in the main flow of the program, using the technique presented in the COMPREHENSIVE EXAMPLE in ACTIVITY 1.6.

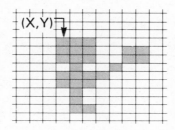

Exhibit 1.7.6

**CHALLENGE**   Rewrite the program that you chose in the CHALLENGE section of ACTIVITY 1.6 so that the diagram can be displayed in a variety of locations on the screen.

# ACTIVITY 1.8   Blinking a Picture of an Object

**LEARNING BY DISCOVERY**   This activity demonstrates how to have a picture of an object flash or blink on the screen.

1. Enter the following commands.

```
NEW
100  HOME : GOTO 500
```

```
150   FOR I = 0 TO 39
165   PLOT I, I : PLOT I, 39 - I
170   NEXT
200   FOR J = 1 TO 500 : NEXT
210   RETURN
500   VTAB 22 : HTAB 15 : PRINT "FLASHING X"
505   GR
510   FOR K = 1 TO 5
520   COLOR = 0 : GOSUB 150
530   COLOR = 2 : GOSUB 150
540   NEXT K
550   TEXT : HOME
RUN
```

Describe the speed and smoothness of the blinking diagram. _____

2. Delete lines 505 and 530 and retype line 520 as follows:

```
505
530
520   GR : COLOR = 2 : GOSUB 150
RUN
```

Compare the speed and smoothness of the blinking diagram with that of Section 1.

_____

3. **Add new lines as follows:**

```
300   GR : COLOR = 10 : REM COLOR BACKGROUND GRAY
310   FOR I = 0 TO 39 : HLIN 0, 39 AT I : NEXT
320   RETURN
505   GOSUB 300
RUN
```

Describe the background for the blinking diagram. _____

4. Retype line 520 and add 530 as follows:

```
520   COLOR = 10 : GOSUB 150
530   COLOR = 2 : GOSUB 150
RUN
```

Compare the background for the blinking diagram with that of Section 3. _____

_____

5. Delete line 200 as follows:

```
200
RUN
```

Compare the speed and smoothness of the blinking diagram with that of Section 4.

_____

**DISCUSSION**   There are basically two procedures by which to blink a diagram on the low resolution screen, if the background color remains black.

One method is to develop a loop where the diagram is drawn successively and repetitively in black and then in the desired color as occurs in Section 1. The subroutine beginning at line 200 provides an appropriate delay between blinks.

Another method is to include the GR command in the loop as is done in Section 2. Since the GR command automatically clears the screen to black, the coloring of the diagram in black as performed in Section 1 is unnecessary.

Although both methods generally blink with the same speed and smoothness, the GR command cannot be used effectively if the background screen is some color other than black as is attempted in Section 3.

Section 4 demonstrates the most desirable procedure is to repetitively alternate the coloring of the object in the background color and then the preferred color for the diagram. Section 5 demonstrates the use of a pause or delay to control the speed of the blink.

These procedures for blinking diagrams will be used in the next activity dealing with the animated movement of these diagrams.

**COMPREHENSIVE EXAMPLE**   Study the following APPLESOFT program to determine the screen display. Check your answer by entering the program into the computer.

```
NEW : HOME
100   REM *****************************************
101   REM *             CE1.8                     *
102   REM *****************************************
120   HOME : GOTO 500
150   COLOR = 1
160   FOR I = 0 TO 8
165   HLIN 11 - I, 28 + I AT I
170   HLIN 11 - I, 28 + I AT 39 - I
175   NEXT
180   FOR I = 0 TO 21
185   HLIN 2, 37 AT 9 + I
190   NEXT
195   RETURN
200   COLOR = C1
210   HLIN 7, 11 AT 18 : HLIN 7, 11 AT 20 : HLIN 7, 11 AT 22 :
      PLOT 7, 19 : PLOT 11, 21 : REM S
215   HLIN 14, 18 AT 18 : VLIN 18, 22 AT 16 : REM T
220   HLIN 21, 25 AT 18 : HLIN 21, 25 AT 22 : VLIN 18, 22 AT
      21 : VLIN 18, 22 AT 25 : REM O
225   HLIN 28, 32 AT 18 : HLIN 28, 32 AT 20 : VLIN 18, 22 AT
      28 : PLOT 32, 19 : REM P
230   FOR K = 1 TO 500 : NEXT
235   RETURN
300   VTAB 24 : HTAB 5
```

```
305   PRINT "HIT THE SPACE BAR TO CONTINUE";
310   GET Q$ : TEXT : HOME : RETURN
500   GR : GOSUB 150
510   VTAB 22 : HTAB 4
515   PRINT "ALWAYS REQUIRES A COMPLETE STOP"
520   FOR I = 1 TO 8
530   C1 = 1 : GOSUB 200
535   C1 = 15 : GOSUB 200
540   NEXT
545   GOSUB 300
550   END
```

**Check Your Comprehension**

What geometric figure is displayed? _____

What message appears within the geometric figure? _____

What lines control the blinking effect? _____

**EXERCISE**   Write an APPLESOFT program that displays the diagram illustrated in Exhibit 1.8.1 in a sequence of four separate frames defined below:

Frame 1: Displays the object and the message, "HI, I AM E.T.";
Frame 2: Blinks the left eye eight times with the message, "I CAN BLINK MY LEFT EYE";
Frame 3: Blinks the right eye eight times with the message, "I CAN BLINK MY RIGHT EYE", and;
Frame 4: Simultaneously blinks both eyes eight times with the message, "I CAN BLINK BOTH MY EYES".

Use a subroutine to color the face brown, the nose black, and the mouth red. Use a separate subroutine to color (and blink) the eyes blue.

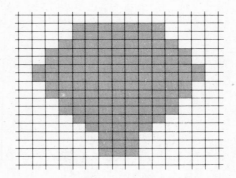

Exhibit 1.8.1

**CHALLENGE**   Write a program which displays the picture of a dragon. Use the blinking techniques demonstrated in this activity to give the effect of the dragon spitting fire.

# ACTIVITY 1.9  Animating Diagrams on a Black Background Screen

**LEARNING BY DISCOVERY**  This activity demonstrates how to provide movement for diagrams which are drawn on a black background screen.

1. Enter the following commands.

```
NEW
100   HOME : GOTO 500
140   REM DRAW ARROW
150   COLOR = C1
160   HLIN X, X + 7 AT Y : HLIN X, X + 7 AT Y + 1 : HLIN X,
      X + 7 AT Y + 2
165   VLIN Y − 2, Y + 4 AT X + 8 : VLIN Y − 1, Y + 3 AT
      X + 9 : VLIN Y, Y + 2 AT X + 10 : PLOT X + 11, Y+ 1
170   RETURN
200   FOR J = 1 TO 500 : NEXT : RETURN
500   Y = 4 : GR
510   FOR X = 0 TO 27 STEP 3
520   C1 = 2 : GOSUB 150 : GOSUB 200
530   GR
540   NEXT
RUN
```

Observe the screen display.

In what direction is the arrow moving? _____

Describe the speed and smoothness of the moving arrow. _____

2. Add line 515 as follows:

```
TEXT : HOME
515 Y = Y + 3
RUN
```

Observe the screen display.

In what direction is the arrow moving? _____

3. Delete line 515 and retype lines 520 and 530 as follows:

```
TEXT : HOME
515
520   C1 = 0 : GOSUB 150 : GOSUB 200
530   C1 = 2 : GOSUB 150 : GOSUB 200
RUN
```

Describe the effectiveness of the animated arrow. _____

4. Retype lines 520 and 530 as follows:

```
TEXT : HOME
520   C1 = 2 : GOSUB 150 : GOSUB 200
530   C1 = 0 : GOSUB 150 : GOSUB 200
RUN
```

Compare the speed and smoothness of the animated arrow with that of Section 1.

---

5. Retype line 530 as follows:

```
TEXT : HOME
530 C1 = 0 : GOSUB 150
RUN
```

Compare the speed and smoothness of the animated arrow with that of Section 4.

---

6. Retype line 200 as follows:

```
TEXT : HOME
200   FOR J = 1 TO 100 : NEXT : RETURN
RUN
```

Compare the speed and smoothness of the animated arrow with that of Section 5.

---

7. Retype lines 200 and 510 as follows:

```
TEXT : HOME
200   FOR J = 1 TO 300 : NEXT : RETURN
510   FOR X = 0 TO 27 STEP 3
RUN
```

Compare the speed and smoothness of the animated arrow with that of Section 5.

---

**DISCUSSION**   The animation of a diagram is the process of first displaying it at some location on the screen, then removing it from the screen, and finally changing the coordinates of it before repeating these steps a determined number of times.

The animation is done incorrectly in Section 3 because the object is removed (by setting C1 = 0) before it is displayed (setting C1 = 2). By interchanging lines 520 and 530 in Section 4, the proper animation effect is achieved. Section 5 improves the animation effect by eliminating the delay after erasing the diagram. Notice this omission of the delay is different from the blinking algorithm where the delay is included twice; after drawing the diagram and after erasing it.

When the background color is black, the diagram can be removed by either recoloring the diagram in black or, more simply, using the GR command to clear the screen to black. Both methods are generally equal in the quality of animation.

The speed and smoothness of the animation can be controlled by using empty delays and by changing the magnitude of the increment (or decrement) used for establishing new coordinates for each subsequent display. The trial and error method is easiest for determining which length of delay and which interval change produces the most appealing animation.

The direction of the animated object can be either horizontal, vertical, or diagonal, depending upon which coordinates are changed (horizontal, vertical, or both).

**COMPREHENSIVE EXAMPLE**   The following program simulates the bouncing of an object (ball) off the walls of an enclosed region. There is one subroutine which controls the horizontal movement and a separate subroutine which controls the vertical movement. Notice the conditions established in lines 640 and 740 to assure that the ball remains inside the region. Study the program and then enter it to observe the motion of the ball.

```
TEXT : HOME : NEW
100   REM ******************************************
101   REM *            CE1.9                       *
102   REM ******************************************
120   HOME : GOTO 800
145   REM PLOT BALL
150   COLOR = C1 : PLOT X, Y : RETURN
195   REM SET CONDITIONS FOR PLOTTING BALL
200   C1 = 2 : X = XN : Y = YN : GOSUB 150 : GOSUB 300
220   C1 = 0 : GOSUB 150
230   RETURN
295   REM DELAY
300   FOR K = 1 TO 100 : NEXT : RETURN
595   REM HORIZONTAL MOVEMENT
600   XN = XO + XM
640   IF XN > 38 OR XN < 1 THEN XM = - 1 * XM : GOTO 600
660   GOSUB 200
670   XO = XN
680   RETURN
695   REM VERTICAL MOVEMENT
700   YN = YO + YM
740   IF YN > 38 OR YN < 1 THEN YM = - 1 * YM : GOTO 700
760   GOSUB 200
770   YO = YN
780   RETURN
795   REM DRAW BORDER
800   GR : COLOR = 15 : HLIN 1, 39 AT 1 : HLIN 1, 39 AT 39 :
      VLIN 1, 39 AT 1 : VLIN 1, 39 AT 39
810   XO = 20 : YO = 20 : XN = 20 : YN = 20 : XM = 2 : YM =
      2 : REM SET INITIAL VALUES
815   VTAB 22 : HTAB 7 : PRINT "THE BALL MOVES HORIZONTALLY"
820   FOR I = 1 TO 50 : GOSUB 600 : NEXT
```

```
825   HOME : VTAB 22 : HTAB 8 : PRINT "THE BALL MOVES
      VERTICALLY"
830   FOR I = 1 TO 50 : GOSUB 700 : NEXT
840   HOME : VTAB 22 : HTAB 7 : PRINT "THE BALL MOVES
      DIAGONALLY"
850   FOR I = 1 TO 75 : GOSUB 600 : GOSUB 700 : NEXT
860   TEXT : HOME
870   END
```

### Check Your Comprehension

Why does line 200 contain "GOSUB 300" whereas line 220 does not? _____

_____

What effect would be obtained if line 300 were deleted? _____

Describe the purpose of the variables, XN, XO, and XM in the subroutine which begins on line 600. _____

**EXERCISE**   Write a program that makes it snow on the screen using the snowflake illustrated in Exhibit 1.9.1. Originally place three snowflakes at coordinates (5, 10), (30, 8), and (18, 2), then allow them to drop seven times, three screen units at a time.

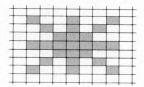

Exhibit 1.9.1

**CHALLENGE**   Write a program that animates a person walking from the left portion of the screen to the right. Use one figure where the legs are in an outstretched position and another where the legs are together to achieve the walking effect.

# ACTIVITY 1.10   Animating Diagrams on a Non-Black Background Screen

**LEARNING BY DISCOVERY**   This activity demonstrates how to provide movement for diagrams which are drawn on non-black background screens.

1. Enter the following commands.

```
NEW
100   HOME : GOTO 500
145   REM DRAW TRUCK
150   COLOR = 4
160   HLIN X, X + 3 AT Y : HLIN X, X + 3 AT Y + 1 : HLIN X,
      X + 3 AT Y + 2
```

```
165  COLOR = 12
170  HLIN X + 4, X + 5 AT Y + 1 : HLIN X + 4, X + 5 AT
     Y + 2
175  COLOR = 5
180  PLOT X + 1, Y + 3 : PLOT X + 4, Y + 3
185  RETURN
200  FOR J = 1 TO 200 : NEXT : RETURN
300  COLOR = 13 : REM COLOR BACKGROUND YELLOW
310  FOR K = 0 TO 39 : HLIN 0, 39 AT K
320  NEXT
330  RETURN
500  GR : Y = 4 : GOSUB 300
510  FOR X = 0 TO 33 STEP 3
520  GOSUB 150 : GOSUB 200
530  GR
540  NEXT
RUN
```

Observe the screen display.

Describe the color of the truck. _____

Does the background remain the same color? _____

2. Retype line 530 as follows:

```
TEXT : HOME
530  GOSUB 150
RUN
```

Observe the screen display.

Does the background remain the same color? _____

Is the effect of a moving truck achieved? _____

3. Retype lines 150, 165, 175, 520, and 530 as follows:

```
TEXT : HOME
155  COLOR = C1
165  COLOR = C2
175  COLOR = C3
520  C1 = 4 : C2 = 12 : C3 = 5 : GOSUB 150 : GOSUB 200
530  C1 = 13 : C2 = 13 : GOSUB 150
RUN
```

Observe the screen display.

Does the background remain the same color? _____

Is the effect of the moving truck achieved? _____

4. Retype line 530 as follows:

```
TEXT : HOME
```

```
530   C1 = 13 : C2 = 13 : C3 = 13 : GOSUB 150
RUN
```

Observe the screen display.

Does the color of the moving truck remain the same? _____

Does the background screen remain the same color? _____

Is the effect of the moving truck achieved? _____

**DISCUSSION**   When the background color is not black, the step in the animation process of removing the diagram from the screen cannot be accomplished by including the GR command in the loop. Since the GR command clears the screen to black, the original background color is destroyed as occurs in Section 1.

Instead, the object must be removed from the screen by recoloring it in the background color. If the diagram includes more than one color (as does the truck), the COLOR = commands in the subroutine which draw the diagram must be assigned variables (e.g. C1, C2, and C3) which either receive the background color (for the removal of the diagram) or receive its true colors (for the display of the diagram) within the loop in the main flow of the program. If any of these important considerations is omitted, errors in the display of the animated object will occur. Sections 2 and 3 are both incorrect because line 530 fails to assign the background color to values C1, C2, and C3 in the removal process. Section 4 produces the desired animated effect.

**COMPREHENSIVE EXAMPLE**   The following program animates a tennis player moving his racket. The two positions are illustrated in Exhibit 1.10.1. Note the non-animated portion of the diagram (player) is one subroutine. A second subroutine is used for displaying the racket in the up position, while another subroutine draws the racket in a horizontal position. Study the program carefully, particularly the coordination between the colors drawn and the displaying and removing of the animated parts. Enter the program to observe the animation.

```
TEXT : HOME : NEW
100   REM *****************************************
101   REM *            CE1.10                     *
102   REM *****************************************
120   HOME : GOTO 500
145   REM DRAW PLAYER
150   COLOR = 11 : REM HEAD, NECK, LEG
160   HLIN X, X + 2 AT Y : HLIN X, X + 2 AT Y + 1 : HLIN X,
      X + 2 AT Y + 2 : PLOT X + 1, Y + 3 : VLIN Y + 5, Y + 7
      AT X + 1
165   COLOR = 1 : HLIN X + 1, X + 2 AT Y + 2 : REM MOUTH
170   COLOR = 2 : PLOT X + 2, Y : REM EYE
175   COLOR = 3 : REM PANTS
180   HLIN X, X + 2 AT Y + 4 : HLIN X, X + 2 AT Y + 5
185   COLOR = 8 : HLIN X + 1, X + 2 AT Y + 8 : REM SHOE
190   RETURN
195   REM DRAW ARM UP
200   COLOR = C1
```

```
220   PLOT X + 3, Y + 4 : PLOT X + 4, Y + 3
230   COLOR = C2
235   HLIN X + 5, X + 6 AT Y + 1 : HLIN X + 5, X + 6 AT
      Y + 2
240   RETURN
245   REM DRAW ARM OUT
250   COLOR = C1
260   HLIN X + 3, X + 4 AT Y + 4
265   COLOR = C2
270   HLIN X + 5, X + 6 AT Y + 3 : HLIN X + 5, X + 6 AT
      Y + 4
275   RETURN
300   FOR K = 1 TO 200 : NEXT : RETURN : REM DELAY
400   COLOR = 12 : REM BACKGROUND SCREEN
405   FOR I = 0 TO 39 : HLIN 0, 39 AT I : NEXT
410   RETURN
500   GR : GOSUB 400
502   X = 5 : Y = 20 : GOSUB 150
505   VTAB 22 : HTAB 12 : PRINT "I'M READY — SERVE!"
510   FOR I = 1 TO 15
515   C1 = 11 : C2 = 8 : GOSUB 200 : GOSUB 300
520   C1 = 12 : C2 = 12 : GOSUB 200
525   C1 = 11 : C2 = 8 : GOSUB 250 : GOSUB 300
530   C1 = 12 : C2 = 12 : GOSUB 250
535   NEXT
540   TEXT : HOME
END
```

## Check Your Comprehension

In which direction is the tennis player facing? _____

What variables are used to control the colors which give the arm animation? \_\_\_\_\_

_____

Which line numbers are used to erase the previous position of the player's arm? \_\_

_____

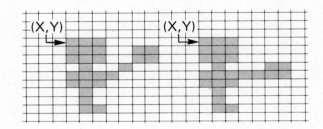

Exhibit 1.10.1

**EXERCISE**   Write a program that animates the flight in a blue sky of the creature illustrated in Exhibit 1.10.2. Color the tail brown (8), the body orange (9), and the head dark green (4) in one subroutine. In another subroutine alternate the drawing of orange (9) and blue (7) wings to give the effect of the wings flapping in the sky. Write an indefinite loop where the creature flaps its wings while moving horizontally from left to right across the middle of the screen. Program the animation to wrap around (start at 0 again) when the right most extremity of the screen is reached.

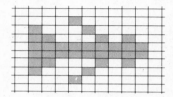

Exhibit 1.10.2

**CHALLENGE**   Write a program that animates a diagram of your choice on a colored background screen. Test your understanding by making the coordination of the diagram on the background screen complex and colorful.

# ACTIVITY 1.11  Drawing Graphic Alphanumerics

**LEARNING BY DISCOVERY**   This activity demonstrates three different techniques to display graphic representations of alphanumeric characters.

1.  Enter the following commands.

```
NEW
100  HOME : GR
110  COLOR = 1
120  HLIN 4, 8 AT 17 : HLIN 4, 8 AT 19 : VLIN 17, 21 AT 4 :
     VLIN 17, 21 AT 8 : REM A
125  COLOR = 2
130  HLIN  11, 15 AT 17 : HLIN 11, 15 AT 19 : VLIN 17, 21 AT
     11 : PLOT 15, 18 : REM P
135  COLOR = 4
140  HLIN 18, 22 AT 17 : HLIN 18, 22 AT 19 : VLIN 17, 21 AT
     18 : PLOT 22, 18 : REM P
145  COLOR = 13
150  VLIN 17, 21 AT 25 : HLIN 25, 29 AT 21 : REM L
155  COLOR = 9
160  HLIN 32, 36 AT 17 : HLIN 32, 36 AT 21 : HLIN 32, 35 AT
     19 : VLIN 17, 21 AT 32
RUN
```

Observe the screen display.

What word is displayed? _____

Describe the speed by which the letters appear. _____

2. Enter the following commands.

```
TEXT : HOME : NEW
100  HOME : GOTO 500
105  HLIN X + 1, X + 4 AT Y : HLIN X + 1, X + 4 AT Y +
     4 : HLIN X + 1, X + 3 AT Y + 2 : VLIN Y, Y + 4 AT X :
     RETURN : REM E
112  VLIN Y, Y + 4 AT X : HLIN X + 1, X + 4 AT Y + 4 :
     RETURN : REM L
116  VLIN Y, Y + 4 AT X : HLIN X + 1, X + 4 AT Y : HLIN X
     + 1, X + 4 AT Y + 2 : PLOT X + 4, Y + 1 : RETURN :
     REM P
201  VLIN Y + 1, Y + 8 AT X : VLIN Y + 1, Y + 8 AT X +
     6 : HLIN X + 1, X + 5 AT Y + 4 : HLIN X + 1, X + 5
     AT Y : RETURN : REM CAP A
500  GR
505  X = 1 : Y = 10 : COLOR = 1 : GOSUB 201
510  Y = 14 : X = X + 9 : COLOR = 2 : GOSUB 116
515  X = X + 6 : COLOR = 4 : GOSUB 116
520  X = X + 6 : COLOR = 13 : GOSUB 112
525  X = X + 6 : COLOR = 9 : GOSUB 105
RUN
```

Observe the screen display.

What word is displayed? _____

How does this display differ from Section 1? _____

3. Retype line 505 and 510 as follows:

```
TEXT : HOME
505  X = 1 : Y = 2 : COLOR = 1 : GOSUB 201
510  Y = 6 : X = X + 9 : COLOR = 2 : GOSUB 116
RUN
```

How does this display differ from Section 2? _____

4. Enter the following commands.

```
TEXT : HOME : NEW
100  HOME : DIM A$ (26) : GR : GOTO 300
200  I = 1
210  FOR V = Y TO Y + 4
220  FOR H = X TO X + 4
230  COLOR = HC * VAL (MID$ (A$(J), I, 1))
240  PLOT H, V
```

```
250   I = I + 1
260   NEXT H
270   NEXT V
280   RETURN
300   A$ (1)  = "0111010001111111000110001"
310   A$ (5)  = "1111110000111101000011111"
320   A$ (12) = "1000010000100001000011111"
330   A$ (16) = "1111110001111111000010000"
400   X = 4 : Y = 10 : HC = 1 : J = 1 : GOSUB 200
410   X = X + 6 : HC = 2 : J = 16 : GOSUB 200
420   X = X + 6 : HC = 4 : J = 16 : GOSUB 200
430   X = X + 6 : HC = 13 : J = 12 : GOSUB 200
440   X = X + 6 : HC = 9 : J = 5 : GOSUB 200
RUN
```

Observe the screen display.

What word is displayed? _____

How does the speed by which the letters appear compare with Sections 1, 2, and 3? _____

**DISCUSSION**   The only convenient way alphanumerics can appear on the graphics portion of low resolution Page 1 is if they are drawn using the traditional APPLESOFT graphics commands. Unfortunately, extensive application of this mode of presentation in a lesson tends to use up valuable memory quite quickly. This activity introduces a technique by which the amount of memory used for coding alphanumeric characters is minimized.

In Section 1, the word APPLE is drawn using specific numbers as coordinates in the HLIN, VLIN, and PLOT commands. This procedure is acceptable and probably memory efficient for limited and specific use. In Section 2, however, the letters are defined in general terms in individual subroutines which did not restrict their placement at a particular location on the screen. By assigning desired X and Y values in the main flow of the program, flexibility is achieved in the positioning of the letter on the screen. Also, in contrast to Section 1, Section 2 does not require the duplication of code for the two letters "P."

Section 4 demonstrates a technique by which alphanumeric characters are coded as a unique string of twenty-five binary digits. The designing of characters in this fashion is illustrated in Exhibits 1.11.1 through 1.11.3. Exhibit 1.11.1 displays the desired formation of the character using twenty-five low resolution graphic positions, arranged as a five by five dot matrix. Exhibit 1.11.2 translates the shaded form of the letter into X's (for 1's) and blanks (for 0's). Finally, Exhibit 1.11.3 displays the translation to binary form. Reading by rows we obtain "1111110001111111000010000" as a unique twenty-five digit string for the letter P.

The drawing of these alphanumeric strings occurs in the subroutine beginning at line 200, which performs string manipulation on character A$ (J). A value of 0 or 1 is obtained for VAL (MID$ (A$(J), I, 1)) when line 230 is executed. Then COLOR is assigned a value of 0 (0 * HC) or HC (1 * HC), where HC (and J) are given values in the main flow of the program prior to accessing the subroutine. When plotting occurs at line 240, the color has been determined to be black (0) or the desired color (HC). The slower appearance of the graphic letters in Section 4, compared with Sections 1, 2, and 3, is due to the time that elapses in plotting twenty-five "bricks" for each character.

APPENDICES 1A, 1B, and 1C provide you with three different codes for the graphic display of the alphabet. APPENDIX 1A provides letters in a 5 by 5 dot matrix form, while APPENDIX 1B includes letters in a 7 by 9 dot matrix form. Notice the easily recallable number scheme used in APPENDIX 1A: 101 (for A), 102 (for B),...126 (for Z). Similar meaningful number schemes are used in APPENDICES 1B and 1C. APPENDIX 1C provides the entire alphabet using the 5 by 5 binary form discussed above.

The user can decide which of the codes, if any, are most appropriate for a particular situation in terms of the memory used and the speed at which the letters are to be displayed.

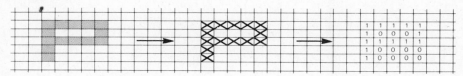

Exhibit 1.11.1          Exhibit 1.11.2          Exhibit 1.11.3

**COMPREHENSIVE EXAMPLE**   Study the following program to determine the graphic alphanumeric message. Check your answer by entering the program in the computer.

```
TEXT : HOME : NEW
100   REM *****************************************
101   REM *              CE1.11                    *
102   REM *****************************************
120   DIM A$ (26) : GOSUB 501 : GOTO 700
150   I = 1
155   FOR V = Y TO Y + 4
160   FOR H = X TO X + 4
165   COLOR = HC * VAL (MID$ (A$(J), I, 1 ))
170   PLOT H, V
175   I = I + 1
180   NEXT H
185   NEXT V
190   RETURN
395   REM DRAW "APPLE"
400   HC = 1 : J = 1 : GOSUB 150
420   X = X + 6 : HC = 2 : J = 16 : GOSUB 150
430   X = X + 6 : HC = 4 : J = 16 : GOSUB 150
440   X = X + 6 : HC = 13 : J = 12 : GOSUB 150
450   X = X + 6 : HC = 9 : J = 5 : GOSUB 150
460   RETURN
500   REM DEFINITION OF ALPHABET
```

```
501   A$ (1) = "0111010001111111000110001"
503   A$ (3) = "0111110000100001000001111"
505   A$ (5) = "1111110000111101000011111"
507   A$ (7) = "1111110000100111000111111"
508   A$ (8) = "1000110001111111000110001"
509   A$ (9) = "1111100100001000010011111"
512   A$ (12) = "1000010001100001000011111"
516   A$ (16) = "1111110001111111000010000"
518   A$ (18) = "1111110001111111001010001"
519   A$ (19) = "1111110000111110000111111"
527   RETURN
595   REM DRAW "GRAPHICS"
600   Y = 0 : HC = 11 : J = 7 : GOSUB 150
610   Y = Y + 6 : HC = 14 : J = 18 : GOSUB 150
615   Y = Y + 6 : HC = 12 : J = 1 : GOSUB 150
617   Y = Y + 6 : HC = 2 : J = 16 : GOSUB 150
620   Y = Y + 6 : HC = 3 : J = 8 : GOSUB 150
625   Y = Y + 6 : HC = 9 : J = 9 : GOSUB 150
630   Y = Y + 6 : HC = 14 : J = 3 : GOSUB 150
635   Y = Y + 6 : HC = 4 : J = 19 : GOSUB 150
640   RETURN
700   GR : POKE - 16302, 0 : CALL - 1998
705   X = 2 : Y = 18 : GOSUB 400
710   X = 8 : GOSUB 600
720   FOR I = 1 TO 5000 : NEXT
730   TEXT : HOME
740   END
```

## Check Your Comprehension

What letter is defined in line 620? _____

What is the color of the graphic letter "C?" _____

What are the screen coordinates for the upper left corner of the graphic letter "A?"

_____

**EXERCISE**   Write a program which displays the alphanumeric message illustrated in Exhibit 1.11.4. Each word is to appear in a different color of your choice.

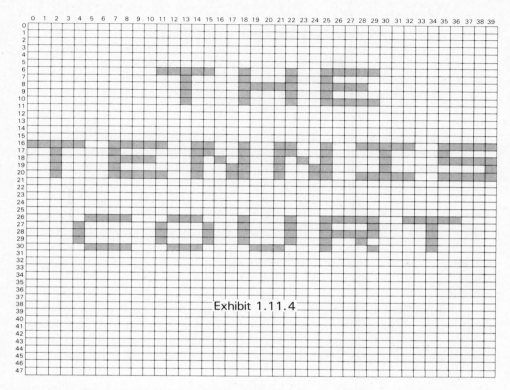

Exhibit 1.11.4

**CHALLENGE**   Define an alphabet where each letter is represented as a unique string of sixty-three binary digits (9 rows by 7 columns). Then write a program which uses an appropriate modification of the COMPREHENSIVE EXAMPLE subroutine beginning at line 150 to successively display each letter of the alphabet.

# MODULE 1C   Putting Low Resolution Graphics All Together

# PUTTING IT ALL TOGETHER: PART 1

**CHAPTER SYNOPSIS**   Congratulations! You survived ACTIVITIES 1.1 through 1.11. CHAPTER 1 introduced you to the Applesoft commands used to obtain low resolution graphic displays. Low resolution graphics is the most rudimentary form of graphics associated with the Apple II Plus or the Apple IIe computer system. This mode of graphics draws diagrams as a composite of rectangular shaped "bricks," or collections of these bricks which appear as thick vertical or horizontal line segments or "bands." In CHAPTER 2, you will discover that low resolution graphics lacks the precision that can be achieved when using high resolution graphics. Nonetheless, low resolution graphics is interesting and fun to explore, has many meaningful and purposeful applications, and is ideal for introducing graphics to the novice computer enthusiast.

Thus far, you have learned to create a variety of graphic displays and effects, but each application was isolated within a particular activity. The purpose of this section is to demonstrate how these individual accomplishments can be integrated into a meaningful sequence of graphic displays. But first, let's summarize what graphics concepts have been covered in CHAPTER 1.

• Obtain mixed graphics mode consisting of 40 rows by 40 columns with a four line text window at the bottom of the screen.
   Examples

```
GR if originally in TEXT mode
POKE −16301, 0 if originally in full graphics mode
```

• Obtain full graphics mode consisting of 48 rows by 40 columns with no text window at the bottom of the screen.
   Example

```
GR : POKE −16302, 0
```

• Select any one of sixteen colors.
   Example

```
COLOR = n where n = 0, 1, 2, ..., 15
```

• Draw a "brick" at any allowable location on the graphics screen.
   Example

```
PLOT 30, 15
```

• Draw a horizontal line (band) at any allowable location on the graphics screen.
   Example

```
HLIN 5, 32 AT 16
```

- Draw a vertical line (band) at any allowable location on the graphics screen.
  Example

  ```
  VLIN 0, 39 AT 4
  ```

- Draw a design at a fixed position on the graphics screen.
  Example

  ```
  HLIN 20, 26 AT 20 : VLIN 17, 29 AT 23
  ```

- Draw a design at any relocatable position on the graphics screen.
  Example

  ```
  X = 20 : Y = 15 : HLIN X, X + 6 AT Y
  X =  5 : Y =  4 : HLIN X, X + 6 AT Y
  ```

- Shade a region in a color.
  Example

  ```
  GR : COLOR = 10
  FOR I = 10 TO 20
  HLIN 20, 30 AT I
  NEXT
  ```

- Blink a diagram by repetitively drawing and erasing it.
  Example

  ```
  GR
  FOR I = 1 TO 20
  COLOR = 6
  HLIN 6, 30 AT 14
  COLOR = 0
  HLIN 6, 30 AT 14
  NEXT
  ```

- Animate a diagram by repetitively drawing and erasing it in a sequence of different screen positions.
  Example

  ```
  GR
  FOR X = 5 TO 30
  COLOR = 6
  HLIN 6, 30 AT X
  COLOR = 0
  HLIN 6, 30 AT X
  NEXT
  ```

- Draw graphic letters by using PLOT, HLIN, and VLIN commands.
- Draw graphic letters by using binary definitions.


**CREATING A COMPUTER STORY**   Now that the review is completed, it is time for you to develop a coordinated lesson or "computer story" which integrates many of the graphics concepts you have learned. Before reading any further, enter and execute the SAMPLE COMPUTER STORY entitled THE TENNIS COURT for an example of what these authors mean by a computer story.

The preparation for a coordinated program, such as THE TENNIS COURT, requires careful planning. The following steps suggest guidelines to follow during the developmental stages of the program.

**Brainstorming:** The first step in developing a program is to decide upon a topic. Let your imagination run wild! Be creative! Think of a computer story which can be presented graphically. Determine which of the low resolution graphics techniques you have learned can be used to achieve your plan.

**Designing:** The next step is to determine more elaborately what you want to present and in what order. Use graph paper to sketch pictorial representations of objects to be included in your program. Develop frames on index cards or pieces of paper which define more precisely each screen display as the program progresses from one stage to the next. Sequence these frames by arranging the cards in a desired order. The sequence of frames used for THE TENNIS COURT is included for your interest. You might wish to execute the program again to observe the coordination between the frame descriptions and the actual screen displays.

**Coding:** The third step is to translate the instructions on each card into the APPLE-SOFT language. TENNIS COURT is fully documented. The reader should LIST the program and study the translation of each frame into its corresponding APPLESOFT code. Pay particular attention to the manner in which the tennis players facing left and right are drawn. Both players are created from the design illustrated in Exhibit A. The right player (Exhibit B) and the left player (Exhibit C) are drawn by shading appropriate parts of the model in Exhibit A. Lines 500 through 640 of the source program constitute the subroutine which draws either player.

**Debugging:** The last step is to test the program by executing it. Correct any errors in the program and modify any frames which are not to your liking.

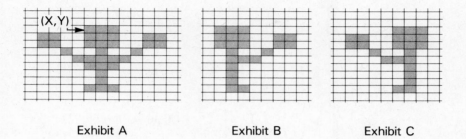

Exhibit A          Exhibit B          Exhibit C

**SAMPLE FRAME DESIGN:**
**THE TENNIS COURT**

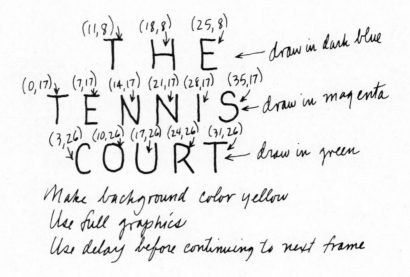

(11,8)  (18,8)  (25,8)

T H E ← draw in dark blue

(0,17) (7,17) (14,17) (21,17) (28,17) (35,17)

T E N N I S ← draw in magenta

(3,26) (10,26) (17,26) (24,26) (31,26)

C O U R T ← draw in green

Make background color yellow
Use full graphics
Use delay before continuing to next frame

*FRAME 1*

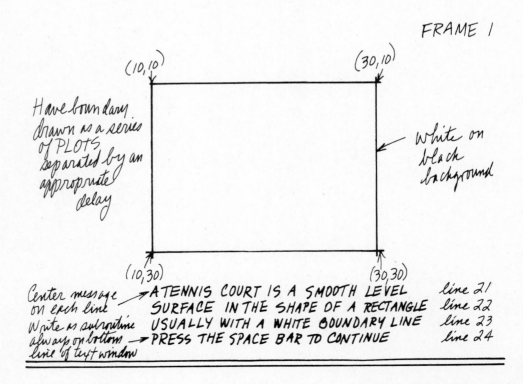

(10,10)                              (30,10)

Have boundary
drawn as a series
of PLOTS
separated by an
appropriate
delay

← White on
black
background

(10,30)                              (30,30)

Center message → A TENNIS COURT IS A SMOOTH LEVEL        line 21
on each line        SURFACE IN THE SHAPE OF A RECTANGLE   line 22
Write as subroutine  USUALLY WITH A WHITE BOUNDARY LINE   line 23
always on bottom → PRESS THE SPACE BAR TO CONTINUE        line 24
line of text window

FRAME 2

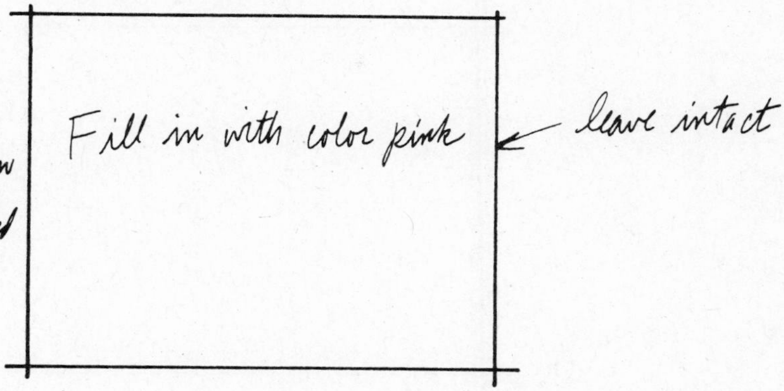

Clear text window then add new message, centered on each line

Fill in with color pink ← leave intact

SOMETIMES THE SURFACE IS    line 21
A PINKISH COLOR CLAY    line 22

PRESS THE SPACE BAR TO CONTINUE    line 24

FRAME 3

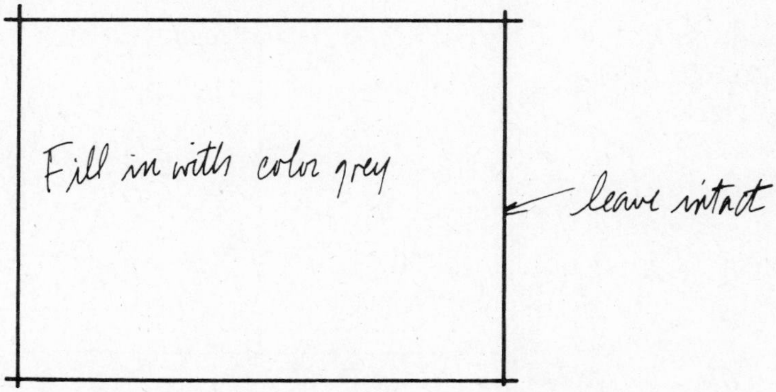

Fill in with color grey ← leave intact

Clear text window then add new message centered on each line

OR SOMETIMES IT IS    line 21
MADE OF GREY MACADAM    line 22

PRESS THE SPACE BAR TO CONTINUE    line 24

*FRAME 4*

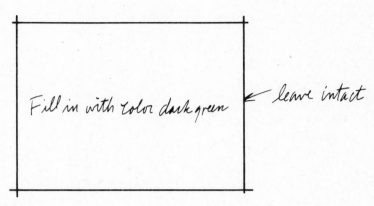

Fill in with color dark green          ← *leave intact*

Clear text window
then add new
message centered
on each line

THE SURFACE IS ALSO MADE OF          *line 21*
A GREEN RUBBER TYPE MATERIAL          *line 22*

PRESS THE SPACE BAR TO CONTINUE          *line 24*

*FRAME 5*

(20,10) add white line
↓

leave boundary
and green interior
intact for
remainder of
program

Clear text window,
then add new
message centered
on each line

THE COURT HAS A NET THAT          *line 21*
DIVIDES IT IN HALF          *line 22*

PRESS THE SPACE BAR TO CONTINUE          *line 24*

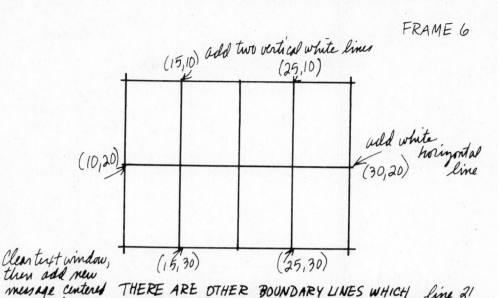

FRAME 6

(15,10) add two vertical white lines (25,10)

(10,20)

add white horizontal line (30,20)

(15,30) (25,30)

Clear text window, then add new message centered on each line

THERE ARE OTHER BOUNDARY LINES WHICH    line 21
ARE IMPORTANT IN THE 'PLAY' OF THE GAME    line 22
     T E N N I S    line 23
PRESS THE SPACE BAR TO CONTINUE    line 24

(10,7) extend line (30,7) FRAME 7
add white line

color dark green | color dark green

(10,35) (30,33) add white line

color dark green | color dark green

Clear text window, then add new message centered on each line

TWO ADDITIONAL HORIZONTAL LINES ARE    line 21
USED TO DETERMINE THE COURT LINES FOR    line 22
'SINGLES PLAY' OR 'DOUBLES PLAY'    line 23
PRESS THE SPACE BAR TO CONTINUE    line 24

FRAME 8

add player facing right
(4,15)

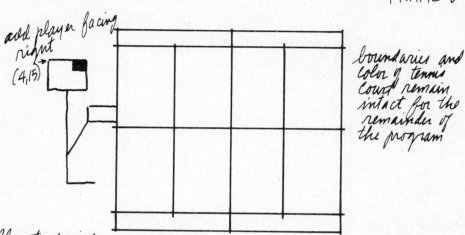

boundaries and color of tennis court remain intact for the remainder of the program

Clean text window, then add new message centered on each line

IN 'SINGLES PLAY' THERE IS ONE PLAYER     line 21
AT THE LEFT END OF THE COURT     line 22

PRESS THE SPACE BAR TO CONTINUE     line 24

FRAME 9

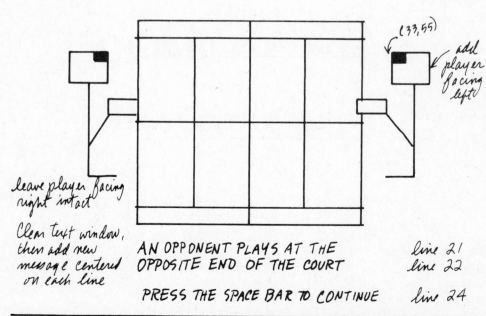

(33,55)
add player facing left

leave player facing right intact

Clean text window, then add new message centered on each line

AN OPPONENT PLAYS AT THE     line 21
OPPOSITE END OF THE COURT     line 22

PRESS THE SPACE BAR TO CONTINUE     line 24

FRAME 10

Erase both
players from frame 9 then add two players facing right

(4,10)

(4,24)

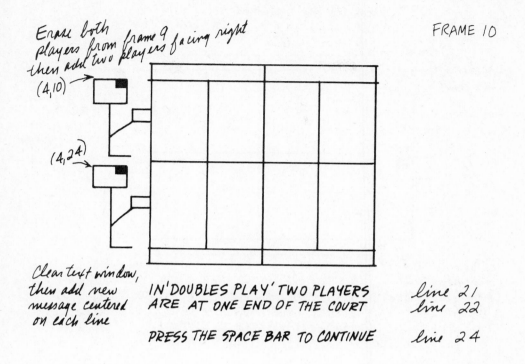

Clear text window,
then add new
message centered
on each line

IN 'DOUBLES PLAY' TWO PLAYERS                line 21
ARE AT ONE END OF THE COURT                 line 22

PRESS THE SPACE BAR TO CONTINUE             line 24


FRAME 11

(33,10)

leave players
facing right
intact

add
players
facing
left

(33,24)

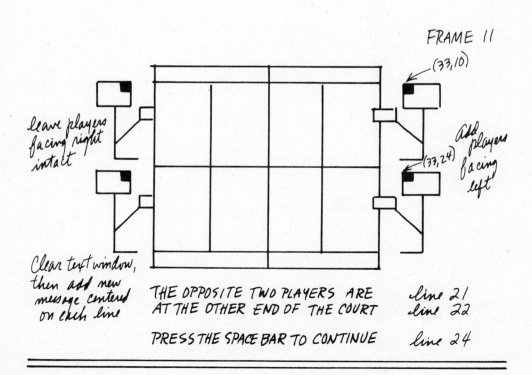

Clear text window,
then add new
message centered
on each line

THE OPPOSITE TWO PLAYERS ARE                line 21
AT THE OTHER END OF THE COURT               line 22

PRESS THE SPACE BAR TO CONTINUE             line 24

Animate the movement of the white
ball moving back and forth hitting paddles
of topmost paddles

FRAME 12

Generate sound
when ball
hits paddle

leave all
players
intact
for the
remainder
of the program

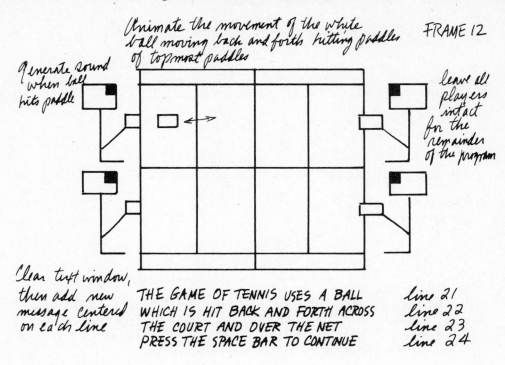

Clear text window,
then add new
message centered
on each line

THE GAME OF TENNIS USES A BALL         line 21
WHICH IS HIT BACK AND FORTH ACROSS     line 22
THE COURT AND OVER THE NET             line 23
PRESS THE SPACE BAR TO CONTINUE        line 24

Animate the movement of the orange ball
moving back and forth hitting the paddles of the
lowermost players

FRAME 13

Generate
sound when
ball hits
paddle

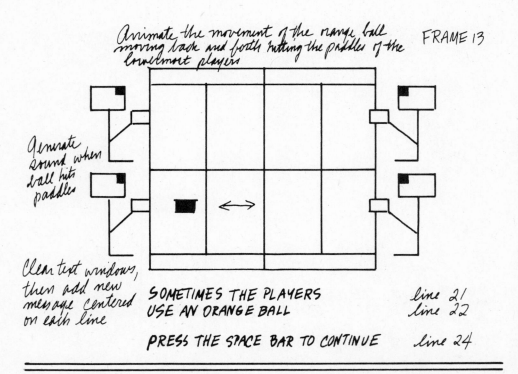

Clear text windows,
then add new
message centered
on each line

SOMETIMES THE PLAYERS                line 21
USE AN ORANGE BALL                   line 22

PRESS THE SPACE BAR TO CONTINUE     line 24

*Animate the movement of red ball moving back and forth hitting paddles: increase horizontal increment by one*  FRAME 14

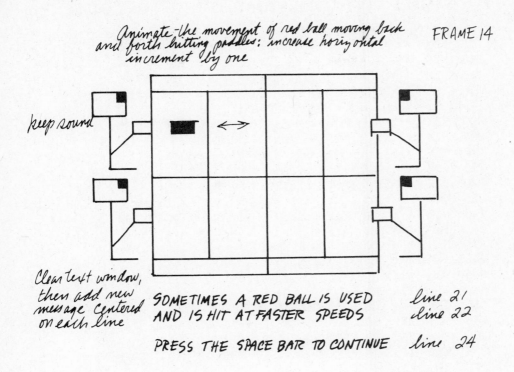

*keep sound*

*Clear text window, then add new message centered on each line*

SOMETIMES A RED BALL IS USED  line 21
AND IS HIT AT FASTER SPEEDS  line 22

PRESS THE SPACE BAR TO CONTINUE  line 24

*Animate the movement of the red ball moving back and forth: increase horizontal increment by three*  FRAME 15

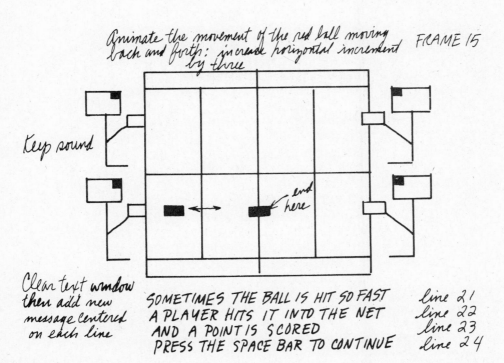

*Keep sound*

*end here*

*Clear text window then add new message centered on each line*

SOMETIMES THE BALL IS HIT SO FAST  line 21
A PLAYER HITS IT INTO THE NET  line 22
AND A POINT IS SCORED  line 23
PRESS THE SPACE BAR TO CONTINUE  line 24

## SAMPLE COMPUTER STORY: THE TENNIS COURT

```
100  REM  ********************************************
110  REM  *              TENNIS COURT               *
120  REM  ********************************************
130  TEXT : HOME : REM  CLEAR SCREEN
140  GOTO 5000: REM  BRANCH TO MAIN FLOW
200  REM  ********************************************
205  REM  *          DEFINITION OF VARIABLES        *
210  REM  ********************************************
215  REM  L : LENGTH OF DELAY
220  REM  D : INDEX FOR DELAY LOOP
225  REM  CA, CB, ...., CL : COLORS FOR PARTS OF TENNIS PLAYER
230  REM  K : CONTROLS PLAYER POSITION : FACING LEFT (I = 1),
     FACING RIGHT (I = 2)
235  REM  X : COLUMN POSITION
240  REM  Y : ROW POSITION
245  REM  A$(1), A$(2), ...., A$(26) : LETTERS OF ALPHABET IN
     BINARY FORM
250  REM  J : CONTROLS GENERAL PURPOSE LOOPS
255  REM  XN : NEW HORIZONTAL POSITION OF BALL
260  REM  XO : OLD HORIZONTAL POSITION OF BALL
265  REM  XI : INCREMENT VALUE FOR HORIZONTAL MOVEMENT OF BALL
270  REM  BALL : COLOR OF BALL
275  REM  M : CONTROLS LOOP FOR SOUND
280  REM  S : MEMORY LOCATION FOR CLICKING SPEAKER
285  REM  B : USED FOR SOUND GENERATION
290  REM  Q$ : VARIABLE FOR USER RESPONSE
295  REM  I : GENERAL INDEX IDENTIFIER
300  REM  ********************************************
305  REM  *             DEFINE ALPHABET             *
310  REM  ********************************************
315  A$(3) = "011111000010000100001111": REM  C
320  A$(5) = "111111000011101000011111": REM  E
325  A$(8) = "100011000111111100011000 1": REM  H
330  A$(9) = "111110010000100001001111 1": REM  I
335  A$(14) = "110011100110101100111001 1": REM  N
340  A$(15) = "011101000110001100010111 0": REM  O
345  A$(18) = "111111000111111100101000 1": REM  R
350  A$(19) = "111111000011111000011111 1": REM  S
355  A$(20) = "111110010000100001000010 0": REM  T
360  A$(21) = "100011000110001100010111 0": REM  U
365  RETURN
400  REM  ********************************************
405  REM  *             DELAY ROUTINE               *
410  REM  ********************************************
```

```
415   FOR D = 1 TO L: NEXT : REM  L = LENGTH OF DELAY
420   RETURN
500   REM  *******************************************
510   REM  *          DRAW TENNIS PLAYER           *
515   REM  *******************************************
520   ON K GOTO 525,535
525   REM  ESTABLISH COLORS FOR PLAYER FACING LEFT
530   CA = 6:CB = 13:CC = 8:CD = 1:CE = 13:CF = 13:CG =
      0:CH = 15: CI = 0:CJ = 0:CK = 3:CL = 9: GOTO 550
535   REM  ESTABLISH COLORS FOR PLAYER FACING RIGHT
540   CA = 13:CB = 6:CC = 0:CD = 13:CE = 1:CF = 0:CG =
      13:CH = 0: CI = 15:CJ = 8:CK = 12:CL = 12
550   REM  DRAW PLAYER
555   COLOR =  CC: HLIN X − 4,X − 3 AT Y + 1: HLIN X − 4,X −
      3 AT Y + 2: REM  DRAW LEFT RACKET : CC = 8 (BROWN) IF
      PLAYER FACES LEFT ; CC = 0 (BLACK) IF PLAYER FACES
      RIGHT
560   COLOR =  CJ: HLIN X + 5,X + 6 AT Y + 1: HLIN X + 5,X +
      6 AT Y + 2: REM  DRAW RIGHT RACKET : CJ = 8 (BROWN) IF
      PLAYER FACES RIGHT; CJ = 0 (BLACK) IF PLAYER FACES
      LEFT
565   COLOR =  CA: PLOT X,Y: REM  DRAW LEFT EYE : CA = 6
      (BLUE) IF PLAYER FACES LEFT; CA = 13 (YELLOW) IF PLAYER
       FACES RIGHT
570   COLOR =  CB: PLOT X + 2,Y: REM  DRAW RIGHT EYE : CB = 6
      (BLUE) IF PLAYER FACES RIGHT; CB = 13 (YELLOW) IF PLAYER
      FACES LEFT
575   COLOR =  CD: PLOT X,Y + 2: REM  DRAW LEFT PART OF MOUTH
      : CD = 1 (MAGENTA) IF PLAYER FACES LEFT ; CD = 13
      (YELLOW) IF PLAYER FACES RIGHT
580   COLOR =  CE: PLOT X + 2,Y + 2: REM  DRAW RIGHT PART OF
      MOUTH : CE = 1 (MAGENTA) IF PLAYER FACES RIGHT; CE = 13
      (YELLOW) IF PLAYER FACES LEFT
585   COLOR =  1: PLOT X + 1,Y + 2: REM  DRAW PART OF MOUTH
      COMMON TO PLAYER FACING IN EITHER DIRECTION
590   COLOR =  13: PLOT X + 1,Y: HLIN X,X + 2 AT Y + 1: REM
      COLOR REMAINING PARTS OF FACE YELLOW
595   PLOT X + 1,Y + 3: REM  COLOR NECK YELLOW
600   VLIN Y + 6,Y + 7 AT X + 1: REM  COLOR LEG YELLOW
605   COLOR =  CF: PLOT X − 2,Y + 3: PLOT X − 1,Y + 4: REM
      DRAW LEFT ARM : CF = 13 ( YELLOW) IF PLAYER FACES LEFT;
      CF = 0 (BLACK) IF PLAYER FACES RIGHT
610   COLOR =  CG: PLOT X + 4,Y + 3: PLOT X + 3,Y + 4: REM
      DRAW RIGHT ARM : CF = 13 (YELLOW) IF PLAYER FACES RIGHT;
      CG = 0 (BLACK) IF PLAYER FACES LEFT
615   COLOR =  CL: HLIN X,X + 2 AT Y + 4: REM  COLOR UPPER
      HALF OF SHORTS EITHER ORANGE (CL = 9, PLAYER FACES LEFT)
```

```
           OR LIGHT GREEN (CL = 12, PLAYER FACES RIGHT)
620   COLOR =   CK: HLIN X,X + 2 AT Y + 5: REM   COLOR LOWER
      HALF OF SHORTS EITHER PURPLE (CK = 3, IF PLAYER FACES
      LEFT) OR LIGHT GREEN (CK = 12, PLAYER FACES RIGHT)
625   COLOR =   15: PLOT X + 1,Y + 8: REM   COLOR PART OF SHOE
      COMMON TO PLAYER FACING EITHER LEFT OR RIGHT WHITE
630   COLOR =   CH: PLOT X,Y + 8: REM   COLOR LEFT PART OF SHOE
      : CH = 13 (WHITE) IF PLAYER FACING LEFT; CH = 0 (BLACK)
      IF PLAYER FACES RIGHT
635   COLOR =   CI: PLOT X + 2,Y + 8: REM   COLOR RIGHT PART OF
      SHOE : CI = 13 (WHITE) IF PLAYER FACING RIGHT; CI = 0
      (BLACK) IF PLAYER FACING LEFT
640   RETURN
700   REM   ANIMATED BALL ROUTINE
705   FOR J = 1 TO 6: REM   BEGIN LOOP : MOVE BALL BACK AND
      FORTH SIX TIMES
710   XN = XO + XI: REM    DETERMINE NEW POSITION (XN) OF BALL
      BY ADDING OLD POSITION (XO) AND INCREMENT (XI) : XI >0,
      MOVES RIGHT; XI <0, MOVES LEFT
715   IF XN >10 AND XN <29 THEN 735: REM    CHECK TO
      ASSURE BALL REMAINS WITHIN COURT BOUNDARIES
720   S= − 16336: FOR M = 1 TO 5:B =  PEEK (S) +
      PEEK (S) +   PEEK (S): NEXT : REM   MAKE NOISE AS BALL HITS
      RACKET
725   XI= − 1 * XI: REM   REVERSE DIRECTION OF BALL
730   GOTO 785: REM   COMPLETE ONE PASS ACROSS COURT
735   COLOR =  BALL: REM   DETERMINE COLOR OF BALL
740   PLOT XN,Y:L = 100: GOSUB 400: REM    PLOT COLORED
      BALL;ENACT DELAY
745   IF XN = 15 OR XN = 20 OR XN = 25 THEN 770: REM
      DETERMINE IF BALL IS AT A WHITE BOUNDARY LINE
750   COLOR = 4: REM   IF NOT AT BOUNDARY LINE, CHANGE COLOR OF
      BALL TO GREEN
755   PLOT XN,Y:L = 100: GOSUB 400: REM   REDRAW MOVING BALL
      GREEN FOR ANIMATED EFFECT; ENACT DELAY
760 XO = XN: REM   ESTABLISH CONDITIONS FOR NEW POSITION OF
      BALL
765   GOTO 710: REM   CONTINUE WITH PROCESS OF ANIMATING THE BALL
770   COLOR =   15: REM   IF A BOUNDARY LINE, CHANGE COLOR OF
      BALL TO WHITE
775   PLOT XN,Y:L = 1: GOSUB 400: REM   REDRAW MOVING BALL WHITE
      FOR ANIMATED EFFECT; ENACT DELAY
777   XO = XN: REM   ESTABLISH CONDITIONS FOR NEW POSITION OF
      BALL
780   GOTO 710: REM   CONTINUE WITH PROCESS OF ANIMATING THE BALL
785   NEXT J: REM    END OF LOOP
790   RETURN : REM   END OF SUBROUTINE; RETURN TO MAIN PROGRAM
```

```
800   REM   ROUTINE FOR DRAWING LETTERS IN BINARY FORM
805   FOR J = 1 TO 25: REM   TWENTY FIVE BITS PER LETTER
810   B$ =  MID$ (A$(I),J,1): REM   ACCESS JTH BIT IN A$ (I)
815   V =  VAL (B$): REM   CONVERT TO NUMERICAL VALUE 0 OR 1
820   R =  INT ((J - 1) / 5): REM   DETERMINE ROW
825   C = J - 5 * R: REM   DETERMINE COLUMN
830   IF V = 0 THEN   COLOR =  BK: REM   COLOR LETTER IN
      BACKGROUND COLOR
835   IF V = 1 THEN   COLOR =  HC: REM   COLOR LETTER IN NON
      BACKGROUND COLOR
840   PLOT X + C - 1,Y + R: REM   DRAW ONE BRICK
845   NEXT J: REM   END OF LOOP
850   RETURN : REM   END OF SUBROUTINE, RETURN TO MAIN PROGRAM
900   REM   ROUTINE TO COMPLETE FRAME
905   VTAB 24: HTAB 4: PRINT "PRESS THE SPACE BAR TO CONTINUE.";
910   GET Q$: REM   WAIT FOR USER RESPONSE
915   HOME : RETURN : REM   CLEAR TEXT WINDOW, RETURN TO MAIN
      PROGRAM
5000  REM   ******************************************
5005  REM   *              MAIN PROGRAM              *
5010  REM   ******************************************
5015  REM   ******************************************
5020  REM   *              TITLE PAGE                *
5025  REM   ******************************************
5027  DIM A$(26): GOSUB 300: REM   DEFINE BINARY ALPHABET
5030  GR : POKE  - 16302,0: REM   ESTABLISH FULL SCREEN LOW RES
      GRAPHICS
5035  COLOR =  13: REM   SET COLOR TO YELLOW
5040  FOR J = 0 TO 47: HLIN 0,39 AT J: NEXT : REM   CREATE
      YELLOW BACKGROUND
5042  BK = 13: REM   SET BACKGROUND COLOR FOR LETTER DRAWING
      SUBROUTINE
5045  HC = 2: REM   CHANGE COLOR TO DARK BLUE
5050  X = 11:Y = 8:I = 20: GOSUB 800: REM   DRAW T
5055  X = 18:I = 8: GOSUB 800: REM   DRAW H
5060  X = 25:I = 5: GOSUB 800: REM   DRAW E
5065  HC = 1: REM   CHANGE COLOR TO MAGENTA
5070  X = 0:Y = 17:I = 20: GOSUB 800: REM   DRAW T
5075  X = 7:I = 5: GOSUB 800: REM   DRAW E
5085  X = 14:I = 14: GOSUB 800: REM   DRAW N
5090  X = 21: GOSUB 800: REM   DRAW N
5095  X = 28:I = 9: GOSUB 800: REM   I
5100  X = 35:I = 19: GOSUB 800: REM   S
5102  HC = 12: REM   CHANGE COLOR TO GREEN
5105  X = 3:Y = 26:I = 3: GOSUB 800: REM   C
5110  X = 10:I = 15: GOSUB 800: REM   O
5115  X = 17:I = 21: GOSUB 800: REM   U
```

```
5120  X = 24:I = 18: GOSUB 800: REM  R
5125  X = 31:I = 20: GOSUB 800: REM  T
5130  L = 5000: GOSUB 400: REM  DELAY SCREEN DISPLAY
5135  REM ****************************************
5140  REM *              FRAME 1               *
5145  REM ****************************************
5147  TEXT : HOME : REM  CLEAR SCREEN
5150  GR : POKE − 16301,0: REM  CLEAR SCREEN, ESTABLISH MIXED
      SCREEN GRAPHICS
5155  COLOR = 15: REM  CHANGE COLOR TO WHITE
5160  REM  PRINT MESSAGE
5165  VTAB 21: HTAB 4: PRINT "A TENNIS COURT IS A SMOOTH LEVEL"
5170  VTAB 22: HTAB 2: PRINT "SURFACE IN THE SHAPE OF A
      RECTANGLE,"
5175  VTAB 23: HTAB 3: PRINT "USUALLY WITH A WHITE BOUNDARY
      LINE."
5180  REM  DRAW BOUNDARY OF TENNIS COURT SLOWLY AS A SERIES OF
      PLOTS
5185  L = 100: REM  ESTABLISH DELAY
5190  FOR J = 10 TO 30: PLOT J,30: GOSUB 400: NEXT : REM  DRAW
      LOWER BOUNDARY
5195  FOR J = 30 TO 10 STEP  − 1: PLOT 30,J: GOSUB 400: NEXT :
      REM  DRAW RIGHT BOUNDARY
5200  FOR J = 30 TO 10 STEP  − 1: PLOT J,10: GOSUB 400: NEXT :
      REM  DRAW UPPER BOUNDARY
5205  FOR J = 10 TO 30: PLOT 10,J: GOSUB 400: NEXT : REM  DRAW
      UPPER BOUNDARY
5210  GOSUB 900: REM  COMPLETE FRAME
5215  REM ****************************************
5220  REM *              FRAME 2               *
5225  REM ****************************************
5230  REM  PRINT MESSAGE
5235  VTAB 21: HTAB 8: PRINT "SOMETIMES THE SURFACE IS"
5240  VTAB 22: HTAB 10: PRINT "A PINKISH COLOR CLAY."
5245  COLOR =  11: REM  CHANGE COLOR TO PINK
5250  FOR J = 11 TO 29: HLIN 11,29 AT J: NEXT : REM  SHADE IN
      RECTANGULAR REGION
5255  GOSUB 900: REM  COMPLETE FRAME
5260  REM ****************************************
5265  REM *              FRAME 3               *
5270  REM ****************************************
5275  REM  PRINT MESSAGE
5280  VTAB 21: HTAB 11: PRINT "OR SOMETIMES IT IS"
5285  VTAB 22: HTAB 10: PRINT "MADE OF GREY MACADAM."
5290  COLOR =  5: REM  CHANGE COLOR TO GREY
5295  FOR J = 11 TO 29: HLIN 11,29 AT J: NEXT J: REM  SHADE IN
      RECTANGULAR REGION
```

```
5300   GOSUB 900: REM   COMPLETE FRAME
5305   REM  ******************************************
5310   REM  *                 FRAME 4               *
5315   REM  ******************************************
5320   REM  PRINT MESSAGE
5325   VTAB 21: HTAB 6: PRINT "THE SURFACE IS ALSO MADE OF"
5330   VTAB 22: HTAB 6: PRINT "A GREEN RUBBER TYPE MATERIAL."
5335   COLOR =  4: REM   CHANGE COLOR TO GREEN
5340   FOR J = 11 TO 29: HLIN 11,29 AT J: NEXT J: REM  SHADE
       RECTANGULAR REGION
5345   GOSUB 900: REM   COMPLETE FRAME
5350   REM  ******************************************
5355   REM  *                 FRAME 5               *
5360   REM  ******************************************
5365   REM  PRINT MESSAGE
5370   VTAB 21: HTAB 8: PRINT "THE COURT HAS A NET THAT"
5375   VTAB 22: HTAB 11: PRINT "DIVIDES IT IN HALF."
5380   COLOR =  15: REM   CHANGE COLOR TO WHITE
5385   VLIN 11,29 AT 20: REM   DRAW NET
5390   GOSUB 900: REM   COMPLETE FRAME
5395   REM  ******************************************
5400   REM  *                 FRAME 6               *
5405   REM  ******************************************
5410   REM  PRINT MESSAGE
5415   VTAB 21: HTAB 2: PRINT "THERE ARE OTHER BOUNDARY LINES
       WHICH"
5420   VTAB 22: HTAB 1: PRINT "ARE IMPORTANT IN THE 'PLAY' OF
       THE GAME"
5425   VTAB 23: HTAB 14: PRINT "T E N N I S."
5430   VLIN 11,29 AT 15: VLIN 11,29 AT 25: REM   DRAW BACKCOURT
       LINES
5435   HLIN 15,25 AT 20: REM   DRAW CENTER COURT LINE
5440   GOSUB 900: REM   COMPLETE FRAME
5445   REM  ******************************************
5450   REM  *                 FRAME 7               *
5455   REM  ******************************************
5460   REM  PRINT MESSAGE
5465   VTAB 21: HTAB 3: PRINT "TWO ADDITIONAL HORIZONTAL LINES
       ARE"
5470   VTAB 22: HTAB 2: PRINT "USED TO DETERMINE THE COURT LINES
       FOR"
5475   VTAB 23: HTAB 4: PRINT "'SINGLES PLAY' OR 'DOUBLES
       PLAY'."
5480   HLIN 10,30 AT 7: HLIN 10,30 AT 33: REM   DRAW HORIZONTAL
       LINES
5485   VLIN 7,33 AT 10: VLIN 7,33 AT 30: REM   DRAW VERTICAL
       LINES
```

```
5490   COLOR =   4: REM   CHANGE COLOR TO GREEN
5495   REM   SHADE NEW BOUNDARIES WITH GREEN
5500   HLIN 11,19 AT 8: HLIN 11,19 AT 9
5505   HLIN 11,19 AT 31: HLIN 11,19 AT 32
5510   HLIN 21,29 AT 8: HLIN 21,29 AT 9
5515   HLIN 21,29 AT 31: HLIN 21,29 AT 32
5520   COLOR =   15: REM   CHANGE COLOR TO WHITE
5525   VLIN 7,33 AT 20: REM   EXTEND DRAWING OF NET
5530   GOSUB 900: REM   COMPLETE FRAME
5535   REM   ******************************************
5540   REM   *                   FRAME 8              *
5545   REM   ******************************************
5550   REM   PRINT MESSAGE
5555   VTAB 21: HTAB 1: PRINT "IN 'SINGLES PLAY' THERE IS ONE
       PLAYER"
5560   VTAB 22: HTAB 6: PRINT "AT THE LEFT END OF THE COURT."
5565   X = 4:Y = 15:K = 2: GOSUB 500: REM   DRAW PLAYER FACING
       RIGHT
5570   GOSUB 900: REM   COMPLETE FRAME
5575   REM   ******************************************
5580   REM   *                   FRAME 9              *
5585   REM   ******************************************
5590   REM   PRINT MESSAGE
5595   VTAB 21: HTAB 9: PRINT "AN OPPONENT PLAYS AT THE"
5600   VTAB 22: HTAB 8: PRINT "OPPOSITE END OF THE COURT."
5605   X = 33:Y = 15:K = 1: GOSUB 500: REM   DRAW PLAYER
       FACING LEFT
5610   GOSUB 900: REM   COMPLETE FRAME
5615   REM   ******************************************
5620   REM   *                   FRAME 10             *
5625   REM   ******************************************
5630   COLOR =   0: REM   CHANGE COLOR TO BLACK
5635   FOR J = 0 TO 39: HLIN 0,9 AT J: HLIN 31,39 AT J: NEXT :
       REM   REMOVE PLAYERS FROM SCREEN
5640   COLOR =   15: REM   CHANGE COLOR TO WHITE
5645   VLIN 10,30 AT 10: VLIN 10,30 AT 30: REM   REDRAW BOUNDARY
       LINES
5650   COLOR =   4: REM   CHANGE COLOR TO GREEN
5655   VLIN 14,19 AT 29: REM   REDRAW SURFACE PREVIOUSLY COVERED
       BY RACKET
5660   REM   PRINT MESSAGE
5665   VTAB 21: HTAB 5: PRINT "IN 'DOUBLES PLAY' TWO PLAYERS"
5670   VTAB 22: HTAB 6: PRINT "ARE AT ONE END OF THE COURT."
5675   X = 4:Y = 10:K = 2: GOSUB 500: REM   DRAW TOP PLAYER
       FACING RIGHT
5680   X = 4:Y = 24:K = 2: GOSUB 500: REM   DRAW BOTTOM PLAYER
       FACING RIGHT
```

```
5685   GOSUB 900: REM   COMPLETE FRAME
5690   REM   *******************************************
5695   REM   *                   FRAME 11              *
5700   REM   *******************************************
5705   REM   PRINT MESSAGE
5710   VTAB 21: HTAB 6: PRINT "THE OPPOSING TWO PLAYERS ARE"
5715   VTAB 22: HTAB 5: PRINT "AT THE OTHER END OF THE COURT."
5720   X = 33:Y = 10:K = 1: GOSUB 500: REM   DRAW TOP PLAYER
       FACING LEFT
5725   X = 33:Y = 24:K = 1: GOSUB 500: REM   DRAW BOTTOM PLAYER
       FACING LEFT
5730   GOSUB 900: REM   COMPLETE FRAME
5735   REM   *******************************************
5740   REM   *                   FRAME 12              *
5745   REM   *******************************************
5750   REM   PRINT MESSAGE
5755   VTAB 21: HTAB 5: PRINT "THE GAME OF TENNIS USES A BALL"
5760   VTAB 22: HTAB 3: PRINT "WHICH IS HIT BACK AND FORTH
       ACROSS"
5765   VTAB 23: HTAB 7: PRINT "THE COURT AND OVER THE NET."
5770   BALL = 15:XI = 1:XO = 10:Y = 12: REM   SET CONDITIONS
       FOR ANIMATED BALL
5775   GOSUB 700: REM   ACCESS ANIMATED BALL ROUTINE
5780   GOSUB 900: REM   COMPLETE FRAME
5785   REM   *******************************************
5787   REM   *                   FRAME 13              *
5790   REM   *******************************************
5800   REM   PRINT MESSAGE
5805   VTAB 21: HTAB 11: PRINT "SOMETIMES THE PLAYERS"
5810   VTAB 22: HTAB 12: PRINT "USE AN ORANGE BALL."
5815   BALL = 9:XI = 1:XO = 10:Y = 26: REM   SET CONDITIONS
       FOR ANIMATED BALL
5820   GOSUB 700: REM   ACCESS ANIMATED BALL ROUTINE
5825   GOSUB 900: REM   COMPLETE FRAME
5830   REM   *******************************************
5835   REM   *                   FRAME 14              *
5840   REM   *******************************************
5845   REM   PRINT MESSAGE
5850   VTAB 21: HTAB 7: PRINT "SOMETIMES A RED BALL IS USED"
5855   VTAB 22: HTAB 7: PRINT "AND IS HIT AT FASTER SPEEDS."
5860   BALL = 1:XI = 2:XO = 10:Y = 12: REM   SET CONDITIONS
       FOR ANIMATED BALL
5865   GOSUB 700: REM   ACCESS ANIMATED BALL ROUTINE
5870   GOSUB 900: REM   COMPLETE FRAME
5875   REM   *******************************************
5880   REM   *                   FRAME 15              *
```

```
5885   REM   ********************************************
5890   REM   PRINT MESSAGE
5895   VTAB 21: HTAB 3: PRINT "SOMETIMES THE BALL IS HIT SO
       FAST"
5900   VTAB 22: HTAB 5: PRINT "A PLAYER HITS IT INTO THE NET"
5905   VTAB 23: HTAB 9: PRINT "AND A POINT IS SCORED."
5910   BALL = 9:XI = 4:XO = 10:Y = 26: REM  SET CONDITIONS
       FOR ANIMATED BALL
5915   GOSUB 700: REM  ACCESS ANIMATED BALL ROUTINE
5920   COLOR = 9: PLOT 20,26: REM  PUT BALL IN NET
5925   GOSUB 900 : REM   COMPLETE FRAME
5930   TEXT : HOME : END : REM  COMPLETE PROGRAM
```

## SUGGESTED PROJECTS

1. Write a computer story which describes the various parts of a head or face. You might include blinking eyes, an alternately happy and sad face, a missing tooth, and a tipping hat.

2. Write a computer story that displays a picture of an apple tree as it progresses from one season to the next. Show how the tree develops leaves in the spring, bears fruit in late summer, loses its fruit in the fall, and defoliates in the winter.

3. Write a computer story which demonstrates how a person jumps rope. Include three different positions: one where the rope is at its highest point and the person is standing on both feet; another where the rope is at its lowest point and both feet of the person are off the ground; and a third where the rope is between its highest and lowest position and one foot of the person is off the ground.

4. Write a computer story which simulates a bowler attempting to throw a strike. Include possibilities where a strike has failed, such as a split, missing the head pin, or throwing a gutter ball.

5. Write a computer story that illustrates a war scene where an aircraft bombs and sinks a battleship.

6. Write a computer story of your creation.

# High Resolution Graphics

## MODULE 2A   Fundamental High Resolution Commands

### ACTIVITY 2.1   Plotting Points on High Resolution
### Page 1

**LEARNING BY DISCOVERY**   This activity introduces the displaying of points on the high resolution screen.

1. Enter the following commands.

   ```
   NEW
   10   HOME
   20   HGR
   RUN
   ```

   Describe what happens. _____

2. Add lines 30 and 40 as follows:

   ```
   TEXT : HOME
   30   HCOLOR = 6
   40   HPLOT 140, 95
   RUN
   ```

   Observe the screen display.
   What geometric object appears? _____
   What color is the object? _____
   Where is the object located? _____

3. Retype line 30 as follows:

   ```
   TEXT : HOME
   ```

```
30   HCOLOR = 5
RUN
```

Describe what happens. _____

4. Retype line 40 as follows:

```
TEXT : HOME
40   HPLOT 139, 95
RUN
```

Describe what happens. _____

5. Retype line 40 as follows:

```
TEXT : HOME
40   HPLOT 280, 95
RUN
```

Describe what happens. _____

6. Retype line 40 as follows:

```
TEXT : HOME
40   HPLOT 139, 160
RUN
```

Describe what happens. _____

7. Retype lines 30 and 40 and add line 50 as follows:

```
TEXT : HOME
30   HCOLOR = 2
40   HPLOT 4, 4
50   PRINT "A VIOLET HI-RES DOT"
RUN
```

Describe what happens. _____

8. Add line 45 as follows:

```
TEXT : HOME
45   VTAB 22
RUN
```

Describe what happens. _____

**DISCUSSION**   The HGR command converts the screen to high resolution mixed graphics mode. Figure 2.1.1 displays the layout and boundary limits of the mixed graphics screen. When HGR is executed, the graphics portion of Page 1 of high resolution graphics is cleared to black, with a four line text window at the bottom of the page. This text window shares the same memory locations as that in low resolution graphics. The text window memory is not affected and the cursor is not moved to the text window area.

HCOLOR = sets the colors for high resolution graphics. Numerals 0 through 7 are used to obtain the various hues. Table 2.1.1 defines the available color codes. Notice the use of H in HGR and HCOLOR for high resolution mode, in contrast to the use of GR and COLOR for low resolution mode.

The HPLOT command displays a dot on the high resolution screen. Care must be taken to coordinate column numbers with color codes. Even numbered color codes must precede an HPLOT with an even column number. Similarly, odd numbered color codes must precede an HPLOT with an odd column number.

For example, the combination of HCOLOR = 6 and HPLOT 140, 95 in Section 2 displays a blue dot, while the combination HCOLOR = 5 and HPLOT 140, 95 in Section 3 does not display an orange dot. An exception to this restriction occurs for the colors black and white (0,3,4 and 7). These colors are available in all columns. Drawing white will be explored more thoroughly in Activities 2.2 and 2.3.

HPLOT 140,95 places a dot at the intersection of column 140 and row 95. HPLOT 280,95 in Section 5 gives an error, since 280 is beyond the allowable column limits of 0 through 279. In Section 6, HPLOT 139,160 gives no graphics display since row 160 is outside the graphics area, in the text window area. Note that the upper left corner of the screen is identified by the coordinate 0,0.

Since the HGR command does not move the cursor to the text window, a VTAB X (where X = 21,22,23, or 24) is necessary for messages from PRINT statements to appear on the screen. Sections 7 and 8 demonstrate how the use of the VTAB command provides better screen control of messages when displaying text in high resolution graphics mode.

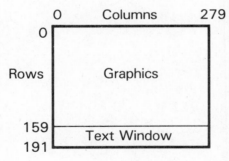

Figure 2.1.1

| COLOR | NUMERAL |
|---------|---------|
| Black 1 | 0 |
| Green | 1 |
| Violet | 2 |
| White 1 | 3 |
| Black 2 | 4 |
| Orange | 5 |
| Blue | 6 |
| White 2 | 7 |

Table 2.1.1

**COMPREHENSIVE EXAMPLE**   Study the following APPLESOFT program to determine the screen display. Check your answer by entering the program into the computer. Note: INT(280 * RND(1)) randomly generates numbers 0 through 279.

```
TEXT : HOME : NEW
10   REM ****************************************
11   REM *            CE2.1                     *
12   REM ****************************************
15   HOME
20   HGR
25   HCOLOR = 3
30   FOR I = 1 TO 50
40   X = INT(280 * RND(1))
50   Y = INT(160 * RND(1))
60   HPLOT X, Y
70   NEXT
80   VTAB 23 : HTAB 14
90   PRINT "A STARRY SKY";
95   GET Q$ : TEXT : HOME
```

**Check Your Comprehension**

How many stars appear in the sky? _____

What colors are the stars? _____

Why is the number 280 used in line 40? _____

**EXERCISE**   Write a program that plots four different colored dots on the four corners of the high resolution mixed graphics screen.

**CHALLENGE**   Write a program that uses a loop to plot violet dots from coordinate (0,0) to coordinate (158,158) with the message "DOTTED VIOLET LINE" centered near the bottom line of the text window.

# ACTIVITY 2.2   Drawing Lines on High Resolution
## Page 1

**LEARNING BY DISCOVERY**   This activity introduces the HPLOT TO command to connect points forming lines.

1. Enter the following commands.

```
NEW
10   HOME : HGR
20   HCOLOR = 3
30   FOR I = 20 TO 260
40   HPLOT I, 90
50   NEXT
RUN
```

Describe what happens. _____

2. Enter the following commands.

```
TEXT : HOME : NEW
10   HOME : HGR
20   HCOLOR = 3
30   HPLOT 20, 90 TO 260, 90
RUN
```

Observe the screen display in comparison to that of Section 1.

What is the result of the HPLOT command? _____

Which line is drawn faster (Section 1 or Section 2)? _____

Estimate the length of the line in terms of dots (pixels). _____

What is the purpose of the 90 in line 30? _____

3. Retype line 20 and 30 as follows:

```
TEXT : HOME
20   HCOLOR = 5
30   HPLOT 105, 10 TO 105, 120
RUN
```

Observe the screen display.

What is the result of the HPLOT command? _____

Estimate the length of the line in terms of pixels. _____

What is the purpose of the 105 in line 30? _____

4. Retype line 20 as follows:

```
TEXT : HOME
20   HCOLOR = 6
RUN
```

Describe what happens. _____

5. Retype lines 20 and 30 as follows:

```
TEXT : HOME
20   HCOLOR = 3
30   HPLOT 106, 10 TO 106, 150
RUN
```

Observe the screen display.
   What color is the vertical line? _____
   What color did you expect? _____

6. Retype lines 20 and 30 as follows:

```
TEXT : HOME
20   HCOLOR = 7
30   HPLOT 105, 10 TO 105, 150
RUN
```

Observe the screen display.
   What color is the vertical line? _____
   What color did you expect? _____

**DISCUSSION**   Besides displaying dots (pixels), the HPLOT command can be combined with TO to draw lines in a much faster fashion than repetitively producing adjacent pixels.

For example, HPLOT 20, 90 TO 260, 90 in Section 2 produces a horizontal line of length 241 (or $(260 - 20) + 1$) dots or pixels at row 90.

Vertical lines can also be drawn, but the same care must be given as occurred when displaying individual dots. For example, in Section 3 an orange vertical line at column 105 of length 111 (or $(120 - 10) + 1$) pixels is drawn by HPLOT 105, 10 TO 105, 120 if preceded by the command HCOLOR = 5; however, no line is visible if the HCOLOR = 6 command is used, as in Section 4. Remember, even numbered colors require even column numbers and odd numbered colors require odd column numbers, except for colors 3 and 7. Sections 5 and 6 demonstrate that any attempt to draw a white (HCOLOR = 3 or 7) vertical line is not successfully displayed regardless of which column number is used, but rather, its displayed color will be either green, violet, orange, or blue. A detailed discussion of drawing white vertical lines is provided in ACTIVITY 2.3.

**COMPREHENSIVE EXAMPLE**   Study the following program to determine the screen display. Check your answer by entering the program in the computer.

```
TEXT : HOME : NEW
10   REM ***************************************
11   REM *              CE2.2                   *
12   REM ***************************************
15   HOME : HGR
```

```
20   HCOLOR = 5
30   FOR J = 0 TO 40
40   HPLOT 135 - J, 60 + J TO 135 + J, 60 + J
50   NEXT
60   VTAB 23 : HTAB 11
70   PRINT "AN EGYPTIAN SUNSET";
80   GET Q$ : TEXT : HOME
```

**Check Your Comprehension**

What geometric figure is drawn? _____

What color is the figure? _____

Why is line 40 included in a loop? _____

**EXERCISE**   Write a program which draws the rectangle illustrated in Figure 2.2.1 blue.

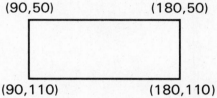

Figure 2.2.1

**CHALLENGE**   Write a program which shades the rectangular region in Figure 2.2.1 violet.

## ACTIVITY 2.3   Drawing with White on the High Resolution Screen

**LEARNING BY DISCOVERY**   This activity demonstrates how to obtain white diagrams on the screen.

Enter the following commands to prepare for the color adjustment of your TV or monitor:

```
NEW
10   HOME : HGR
20   HCOLOR = 1 : HPLOT 50, 10 TO 200, 10
30   HCOLOR = 2 : HPLOT 50, 100 TO 200, 100
40   HCOLOR = 5 : HPLOT 53, 25 TO 53, 85
50   HCOLOR = 6 : HPLOT 190, 25 TO 190, 85
RUN
```

Adjust your color controls so the upper horizontal line is green, the lower horizontal line is violet, the left vertical line is orange, and the right vertical line is blue. Some of these colors may vary due to differences among TV's and monitors.

1. Enter the following commands.

```
TEXT : HOME : NEW
10   HOME : HGR
20   HCOLOR = 3
30   HPLOT 139, 50 TO 139, 150
RUN
```

What color is the line? _____

2. Retype line 30 as follows:

```
TEXT : HOME
30   HPLOT 140, 50 TO 140, 150
RUN
```

What color is the line? _____

3. Retype line 20 as follows:

```
TEXT : HOME
20   HCOLOR = 7
RUN
```

What color is the line? _____

4. Retype line 30 as follows:

```
TEXT : HOME
30   HPLOT 139, 50 TO 139, 150
RUN
```

What color is the line? _____

5. Add line 40 as follows:

```
TEXT : HOME
40   HPLOT 140, 50 TO 140, 150
RUN
```

What color is the line? _____

**DISCUSSION**   The plotting of any high resolution white dot appears on the screen without concern as to whether the X coordinate of the HPLOT command is odd or even, as is the case with HCOLORS of 1,2,5, and 6 (refer to ACTIVITY 2.1); however, it will not be white. Either a violet, green, blue or orange dot will occur, depending upon whether HCOLOR = 3 or 7 and whether the X coordinate of the HPLOT is odd or even. Two dots must be plotted horizontally adjacent to each other to appear white. Table 2.3.1 summarizes this peculiar occurrence.

|  | ODD<br>X COORDINATE | EVEN<br>X COORDINATE | TWO ADJACENT<br>X COORDINATES |
|---|---|---|---|
| HCOLOR = 3 | Green | Violet | White |
| HCOLOR = 7 | Orange | Blue | White |

Table 2.3.1

**COMPREHENSIVE EXAMPLE**  Study the following program to determine the screen display. Check your answer by entering the program into the computer.

```
TEXT : HOME : NEW
10   REM ****************************************
11   REM *              CE2.3                   *
12   REM ****************************************
15   HOME : HGR : HCOLOR = 3
20   FOR I = 19 TO 119 STEP 2
40   HPLOT I, I
50   NEXT
60   FOR I = 40 TO 140 STEP 2
70   HPLOT I, I - 20
80   NEXT
90   VTAB 21: HTAB 12
95   PRINT "PARALLEL COLORS";
98   GET Q$ : TEXT : HOME
```

**Check Your Comprehension**

What is the color of the first dotted line segment that is drawn? _____

What is the color of the second dotted line segment that is drawn? _____

Why are these dotted line segments not white? _____

**EXERCISE**  Write a program that frames the high resolution mixed screen in white.

**CHALLENGE**  Write a program that draws a 10 × 10 white grid.

# ACTIVITY 2.4  More on the HPLOT TO Command

**LEARNING BY DISCOVERY**  This activity demonstrates additional features of the HPLOT TO command which will facilitate your drawing of diagrams.

1. Enter the following commands.

```
NEW
10   HOME : HGR
20   HCOLOR = 3
30   HPLOT 0, 0 TO 279, 0
40   HPLOT 279, 0 TO 279, 159
50   HPLOT 279, 159 TO 0, 0
RUN
```

Describe what happens. _____

2. Enter the following commands.

```
TEXT : HOME : NEW
10   HOME : HGR
20   HCOLOR = 3
30   HPLOT 0, 0 TO 279, 0 TO 279, 159 TO 0, 0
RUN
```

Observe the screen display in comparison to that of Section 1.

How do they compare? _____

3. Enter the following commands.

```
TEXT : HOME : NEW
10   HOME : HGR
20   HCOLOR = 3
30   HPLOT TO 279, 0
RUN
```

Describe what happens. _____

4. Add line 25 as follows:

```
TEXT : HOME
25   HPLOT 0, 159
RUN
```

Describe what happens. _____

5. Enter the following commands.

```
TEXT : HOME : NEW
10   HOME : HGR
20   HCOLOR = 3
30   FOR I = 1 TO 5
40   READ X, Y
50   HPLOT TO X, Y
60   NEXT
70   DATA 100, 50, 150, 100, 125, 150, 75, 150, 50, 100
RUN
```

Describe what happens. _____

6. Add line 25 as follows:

```
TEXT : HOME
25  HPLOT 50, 100
RUN
```

Describe what happens. _____

**DISCUSSION**   The HPLOT command has some additional powerful options. Prior to this lesson, you learned the HPLOT command displays a point and the HPLOT TO command draws both vertical and horizontal lines.

HPLOT TO will also draw diagonal lines, as demonstrated by HPLOT 279, 159 TO 0, 0. A series of lines can be drawn by using one HPLOT command with the syntax: HPLOT X1, Y1, TO X2, Y2 TO X3, Y3... . A triangle is displayed in the upper right part of the screen by HPLOT 0, 0 TO 279, 0 TO 279, 159 TO 0, 0 in Section 2.

A series of line segments can be connected successively by placing an HPLOT TO X, Y command in a loop where appropriate values for X and Y are supplied as predetermined data. For example, the combination of Sections 5 and 6 provide instructions which will display the diagram in Figure 4.1 by sequentially entering (READ X, Y) and connecting (HPLOT  TO X, Y) its vertices.

Due to another peculiarity of APPLESOFT, the HPLOT 50, 100 used in Section 6 is necessary for the screen display to appear. When HCOLOR is first defined, it is not internally established until the high resolution cursor is given starting coordinates. Therefore, any HPLOT TO X, Y command must be initiated by some HPLOT X, Y. The necessary prerequisite HPLOT X, Y to the HPLOT TO command is also demonstrated in Sections 3 and 4.

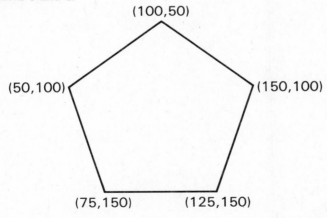

Figure 2.4.1

**COMPREHENSIVE EXAMPLE**   Study the following program to determine the screen display. Check your answer by entering the program in the computer.

```
TEXT : HOME : NEW
10   REM ****************************************
11   REM *              CE2.4                   *
```

```
12   REM *******************************************
15   HOME : HGR
20   HCOLOR = 3
30   HPLOT 0, 0 TO 279, 0 TO 279, 159 TO 0, 159 TO 0, 0
40   FOR I = 1 TO 5
50   READ X, Y
60   HPLOT TO X, Y
70   NEXT
80   DATA 279, 159, 278, 159, 278, 0, 1, 159, 1, 0
90   VTAB 22 : HTAB 11
95   PRINT "X IN A WHITE FRAME";
98   GET Q$ : TEXT : HOME
```

## Check Your Comprehension

What is the purpose of line 30? _____

What diagram is drawn by the loop? _____

Why does the HPLOT TO command in line 60 not need an initial HPLOT command? _____

**EXERCISE**   Write a program that draws the star illustrated in Figure 2.4.2 with the given coordinates, by using HPLOT X1, Y1 TO X2, Y2 TO X3, Y3 ... only once.

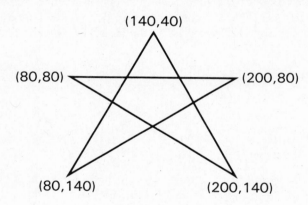

(140,40)

(80,80)         (200,80)

(80,140)       (200,140)

Figure 2.4.2

**CHALLENGE**   Write a program that draws the star illustrated in Figure 2.4.2 by using the HPLOT TO X, Y command in a loop and with the coordinates of the star as data.

# ACTIVITY 2.5   Obtaining Full Screen Graphics on Page 1

**LEARNING BY DISCOVERY**   This activity shows how to obtain full screen graphics on Page 1 of the high resolution screen.

Note: The next seven activities will demonstrate the use of Apple memory locations specifically reserved for controlling various screen display situations. A comprehensive discussion of all of these "soft switches" is given in the Synopsis section of Putting It All Together: Part 2.

1. Enter the following commands.

```
NEW
10   HOME
20   HGR
30   HCOLOR = 3
40   HPLOT 0, 191 TO 279, 191
RUN
```

Describe what happens. _____

2. Add line 25 as follows:

```
TEXT : HOME
25   POKE −16302, 0
RUN
```

Describe what happens. _____

3. Add lines 50 and 60 as follows:

```
TEXT : HOME
50   VTAB 22
60   PRINT "A STRAIGHT LINE"
RUN
```

Describe what happens. _____

4. Retype line 25 as follows:

```
TEXT : HOME
25   POKE −16301, 0
RUN
```

Describe what happens. _____

5. Retype line 25 as follows:

```
TEXT : HOME
25   POKE 49234, 0
RUN
```

Describe what happens. _____

6. Add lines 25 and 35 as follows:

```
TEXT : HOME
25  POKE 49235, 0
35  HPLOT 0, 159 TO 279, 159
RUN
```

Describe what happens. _____

**DISCUSSION**   In ACTIVITY 2.1, we learned that the HGR command causes Page 1 of the high resolution screen to be cleared to black and put into the mixed graphics mode (graphics & text). Any attempt to draw in the text area, such as HPLOT 0, 191 TO 279, 191, will not be displayed.

APPLESOFT does allow for full screen graphics by using a POKE −16302, 0 command after the HGR command. While in high resolution graphics, POKE −16302, 0 switches high resolution graphics from a 280 by 160 grid to a 280 by 192 grid.

Once in full screen graphics, messages from PRINT statements will not be displayed, as demonstrated in Section 3, unless certain conditions are established. Writing on the high resolution graphics screen will be discussed in CHAPTER 3.

The POKE −16301, 0 command switches the video display back to mixed screen graphics from full screen graphics. The number −16301 is an artificial representation of memory location 49235 (i.e. −16301 = 49235 − 65536) which is consistently used in Integer BASIC and is often used in APPLESOFT. Similarly, POKE −16302, 0 and POKE 49234, 0 are equivalent. POKE −16301 and POKE −16302 coordinate in tandem as "soft switches" illustrated in Table 2.5.1. A POKE at one address switches the adjacent address as well.

|   | MEMORY | LOCATION |
|---|---|---|
|   | − 16301 | − 16302 |
|   | 49235 | 49234 |
|   | MIXED SCREEN | FULL SCREEN |
| STATUS OF SWITCH | ON | OFF |
|   | OFF | ON |

Table 2.5.1

**COMPREHENSIVE EXAMPLE**   Study the following program to determine the screen display. Check your answer by entering the program into the computer.

```
TEXT  : HOME : NEW
10    REM ****************************************
11    REM *            CE2.5                     *
12    REM ****************************************
15    HOME
20    HGR : POKE -16302, 0
30    HCOLOR = 5
40    FOR I = 1 TO 100
50    HPLOT 140, 96
60    X = INT (280 * RND (1))
70    Y = INT (192 * RND (1))
80    HPLOT TO X, Y
90    NEXT
95    GET Q$ : TEXT : HOME
```

**Check Your Comprehension**

What diagram is drawn? _____

What is the purpose of the 192 in line 70? _____

What is the purpose of line 40? _____

**EXERCISE**  Write a program which draws a blue outline of the rocket illustrated in Figure 2.5.1 at the given coordinates on Page 1 of the high resolution screen.

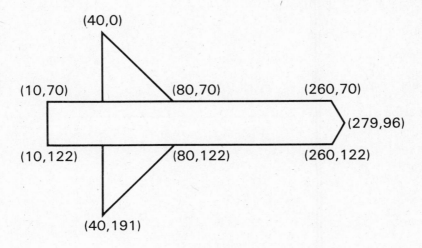

Figure 2.5.1

**CHALLENGE**  Write a program which draws an outline of a diagram of your choice using the full screen dimensions of high resolution Page 1.

# ACTIVITY 2.6   Drawing on High Resolution Page 2

**LEARNING BY DISCOVERY**   This activity demonstrates the techniques used for obtaining the possible screen displays on high resolution Page 2.

1. Enter the following commands.

```
NEW
10   HOME
20   HGR2
30   HCOLOR = 3
40   HPLOT 0, 191 TO 279, 191
RUN
```

Describe what happens. _____

2. Add lines 50 and 60 as follows:

```
TEXT : HOME
50   VTAB 22
60   PRINT "A STRAIGHT LINE"
RUN
```

Describe what happens. _____

3. Add line 25 as follows:

```
TEXT : HOME
25   POKE −16301, 0
RUN
```

Describe what happens. _____

4. Retype line 25 as follows:

```
TEXT : HOME
25   POKE −16302, 0
RUN
```

Describe what happens. _____

**DISCUSSION**   In Section 1, HGR2 clears the entire screen to black and switches to Page 2 of high resolution graphics. Unlike the HGR command, HGR2 creates a full screen graphics mode, rather than a mixed graphics screen. Section 2 demonstrates that any attempt to display messages from PRINT statements following an HGR2 command is futile, as was the situation with full screen graphics on high resolution Page 1. POKE −16301, 0, in Section 3, switches Page 2 back to mixed screen graphics; however, this attempt to PRINT in the text area results in unexpected nonsense. POKE −16302,0 in Section 4 switches Page 2 back to full screen graphics mode.

Page 2 of high resolution graphics does not allow for messages, either in mixed screen or full screen mode, by conventional methods. PRINTing can occur on both full screen pages but this discussion will be postponed until CHAPTER 3.

The benefits obtained from selecting either Page 1 or Page 2 will become clear as you proceed through the book.

**COMPREHENSIVE EXAMPLE**   Study the following program to determine the screen display. Check your answer by entering the program into the computer.

```
TEXT : HOME : NEW
10   REM ****************************************
11   REM *            CE2.6                    *
12   REM ****************************************
20   HOME : HGR2
30   HCOLOR = 6
40   HPLOT 110, 0 TO 110, 120 TO 0, 191 TO 110, 120 TO 279, 120
50   HCOLOR = 3
60   HPLOT 210, 124 TO 216, 130
70   HPLOT 216, 124 TO 210, 130
80   HPLOT 114, 60 TO 117, 63 TO 117, 66 TO 117, 63 TO 120, 60
90   HPLOT 70, 156 TO 76, 156 TO 70, 162 TO 76, 162
95   GET Q$ : TEXT : HOME
```

**Check Your Comprehension**

What diagram is drawn in blue? _____

What diagram is drawn in white? _____

Explain why no PRINT statements appear in the program. _____

**EXERCISE**   Write a program that draws the letters spelling APPLE forty pixels high, 30 pixels wide, and centered on Page 2 of the high resolution screen as show in Figure 2.6.1.

Figure 2.6.1

**CHALLENGE**   Write a program that colors in orange high resolution Page 2 in full graphics mode.

# ACTIVITY 2.7   Page Flipping with High Resolution Graphics

**LEARNING BY DISCOVERY**   This activity demonstrates how to alternate viewing of drawings on Page 1 and 2 of the high resolution screen. Let us assume that we first want to draw the diagram on Page 1 followed by that on Page 2 as illustated in Figure 2.7.1. Then, we want to successively view each of the diagrams by switching (flipping) back and forth between pages.

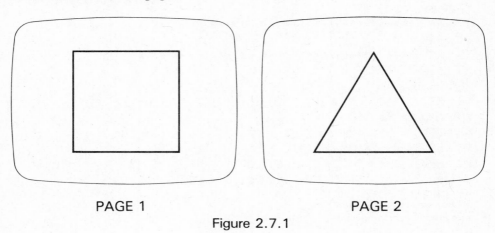

PAGE 1                                      PAGE 2

Figure 2.7.1

1. Obtain the diagrams on Page 1 and 2 by entering the following commands.

```
NEW
10   HOME
15   REM DRAW ON PAGE 1
20   HGR
25   HCOLOR = 2
30   HPLOT 90, 30 TO 190, 30 TO 190, 120 TO 90, 120 TO 90, 30
35   REM HIT ANY KEY TO CONTINUE
40   GET Q$
45   REM DRAW ON PAGE 2
50   HGR2
60   HPLOT 140, 30 TO 190, 120 TO 90, 120 TO 140, 30
RUN
```

2. Now try to flip pages five times by entering the following commands.

```
TEXT : HOME
65   FOR I = 1 TO 5
70   HGR
75   REM DELAY BETWEEN EACH FLIP
80   FOR J =  1 TO 500 : NEXT J
85   HGR2
```

```
87  FOR J = 1 TO 500 : NEXT J
90  NEXT I
RUN
```

Observe the sequence of screen displays.

Does the page flipping occur as we want? _____

Can you explain the results? _____

3. Now retype lines 70 and 85 as follows:

```
TEXT : HOME
70  POKE −16300, 0
85  POKE −16299, 0
RUN
```

Does the page flipping occur as we want? _____

**DISCUSSION**    The HGR and HGR2 commands establish a proper environment for initial drawing on Page 1 and Page 2, respectively. Since both of these commands clear their respective pages, they are not effectively used in a situation where subsequent viewing of diagrams on these pages is desired, as occurs in Section 2. Instead, what is needed are commands which allow for the visual display of a page without erasing the previous contents of it. Memory locations 49236 (or −16300) and 49237 (or −16299) are reserved for this purpose.

In Section 3, the POKE −16300, 0 command sets conditions for the display of Page 1 while the POKE −16299, 0 displays Page 2 on the screen. Memory locations −16299 and −16300 coordinate as another one of several "soft switches" used to control the screen display in APPLESOFT. Table 2.7.1 illustrates this switch-like function.

By placing both of these POKE commands in a loop with an appropriate delay between them, a consistent, continual "flipping" between both high resolution pages is easily obtained.

| | MEMORY | LOCATION |
|---|---|---|
| | − 16300 | − 16299 |
| | 49236 | 49237 |
| | PAGE 1 | PAGE 2 |
| STATUS OF SWITCH | ON | OFF |
| | OFF | ON |

Table 2.7.1

**COMPREHENSIVE EXAMPLE**   Study the following program to determine the screen display. Check your answer by entering the program in the computer.

```
TEXT : HOME : NEW
10  REM *****************************************
11  REM *              CE2.7                    *
12  REM *****************************************
15  HOME
20  HGR
25  HCOLOR = 3
30  HPLOT 100, 80 TO 130, 50 TO 160, 50 TO 190, 80 TO 160, 110
    TO 130, 110 TO 100, 80
35  GET Q$
40  HGR2
45  HPLOT 131, 90 TO 131, 70 TO 145, 90 TO 145, 70
50  HPLOT 149, 90 TO 149, 70 TO 163, 70 TO 163, 90 TO 149, 90
55  GET Q$
60  FOR I = 1 TO 20
65  POKE -16300, 0
70  FOR J = 1 TO 100 : NEXT J
75  POKE -16299, 0
78  FOR J = 1 TO 100 : NEXT J
80  NEXT I
90  GET Q$ : TEXT : HOME
```

### Check Your Comprehension

What diagram is displayed on Page 1? _____

What diagram is displayed on Page 2? _____

What is the purpose of line 65? _____

What is the purpose of line 78? _____

**EXERCISE**   Write a program which first draws the pictures illustrated in Figure 2.7.2 on high resolution Pages 1 and 2, and then repeatedly flips between the two pages 10 times with appropriate pauses between page viewing to give the appearance of a swinging sign.

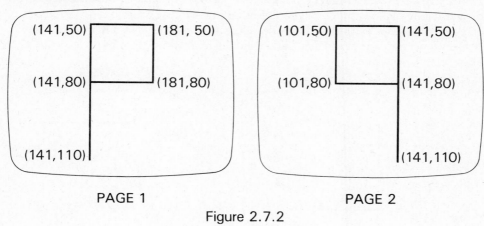

Figure 2.7.2

**CHALLENGE**   Write a program which creates the appearance of a flashing amber warning light by repeatedly flipping on high resolution Pages 1 and 2 the rectangular orange shaded diagrams illustrated in Figure 2.7.3.

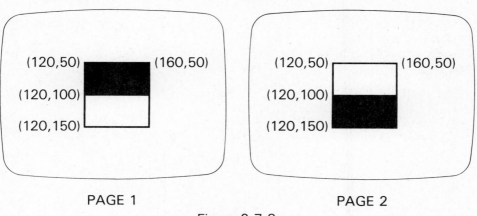

Figure 2.7.3

# ACTIVITY 2.8   Subsequent Drawing on High Resolution Pages 1 & 2

**LEARNING BY DISCOVERY**   This activity demonstrates how to continue to draw on alternating high resolution pages. Let us assume we first want to draw the diagram on Page 1 followed by that on Page 2 as illustrated in Phase 1 of Figure 2.8.1 below. Then, we want to return to Page 1 and continue to draw on these pages as depicted in Phase 2.

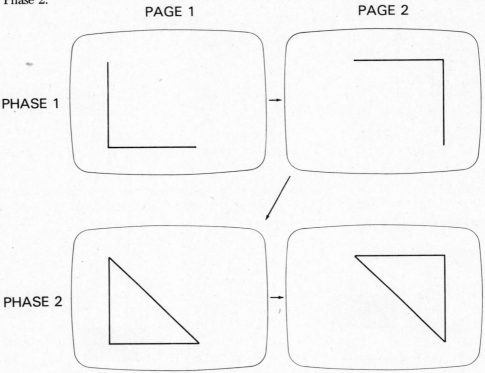

Figure 2.8.1

1. Obtain the diagrams in Phase 1 by entering the following commands.

```
NEW
10   HOME
15   REM DRAW ON PAGE 1
20   HGR
25   HCOLOR = 3
30   HPLOT 3, 10 TO 3, 159 TO 140, 159
35   REM HIT ANY KEY TO CONTINUE
40   GET Q$
45   REM DRAW ON PAGE 2
50   HGR2
60   HPLOT 140, 10 TO 278, 10 TO 278, 160
RUN
```

2. Now try to obtain the display in Phase 2 by entering the following commands.

```
TEXT : HOME
62   REM PAUSE BETWEEN PAGE 1 AND PAGE 2
64   GET Q$
65   REM CONTINUE TO DRAW ON PAGE 1
70   HGR
75   HPLOT 3, 10 TO 140, 159
80   REM PAUSE BETWEEN PAGES
85   GET Q$
90   REM CONTINUE TO DRAW ON PAGE 2
95   HGR2
99   HPLOT 140, 10 TO 278, 160
RUN
```

Observe the sequence of screen displays.

Does the display on Page 1 occur as we want? _____

Does the display on Page 2 occur as we want? _____

Can you explain the results? _____

3. Now retype lines 70 and 95 as follows:

```
TEXT : HOME
70   POKE −16300, 0
95   POKE −16299, 0
RUN
```

Does the sequence of screen displays occur as we want? _____

4. Now retype lines 70 and 95 as follows:

```
TEXT : HOME
70   POKE −16300, 0 : POKE 230, 32
95   POKE −16299, 0 : POKE 230, 64
```

RUN

Does the sequence of screen displays occur as we want? _____

**DISCUSSION**   By now, writing the commands in Section 1 to obtain the diagrams displayed on Page 1 and Page 2 of Phase 1 should cause no difficulty. The HGR and HGR2 commands are used in Section 2 to establish the proper conditions for drawing on these pages. However, the HGR and HGR2 commands cannot be used for continued extensions of previous drawings because these commands clear both pages to black.

  Also, the attempt in Section 3 to replace the HGR command with POKE −16300, 0 and the HGR2 command with POKE −16299, 0 was unsuccessful in obtaining Phase 2. POKE −16300, 0 only establishes the condition for displaying Page 1, but not for drawing on it. An analogous condition is set with POKE −16299, 0 and Page 2 of the high resolution screen.

  The content of memory location 230 determines which graphics page is to be used for drawing. POKE 230, 32 identifies Page 1 for drawing while POKE 230, 64 identifies Page 2. The selection of numbers 32 and 64 will remain a mystery until later activities, where a detailed analysis of Apple memory will be explored. If the POKE 230,--command is not used, the page used for drawing is determined by the most recently used HGR (Page 1) or HGR2 (Page 2) command.

  The attempt in Section 3 to create the screen displays in Phase 2 resulted with all drawings on Page 2 because the HGR2 was the most recent command used. The combination, POKE −16300, 0 : POKE 230, 32, in Section 4 displays the previously used Page 1 and sets the successful condition for additional drawing on it.

**COMPREHENSIVE EXAMPLE**   Study the following program to determine the screen display. Check your answer by entering the program into the computer.

```
TEXT : HOME : NEW
10   REM ****************************************
11   REM *            CE2.8                     *
12   REM ****************************************
15   HOME
18   HGR
20   HCOLOR = 3
25   HPLOT 100, 60 TO 160, 60 TO 160, 100 TO 100, 100 TO 100, 60
30   GET Q$
35   HGR2
40   HPLOT 130, 70 TO 160, 100 TO 100, 100 TO 130, 70
45   GET Q$
50   POKE −16300, 0 : POKE −16301, 0 : POKE 230, 32
55   FOR I = 1 TO 40
60   HPLOT 100, 100 − I TO 160, 100 − I
65   NEXT I
67   VTAB 22 : HTAB 11
68   PRINT "FILLED TO THE BRIM";
70   GET Q$
75   POKE −16299, 0 : POKE −16302, 0 : POKE 230, 64
```

```
80   FOR I = 1 TO 30
85   HPLOT 100 + I, 100 − I TO 160 − I, 100 − I
90   NEXT I
95   GET Q$ : TEXT : HOME
```

**Check Your Comprehension**

What diagram is drawn on high resolution Page 2? _____

What do lines 55 through 65 accomplish? _____

What is the purpose of line 75? _____

**EXERCISE**   Using the diagrams illustrated in Figure 2.8.2, write a program that first draws the green regions on Page 1 and Page 2 and then demonstrates their decay or destruction by erasing (coloring black) successive horizontal lines comprising each object. Design the program so the gradual elimination of the objects occurs simultaneously by alternating the viewing of each page.

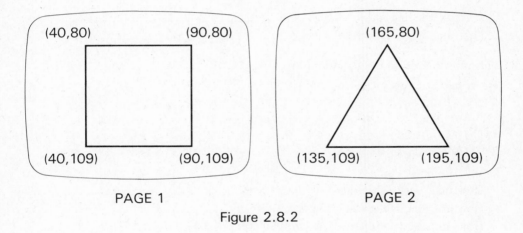

PAGE 1                                    PAGE 2

Figure 2.8.2

**CHALLENGE**   Modify the program for the previous exercise so the decay of the diagrams is followed by their growth or construction. Develop a loop that controls the successive decay and growth of the diagrams five times.

# ACTIVITY 2.9   Switching Between High & Low Resolution Screens

**LEARNING BY DISCOVERY**   This activity demonstrates how to coordinate the alternate viewing of the low resolution and either of the two high resolution screens.

1. Enter the following commands.

```
NEW
10   HOME
15   GR : COLOR = 9
20   FOR I = 15 TO 25 : HLIN 15, 25 AT I : NEXT I
25   GET Q$
30   HGR : HCOLOR  = 2
35   FOR I = 60 TO 103 : HPLOT 105, I TO 181, I : NEXT I
RUN
```

Describe the first screen display. _____

Describe the second screen display. _____

2. Now add lines 40 through 55 as follows:

```
TEXT : HOME
40   GET Q$
45   POKE −16298, 0
50   GET Q$
55   POKE −16297, 0
RUN
```

How many successive screen displays appear? _____

How are alternate screen displays similar? _____

How are alternate screen displays different? _____

3. Enter the following commands.

```
TEXT : HOME : NEW
10   HOME
15   HGR2 : HCOLOR = 3
20   HPLOT 0, 0 TO 279, 0 TO 279, 191 TO 0, 191 TO 0, 0
25   GET Q$
35   GR : COLOR = 9
40   HLIN 0, 39 AT 0 : HLIN 0, 39 AT 39
45   VLIN 0, 39 AT 0 : VLIN 0, 39 AT 39
RUN
```

Describe what appears on the first screen display. _____

Describe what appears on the second screen display. _____

4. Now add line 37 as follows:

```
TEXT : HOME
37  POKE  −16300, 0
RUN
```

Again, describe what appears on the second screen display. _____

5. Now delete line 37 and add line 30 as follows:

```
TEXT : HOME
37
30  POKE  −16300, 0
RUN
```

What difference does this make on what appears on the second screen display? ___
_____

6. Retype line 30 as follows:

```
TEXT : HOME
30  TEXT
RUN
```

Does this change have any effect on the second screen display? _____

**DISCUSSION**   Occasions might arise where a programmer wishes to alternate between using low and high resolution graphics. APPLESOFT has another "soft switch" which selects the display of either low or high resolution  graphics without destroying any current contents. Previously drawn low or high resolution graphics can be viewed at a later time by respectively POKing memory locations −16298 or −16297. Table 2.9.1 illustrates the characteristics of this switch.

There is no difficulty alternating between low and high resolution graphics when the GR and HGR commands are used. Since GR uses low resolution Page 1 and HGR uses high resolution Page 1, the "soft switch" which controls the screen display (memory locations −16299 and −16300) is already established. Thus, immediate viewing can be observed. Section 2 demonstrates the successful coordination of these two modes of graphics display.

When switching from high to low resolution graphics, the GR command cannot immediately follow the HGR2 command, as in Section 3, since HGR2 uses high resolution Page 2 and graphics cannot be drawn conveniently on low resolution Page 2. Sections 5 and 6 demonstrate the user must first select Page 1 for the screen display by using either the POKE −16300, 0 or TEXT commands. The TEXT command automatically establishes Page 1 as the next used page. Placing either of these commands ahead of the GR command eliminates a brief but annoying flash of garbage that occurs in Section 4.

|  MEMORY | LOCATIONS |
|---|---|
| − 16298 | − 16297 |
| 49238 | 49239 |
| **LOW RES** | **HIGH RES** |
| ON | OFF |
| OFF | ON |

STATUS OF SWITCH

Table 2.9.1

**COMPREHENSIVE EXAMPLE**  Study the following program to determine the screen displays. Check your answer by entering the program into the computer.

```
TEXT : HOME : NEW
10   REM ******************************************
11   REM *              CE2.9                      *
12   REM ******************************************
14   HOME
15   GR : COLOR = 4
20   FOR I = 0 TO 10
25   PLOT 10 + I, 15 − I : PLOT 30 − I,
     15 −I : PLOT 10 + I, 15 + I : PLOT 30 − I, 15 + I
30   NEXT I
35   VTAB 22 : HTAB 9
40   PRINT "A LOW QUALITY DIAMOND";
45   GET Q$ : HOME
50   HGR : HCOLOR = 1
55   HPLOT 100, 80 TO 140, 40 TO 180, 80 TO 140, 120 TO 100, 80
60   VTAB 22 : HTAB 9
65   PRINT "A HIGH QUALITY DIAMOND";
70   GET Q$ : HOME
75   VTAB 22 : HTAB 12
80   PRINT "DAZZLING DIAMONDS";
82   FOR I = 1 TO 5
85   POKE −16298, 0
88   FOR J = 1 TO 500 : NEXT J
90   POKE −16297, 0
```

```
95   FOR J = 1 TO 500 : NEXT J
98   NEXT I
99   GET Q$ : TEXT : HOME
RUN
```

**Check Your Comprehension**

How does the "high quality diamond" differ from the "low quality diamond?" _____
What line numbers control the viewing of the different pages? _____
Why is the HOME command included in lines 45 and 70? _____

**EXERCISE**   Write a program which first draws an orange arrow on high resolution Page 2 and then draws a magenta arrow on low resolution Page 1.

**CHALLENGE**   Modify the program from the previous exercise so ten successive screen displays alternate the viewing of the orange arrow on high resolution Page 2 with the magenta arrow on low resolution Page 1.

# ACTIVITY 2.10   Switching Between Text & the Graphics Screen

**LEARNING BY DISCOVERY**   This activity demonstrates how to coordinate the alternate viewing of the text page and either of the two high resolution pages.

1. Enter the following commands.

```
NEW
10   HOME
15   VTAB 13 : HTAB 11
20   PRINT "COMPUTER GRAPHICS"
25   GET Q$
30   HGR : HCOLOR = 1
35   HPLOT 100, 50 TO 150, 100
40   HPLOT 100, 100 TO 150, 50
45   VTAB 22 : HTAB 14
50   PRINT "A SMALL X"
RUN
```

Describe the first screen display. _____
Describe the second screen display. _____

2. Now add the lines 55 through 70 as follows:

```
TEXT : HOME
55   GET Q$
60   POKE −16303, 0
65   GET Q$
```

```
 70  POKE −16304, 0
RUN
```

You should have obtained four successive screen displays.

Describe the first screen display. _____

Describe the second screen display. _____

Describe the third screen display. _____

Describe the fourth screen display. _____

3. Enter the following commands.

```
TEXT : HOME : NEW
10   HOME
15   HGR : HCOLOR = 2
20   HPLOT 0, 0 TO 150, 150
25   VTAB 22 : HTAB 15
30   PRINT "A PURPLE LINE"
35   GET Q$
40   HGR2 : HCOLOR = 5
45   HPLOT 0, 150 TO 150, 0
RUN
```

Describe the first screen display. _____

Describe the second screen display. _____

4. Now let's attempt to get the picture from the first screen display to appear on a third screen by entering the following commands.

```
TEXT : HOME
60   GET Q$
65   POKE −16300, 0
RUN
```

Is the third screen display the same as the first? _____

5. Retype line 65 as follows:

```
TEXT : HOME
65   POKE −16303, 0
RUN
```

Now is the third screen display the same as the first? _____

6. Retype line 65 as follows:

```
TEXT : HOME
65   POKE −16301, 0
RUN
```

Do we achieve our desired screen this time? _____

7. Now add line 65 as follows:

```
TEXT : HOME
65 POKE −16300, 0 : POKE −16301, 0
RUN
```

How about this time? _____

**DISCUSSION**  APPLESOFT has one last "soft switch" which is used to select text or graphics mode. Memory locations −16303 and −16304 are reserved for this purpose and are illustrated in Table 2.10.1.

Text and low resolution graphics share the same memory locations. Therefore, both of these modes cannot be functioning at the same time, except for mixed screen, low resolution graphics which uses the bottom four lines of low resolution Page 1 for the text window. Recall that HGR establishes a mixed screen, high resolution graphics mode. Surprisingly, the text window area for the high resolution Page 1 also resides in the bottom four lines of low resolution Page 1. This explains why both messages, "COMPUTER GRAPHICS" and "A SMALL X" appear in the text area following the POKE −16303, 0 command in Section 2.

The programmer must pay close attention to the effects various commands have on the "soft switches."  In Section 3, the HGR2 command establishes a full screen graphics mode on high resolution Page 2. The POKE −16300, 0 command (view Page 1) in Section 4 does not create the desired display because full screen graphics is still in effect. Similarly, POKE −16301, 0 (select mixed screen), by itself in Section 6, is another futile attempt. Both of the commands are necessary to first switch to high resolution Page 1 and to then establish a mixed graphics screen, as occurs in Section 7. Note that POKE −16303, 0 clears the entire screen to text, losing the picture altogether.

|  | MEMORY | LOCATIONS |
|---|---|---|
|  | − 16303 | − 16304 |
|  | 49233 | 49232 |
|  | TEXT | GRAPHICS |
| STATUS OF SWITCH | ON | OFF |
|  | OFF | ON |

Table 2.10.1

**COMPREHENSIVE EXAMPLE**   The following program demonstrates how the text page can be used to display a menu which controls  access to either page of the high resolution graphics screen. Study and enter the program to observe the effects.

```
TEXT : HOME : NEW
10   REM ******************************************
11   REM *             CE2.10                      *
12   REM ******************************************
14   HOME
15   REM DRAW ON PAGE 1
20   HGR : HCOLOR = 1 : HPLOT 101, 150 TO 101, 50 TO 181, 50 TO
     181, 100 TO 101, 100
25   GET Q$
30   REM DRAW ON PAGE 2
35   HGR2 : HCOLOR = 5 : HPLOT 101, 50 TO 101, 150
     TO 181, 150 TO 181, 100 TO 101, 100
40   GET Q$
45   REM PREPARE A MENU
50   TEXT
52   VTAB 12 : HTAB 1 : PRINT "TYPE THE NUMBER OF THE DESIRED
     SCREEN"
55   VTAB 13 : HTAB 3 : PRINT "HIT ANY KEY TO RETURN TO THE
     MENU"
60   VTAB 16 : HTAB 12 : PRINT "1. A LETTER"
65   VTAB 17 : HTAB 12 : PRINT "2. A NUMBER"
68   VTAB 18 : HTAB 12 : PRINT "3. END PROGRAM"
70   VTAB 20 : HTAB 1 : INPUT N
72   POKE -16304, 0
75   IF N = 1 THEN POKE -16300, 0 : GET Q$ : GOTO 50
80   IF N = 2 THEN POKE -16299, 0 : GET Q$ : GOTO 50
85   TEXT : HOME : END
```

### Check Your Comprehension

What diagram appears on Page 1? _____

What diagram appears on Page 2? _____

In what page of memory is the menu stored? _____

What is the purpose of line 80? _____

**EXERCISE**   Lines 75 and 80 of the COMPREHENSIVE EXAMPLE cause the text page to be rewritten rather than, more efficiently, to view the previously set screen. Change lines 75 and 80 and any other lines to make this efficiency improvement by adding the appropriate POKE commands and replacing GOTO 50 with GOTO 70.

**CHALLENGE**   Write a menu driven program which permits you to view diagrams of your choice that are to be displayed on high resolution Pages 1 and 2. How imaginative can you be in creating the diagrams?

# ACTIVITY 2.11   Alternatives to HGR & HGR2

**LEARNING BY DISCOVERY**   Graphics can be accomplished without using the HGR and HGR2 commands. This activity demonstrates the equivalent set of statements for each of these commands.

1. Boot the system. Then enter the following commands.

```
NEW
10   HOME
20   POKE −16304, 0
25   POKE −16301, 0
30   POKE −16300, 0
35   POKE −16297, 0
60   HCOLOR = 3
65   HPLOT 0, 0 TO 279, 191 TO 0, 191 TO 279, 0
70   VTAB 22 : HTAB 13
75   PRINT "A LARGE X"
RUN
```

   Describe what appears on the screen display. _____

2. Now enter line 40 as follows:

```
TEXT : HOME
40   POKE 230, 32
RUN
```

   Describe what appears on the screen display. _____

3. Now enter line 45 as follows:

```
TEXT : HOME
45   CALL 62450
RUN
```

   Describe what appears on the screen display. _____
   What high resolution page is being used? _____

4. Now retype line 25 as follows:

```
TEXT : HOME
25   POKE −16302, 0
RUN
```

   Describe what appears on the screen display. _____
   What high resolution page is being used. _____

**DISCUSSION**   As you learned in earlier activities, execution of the HGR command creates a screen display with the following characteristics:

1. Establishes high resolution mixed graphics mode for the screen;

2. Selects, clears to black, and displays Page 1 of high resolution graphics, and;

3. Identifies Page 1 of high resolution graphics as the next page where plotting will occur.

In this activity we are attempting to draw graphics on high resolution Page 1 without using the HGR command. The APPLESOFT program in Section 1 POKEd the appropriate memory locations from each of the four "soft switches" to obtain what we might expect to be the equivalent of the HGR command. However, the toggling of these switches is not sufficient without including POKE 230, 32, which identifies Page 1 as the next page on which to plot, and CALL 62450, which clears the current screen display to black. Table 2.11.1 displays the commands which collectively are equivalent to HGR and HGR2.

| HGR | HGR2 |
|---|---|
| POKE −16304,0 | POKE −16304,0 |
| POKE −16301,0 | POKE −16302,0 |
| POKE −16300,0 | POKE −16299,0 |
| POKE −16297,0 | POKE −16297,0 |
| POKE   230,32 | POKE   230,64 |
| CALL   62450 | CALL   62450 |

Table 2.11.1

**COMPREHENSIVE EXAMPLE**   The following program draws a dotted outline of an imperfect circle with a radius of 75 and a center located at (140, 80) using trigonometric functions. The circle is drawn on high resolution Page 1, but without using the HGR command. Lines 50 through 80 draw the circle. The relationship of using the sine(SIN) and cosine(COS) functions for generating the circles and a technique for perfecting the shape of the circle will be presented in CHAPTER 4.

```
TEXT : HOME : NEW
10   REM ****************************************
11   REM *              CE2.11                   *
12   REM ****************************************
14   HOME
15   POKE −16304, 0 : POKE −16301, 0 : POKE −16300, 0 : POKE
     −16297, 0 : POKE 230, 32 : CALL 62450
20   HCOLOR = 3
30   H = 140 : V = 80 : R = 75
40   REM PLOT CIRCLE POINTS
50   FOR I = 0 TO 6.30 STEP .1
60   X = R * COS (I) : Y = R * SIN (I)
```

```
70   HPLOT H + X, V + Y
80   NEXT I
85   GET Q$ : TEXT : HOME
RUN
```

## Check Your Comprehension

On what high resolution page is the circle drawn? _____

Where is the center of the circle? _____

What is the radius of the circle? _____

**EXERCISE**   Write a program that draws a circle with a radius of 30 and center located at (60, 40) on high resolution Page 2 without using the HGR2 command.

**CHALLENGE**   Write a program that uses R in a FOR - NEXT loop to draw ten concentric circles located near the center of high resolution Page 1 without using the HGR command.

# MODULE 2B   Special Effects with High Resolution Graphics

## ACTIVITY 2.12   Coloring the Background Screen

**LEARNING BY DISCOVERY**   This activity demonstrates several approaches for coloring the entire screen.

1. Enter the following commands.

```
NEW
10  HOME : HGR : HCOLOR = 6
20  FOR I = 0 TO 159
30  HPLOT 0, I TO 279, I
40  NEXT I
RUN
```

Describe the pattern by which the screen turns blue. _____

2. Retype lines 20 and 30 as follows:

```
TEXT : HOME
20  FOR I = 0 TO 279
30  HPLOT I, 0 TO I, 159
RUN
```

Describe the pattern by which the screen turns blue. _____
Does the speed at which the screen turns blue in either of the two techniques meet your satisfaction? _____

3. Enter the following commands.

```
TEXT : HOME : NEW
10  HOME : HGR
20  HCOLOR = 6
30  CALL 62454
RUN
```

Describe the screen display. _____

4. Now enter line 25 as follows:

```
TEXT : HOME
25  HPLOT 0, 0
RUN
```

Describe the screen display. _____

Is the speed at which the screen now turns blue more satisfactory than before?

_____

5. Now enter line 15 as follows:

```
TEXT : HOME
15   POKE −16302, 0
RUN
```

What change in the screen display occurs? _____

**DISCUSSION**   Establishing a quickly colored background screen can be quite useful when using graphics. Sections 1 and 2 successfully complete the task but too slowly.

The CALL 62454 command is used to establish instantaneous coloring of the entire screen, in either mixed or full graphics mode. This command colors the screen to the HCOLOR most recently HPLOTed. Section 3 demonstrates failure to perform an HPLOT before CALL 62454 will result in a black screen. Section 4 corrects this omission by inserting HPLOT 0, 0 prior to CALL 62454. Drawing with other colors on a colored background screen will be considered in the next activity.

**COMPREHENSIVE EXAMPLE**   Study the following program to determine the screen displays. Check your answer by entering the program in the computer.

```
TEXT : HOME : NEW
10   REM ****************************************
11   REM *              CE2.12                  *
12   REM ****************************************
15   HOME : HGR2
20   FOR I = 1 TO 10
30   X = INT (6 * RND (1)) + 1
40   IF X = 0 OR X = 4 THEN 30
50   HCOLOR =  X
60   HPLOT 0, 0
70   CALL 62454
80   FOR J = 1 TO 1000 : NEXT J
90   NEXT I
95   GET Q$ : TEXT : HOME
RUN
```

**Check Your Comprehension**

Describe the screen displays. _____

What is the purpose of line 30? _____

What is the purpose of line 40? _____

What is the purpose of line 60? _____

**EXERCISE**   Write a program which alternates (five times) the full screen display of green on Page 1 and orange on Page 2 on the high resolution screen by successively flipping between the pages.

**CHALLENGE**  Write a three-option menu-driven program which permits you to view either an orange Page 1, a green Page 2, or to terminate the program.

# ACTIVITY 2.13   Drawing on a Non-Black Background Screen

**LEARNING BY DISCOVERY**  This activity explores the possibilities for drawing in color on a screen which has a colored background.

1. Enter the following commands.

```
NEW
10   HOME : HGR
20   HCOLOR = 3
30   HPLOT 0, 0 : CALL 62454
40   HCOLOR = 4
50   HPLOT 110, 90 TO 170, 90 TO 170, 140 TO 110, 140 TO 110,
     90
RUN
```

What color is the background screen? _____

What color are the  vertical sides of the square? _____

What color are the horizontal sides of the square? _____

2. Retype line 50 as follows:

```
TEXT : HOME
50   HPLOT 111, 90 TO 171, 90 TO 171, 140 TO 111, 140 TO 111,
     90
RUN
```

What color are the vertical sides of the square? _____

What color are the horizontal sides of the square? _____

3. Now retype lines 20 and 40 as follows:

```
TEXT : HOME
20   HCOLOR = 5
40   HCOLOR = 6
RUN
```

What color is the background screen? _____

What color are the vertical sides of the square? _____

What color are the horizontal sides of the square? _____

4. Retype line 50 as follows:

```
TEXT : HOME
```

```
50  HPLOT 110, 90 TO 170, 90 TO 170, 140 TO 110, 140 TO 110,
    90
RUN
```

Now what color are the vertical sides of the square? _____

What color are the horizontal sides of the square? _____

5. Once again, retype lines 20 and 40 as follows:

```
TEXT : HOME
20  HCOLOR = 1
40  HCOLOR = 0
RUN
```

What color is the background screen? _____

What color are the horizontal lines of the square? _____

Do the vertical lines of the square appear? _____

6. Retype line 40 as follows:

```
TEXT : HOME
40  HCOLOR = 6
RUN
```

Describe the appearance of the square. _____

7. Retype line 40 as follows:

```
TEXT : HOME
40  HCOLOR = 3
RUN
```

Now, describe the appearance of the square. _____

8. Retype line 40 as follows:

```
TEXT : HOME
40  HCOLOR = 7
RUN
```

Describe the appearance of the screen. _____

9. Retype line 20 as follows:

```
TEXT : HOME
20  HCOLOR = 5
RUN
```

Again, describe the appearance of the screen display. _____

**DISCUSSION**    Thus far, all graphics have been performed on a black screen. Diagrams can also be drawn on a colored screen, but with several limitations. This activity illustrates several of the peculiar screen displays which occur when drawing one color on another.

The careful observer should recognize that the horizontal lines of the square are always the same color designated by the HCOLOR command. The vertical lines, however, result in either unexpected colors (Sections 1 through 4), strange wide multi-colored bands (Section 6), or do not appear at all (Section 5). To complicate matters, the switching of odd and even column coordinates results in different displays. Table 2.13.1 identifies the expected color displays when considering all possible combinations of background colors, overlay colors, and column coordinates. Empty entries within the table indicate that either a vertical line is not drawn or it results in an undesired, wide band.

It should be noted that there are only a few possibilities for drawing a diagram with only one color on a non-black display screen. Section 7 displays one of these possibilities, where a white (HCOLOR = 3) square is drawn on a green (HCOLOR = 1) background. Notice what happens in Section 8, where white (HCOLOR = 7) is drawn on a green (HCOLOR = 1) background. The distorted vertical lines are due to mixing groups of colors. It is advisable to work only with colors 0, 1, 2, and 3 as one group or with colors 4, 5, 6, and 7 as another group. Section 9 corrects the problem in Section 8 by changing the background color to orange (HCOLOR = 5), so colors 5 and 7 are within the same color group. Table 2.13.2 depicts all possibilities of overlaying colors on a non-black background screen, indicating the proper column coordinate mode which must be used.

Background Colors

Overlay Colors

| Color | Column Coordinate | 0 | 1 | 2 | 3 | 4 | 5 | 6 | 7 |
|---|---|---|---|---|---|---|---|---|---|
| 0 | odd | | black | | violet | | | | violet |
| 0 | even | | | black | green | | | | green |
| 1 | odd | green | | white | | green | | | |
| 1 | even | | | black | green | | | | green |
| 2 | odd | | black | | violet | | | | violet |
| 2 | even | violet | white | | | violet | | | |
| 3 | odd | green | | white | | green | | | |
| 3 | even | violet | white | | | violet | | | |
| 4 | odd | | | | blue | | black | | blue |
| 4 | even | | | | orange | | | black | orange |
| 5 | odd | orange | | | | orange | | white | |
| 5 | even | | | | orange | | | black | orange |
| 6 | odd | | | | blue | | black | | blue |
| 6 | even | blue | | | | blue | white | | |
| 7 | odd | orange | | | | orange | | white | |
| 7 | even | blue | | | | blue | white | | |

Table 2.13.1

Non-Black Background Colors

| Overlay Colors | Green 1 | Violet 2 | White 3 | Orange 5 | Blue 6 | White 7 |
|---|---|---|---|---|---|---|
| Black (0) | odd | even | | | | |
| Green (1) | | | even | | | even |
| Violet (2) | | | odd | | | |
| White (3) | even | odd | | | | |
| Black (4) | | | | odd | even | |
| Orange (5) | | | even | | | even |
| Blue (6) | | | | | | odd |
| White (7) | | | | even | odd | |

Table 2.13.2

**COMPREHENSIVE EXAMPLE** Study the following program to determine the screen display. Check your answer by entering the program into the computer.

```
TEXT : HOME : NEW
10  REM **************************************
11  REM *               CE2.13               *
12  REM **************************************
15  HOME : HGR : POKE -16302, 0
20  HCOLOR = 5
30  HPLOT 0, 0: CALL 62454
40  HCOLOR = 4
50  FOR I = 1 TO 8
60  HPLOT 61 + X, 20 + X TO 221 - X, 20 + X TO 221 -X, 160
    -X TO 61 + X, 160 -X TO 61 + X, 20 + X
70  FOR J = 1 TO 500 : NEXT
75  X = X + 8
80  NEXT I
85  HCOLOR = 7
88  FOR I = 77 TO 103
90  HPLOT 118, I TO 164, I
95  NEXT I
96  HCOLOR = 1
98  HPLOT 119, 78 TO 162, 102 : HPLOT 119, 102 TO 162, 78
```

```
99  GET Q$ : TEXT : HOME
RUN
```

**Check Your Comprehension**

What color is the background screen? _____

What diagram is first drawn on the screen? _____

What is the final drawing on the screen? _____

**EXERCISE**   Write a program which displays on Page 2 of the high resolution screen a picture of a green tick-tack-toe board, with the nine cells and frame outlined in white, and with black X's making a "tick-tack-toe" along the diagonal from the upper left to the lower right corner.

**CHALLENGE**   Write a program which draws a sixteen-paneled (4 rows by 4 columns) quilt with alternating orange and blue squares. Draw small white triangles within each square of the quilt.

# ACTIVITY 2.14   Blinking a Picture of an Object

**LEARNING BY DISCOVERY**   This activity demonstrates several techniques by which a graphics diagram can repetitively appear and disappear.

1. Enter the following commands.

```
NEW
100  HOME : GOTO 500
200  HCOLOR = C1
210  HPLOT X, Y TO X + 20, Y TO X + 20, Y +
     30 TO X, Y + 30 TO X,Y
220  RETURN
295  REM DELAY BETWEEN BLINKS
300  FOR J = 1 TO 500 : NEXT J
320  RETURN
495  REM BLINK BY RE-ESTABLISHING SCREEN
500  C1 = 3 : X = 129 : Y = 70
520  FOR I = 1 TO 10
530  HGR : GOSUB 200 : GOSUB 300
550  NEXT I
RUN
```

Describe the speed, smoothness, and clarity of the blinking square on the screen.

_____

2. Retype line 495 and add line 540 as follows:

```
TEXT : HOME
495  REM BLINK BY DRAWING ON TWO PAGES
```

```
540  HGR 2  : GOSUB 200 : GOSUB 300
RUN
```

Observe the screen display and compare the speed, smoothness, and clarity of the blinking square with the previous method. _____

3. Retype lines 495, 500, 530 and 540 as follows:

```
TEXT : HOME
495  REM BLINK BY DRAWING BLACK AND WHITE
500  HGR : X = 129 : Y = 70
530  C1 = 3 : GOSUB 200 : GOSUB 300
540  C1 = 0 : GOSUB 200 : GOSUB 300
RUN
```

Observe the screen display and compare the speed, smoothness, and clarity of the blinking square with the previous methods. _____
Which of the previous "blinking" methods gives the best effect? _____

**DISCUSSION**   The capability of blinking an object on the display screen can be used to accomplish animation, a future topic. This activity demonstrates three different techniques which can be used to blink an object on the high resolution screen. The subroutine beginning at line 200 draws a small square at any position on the screen as specified by the user. Lines 300 through 320 represent a delay subroutine.

Sections 1 and 2 demonstrate the blinking of a diagram by using either the HGR command (for one page) or both HGR and HGR2 commands (for page flipping). Since the execution of both of these commands erases their corresponding screens, they give the effect of blinking by successively clearing the screen and then redrawing on it. There is, however, a displeasing, slow clearing of the screen which detracts from the asthetic quality of the desired blinking object.

Instead, Section 3 provides a method by which the lag in the erasing of the previous object on the screen disappears. This more pleasing technique alternates the drawing of the object in some color followed by a redrawing of the same object with the black screen color. The speed of the "blink" is controlled by the length of the delay and must be placed after each drawing.

**COMPREHENSIVE EXAMPLE**   Study the following program to determine the screen display. Check your answer by entering the program in the computer.

```
TEXT : HOME : NEW
100  REM ****************************************
101  REM *              CE2.14                  *
102  REM ****************************************
150  HOME : GOTO 500
200  HPLOT X, Y TO X + 20, Y − 30 TO X + 40, Y TO X, Y
250  FOR J = 1 TO 500 : NEXT J
260  RETURN
500  HGR : HCOLOR = 2
510  HPLOT 0, 0 : CALL 62454
```

```
515   X = 120 : Y = 70
520   FOR I = 1 TO 10
530   HCOLOR = 3 : GOSUB 200
540   HCOLOR = 2 : GOSUB 200
550   NEXT I
560   GET Q$ : TEXT : HOME
RUN
```

**Check Your Comprehension**

What color is the background? _____

What diagram blinks on the screen? _____

What color is the diagram? _____

What is the purpose of line 540? _____

**EXERCISE**   Write a program that frames high resolution Page 2 in blue and blinks a full screen orange X within the frame 15 times.

**CHALLENGE**   Write a program that alternates the blinking of a black rectangle and a white triangle on a violet background using full screen graphics of high resolution Page 1.

# ACTIVITY 2.15   Animating Simply Drawn Pictures

**LEARNING BY DISCOVERY**   This activity demonstrates several techniques for moving a diagram around the screen.

1.  Enter the following commands.

```
NEW
100   HOME : GO TO 500
200   HCOLOR = C1
210   HPLOT X, Y TO X + 20, Y TO X + 20, Y + 30 TO X, Y +
      30 TO X,Y
220   FOR J = 1 TO 50 : NEXT J
230   RETURN
495   REM CLEAR PAGE METHOD
500   C1 = 3 : Y = 90
520   FOR X = 30 TO 180 STEP 10
530   HGR : GOSUB 200
550   NEXT X
RUN
```

Describe the smoothness of the animated rectangle as it moves across the screen.

_____

2. Retype lines 495 through 550 as follows:

```
TEXT : HOME
495   REM DRAWING ON TWO PAGES
500   X = 20 : Y = 90 : C1 = 3
520   FOR L = 1 TO 10
530   X = X + 10 : HGR : GOSUB 200 : HGR : REM DRAW ON PAGE
      1
540   X = X + 10 : HGR2 : GOSUB 200 : HGR2 : REM DRAW ON
      PAGE 2
550   NEXT L
RUN
```

Describe the smoothness of the animated rectangle in comparison with the previous method. _____

3. Retype lines 495 through 550 as follows:

```
TEXT : HOME
495   REM DRAWING BLACK AND WHITE
500   Y = 90 : HGR
520   FOR X = 30 TO 180 STEP 10
530   C1 = 3 : GOSUB 200 : REM DRAW OBJECT WHITE
540   C1 = 0 : GOSUB 200 : REM DRAW OBJECT BLACK
550   NEXT X
```

Describe the smoothness of the animated rectangle in comparison with the previous methods. _____

Which of these methods animates the rectangle most effectively? _____

**DISCUSSION**   Computer animation is the process of moving a picture of some object around the screen either horizontally, vertically or diagonally (simultaneously moving both horizontally and vertically).

The effect of animation is accomplished by successively drawing the picture, then removing it after some appropriate pause, and finally drawing it again in a new position by either incrementing or decrementing a variable designated for controlling the location of the object. For diagonal animation, two variables are needed, one for the control of the horizontal position and a second for the control of the vertical position.

Due to the unpleasant lag in erasing the screen, using HGR or HGR2 to remove previous drawings, as occurs in Sections 1 and 2, does not yield a smooth movement of the object. In Section 3, the effect of drawing an object in a color, then drawing it again in the background color in the same position after an appropriate delay, and looping this procedure offers a more satisfactory animation effect, at least for the simply constructed square which is used. The next activity explores the most appropriate technique for animation when more complex diagrams are involved.

**COMPREHENSIVE EXAMPLE**   Study the following program to determine the screen display. Check your answer by entering the program into the computer.

```
TEXT : HOME : NEW
100  REM ******************************************
101  REM *              CE2.15                    *
102  REM ******************************************
110  HOME : GOTO 500
200  HCOLOR = C1
210  HPLOT X, Y TO X + 20, Y  TO X, Y + 20 TO X, Y
220  FOR J = 1 TO 250 : NEXT J
230  RETURN
500  Y = 20 : HGR
510  FOR X = 30 TO 180 STEP 10
525  Y = Y + 5
530  C1 = 3 : GOSUB 200
540  C1 = 0 : GOSUB 200
550  NEXT X
560  GET Q$ : TEXT : HOME
RUN
```

**Check Your Comprehension**

In what direction does the animated picture move? _____

What is the purpose of line 525? _____

What is the purpose of line 530? _____

**EXERCISE**   Write a program to animate (using the white/black drawing method) a small triangle 5 times, in increments of 20, from the bottom left corner towards the upper right corner of high resolution Page 2.

**CHALLENGE**   Write a program to animate a black rectangle on an orange background screen so the path of the rectangle follows the pattern of a V.

# ACTIVITY 2.16   Quick Display of Slowly Drawn Pictures

**LEARNING BY DISCOVERY**   This activity demonstrates how a diagram which is time consuming to draw can be instantaneously displayed on the screen.

1. Enter the following commands.

```
NEW
100  GOTO 500
200  FOR I = 0 TO 6.3 STEP .1
210  X = R * COS (I) : Y = R * SIN (I)
220  HPLOT H + X, V + Y
230  NEXT I
240  RETURN
500  TEXT : HOME
```

```
505   VTAB 12 : HTAB 13 : PRINT "A SMALL CIRCLE"
510   FOR J = 1 TO 1000 : NEXT J
520   HGR : HCOLOR = 3
530   V = 80 : H = 140 : R = 10
540   GOSUB 200
RUN
```

Describe the screen display. _____

Are you pleased with the speed at which the circle is drawn? _____

2. Retype lines 500 and 520 and add line 550 as follows:

```
TEXT : HOME
500   HGR : HCOLOR = 3 : TEXT : HOME
520   POKE 230, 32
550   POKE −16304, 0 : POKE −16300, 0
RUN
```

Does the circle appear more quickly than before? _____

3. Now add line 560 through 600 as follows:

```
TEXT : HOME
560   FOR J = 1 TO 1000 : NEXT J
570   TEXT : HOME : VTAB 12 : HTAB 13 : PRINT "A LARGE
      CIRCLE "
580   POKE 230, 64 : CALL 62450
590   R = 80 : GOSUB 200
600   POKE −16304, 0 : POKE −16302, 0 : POKE −16299, 0
RUN
```

Are you pleased with the improved speed with which the circles appear on the screen?_____

**DISCUSSION**   The slower drawing of more complex diagrams can be distractive if an instantaneous display is desired. The drawing of a circle is particularly time consuming since, as in this activity, over 600 points are calculated. Changing the STEP function from .1 to .01 would have yielded a circle with more closely packed pixels, but would also have been considerably more time consuming to plot than that which is demonstrated. Fortunately, there is a technique by which one can draw on one page of memory while viewing another.

In Section 2, the quick display of the small circle occurs by drawing the picture on high resolution Page 1 while Page 1 of TEXT is being viewed. The combination of POKE −16304, 0 and POKE −16300, 0 establishes a graphics mode and the viewing of high resolution Page 1. The large circle is quickly displayed in Section 3 by drawing on high resolution Page 2 while viewing text. The HGR command which is added on line 500 clears high resolution Page 1 and sets the "soft switches" appropriately for graphics. Line 580 uses CALL 62450 to clear high resolution Page 2.

**COMPREHENSIVE EXAMPLE**    Study the following program to determine the screen display. Check your answer by entering the program into the computer.

```
TEXT : HOME : NEW
100  REM ******************************************
101  REM *              CE2.16                     *
102  REM ******************************************
105  HOME : GOTO 500
110  REM ESTABLISH BACKGROUND COLOR ON PAGE 1
120  POKE 230, 32
130  HCOLOR = 2 : HPLOT 0, 0 : CALL 62454
150  REM DRAW DESIGN
160  HCOLOR = 3
170  FOR I = 1 TO 10
180  HPLOT X, 0 TO 278, 191 — X
190  HPLOT 0, X TO 278 —·X, 191
200  X = X + 20
205  NEXT I
207  X = 0
210  FOR I = 1 TO 10
220  HPLOT 0, 191 — X TO 278 — X, 0
230  HPLOT X, 191 TO 278, X
240  X = X + 20
250  NEXT I
260  RETURN
300  FOR J = 1 TO 500 : NEXT : RETURN
500  HGR : HGR2 : REM CLEAR HI RES SCREENS AND SET SOFT
     SWITCHES
510  TEXT : HOME : VTAB 12 : HTAB 15 : INVERSE : PRINT
     "DRAWING" : NORMAL
515  GOSUB 120 : GOSUB 300
520  REM CREATE BLINKING OF DESIGN
525  POKE —16304, 0
530  FOR I = 1 TO 5
540  POKE —16300, 0 : GOSUB 300
550  POKE —16299, 0 : GOSUB 300
560  NEXT I
570  GET Q$ : TEXT : HOME
RUN
```

**Check Your Comprehension**

Describe the screen display. _____

On what high resolution page is the picture drawn? _____

What is the purpose of line 550? _____

**EXERCISE**    Use the HPLOT TO command to quickly display on high resolution Page 2 (but not view while drawing) smooth (connected points) concentric circles with radii of 70 and 40 units.

**CHALLENGE**   Use the techniques introduced in this activity to blink a rectangular region shaded in orange on a white background screen.

# ACTIVITY 2.17   Animating Slowly Drawn Pictures

**LEARNING BY DISCOVERY**   This activity demonstrates several techniques which attempt to effectively animate the movement of a circle diagonally across the screen.

1. Enter the following commands.

```
NEW
100   REM DRAW /REMOVE METHOD
110   HOME : GOTO 500
200   HCOLOR = C1
210   FOR I = 0 TO 6.3 STEP .1
220   X = R * COS (I) : Y = R * SIN (I)
230   HPLOT H + X, V + Y
240   NEXT I
250   RETURN
300   FOR J = 1 TO 500 : NEXT J : RETURN
500   R = 30 : V = 40 : HGR
510   FOR H = 90 TO 210 STEP 30
520   C1 = 3 : GOSUB 200 : GOSUB 300
530   C1 = 0 : GOSUB 200
540   V = V + 15
550   NEXT H
RUN
```

Describe the process of animation that is displayed. _____

Are you pleased with the speed of the animation? _____

2. Retype lines 100 and 500 through 560 as follows:

```
TEXT : HOME
100   REM DRAWING ON ONE PAGE WHILE VIEWING ANOTHER METHOD
500   HOME : R = 30 : V = 40 : H = 40 : HGR : HGR2
510   FOR L = 1 TO 5
520   C1 = 0 : POKE 230, 32 : GOSUB 200
525   V = V + 10 : H = H + 30
530   C1 = 3 : GOSUB 200
540   POKE −16300, 0
550   C1 = 0 : POKE 230, 64 : GOSUB 200
555   V = V + 10 : H = H + 30
560   C1 = 3 : GOSUB 200
570   POKE -16299, 0
575   V = V − 10 : H = H − 30
580   NEXT L
RUN
```

Compare the animation process with the previous method. _____

Are you pleased with the speed of the animation? _____

3. Modify the previous program by entering the following commands.

```
TEXT : HOME
110  DIM X (63), Y (63)
200  HOME : R = 30
210  VTAB 10 : HTAB 15 : PRINT "CALCULATING"
220  FOR I = 0 TO 63
230  X (I) = R * COS (I/10) : Y (I) = R * SIN (I/10)
240  NEXT I
250  GOTO 500
400  HCOLOR = C1
410  FOR I = 1 TO 63
420  HPLOT X (I) + H, Y (I) + V
430  NEXT I
440  RETURN
520  C1 = 0 : POKE 230, 32 : GOSUB 400
530  C1 = 3 : GOSUB 400
550  C1 = 0 : POKE 230, 64 : GOSUB 400
560  C1 = 3 : GOSUB 400
RUN
```

Compare the animation process with the previous method. _____

Are you pleased with the speed of the animation? _____

4. Retype lines 510, 520 and 550 and delete line 575 as follows:

```
TEXT : HOME
510  FOR L = 1 TO 3
520  POKE 230, 32 : CALL 62450
550  POKE 230, 64 : CALL 62450
RUN
```

Does this improve the speed of animation? _____

**DISCUSSION** Diagrams which are time consuming to draw are difficult to animate in a smooth and quick manner using the HPLOT command. The most effective procedure using the HPLOT command is to draw the picture on one page while viewing the other, which is demonstrated in Sections 2, 3, and 4. The successive drawing and removing of an object at different locations on the same page, as demonstrated in Section 1, is not an effective technique for animation, unless the viewing of the actual drawing process is desired. This method, however, is quite adequate when the diagrams are quickly drawn.

The procedure used in Section 2 is to draw (HCOLOR = 3) and remove (HCOLOR = 0) the diagram from one page while the other is being viewed. Lines 525, 555, and 575 control the new positions for the picture. The annoying delay is due to the unnecessary continued calculations for determining the points of the circle which occur at lines 200 through 250.

In Section 3, these points are calculated once and stored in arrays X and Y. The animation process then only needs to plot, not calculate and plot, the points for each new circle on the screen display.

Section 4 provides a slightly faster animation by clearing the screen on lines 520 and 550 with CALL 62450, instead of redrawing the circles in black.

The reader is most likely dissatisfied with the speed at which the most effective procedure, Section 4, animates the circles. Fortunately, Apple graphics provides another alternative, known as creating "shapes," which will be discussed in CHAPTER 3. For now, additional experience with the technique of "viewing on one page while drawing on another," regardless of the complexity of the picture, will be pursued.

**COMPREHENSIVE EXAMPLE**   Study the following program to determine the screen display. Check your answer by entering the program into the computer.

```
TEXT : HOME : NEW
105   HOME : GOTO 500
200   HCOLOR = C1
210   HPLOT X, Y TO X + 20, Y TO X + 20, Y + 10
      TO X, Y + 10 TO X, Y
220   HPLOT X + 20, Y + 5 TO X + 26, Y + 5 TO X + 26, Y + 10
      TO X + 20, Y +10
230   HPLOT X + 2, Y + 10 TO X + 2, Y + 12
      TO X + 4, Y + 12 TO X + 4, Y + 10
240   HPLOT X + 22, Y + 10 TO X + 22, Y +
      12 TO X + 24, Y + 12 TO X + 24, Y + 10
250   RETURN
300   FOR J = 1 TO 10 : NEXT : RETURN
500   X = 2 : Y = 80 : HGR : HGR2 : C1 = 3
510   FOR L = 1 TO 6
520   POKE 230, 32 : CALL 62450
525   X = X + 20
530   GOSUB 200 : GOSUB 300
540   POKE -16300, 0
550   POKE 230, 64 : CALL 62450
555   X = X + 20
560   GOSUB 200 : GOSUB 300
570   POKE -16299, 0
580   NEXT L
590   GET Q$ : TEXT : HOME.
RUN
```

**Check Your Comprehension**

What picture is animated? _____

What is the purpose of line 500? _____

What is the purpose of line 550? _____

What is the purpose of line 570? _____

**EXERCISE** Write a program that animates a shooting star, as illustrated in Figure 2.17.1, diagonally from the upper left corner to the lower right corner with horizontal increments of 20 and vertical increments of 15. Use the method of drawing on one page while viewing the other. Begin the animation at coordinate (10, 30).

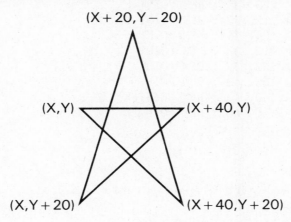

$(X+20, Y-20)$

$(X, Y)$        $(X+40, Y)$

$(X, Y+20)$        $(X+40, Y+20)$

Figure 2.17.1

**CHALLENGE** Write a program that draws the star in Figure 2.17.1 in white and animates it on a blue background screen using the animation method emphasized in this activity.

# ACTIVITY 2.18   Designing Artistic Graphics

**LEARNING BY DISCOVERY** The purpose of this activity is to present a procedure by which creative graphics can first be designed and then displayed on the screen.

1. The following DATA statements contain coordinates which determine a rather rough outline of the cursive letter L. The points are plotted in Exhibit 2.18.1. Take a straightedge and complete the connecting of points in alphabetical order to draw the picture of the L. Then enter the following commands to display the diagram on the screen.

```
NEW
100   HOME : HGR : HCOLOR = 3
110   READ X, Y
120   HPLOT X, Y
130   READ X, Y
140   IF X=-1 THEN 999
150   HPLOT TO X, Y
160   GOTO 130
500   DATA 118, 24 : REM POINT A
505   DATA 130, 25 : REM POINT B
```

```
510  DATA 140, 19 : REM POINT C
515  DATA 140, 12 : REM POINT D
520  DATA 134, 18 : REM POINT E
525  DATA 130, 25 : REM POINT B
530  DATA 120, 35 : REM POINT F
535  DATA 112, 37 : REM POINT G
540  DATA 104, 35 : REM POINT H
545  DATA 112, 33 : REM POINT I
550  DATA 120, 35 : REM POINT F
555  DATA 128, 40 : REM POINT J
560  DATA 140, 42 : REM POINT K
565  DATA 146, 40 : REM POINT L
570  DATA -1, -1
999  END
RUN
```

Are you pleased with the shape of the cursive L? _____

2. Change lines 500 through 570 as follows:

```
TEXT : HOME
500  DATA 112, 78, 114, 79, 116, 79
505  DATA 118, 80, 120, 80, 122, 80, 124, 80, 126, 80, 128,
     80, 130, 80
510  DATA 132, 79, 134, 79, 136, 78, 138, 78, 140, 77, 142,
     75, 143, 73
515  DATA 144, 72, 144, 70, 144, 68
520  DATA 142, 67, 140, 68, 138, 69, 136, 70, 135, 72, 134,
     74, 133, 76, 132, 77, 131, 79, 130, 80
525  DATA 128, 81, 126, 83, 125, 84, 124, 84, 123, 86, 122,
     87, 121, 88, 120, 90, 118, 91, 116, 92
530  DATA 114, 93, 112, 93, 110, 93, 108, 93
535  DATA 106, 92, 105, 90, 106, 88, 107, 87, 108,
     86, 110, 86, 112, 87, 114, 87, 116, 88, 118, 89, 120,
     90, 122, 91, 124, 92, 126, 93
540  DATA 128, 94, 130, 96, 132, 97, 134, 98
545  DATA 136, 99, 138, 99, 140, 99
550  DATA 142, 98, 144, 98, 146, 97
DEL 555, 565
RUN
```

Are you pleased with the appearance of the script L? _____

3. Retype lines 505, 515, 530 and 545 as follows:

```
TEXT : HOME
505    DATA 118, 80, 130, 80
515    DATA 144, 72, 144, 68
530    DATA 114, 93, 108, 93
545    DATA 136, 99, 140, 99
RUN
```

Does the appearance of the script L change? _____

4. Now add line 155 as follows:

```
TEXT : HOME
155    FOR I = 1 TO 100 : NEXT
RUN
```

How does the appearance of the script L change? _____

5. Retype line 100 as follows:

```
TEXT : HOME
100   HOME : HGR : HCOLOR = 2
RUN
```

Are you pleased with the appearance of the violet script L? _____

**DISCUSSION**   This activity introduces you to a tedious but useful tool for designing your graphics screen display. The provided graph paper emulates the raster display of pixels. That is, any diagram which is drawn on the graph paper can be displayed on the screen with the same approximate size, shape and location by appropriately labelling the coordinates of the graph paper cells used in the picture. These coordinates then serve as data to be entered for plotting.

The graph paper has 140 columns (one half of 280) and 96 rows (one half of 192). Each column cell can be labelled with either even or odd numbered coordinates. When using color (other than white) no degree of screen display resolution is lost because of the odd/even limitations you have already encountered. Any apparent loss of resolution is due to points being plotted in inappropriate columns. When using drawings which appear in white, both odd and even column numbers can be used by allowing the vertical lines between adjacent cells to approximate the opposite type number.

Section 1 first displays a crude representation of the script letter L. Section 2 displays a more highly precisioned drawing (illustrated in Exhibit 2.18.2) by including the plotting of many more points, determined by finding the coordinates of each graph cell used.

Note the mixing of odd and even column numbers used in lines 520 and 535 when drawing the white L. The changing of lines 505, 515, 530 and 545 in Section 3 eliminates the repetition of needless data; since the HPLOT TO command is used, only the initial and terminal points are necessary. The addition of line 155 in Section 4 controls the speed at which the cursive letter is drawn. Section 5 demonstrates the incomplete drawing obtained when color other than white is used.

There is another alternative for designing more elaborate diagrams than the cumbersome procedure presented here. In the next chapter the creating of "shapes" and "shape tables" will be discussed. By preparing pictures as "shapes," some interesting and versatile procedures for displaying diagrams, as well as quick and easy methods for storage and retrieval, will be available. However, the method discussed in this activity is practical if the drawing process is to be simulated, such as demonstrating the handwriting of the script letter L.

**COMPREHENSIVE EXAMPLE** The following program draws the football illustrated in Exhibit 2.18.3. Match the data points with the coordinates of the diagram. Enter the program to view the football.

```
TEXT : HOME : NEW
100  REM ****************************************
101  REM *              CE2.18                  *
102  REM ****************************************
105  HOME : HGR : HCOLOR = 3
110  READ X, Y
120  HPLOT X, Y
130  READ X, Y
140  IF X = -1 THEN 170
150  HPLOT TO X, Y
160  GOTO 130
170  FOR I = 1 TO 3
180  READ X, Y, W
190  HPLOT X, Y TO W, Y
200  NEXT I
210  FOR I = 1 TO 4
220  READ X, Y, W
230  HPLOT X, Y TO X, W
240  NEXT I
250  GET Q$ : TEXT : HOME
500  DATA 104, 134, 106, 132, 108, 130, 110, 130, 112, 128,
     114, 128, 116, 126, 118, 126, 120, 125, 122, 124, 124, 124
505  DATA 126, 123, 130, 123
510  DATA 132, 122, 148, 122
520  DATA 156, 124, 158, 124, 160, 125, 162, 126, 164, 127,
     166, 128, 168, 129, 170, 130, 172, 132, 174, 133
525  DATA 176, 134, 176, 140
530  DATA 174, 142, 172, 143, 170, 144, 168, 146, 166, 147,
     164, 148, 162, 148, 162, 149, 158, 150, 156, 150, 154,
     151, 152, 151, 150, 152, 148, 152, 146, 152
535  DATA 144, 153, 134, 153
540  DATA 132, 152, 130, 152, 128, 152, 126, 151, 124, 151,
     122, 150, 120, 150, 118, 149, 116, 148, 114, 147, 112,
     146, 110, 145, 108, 144, 106, 143, 104, 141, 104, 138,
     104, 136, 104, 134
```

```
550  DATA  -1, -1
560  DATA  104, 137, 176
570  DATA  126, 136, 152
580  DATA  126, 138, 152
590  DATA  130, 134, 140
600  DATA  136, 134, 140
610  DATA  142, 134, 140
620  DATA  148, 134, 140
999  END
```

**Check Your Comprehension**

What is the purpose of line 120? _____

What is the purpose of line 140? _____

What part of the football do lines 220, 230 and 240 draw? _____

**EXERCISE**   Write a program that draws a picture of an object of your choice. Prepare the data by finding coordinates from the outline of the diagram on the provided blank sheet of graph paper. The authors created a picture of a koala for your interest. Refer to Exhibit 2.18.4.

**CHALLENGE**   Write another program that draws a picture of your choice following the directions of the previous exercise.

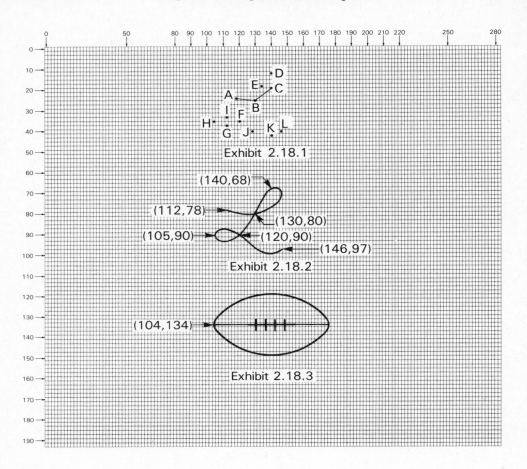

Exhibit 2.18.1

Exhibit 2.18.2

Exhibit 2.18.3

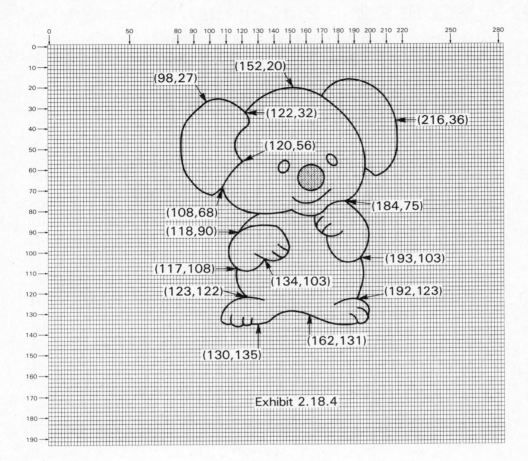

Exhibit 2.18.4

# MODULE 2C   Putting High Resolution Graphics All Together

## PUTTING IT ALL TOGETHER: PART 2

**CHAPTER SYNOPSIS**   CHAPTER 1 introduced you to the commands and techniques associated with low resolution graphics. Each graphics display was a collection of small rectangles, referred to as "bricks." In CHAPTER 2 you examined high resolution graphic designs where each display was a collection of points or dots, or more sophisticatedly, entities called pixels. The difference between low resolution and high resolution graphics is the number of primary components that can be displayed on the screen at one time. Low resolution graphics can provide a maximum of 1920 (or 48 $\times$ 40) "bricks," whereas high resolution graphics can provide a maximum of 53760 (280 $\times$ 192) "pixels." Thus, high resolution graphics provides higher quality or finer resolution than low resolution graphics.

While high resolution graphics offers more precise screen displays, it is also more difficult to use than low resolution graphics. The major difficulties one encounters throughout the chapter activities include the use of two display pages, the availability of "soft switches," and the coordination of color displays with proper column coordinates and with common color groups.

The quickest access into high resolution graphics mode is to use either the HGR or HGR2 commands. However, APPLESOFT has four of what are commonly called "soft switches" or "display switches" which provide more versatile control over screen displays than solely using the HGR and HGR2 commands. Each "switch" consists of two memory locations which work in tandem and are accessed by POKing these memory locations. Although no physical switch is involved, they are appropriately named since POKing one memory location (turning it on, for example) has the effect of POKing the partner location (turning it off). Table 2A classifies the four switches and identifies the corresponding pairs of memory locations for each switch.

| SWITCH | 1 | | 2 | | 3 | | 4 | |
|---|---|---|---|---|---|---|---|---|
| FUNCTION | TEXT | GRAPHICS | MIXED SCREEN | FULL SCREEN | PAGE 1 | PAGE 2 | LOW RES | HIGH RES |
| MEMORY LOCATION | −16303 49233 | −16304 49232 | −16301 49235 | −16302 49234 | −16300 49236 | −16299 49237 | −16298 49238 | −16297 49239 |
| STATUS OF SWITCH | ON | OFF | ON | OFF | ON | OFF | ON | OFF |

Table 2A

A description of each of these memory locations follows. While POKing these memory locations can occur for any number 0 through 255, 0 has become the customary practice with most programmers.

POKE −16303, 0—Selects and displays the screen in text mode. The page selected depends upon the status of switch 3. The status of switch 2 and 4 are irrelevant to the visual effects when in TEXT mode. Thus, there are effectively two (2) text modes, text Page 1 and text Page 2. Text Page 1 is the more convenient one to use and is the page used for printed messages when TEXT mode or mixed graphics mode is in effect.

POKE −16304, 0—Selects and displays the screen in graphics mode without clearing the screen to black. The status of the remaining three switches determines whether the graphics display is to be low resolution or high resolution, Page 1 or Page 2, and in full screen graphics or mixed screen graphics. While this results in eight (8) possible graphics modes, use of low resolution graphics on Page 2 in either mixed or full screen mode is not practical. Also, high resolution Page 2 does not easily function in mixed graphics mode.

The careful reader will notice that the two text modes and eight graphics modes provide a total of ten different screen displays. However, only six (6) of these ten are conveniently used by conventional programming commands and are highlighted below.

Text on Page 1

Low Resolution, mixed screen graphics on Page 1

Low Resolution, full screen graphics on Page 1

High Resolution, mixed screen graphics on Page 1

High Resolution, full screen graphics on Page 1

High Resolution, full screen graphics on Page 2

POKE −16301, 0—Establishes mixed screen graphics mode by opening a four-line text window at the bottom of the screen, conveniently visible only on Page 1 and only after being preceded by POKE −16304, 0.

POKE −16302, 0—Establishes full screen graphics by closing the text window at the bottom of the screen. POKE −16304, 0 is necessary first to view the graphics screen. The status of switches 3 and 4 determine the other display characteristics, but full screen, low resolution graphics on Page 2 is not easily visible to the user.

POKE −16300, 0—Displays Page 1 of the screen in either graphics or text mode without destroying the previous contents. The status of switches 2 and 4 determine which APPLE memory locations are viewed. Table 2B identifies these possible memory locations.*

| MODE | DECIMAL | HEXADECIMAL |
|---|---|---|
| Text | 1047 – 2047 | $400 – $7FF |
| Low Res | 1024 – 2047 | $400 – $7FF |
| High Res | 8192 – 16383 | $2000 – $3FFF |

Table 2B

POKE  −16299, 0—Displays Page 2 of the screen without destroying the present contents. The status of switches 2 and 4 determine which APPLE memory locations are viewed. Table 2C identifies these possible memory locations.* Remember, Page 2 has no easily obtained practical applications in text or low resolution graphics mode.

| MODE | DECIMAL | HEXADECIMAL |
|------|---------|-------------|
| Text | 2048 – 3071 | $800 – $BFF |
| Low Res | 2048 – 3071 | $800 – $BFF |
| High Res | 16384 – 24575 | $4000 – $5FFF |

Table 2C

POKE  −16298, 0—Selects and displays low resolution graphics (memory area 1024-2047) without erasing the previous contents, but is not visible until memory location  −16304 is accessed. Viewing memory area 2048-3071 (for Page 2) is not easily obtained.

POKE  −16297, 0—Selects and displays one of the high resolution screens, determined by switch 3, without erasing the previous contents. Switch 2 determines whether mixed or full screen graphics is in effect and POKE  −16304, 0 is necessary for the screen to be visible.

Various combinations of POKE commands using the soft switches provide many possible screen displays. Exhibit 2A summarizes these possibilities in flow chart form.

*CHAPTER 3 presents a more comprehensive discussion of the APPLE memory organization.*

## MODES OF APPLE SCREEN DISPLAY.

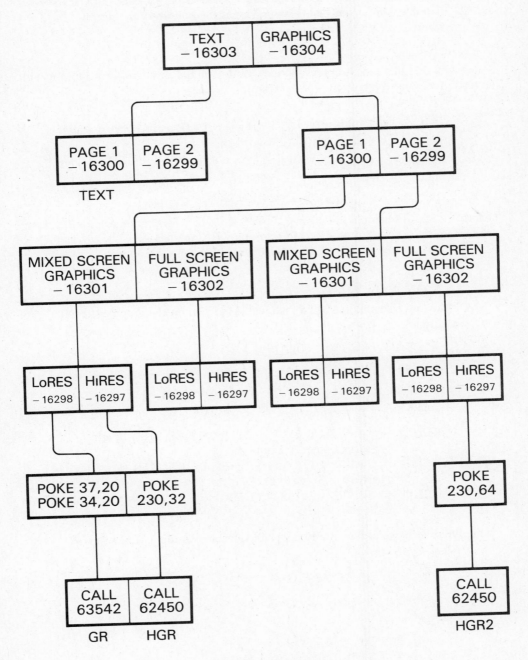

Exhibit 2A

Let's now review the graphics concepts covered in CHAPTER 2 and summarize some of the more commonly used screen displays.

• Obtain mixed graphics mode on high resolution Page 1 consisting of 160 rows and 280 columns with a four line text window at the bottom of the screen.

Example

```
HGR
```

• Obtain full screen graphics mode consisting of 192 rows and 280 columns with no text window at the bottom of the screen.

Examples

```
HGR : POKE −16301, 0, if using high resolution Page 1
HGR2, if using high resolution Page 2
```

• Select any one of eight colors.

Example

```
HCOLOR = N where N=0, 1, 2, ..., 7.
```

Colors 0, 1, 2, 3, form one color group; colors 4, 5, 6, 7 form another group. Mixing colors from different color groups can cause some bleeding effects.

• Draw a "pixel" at any allowable location on the graphics screen.

Example

```
HPLOT 100, 96
```

• Draw a horizontal line at any allowable location on the graphics screen.

Example

```
HPLOT 75, 35, TO 250, 35
```

• Draw a vertical line at any allowable location on the graphics screen. Coordination between color numbers and column coordinators must occur.

Examples

```
HCOLOR = 1 : HPLOT 87, 10 TO HPLOT 87, 150 draws a
        vertical green line
HCOLOR = 2 : HPLOT 87, 10 TO HPLOT 87, 150 does not
        display the vertical line
HCOLOR = 6 : HPLOT 158, 50 TO 158, 151 draws a blue
        vertical line
```

• Draw a diagonal line at any allowable location on the graphics screen.

Example

```
HPLOT 10, 30 TO 260, 147
```

• Shade a region in color.

Example

```
HGR : HCOLOR = 5
FOR I = 60 TO 120
HPLOT 100, I TO 200, I
```

```
NEXT
```

• Blink a diagram by repetitively drawing and erasing it.

Example

```
HGR
FOR I = 1 TO 10
HCOLOR = 5
HPLOT 10, 30 TO 260, 140
FOR J = 1 TO 200 : NEXT
HCOLOR = 4
HPLOT 10, 30 TO 260, 140
FOR J = 1 TO 200 : NEXT
NEXT
```

• Blink a diagram by using page flipping.

Example

```
HGR : HCOLOR = 5
HPLOT 10, 30 TO 260, 140
FOR I = 1 TO 10
HGR2
FOR J = 1 TO 200 : NEXT
POKE -16300, 0 : POKE -16301, 0
FOR J = 1 TO 200 : NEXT
NEXT
```

• Animate a diagram by repetitively drawing and erasing it in a sequence of different screen positions.

Example

```
HGR : Y = 100
FOR X = 50 TO 100 STEP 5
HCOLOR = 2
HPLOT X, Y TO X + 50, Y + 50
FOR J = 1 TO 200 : NEXT
HCOLOR = 0
HPLOT X, Y TO X + 50, Y + 50
NEXT
```

• Animate a diagram by using page flipping.

Example

```
X = 50 : Y = 100 : HGR : HGR 2
HCOLOR = 3
FOR L = 1 TO 8
POKE 230, 32 : CALL 62450
X = X + 10
HPLOT X, Y TO X + 50, Y + 50
POKE -16300, 0
FOR J = 1 TO 200 : NEXT
```

```
POKE 230, 64 : CALL 62450
X = X + 10
HPLOT X, Y TO X + 50, Y + 50
POKE -16299, 0
FOR J = 1 TO 200 : NEXT
NEXT
```

**CREATING A COMPUTER STORY**   In CHAPTER 1, a computer story entitled THE TENNIS COURT was used to review low resolution graphics and to demonstrate a model for developing a meaningful sequence of screen displays. In this chapter, the high resolution story, THE SHADOW BOX, is presented. While the story does not include all of the graphing techniques presented in the chapter, it does provide motivation for reading CHAPTER 3. Figure 2A includes the details for the animated robot.

The statements and variables used to program THE SHADOW BOX almost extend into the memory reserved for high resolution Page 1. After executing the statements for THE SHADOW BOX, enter the four lines of commands at the end of the program listing. Then RUN the program again to observe what happens when the program becomes large enough to interfere with the Page 1 display. CHAPTER 3 resolves this problem by demonstrating how to relocate where the program resides in memory.

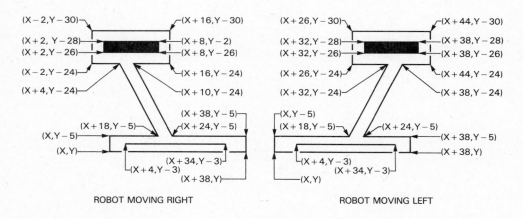

ROBOT MOVING RIGHT                    ROBOT MOVING LEFT

Figure 2A

**SAMPLE FRAME DESIGN:**
**THE SHADOW BOX**

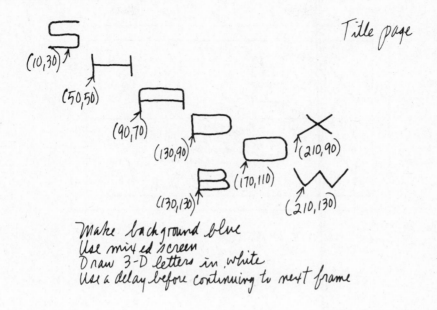

Title page

(10,30)
(50,50)
(90,70)
(130,90)
(170,110)
(210,90)
(130,130)
(210,130)

Make background blue
Use mixed screen
Draw 3-D letters in white
Use a delay before continuing to next frame

FRAME 1

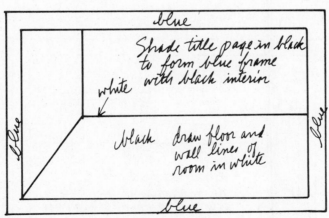

blue
Shade title page in black
to form blue frame
with black interior
white
blue
black   draw floor and
wall lines of
room in white
blue
blue
blue

Center messages
on each line

HERE IS THE BEGINNING OF THE
S H A D O W   B O X

PRESS THE SPACE BAR TO CONTINUE

line 21
line 22

line 24

FRAME 2

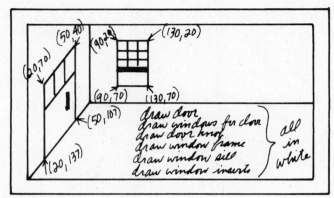

*Center messages on each line*

THE ROOM NEEDS A      *line 21*
DOOR AND A WINDOW      *line 22*

PRESS THE SPACE BAR TO CONTINUE    *line 24*

FRAME 3

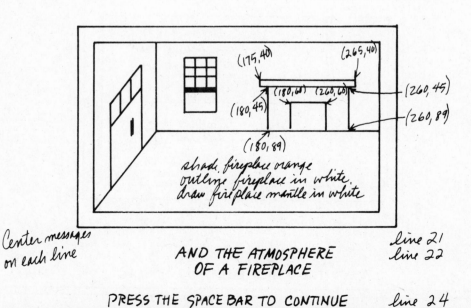

*Center messages on each line*

AND THE ATMOSPHERE      *line 21*
OF A FIREPLACE      *line 22*

PRESS THE SPACE BAR TO CONTINUE    *line 24*

FRAME 4

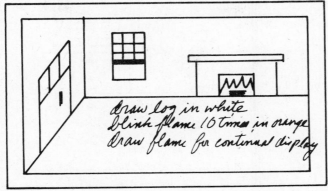

draw log in white
blink flame 10 times in orange
draw flame for continual display

Center messages on each line

AND THE WARMTH                    line 21
OF A FIRE                              line 22

PRESS THE SPACE BAR TO CONTINUE   line 24

FRAME 5

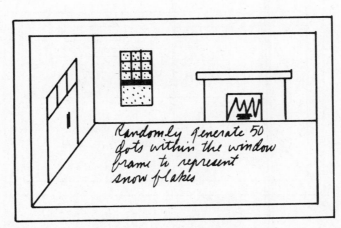

Randomly generate 50
dots within the window
frame to represent
snow flakes

Center messages on each line

DURING THE WINTER               line 21
SNOW STORM                         line 22

PRESS THE SPACE BAR TO CONTINUE  line 24

FRAME 6

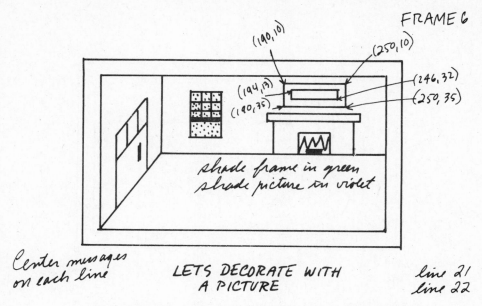

(190,10)
(250,10)
(194,13)
(246,32)
(190,35)
(250,35)

*shade frame in green*
*shade picture in violet*

*Center messages*
*on each line*

LETS DECORATE WITH
A PICTURE

*line 21*
*line 22*

PRESS THE SPACE BAR TO CONTINUE *line 24*

FRAME 7

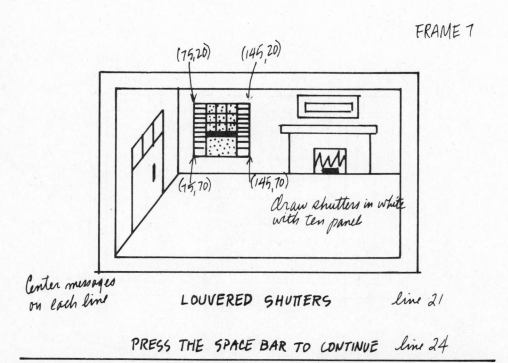

(75,20)     (145,20)

(75,70)     (145,70)

*Draw shutters in white*
*with ten panel*

*Center messages*
*on each line*

LOUVERED SHUTTERS          *line 21*

PRESS THE SPACE BAR TO CONTINUE  *line 24*

FRAME 8

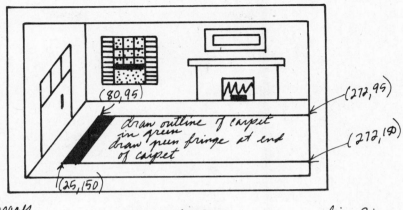

(80,95)

(272,95)

(272,150)

draw outline of carpet
in green
draw green fringe at end
of carpet

(25,150)

Center messages
on each line

AND A CARPET          line 21

PRESS THE SPACE BAR TO CONTINUE   line 24

FRAME 9

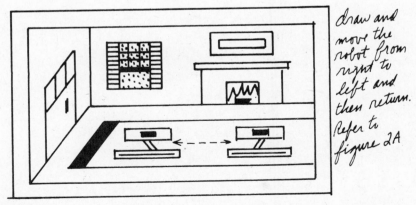

draw and
move the
robot from
right to
left and
then return.
Refer to
figure 2A

Center messages
on each line

WHICH NEEDS TO BE CLEANED BY     line 21
THE ROBOT SWEEPER                line 22

line 24

PRESS THE SPACE BAR TO CONTINUE

## SAMPLE COMPUTER STORY: THE SHADOW BOX

```
100   REM   ****************************************
110   REM   *            SHADOW  BOX               *
120   REM   ****************************************
130   TEXT : HOME : REM   CLEAR SCREEN
140   GOTO 5000
205   REM   *         DEFINE LETTERS               *
215   HPLOT X,Y TO X,Y − 18 TO X + 3,Y − 21 TO X + 17,Y
      − 21 TO X + 20,Y − 18 TO X + 20,Y: HPLOT X,Y
      − 10 TO X + 20,Y − 10: RETURN : REM    A
220   HPLOT X,Y TO X,Y − 21 TO X + 20,Y − 21 TO X + 20,Y −
      14 TO X + 15,Y − 10 TO X + 20,Y − 6 TO X + 20,Y TO
      X,Y: HPLOT X,Y − 10 TO X + 15,Y − 10: RETURN :
      REM   B
225   HPLOT X,Y TO X,Y − 21 TO X + 15,Y − 21 TO X + 20,Y −
      17 TO X + 20,Y − 4 TO X + 15,Y TO X,Y: RETURN : REM   D
230   HPLOT X,Y TO X,Y − 21: HPLOT X + 20,Y TO X + 20,Y
      − 21: HPLOT X,Y − 10 TO X + 20,Y − 10: RETURN : REM   H
235   HPLOT X,Y − 3 TO X,Y − 18 TO X + 3,Y − 21 TO X + 17,
      Y − 21 TO X + 20,Y − 18 TO X + 20,Y − 3 TO X + 17,Y
      TO X + 3,Y TO X,Y − 3: RETURN : REM   O
240   HPLOT X,Y TO X + 17,Y TO X + 20,Y − 3 TO X + 20,Y − 8
      TO X + 17,Y − 10 TO X + 3,Y − 10 TO X,Y − 12 TO X,Y −
      18 TO X + 3,Y − 21 TO X + 20,Y − 21: RETURN : REM    S
245   HPLOT X,Y − 21 TO X,Y TO X + 9,Y − 10 TO X + 20,Y TO X
      + 20,Y − 21: RETURN : REM    W
250   HPLOT X,Y − 21 TO X + 20,Y: HPLOT X,Y TO X + 20,Y − 21:
      RETURN : REM    X
296   REM   *         FRAME CONTROL ROUTINE        *
300   VTAB 24: HTAB 5
305   PRINT "PRESS THE SPACE BAR TO CONTINUE";
310   GET Q$: HOME
315   RETURN
396   REM   *              FIRE                     *
400   HPLOT 205,89 TO 208,80 TO 210,85 TO 220,70 TO 225,86 TO
      230,78 TO 233,80 TO 235,84 TO 238,89: RETURN
495   REM   *  DRAW ROBOT MOVING RIGHT              *
500   HPLOT X,Y TO X + 38,Y TO X + 38,Y − 5 TO X + 24,Y − 5
      TO X + 38,Y − 24 TO X + 44,Y − 24 TO X + 44,Y − 30 TO
      X + 26,Y − 30 TO X + 26,Y − 24 TO X + 32,Y − 24 TO
      X + 18,Y −  5 TO X,Y − 5 TO X,Y
510   HPLOT X + 4,Y − 3 TO X + 34,Y − 3: HPLOT X + 32,Y − 28
      TO X + 38,Y − 28: HPLOT X + 32,Y − 27 TO X + 38,Y −
      27: HPLOT X + 32,Y − 26 TO X + 38,Y − 26
520   RETURN
```

```
595   REM  *   DRAW ROBOT MOVING LEFT            *
600   HPLOT X,Y TO X + 38,Y TO X + 38,Y - 5 TO X + 24,Y - 5
      TO X + 10,Y - 24 TO X + 16,Y - 24 TO X + 16,Y - 30 TO
      X - 2,Y - 30 TO X - 2,Y - 24 TO X + 4,Y - 24 TO X +
      18,Y - 5 TO X,Y - 5 TO X,Y
610   HPLOT X + 4,Y - 3 TO X + 34,Y - 3: HPLOT X + 2,Y - 28
      TO X + 8,Y - 28: HPLOT X + 2,Y - 27 TO X + 8,Y - 27:
      HPLOT X + 2,Y - 26 TO X + 8,Y - 26
620   RETURN
4030  GOSUB 220
5000  REM  ******************************************
5005  REM  *            MAIN PROGRAM             *
5010  REM  ******************************************
5012  REM  ******************************************
5013  REM  *             TITLE PAGE              *
5014  REM  ******************************************
5020  HGR : REM     SELECT PAGE 1
5025  HCOLOR = 6: HPLOT 0,0: CALL 62454: REM   COLOR SCREEN
      BLUE
5030  HCOLOR = 7: REM   COLOR LETTERS WHITE
5032  REM  DRAW 3D S
5035  X = 10:Y = 30
5040  FOR I = 1 TO 4
5045  X = X + 1:Y = Y + 1: GOSUB 240
5050  NEXT
5052  REM  DRAW 3D H
5055  X = 50:Y = 50
5060  FOR I = 1 TO 4
5065  X = X + 1:Y = Y + 1: GOSUB 230
5070  NEXT
5072  REM  DRAW 3D A
5075  X = 90:Y = 70
5080  FOR I = 1 TO 4
5085  X = X + 1:Y = Y + 1: GOSUB 215
5090  NEXT
5092  REM  DRAW 3D D
5095  X = 130:Y = 90
5100  FOR I = 1 TO 4
5105  X = X + 1:Y = Y + 1: GOSUB 225
5110  NEXT
5112  REM  DRAW 3D O
5115  X = 170:Y = 110
5120  FOR I = 1 TO 4
5125  X = X + 1:Y = Y + 1: GOSUB 235
5130  NEXT
5132  REM  DRAW 3D W
5135  X = 210:Y = 130
```

```
5140    FOR I = 1 TO 4
5145    X = X + 1:Y = Y + 1: GOSUB 245
5150    NEXT
5152    REM   DRAW 3D B
5155    X = 130:Y = 130
5160    FOR I = 1 TO 4
5165    X = X + 1:Y = Y + 1: GOSUB 220
5170    NEXT
5172    REM   DRAW 3D X
5175    X = 210:Y = 90
5180    FOR I = 1 TO 4
5185    X = X + 1:Y = Y + 1: GOSUB 250
5190    NEXT
5195    FOR J = 1 TO 2500: NEXT : REM   DELAY
5197    REM   *****************************************
5198    REM   *              FRAME 1                  *
5199    REM   *****************************************
5200    REM   SHADE IN BLACK TO FORM SHADOW BOX
5202    HCOLOR = 4
5205    FOR I = 5 TO 154
5210    HPLOT 5,I TO 272,I
5215    NEXT
5217    REM   DRAW 3D OUTLINE OF ROOM
5220    HCOLOR = 7
5225    HPLOT 6,153 TO 70,90 TO 271,90: HPLOT 70,90 TO 70,6:
        HPLOT 69,90 TO 69,6
5230    VTAB 21: HTAB 6
5235    PRINT "HERE IS THE BEGINNING OF THE"
5240    VTAB 22: HTAB 12
5245    PRINT "S H A D O W   B O X"
5250    GOSUB 300
5255    REM   *****************************************
5256    REM   *              FRAME 2                  *
5257    REM   *****************************************
5259    REM   DRAW DOOR FRAME
5260    HPLOT 20,137 TO 20,70 TO 50,40 TO 50,107: HPLOT 44,85 TO
        47,82: HPLOT 44,86 TO 47,83: HPLOT 44,87 TO 47,84
5262    REM   DRAW WINDOW FRAME
5265    HPLOT 90,70 TO 90,20 TO 130,20 TO 130,70 TO 90,70
5267    REM   DRAW DOOR WINDOW
5268    HPLOT 20,85 TO 50,55: HPLOT 30,60 TO 30,75: HPLOT 40,50
        TO 40,65
5270    FOR I = 42 TO 46
5275    HPLOT 90,I TO 130,I
5280    NEXT
5283    REM   DRAW WINDOW INSERTS
5285    HPLOT 90,31 TO 130,31: HPLOT 103,20 TO 103,42: HPLOT
```

```
          116,20 TO 116,42
5290  VTAB 21: HTAB 12
5295  PRINT "THE ROOM NEEDS A"
5300  VTAB 22: HTAB 12
5305  PRINT "DOOR AND A WINDOW"
5310  GOSUB 300
5315  REM  *****************************************
5316  REM  *              FRAME 3                  *
5317  REM  *****************************************
5320  REM   COLOR FIREPLACE ORANGE
5325  HCOLOR = 5
5330  FOR I = 45 TO 60
5335  HPLOT 180,I TO 260,I
5340  NEXT
5345  FOR I = 60 TO 89
5350  HPLOT 180,I TO 200,I: HPLOT 240,I TO 260,I
5355  NEXT
5357  REM   OUTLINE FIREPLACE
5360  HCOLOR = 7
5365  HPLOT 180,90 TO 180,45 TO 260,45 TO 260,90
5370  HPLOT 200,90 TO 200,60 TO 240,60 TO 240,90
5372  REM   DRAW FIREPLACE MANTEL
5375  FOR I = 40 TO 45
5380  HPLOT 175,I TO 265,I
5385  NEXT
5390  VTAB 21: HTAB 11
5395  PRINT "AND THE ATMOSPHERE"
5400  VTAB 22: HTAB 13
5405  PRINT "OF A FIREPLACE"
5410  GOSUB 300
5415  REM  *****************************************
5416  REM  *              FRAME 4                  *
5417  REM  *****************************************
5420  VTAB 21: HTAB 13
5425  PRINT "AND THE WARMTH"
5430  VTAB 22: HTAB 16
5435  PRINT "OF A FIRE"
5437  REM   DRAW LOG
5440  FOR I = 85 TO 89
5445  HPLOT 210,I TO 230,I
5450  NEXT
5452  REM   BLINK FLAME
5455  FOR I = 1 TO 10
5460  HCOLOR = 5
5462  GOSUB 400
5465  FOR J = 1 TO 200: NEXT
5467  HCOLOR = 4
```

```
5470   GOSUB 400
5472   FOR J = 1 TO 200: NEXT
5480   NEXT I
5485   REM    DRAW FLAME
5490   HCOLOR = 5: GOSUB 400
5495   GOSUB 300
5500   REM  ****************************************
5501   REM  *              FRAME 5                 *
5502   REM  ****************************************
5505   VTAB 21: HTAB 13
5510   PRINT "DURING A WINTER"
5515   VTAB 22: HTAB 15
5520   PRINT "SNOW STORM"
5525   HCOLOR = 7
5530   FOR I = 1 TO 50
5535   X = 40 *  RND (1) + 90
5540   Y = 50 *  RND (1) + 20
5545   HPLOT X,Y
5550   NEXT
5555   GOSUB 300
5560   REM  ****************************************
5561   REM  *              FRAME 6                 *
5562   REM  ****************************************
5564   REM  SHADE FRAME IN GREEN
5565   HCOLOR = 1
5570   FOR I = 10 TO 35
5575   HPLOT 190,I TO 250,I
5580   NEXT
5582   REM  SHADE PICTURE IN VIOLET
5585   HCOLOR = 2
5590   FOR I = 13 TO 32
5595   HPLOT 194,I TO 246,I
5597   NEXT
5605   VTAB 21: HTAB 12
5610   PRINT "LET'S DECORATE WITH"
5615   VTAB 22: HTAB 16
5620   PRINT "A PICTURE"
5625   GOSUB 300
5630   REM  ****************************************
5631   REM  *              FRAME 7                 *
5632   REM  ****************************************
5640   HCOLOR = 7
5645   HPLOT 90,70 TO 75,70 TO 75,20 TO 90,20
5647   HPLOT 130,70 TO 145,70 TO 145,20 TO 130,20
5650   FOR I = 25 TO 65 STEP 5
5655   HPLOT 75,I TO 90,I
5657   HPLOT 130,I TO 145,I
```

```
5660   NEXT
5665   VTAB 21: HTAB 12
5670   PRINT "LOUVERED SHUTTERS"
5675   GOSUB 300
5680   REM  ****************************************
5681   REM  *            FRAME 8                   *
5682   REM  ****************************************
5700   HCOLOR = 1
5702   REM   DRAW OUTLINE OF CARPET
5705   HPLOT 272,150 TO 25,150 TO 80,95 TO 272,95
5706   REM  DRAW FRINGE OF CARPET
5707   FOR I = 26 TO 31
5708   HPLOT I,150 TO I + 55,95
5709   NEXT
5710   VTAB 21: HTAB 14
5715   PRINT "AND A CARPET"
5720   GOSUB 300
5725   REM  ****************************************
5726   REM  *            FRAME 9                   *
5727   REM  ****************************************
5730   VTAB 21: HTAB 6
5732   PRINT "WHICH NEEDS TO BE CLEANED BY"
5735   VTAB 22: HTAB 12
5737   PRINT "THE ROBOT SWEEPER"
5740   Y = 140
5742   REM  SET CONDITIONS FOR ROBOT MOVING RIGHT
5745   FOR X = 225 TO 90 STEP  - 5
5750   HCOLOR = 7: GOSUB 500: REM  DISPLAY ROBOT
5755   HCOLOR = 4: GOSUB 500: REM  ERASE ROBOT
5760   NEXT
5762   REM  SET CONDITIONS FOR ROBOT MOVING LEFT
5765   FOR X = 90 TO 225 STEP 5
5770   HCOLOR = 7: GOSUB 600: REM  DISPLAY ROBOT
5775   HCOLOR = 4: GOSUB 600: REM  ERASE ROBOT
5780   NEXT
5782   REM  DRAW ROBOT FOR LAST VIEW
5785   HCOLOR = 7: GOSUB 600
5790   GOSUB 300: TEXT : HOME
5795   END
```

Now enter the next four lines of APPLESOFT commands, RUN the new program, and observe the sequence of screen displays.

```
5599   REM DRAW PICTURE DESIGN
5600   HCOLOR = 0
5602   HPLOT 195, 33 TO 220, 14 TO 245, 33
5603   HPLOT 195, 14 TO 220, 33 TO 245, 14
       RUN
```

**SUGGESTED PROJECTS**
1. Write a computer story that pictorially describes the layout of a baseball field, indicating the various positions where offensive and defensive players are located.
2. Write a computer story that imitates the action of a scoreboard one often finds at a professional sports event.
3. Write a computer story which develops a favorite TV show by first drawing a picture of a TV set with knobs and other controls, and finally animating the various portions of the show on the TV tube.
4. Write a computer story which describes an outdoor neighborhood scene consisting of a house, some trees, a street, a sidewalk, a bird flying to a tree, and any other creative idea you might have.
5. Write a computer story of your choice.

# More Advanced Topics in Graphics

## MODULE 3A    Memory Usage with Graphics

### ACTIVITY 3.1    Text & Low Resolution Memory Locations

**LEARNING BY DISCOVERY**    This activity will demonstrate how computer memory addresses are used to display text and low resolution "bricks," and where this memory resides within the computer. It is assumed that the reader understands the relationship between the decimal, binary, and hexadecimal number systems and is familiar with the meaning of the terms bits, nybbles, bytes, and high order and low order nybbles and bytes. If not, APPENDIX 3A should be studied prior to performing this activity.

1.  Enter the following commands.

    ```
    NEW
    10   HOME
    20   POKE 1725, 197
    RUN
    ```

    What symbol appears on the screen? _____

2.  Add line 30 as follows:

    ```
    HOME
    30   POKE 1498, 69
    RUN
    ```

    What new symbol appears on the screen? _____

3. Add line 40 as follows:

```
HOME
40   POKE 1290, 5
RUN
```

What new symbol appears on the screen? _____

4. Enter the following commands.

```
HOME : NEW
10   HOME
20   FOR X = 1024 TO 2047
30   POKE X, 163
40   NEXT
RUN
```

Observe the screen display.

What symbol appears on the screen? _____

Describe the pattern by which the symbol appears repetitively. _____

5. Enter the following commands.

```
HOME : NEW
10   HOME : GR
20   POKE  1683, 114
RUN
```

Observe the screen display.

How many bricks appear? _____

What color is the upper brick? _____

What color is the lower brick? _____

6. Retype line 20 as follows:

```
TEXT : HOME
20   POKE 1125, 207
RUN
```

Observe the screen display.

What color is the upper brick? _____

What color is the lower brick? _____

**DISCUSSION**   Apple reserves memory locations (or addresses) 1024 through 2047 (or hexadecimal $400 through $7FF) for both the display of text and low resolution graphics. Exhibit 3.1.1 illustrates the structure of the address map associated with this part of the Apple memory.

In Section 1, the POKE 1725, 197 causes the letter E to appear on the screen, identified by the placement of the E in Exhibit 3.1.1. The address 1725 is determined by taking the corresponding row decimal number (1704) and adding the corresponding column number (21) to obtain the sum 1725 (or 1704 + 21). The number 197 in POKE 1725, 197 is the decimal numerical code for the normal display of the ASCII (American Standard Code for Information Interchange) screen character E.

In Sections 2 and 3, the numbers 69 and 5 result, respectively, in a flashing E and an inverse video E (black on white). Table 3.1.1 provides the numerical codes for all ASCII screen characters by adding row and column numbers in a manner identical to that used for locating memory addresses in Exhibit 3.1.1.

You should have noticed the peculiar manner in which the screen filled with # 's in Section 4. The memory addresses are not numbered consecutively from row to row. Section 4 demonstrates, as the memory map in Exhibit 3.1.1 suggests, that rows 1, 9, and 17 are filled first and in that order, followed by rows 2, 10, and 18, and so on until rows 8, 16, and 24 finally complete the filling of the screen.

In Section 5, when the activity changes from text to graphics mode, another phenomenon occurs. Two "bricks," in contrast to one letter, are displayed. This explains why APPLESOFT provides 24 lines of text and 48 lines (twice 24) of graphic "bricks."

Perhaps you are surprised the bricks appear in two different colors. By first converting the number 114 in Section 5 to its hexadecimal equivalent, $72, APPLE-SOFT defines the high order nybble (7) to be the color of the lower brick and the number of the low order nybble (2) to determine the color of the upper brick. Since COLOR = 7 and COLOR = 2 correspond to the colors light blue and dark blue respectively, the lower and upper bricks appear in these colors.

Similarly, in Section 6, the decimal number 207 corresponds to the hexadecimal number $CF. Therefore, the color of the lower brick is light green (COLOR = 12 for C) and the color of the upper brick is white (COLOR = 15 for F).

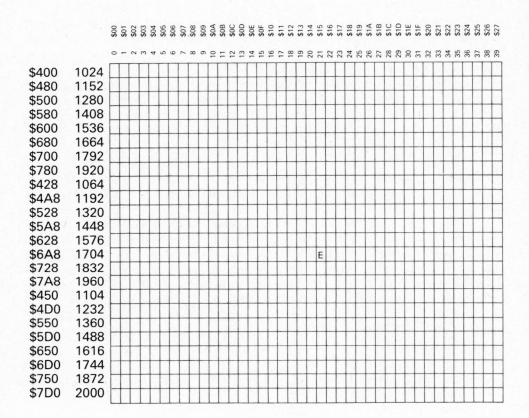

Exhibit 3.1.1

| ASCII Screen Characters | | | | | | | | | | | | | | | | |
|---|---|---|---|---|---|---|---|---|---|---|---|---|---|---|---|---|
| | Inverse | | | | Flashing | | | | Control | Normal | | | | | Lowercase | |
| Decimal | 0 | 16 | 32 | 48 | 64 | 80 | 96 | 112 | 128 | 144 | 160 | 176 | 192 | 208 | 224 | 240 |
| 0 | @ | P | | 0 | @ | P | | 0 | @ | P | | 0 | @ | P | | 0 |
| 1 | A | Q | ! | 1 | A | Q | ! | 1 | A | Q | ! | 1 | A | Q | ! | 1 |
| 2 | B | R | " | 2 | B | R | " | 2 | B | R | " | 2 | B | R | " | 2 |
| 3 | C | S | # | 3 | C | S | # | 3 | C | S | # | 3 | C | S | # | 3 |
| 4 | D | T | $ | 4 | D | T | $ | 4 | D | T | $ | 4 | D | T | $ | 4 |
| 5 | E | U | % | 5 | E | U | % | 5 | E | U | % | 5 | E | U | % | 5 |
| 6 | F | V | & | 6 | F | V | & | 6 | F | V | & | 6 | F | V | & | 6 |
| 7 | G | W | ' | 7 | G | W | ' | 7 | G | W | ' | 7 | G | W | ' | 7 |
| 8 | H | X | ( | 8 | H | X | ( | 8 | H | X | ( | 8 | H | X | ( | 8 |
| 9 | I | Y | ) | 9 | I | Y | ) | 9 | I | Y | ) | 9 | I | Y | ) | 9 |
| 10 | J | Z | * | : | J | Z | * | : | J | Z | * | : | J | Z | * | : |
| 11 | K | [ | + | ; | K | [ | + | ; | K | [ | + | ; | K | [ | + | ; |
| 12 | L | \ | , | < | L | \ | , | < | L | \ | , | < | L | \ | , | < |
| 13 | M | ] | - | = | M | ] | - | = | M | ] | - | = | M | ] | - | = |
| 14 | N | ^ | . | > | N | ^ | . | > | N | ^ | . | > | N | ^ | . | > |
| 15 | O | - | / | ? | O | - | / | ? | O | - | / | ? | O | - | / | ? |

Table 3.1.1

**COMPREHENSIVE EXAMPLE**   Using Table 3.1.1, study the following APPLE-
SOFT program to determine the screen display. Check your answer by entering the
program into the computer.

```
TEXT : HOME : NEW
100  REM ***************************************
101  REM *              CE 3.1                 *
102  REM ***************************************
105  HOME
110  FOR X = 1080 TO 1088 STEP 2
120  READ Y
130  POKE X, Y
140  NEXT X
150  FOR X = 1336 TO 1344 STEP 2
160  READ Y
170  POKE X, Y
180  NEXT X
```

```
190   DATA 65, 208, 208, 204, 5
200   DATA 67, 73, 68, 69, 82
210   GET Q$ : HOME
```

**Check Your Comprehension**

What message is displayed by executing the loop defined by lines 110 through 140?

_____

What message is displayed by executing the loop defined by lines 150 through 180?

_____

What is the purpose of variable X in the program? _____

What is the purpose of variable Y in the program? _____

**EXERCISE**   Write an APPLESOFT program that places two "bricks" at location 1468 on the low resolution screen, without using the PLOT command, so the upper brick is yellow and the lower brick is dark green, and then prints "BRICK" centered on line 22 of the text window, without using the PRINT command.

**CHALLENGE**   Write an APPLESOFT program that randomly places ten randomly colored "bricks" at any location on the low resolution mixed screen without using the PLOT command. Then center the display of "RANDOM" on line 22 and "BRICKS" on line 23 of the text window without using the PRINT command.

# ACTIVITY 3.2   High Resolution Memory Locations

**LEARNING BY DISCOVERY**   This activity will demonstrate how computer memory addresses are used to display high resolution graphics and where this memory resides within the computer.

1. Enter the following commands.

```
NEW
100   HOME : HGR
110   FOR X = 1024 TO 2047
120   POKE X, 163
130   NEXT
RUN
```

   Observe the screen display.

   What appears in the graphics portion of the screen? _____

   What appears in the text window? _____

2. Retype line 100 as follows:

```
TEXT : HOME
100   HOME : HGR2
RUN
```

Observe the screen display.

What appears in the graphics portion of the screen? _____

What appears in the text window? _____

3. Enter the following commands.

```
TEXT : HOME : NEW
100   HOME : HGR
110   FOR X = 8192 TO 16383
120   POKE X, 193
130   NEXT
RUN
```

Observe the screen display.

What image appears on the screen? _____

Describe the order in which this image appears repetitively. _____

4. Retype lines 100 and 110 as follows:

```
TEXT : HOME
100   HOME : HGR2
110   FOR X = 16384 TO 24575
RUN
```

Observe the screen display.

What image appears on the screen? _____

Describe the order in which this image appears repetitively. _____

5. Enter the following commands.

```
TEXT : HOME : NEW
100   HOME : HGR
110   FOR X = 8636 TO 14780 STEP 1024
120   READ Y
130   POKE X, Y
140   NEXT
150   DATA 63, 65, 65, 63, 17, 33, 65
RUN
```

What symbol appears on the screen? _____

**DISCUSSION**  Apple reserves memory locations 8192 through 16383 (or hexadecimal $2000 through $3FFF) for the display of high resolution Page 1, and memory locations 16384 through 24575 (hexadecimal $4000 through $5FFF) for the display of high resolution Page 2. The appearance of the four lines in the text window in Section 1 demonstrates that the mixed graphics screen initiated by the HGR command uses text Page 1 for the text window. In contrast, the empty screen display in Section 2 reinforces our previous discovery that HGR2 command does not initiate this text window display.

Sections 3 and 4 illustrate the peculiar manner in which the memory addresses are sequenced for both pages of the high resolution screen, similar to the manner discovered in ACTIVITY 3.1 for the low resolution screen. Exhibit 3.2.1 illustrates the structure of the address map associated with high resolution Page 1.

In Section 5, the letter R in the cell indicated in Exhibit 3.2.1 is displayed. In high resolution graphics each of these cells consists of eight bytes, with each byte containing eight bits. The right most bit is used for determining color, and therefore is not displayed. This situation leaves 8 rows of 7 pixels each for each cell, as depicted in Exhibit 3.2.2.

Notice these row addresses are incremented by a magnitude of 1024. Some simple arithmetic now provides some meaningful results. Recall that the high resolution screen consists of 192 rows, with each row having 280 columns. The intersection of each row and column defines a pixel. The 192 is the result of the product $(24 \times 8)$, since there are 24 rows of cells and each cell has 8 rows. Similarly, the 280 is the result of the product $40 \times 7$, since there are 40 columns of cells and each column is divided into 7 smaller columns.

Exhibits 3.2.3 through 3.2.6 illustrate the procedure by which the character R is developed. Exhibit 3.2.3 displays the letter R as 7 pixels long by 7 pixels high which fills one cell, except for the bottom row. Exhibit 3.2.4 translates the shaded R into binary code by writing a 1 if a pixel is shaded and a 0 if it is not shaded. Exhibit 3.2.5 puts each row of bits in reverse order because Apple graphics displays show the bits in reverse order. Exhibit 3.2.6 converts each row of bits to its equivalent decimal number. These decimal numbers can then be used as data to be entered with a READ statement and POKEd into the desired memory address as occur in Section 5. The value 14780 is determined by the computation $8636 + 6 * 1024$ since there are 7 rows used in the letter R.

This activity demonstrates a procedure by which alphanumeric characters can be displayed on the high resolution screen, but not with the ease of simply using a PRINT command. This is the method you must use unless you have special software packages available. We will examine one of these high resolution character generator packages later in CHAPTER 3, which will finally permit us to write on the high resolution screen with PRINT statements.

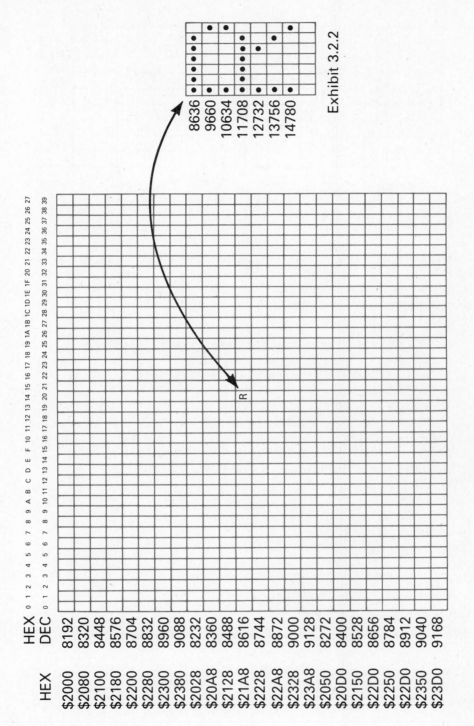

Exhibit 3.2.2

Exhibit 3.2.1

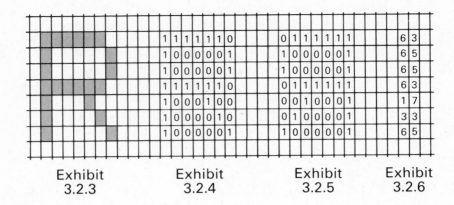

Exhibit
3.2.3

Exhibit
3.2.4

Exhibit
3.2.5

Exhibit
3.2.6

**COMPREHENSIVE EXAMPLE**   The following APPLESOFT program displays the larger and thicker H illustrated in Exhibit 3.2.7 using four memory addresses. Check the accuracy of the DATA values as they relate to the picture. Study and enter the program to observe the screen display.

```
TEXT : HOME : NEW
100  REM ****************************************
101  REM *                CE 3.2                *
102  REM ****************************************
105  HOME : HGR
110  FOR Z = 1 TO 4 : REM CONTROL FOUR CELLS
115  READ A, B : REM DETERMINE FIRST AND LAST ROW ADDRESS
     WITHIN CELL
120  FOR X = A TO B STEP 1024
130  READ Y : REM ENTER BYTE FOR ROW
150  POKE X, Y
160  NEXT X
200  NEXT Z
210  DATA 8636, 15804, 3, 3, 3, 3, 3, 3, 3, 127
220  DATA 8637, 15805, 96, 96, 96, 96, 96, 96, 96, 127
230  DATA 8764, 15932, 127, 3, 3, 3, 3, 3, 3, 3
240  DATA 8765, 15933, 127, 96, 96, 96, 96, 96, 96, 96
250  GET Q$ : TEXT : HOME
```

**Check Your Comprehension**

What is the significance of the numbers 8636 and 15804 in line 210? _____

How many times is line 130 executed? _____

Why does line 120 contain STEP 1024? _____

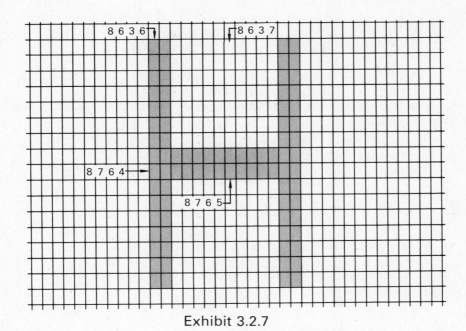

Exhibit 3.2.7

**EXERCISE**  Write an APPLESOFT program which displays the 7 × 7 pixel characters, B S C, centered on the screen.

**CHALLENGE**  Write an APPLESOFT program which displays all base ten digits on one line, beginning at memory location 9009, and with one screen column separating each digit.

# ACTIVITY 3.3  Relocating APPLESOFT Programs

**LEARNING BY DISCOVERY**  This activity demonstrates procedures for making more efficient use of Apple memory.

1. Boot your computer system with the DOS 3.3 System Master. Insert a diskette which is not write protected. Then enter the following commands in immediate mode and record the printed values in the provided space.

```
NEW
PRINT 256 * PEEK (104) + PEEK (103) _____
PRINT PEEK (2048)                      _____
PRINT 256 * PEEK (106) + PEEK (105) _____
PRINT 256 * PEEK (116) + PEEK (115) _____
```

2. Enter the following APPLESOFT commands.

```
10 HOME : HGR : HCOLOR = 3
20 FOR I = 60 TO 100 : HPLOT 120, I TO 160, I :
   NEXT
SAVE DEMO
```

Enter the following commands in immediate mode and record the printed values in the provided space.

```
PRINT 256 * PEEK (104) + PEEK (103) _____
PRINT 256 * PEEK (106) + PEEK (105) _____
PRINT 256 * PEEK (116) + PEEK (115) _____
```

3. Enter the following commands in immediate mode.

```
NEW
POKE 104, 64
POKE 103, 1
POKE 16384, 0
RUN DEMO
```

Enter the following commands in immediate mode and record the printed values in the provided space.

```
TEXT
PRINT 256 * PEEK (104) + PEEK (103) _____
PRINT PEEK (16384)                  _____
PRINT 256 * PEEK (106) + PEEK (105) _____
```

4. Enter the following commands.

```
NEW
10 HOME
20 POKE 104, 96
30 POKE 103, 1
40 POKE 24576, 0
SAVE RELOCATE
RUN RELOCATE
RUN DEMO
```

Enter the following commands in immediate mode and record the printed values in the provided space.

```
TEXT
PRINT 256 * PEEK (104) + PEEK (103) _____
PRINT PEEK (24596)                  _____
PRINT 256 * PEEK (106) + PEEK (105) _____
PRINT 256 * PEEK (116) + PEEK (115) _____
```

**DISCUSSION**   As one begins to write long programs on any microcomputer, availability of sufficient memory becomes of concern. In particular, the awkward arrangement of Apple memory prevents straightforward writing of long programs which include high resolution graphics. The following comments refer to the use of DOS 3.3 on an Apple II Plus (Apple IIe, Franklin ACE 1000) system with 48K bytes of RAM.

Table 3.3.1 illustrates the memory map of an Apple II Plus system with 48K bytes of RAM and 16K bytes of ROM, with the memory locations designated in both decimal and hexadecimal form. Of interest to graphics programmers is the location of low resolution Page 1 (1024 − 2047), high resolution Page 1 (8192 − 16383), and high resolution Page 2 (16384 − 24576). Also notice DOS 3.3 uses almost 11K bytes of RAM, and BASIC programs begin at memory location 2048.

When writing programs which include only low resolution graphics, the programmer has 36,352 bytes (from 2048 to 38399) of memory available, since low resolution Page 1 is below memory location 2048. Problems arise when high resolution graphics are used. The inconveniently placed locations for Pages 1 and 2 only permit programs of length 6K bytes (2048 − 8192). Longer programs will extend into high resolution Page 1, which will result in an upsetting display of colorful nonsense on the screen as your program statements and/or numeric variables get clobbered.

Table 3.3.2 identifies several memory addresses used in the activity to demonstrate how BASIC programs can be relocated in Apple memory. The PEEK command is used for "looking" at the value in a particular address.

Memory locations 103 and 104 are used in tandem to determine where the BASIC program is loaded. Section 1 demonstrates BASIC programs normally begin at location 2049; a 0 must be placed in memory (2048) immediately ahead of where the program will load.

Memory addresses 105 and 106 collectively define a location called LOMEM. LOMEM is set at the end of the BASIC program and increases as the program increases in size, as shown in Section 2. Simple variables are stored from LOMEM upward.

Memory positions 115 and 116 are used to determine HIMEM, the top end of available memory. Strings are stored from HIMEM downward to lower memory locations. HIMEM remained at 38400 throughout this activity as our modifications did not affect this area of memory.

In Section 3 the APPLESOFT program was relocated to begin at location 16385, immediately above high resolution Page 1. The number 64 in POKE 104, 64 is determined by the formula INT (Address/256) = INT (16385/256) = 64. The remainder, 1, is POKEd into location 103. The position just ahead of where the program is to be loaded, 16384, has a 0 placed in it with POKE 16384,0.

The technique of POKing memory locations in immediate mode prior to RUNning a program is inconvenient and unnecessary. Section 4 demonstrates an alternative technique by which the POKing is accomplished in a separate program, which is executed before the RUN of the desired APPLESOFT program.

While it is not shown here, these POKE's could have been included in the HELLO program on the diskette so the APPLESOFT program could be executed immediately following the booting of the system. Notice in Section 4 the program is loaded above Page 2, beginning at location 24577.

By relocating the program above Page 2, approximately 14K (or 38999 − 24576) bytes of RAM is available. If Page 2 is not needed, then the program can be loaded immediately above Page 1, giving 22K (or 14K + 8K) bytes of RAM. Notice the vacant 6K bytes of memory between locations 2049 and 8192 appear to be wasted. This memory can be used for loading larger shape tables or other special purpose routines.

**COMPREHENSIVE EXAMPLE**    The following commands demonstrate a technique by which an APPLESOFT program can be loaded at a specified memory location by using the DOS 3.3 EXEC command. The following program (MAKELOAD) creates a TEXT file (LOAD) which establishes the conditions necessary for relocating the program (DEMO). The command EXEC LOAD loads DEMO beginning at location 24577, just above high resolution Page 2. Enter the following commands in the given order to observe the effects of this technique.

```
NEW
10    REM ****************************************
11    REM *           MAKELOAD CE 3.3            *
12    REM ****************************************
15    D$ = CHR$ (13) + CHR$ (4)
20    PRINT D$; "OPEN LOAD" : PRINT D$ ; "DELETE LOAD"
30    PRINT D$; "OPEN LOAD" : PRINT D$; "WRITE LOAD"
40    PRINT "NEW"
50    PRINT "POKE 104, 96"
60    PRINT "POKE 103, 1"
70    PRINT "POKE 24576, 0"
80    PRINT "RUN DEMO"
90    PRINT "CLOSE"
95    END
RUN (First insert your non-write-protected diskette.)
TEXT
EXEC LOAD
TEXT
PRINT 256 * PEEK (104) + PEEK (103)
```

**Check Your Comprehension**

What is the purpose of line 10? _____

What is the purpose of lines 50 and 60? _____

What is the purpose of line 70? _____

**EXERCISE**    Modify the technique used in the COMPREHENSIVE EXAMPLE to load DEMO just above high resolution Page 1 using the command EXEC LODE.

**CHALLENGE**    Design your diskette greeting program to load a program above a high resolution page of your choice by simply booting the system.

| Memory Location | | Memory Purpose | |
|---|---|---|---|
| 65535 | $FFFF | monitor & APPLESOFT Interpretor | 16K Bytes ROM |
| 53248 | $D000 | | |
| 53247 | $CFFF | I/O, Speaker, Paddles | |
| 49152 | $C000 | | |
| 49151 | $BFFF | Disk Operating System | 48K Bytes RAM |
| 38400 | $9600 | | |
| 38399 | $95FF | Free Memory | |
| 24576 | $6000 | | |
| 24575 | $5FFF | High Res Page 2 | |
| 16384 | $4000 | | |
| 16383 | $3FFF | High Res Page 1 | |
| 8192 | $2000 | | |
| 8191 | $1FFF | BASIC begins here | |
| 3072 | $C00 | | |
| 3071 | $BFF | Text/Low Res Page 2 | |
| 2048 | $800 | | |
| 2047 | $7FF | Text/Low Res Page 1 | |
| 1024 | $400 | | |
| 1023 | $3FF | Special Monitor Addresses | |
| 1008 | $3F0 | | |
| 1007 | $3EF | Shape Tables & Machine Language Programs | |
| 768 | $300 | | |
| 767 | $2FF | Keyboard Buffer | |
| 0 | $0 | | |

Table 3.3.1

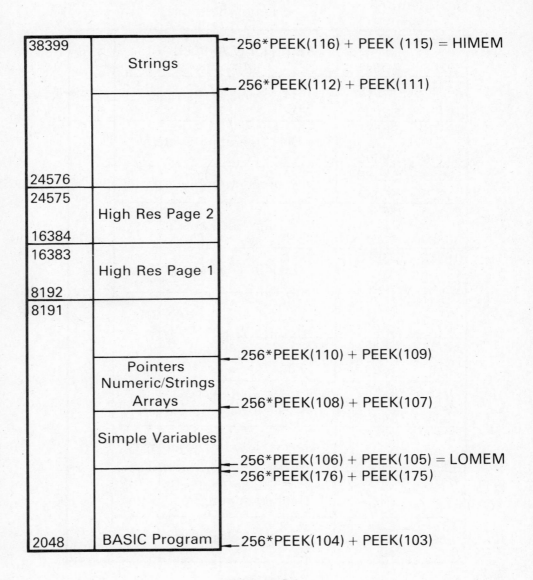

Table 3.3.2

# MODULE 3B   Shapes

## ACTIVITY 3.4   Defining Shapes

**LEARNING BY DISCOVERY**   This activity introduces how to design and create two-dimensional shapes in high resolution graphics mode.

1. Enter the following commands.

```
NEW
100   GOTO 500
200   HIMEM : 37888 : REM ENTER THE SHAPE
205   POKE 233, 148 : POKE 232,0
210   FOR I = 37888 TO 37904
215   READ J
220   POKE I, J
225   NEXT I
230   RETURN
300   DATA 1, 0, 4, 0
310   DATA 63, 36, 63, 36, 45, 36, 45, 54, 45, 54, 63, 54, 0
500   GOSUB 200
510   HGR : HCOLOR = 3
520   X = 140 : Y = 90
530   SCALE = 1 : ROT = 0
540   DRAW 1 AT X, Y
RUN
```

Describe the diagram which appears on the screen. _____

2. Retype lines 210 and 310 as follows:

```
TEXT : HOME
210   FOR I = 37888 TO 37905
310   DATA 73, 60, 39, 60, 55, 62, 55, 46, 53, 46, 37, 44, 37,
      0
RUN
```

Describe the diagram which appears on the screen. _____

3. Retype lines 210 and 310 as follows:

```
TEXT : HOME
210   FOR I = 37888 TO 37902
310   DATA 231, 100, 45, 21, 246, 14, 246, 63, 28, 36, 0
RUN
```

Describe the diagram which appears on the screen. _____

4. Retype lines 210 and 310 as follows:

```
TEXT : HOME
210   FOR I = 37888 TO 37900
310   DATA 12, 12, 12, 12, 12, 12, 12, 4, 0
RUN
```

Describe the diagram which appears on the screen. _____

5. Retype line 310 as follows:

```
TEXT : HOME
310   DATA 5, 5, 5, 5, 5, 5, 5, 5, 0
RUN
```

Describe the diagram which appears on the screen. _____

**DISCUSSION**   The use of shapes provides another alternative for drawing diagrams on the high resolution screen other than using HPLOT commands. Future activities will demonstrate there is a more versatile screen display when drawing shapes; however, the design and creating of shapes is a most tedious process.

A high resolution shape is created by executing a sequence of instruction codes known as "plotting vectors." Each vector indicates movement either up, down, right, or left. Vectors can either be "plotted" or "not plotted," which gives a combination of eight vector outcomes or actions.

Each vector action is represented symbolically in binary code as a 3-bit entity. The left most bit is used to define whether the vector is to be plotted (coded 1) or not plotted (coded 0). The remaining two bits are used to indicate direction: Up is coded 00, right is coded 01, down is coded 10, and left is coded 11. Table 3.4.1 summarizes these vectors by indicating the vector symbol, its resulting action and its corresponding binary code. Notice the heavily shaded dot at the tail of the arrow to indicate a plotting vector and the absence of the dot to indicate a non-plotting vector.

These vectors are assembled into a sequence of bytes (eight bits), converted to equivalent decimal numbers, and finally POKEd into designated memory locations as DATA in coordination with a READ statement. Table 3.4.2 illustrates the byte configuration, where at most three vectors can define a byte. Section A is used to represent the first vector, Section B the second, and Section C the third (if possible).

Notice that Section C has only two bits while Sections A and B have three each. Section C is missing the bit which determines whether the vector is to be plotted ($P = 1$) or not plotted ($P = 0$). By default, only non-plotting ($P = 0$) vectors can be placed in Section C since the third bit is not available. Thus, it is possible that Section C may remain empty in some bytes when the sequence of bytes is being assembled. APPLE-SOFT executes each byte by moving in the order from Section A to B to C.

The first step in creating a shape is to draw the shape on graph paper as illustrated in Exhibit 3.4.1. This drawing then is translated into a series of plotting vectors (A through X) as illustrated in Exhibit 3.4.2. Although the starting point is arbitrary, later activities will demonstrate that position becomes important when manipulating the shape.

Table 3.4.3 shows the sequence of vectors, their corresponding actions, and their symbolic binary codes which correspond to the shape. Table 3.4.4 depicts the assembling of these bits into the sequence of bytes, which finally defines the shape.

The corresponding binary, hexadecimal, and decimal representations of these bytes are also given. Notice Section C of each byte is empty, since the shape contains no non-plotting vectors. The last column of decimal numbers represents the sequence of bytes which are the data in line 310 of the program.

The program entered in Section 1 draws the defined shape in the center of the screen. There are 17 pieces of data to be entered from lines 300 and 310 by POKing memory locations 37888 to 37904. The number 37904 is derived by 37888 + 17 − 1. The data in line 310 are the decimal numbers from Table 3.4.4. Line 300 contains data to set initial conditions for the shape. This and other remaining details of the program will be presented in the next several activities. It is the purpose of this activity to learn only how to design and create shapes.

Section 2 demonstrates that the same shape can be drawn but with a different sequence of vectors and with a different starting point. Exhibits 3.4.3 and 3.4.4 and Tables 3.4.5 and 3.4.6 present the necessary details for redefining the shape, in a fashion similar to that in Section 1.

Note that inclusion of three successive non-plotting vectors provides an example in byte 1 of how Section C is used in the assembling of vectors into bytes. The reader is encouraged to study both of the presented examples with thorough understanding before proceeding any further with the discussion.

The drawing of the numeral 8 in Section 3 represents an example where vector patterns include diagonally oriented drawings. Notice that in order to move from Point A to Point B in Exhibit 3.4.6, an upward plot vector is followed by a left non-plot vector. Also, movement from Point C to Point D occurs by an upward plot vector followed by a right non-plot vector.

Other similar situations occur in the diagram where the rounding or smoothing of corners is desired. The reader should again study every detail in coordinating the steps illustrated in Exhibits 3.4.5 and 3.4.6 and Table 3.4.7.

An attempt is made to draw the shape illustrated in Exhibit 3.4.7 in Sections 4 and 5. Section 4 is successful; Section 5 is not. Section 4 uses the vector sequence illustrated in Table 3.4.8, while Section 5 uses the sequence shown in Table 3.4.9. Section 5 results in a horizontal line, as only Section A (101) of each byte is drawn. Sections B and C are essentially ignored. In general, APPLESOFT ignores all leading zero vectors: 00 (Section C) and 000 (Section B). Section 4 avoids the leading zero problem by moving diagonally with a plot up vector followed by a non-plot right vector (001100).

The zero byte (00000000) is used to end the definition of a shape. Thus, no shape can have three consecutive non-plot up vectors, since this would result in the zero vector, and end the shape.

**COMPREHENSIVE EXAMPLE**  The following program draws the rocket shape illustrated in Exhibit 3.4.8. Study these vector plots with the sequence of bytes in Table 3.4.10 to verify the data in lines 310 and 320. Enter the program to observe the shape.

```
TEXT : HOME : NEW
100  REM ******************************************
```

```
101   REM *                CE3.4                      *
102   REM ******************************************
105   HOME : GOTO 500
200   HIMEM : 37888
205   POKE 233, 148 : POKE 232, 0
210   FOR I = 37888 TO 37937
215   READ J
220   POKE I, J
225   NEXT
230   RETURN
300   DATA 1, 0, 4, 0
310   DATA 63, 63, 71, 192, 36, 36, 140, 14, 14, 14, 62, 63, 63,
      63, 54, 54, 54, 45, 53, 9, 9
320   DATA 30, 30, 30, 30, 36, 36, 44, 45, 45, 45, 45, 45, 45,
      37, 33, 33, 33, 227, 28, 63, 63, 63, 63, 63, 0
500   GOSUB 200
510   HGR : HCOLOR = 3
520   X = 140 : Y = 90
530   SCALE = 1 : ROT = 0
540   DRAW 1 AT X, Y
550   GET Q$ : TEXT : HOME
```

## Check Your Comprehension

How is the number 37937 selected in line 210? _____

What is the purpose of the data in line 300? _____

Explain the significance of POKE I, J in line 220? _____

**EXERCISE**   Using vectors, determine the DATA for lines 310 and 320 to obtain the shape of the "3" illustrated in Exhibit 3.4.9. Don't forget to establish the proper length of the loop in line 210.

**CHALLENGE**   The numerals 8 and 3 illustrated in Exhibits 3.4.5 and 3.4.9 are 5 pixels wide by 7 pixels long. Using vectors, determine the data for lines 310 and 320 to obtain the shapes of the remaining digits: 0, 1, 2, 4, 5, 6, 7, and 9. Then modify the program given in the COMPREHENSIVE EXAMPLE so it executes once to display the eight new digits. The starting and ending numbers in line 210 should be entered as data.

| Symbol | Action | Binary Code |
|--------|--------|-------------|
| ↑ | Move up without plotting | 000 |
| → | Move right without plotting | 001 |
| ↓ | Move down without plotting | 010 |
| ← | Move left without plotting | 011 |
| ↑ | Move up with plotting | 100 |
| → | Move right with plotting | 101 |
| ↓ | Move down with plotting | 110 |
| ← | Move left with plotting | 111 |

Table 3.4.1

Shape Table Byte

| Bit | Section C | | Section B | | | Section A | | |
|-----|-----------|---|-----------|---|---|-----------|---|---|
| | 7 | 6 | 5 | 4 | 3 | 2 | 1 | 0 |
| D = Direction bit<br>P = Plot/No plot bit | D | D | P | D | D | P | D | D |

DD = 00   move up          P = 0   do not plot
DD = 01   move right       P = 1   do plot
DD = 10   move down
DD = 11   move left

Table 3.4.2

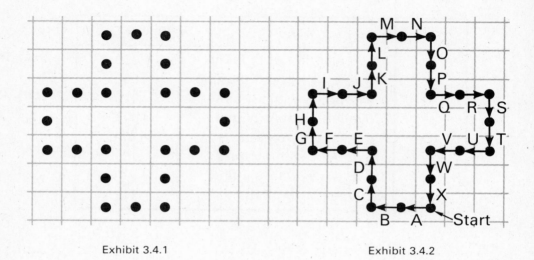

Exhibit 3.4.1                                    Exhibit 3.4.2

| Vector | Action | Binary Rep. | Vector | Action | Binary Rep. |
|--------|--------|-------------|--------|--------|-------------|
| A | ← | 111 | M | → | 101 |
| B | ← | 111 | N | → | 101 |
| C | ↑ | 100 | O | ↕ | 110 |
| D | ↕ | 100 | P | ↕ | 110 |
| E | ← | 111 | Q | → | 101 |
| F | ← | 111 | R | → | 101 |
| G | ↑ | 100 | S | ↓ | 110 |
| H | ↕ | 100 | T | ↕ | 110 |
| I | → | 101 | U | ← | 111 |
| J | → | 101 | V | ← | 111 |
| K | ↑ | 100 | W | ↓ | 110 |
| L | ↕ | 100 | X | ↓ | 110 |

Table 3.4.3

## Byte Configuration of the Shape

| Byte # | Section C | Section B | Section A | Bin. Rep. | Hex. Rep. | Dec. Rep. |
|--------|-----------|-----------|-----------|-----------|-----------|-----------|
| 1 | — | B | A | 00111111 | 3F | 63 |
| 2 | — | D | C | 00100100 | 24 | 36 |
| 3 | — | F | E | 00111111 | 3F | 63 |
| 4 | — | H | G | 00100100 | 24 | 36 |
| 5 | — | J | I | 00101101 | 2D | 45 |
| 6 | — | L | K | 00100100 | 24 | 36 |
| 7 | — | N | M | 00101101 | 2D | 45 |
| 8 | — | P | O | 00110110 | 36 | 54 |
| 9 | — | R | Q | 00101101 | 2D | 45 |
| 10 | — | T | S | 00110110 | 36 | 54 |
| 11 | — | V | U | 00111111 | 3F | 63 |
| 12 | — | X | W | 00110110 | 36 | 54 |

Table 3.4.4

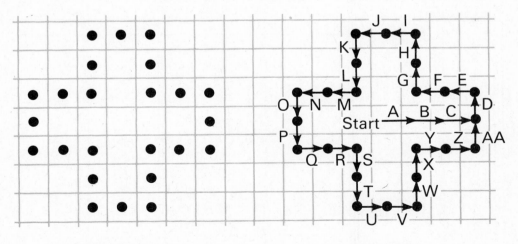

Exhibit 3.4.3                              Exhibit 3.4.4

| Vector | Action | Binary Rep. | Vector | Action | Binary Rep. |
|--------|--------|-------------|--------|--------|-------------|
| A | → | 001 | N | ↔ | 111 |
| B | → | 001 | O | ↕ | 110 |
| C | → | 001 | P | ↕ | 110 |
| D | ↕ | 100 | Q | ↔ | 101 |
| E | ↔ | 111 | R | ↔ | 101 |
| F | ↔ | 111 | S | ↕ | 110 |
| G | ↕ | 100 | T | ↕ | 110 |
| H | ↕ | 100 | U | ↔ | 101 |
| I | ↔ | 111 | V | ↔ | 101 |
| J | ↔ | 111 | W | ↕ | 100 |
| K | ↕ | 110 | X | ↕ | 100 |
| L | ↕ | 110 | Y | ↔ | 101 |
| M | ↔ | 111 | Z | ↔ | 101 |
|   |   |   | AA | ↕ | 100 |

Table 3.4.5


Byte Configuration of the Shape

| Byte # | Section C | Section B | Section A | Bin. Rep. | Hex. Rep. | Dec. Rep. |
|--------|-----------|-----------|-----------|-----------|-----------|-----------|
| 1 | C | B | A | 01001001 | 49 | 73 |
| 2 | — | E | D | 00111100 | 3C | 60 |
| 3 | — | G | F | 00100111 | 2F | 39 |
| 4 | — | I | H | 00111100 | 3C | 60 |
| 5 | — | K | J | 00110111 | 37 | 55 |
| 6 | — | M | L | 00111110 | 3E | 62 |
| 7 | — | O | N | 00110111 | 37 | 55 |
| 8 | — | Q | P | 00101110 | 2E | 46 |
| 9 | — | S | R | 00110101 | 35 | 53 |
| 10 | — | U | T | 00101110 | 2E | 46 |
| 11 | — | W | V | 00100101 | 25 | 37 |
| 12 | — | Y | X | 00101100 | 2C | 44 |
| 13 | — | AA | Z | 00100101 | 25 | 37 |

Table 3.4.6

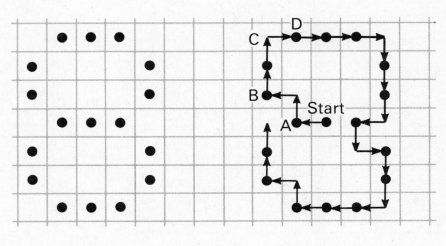

Exhibit 3.4.5                                    Exhibit 3.4.6

## Byte Configuration of the Shape

| Byte # | Section C | Section B | Section A | Bin. Rep. | Hex. Rep. | Dec. Rep. |
|--------|-----------|-----------|-----------|-----------|-----------|-----------|
| 1 | ← | ↕ | ↔ | 11100111 | E7 | 231 |
| 2 | → | ↕ | ↕ | 01100100 | 64 | 100 |
| 3 | ↔ | ↔ | ↔ | 00101101 | 2D | 45 |
| 4 | ↕ | ↕ | ↔ | 00010101 | 15 | 21 |
| 5 | ← | ↕ | ↕ | 11110110 | F6 | 246 |
| 6 | → | → | ↕ | 00001110 | 0E | 14 |
| 7 | ← | ↕ | ↕ | 11110110 | F6 | 246 |
| 8 | ↔ | ↔ | ↔ | 00111111 | 3F | 63 |
| 9 | ← | ← | ↕ | 00011100 | 1C | 28 |
| 10 | | ↕ | ↕ | 00100100 | 24 | 36 |

Table 3.4.7

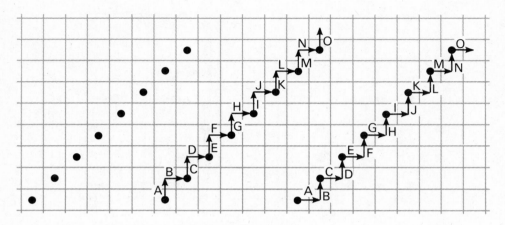

Exhibit 3.4.7

| Vectors | | Bin. Rep. | Dec. Rep. |
|:---:|:---:|:---:|:---:|
| B | A | 00001100 | 12 |
| D | C | 00001100 | 12 |
| F | E | 00001100 | 12 |
| H | G | 00001100 | 12 |
| J | I | 00001100 | 12 |
| L | K | 00001100 | 12 |
| N | M | 00001100 | 12 |
| | O | 00000100 | 4 |

Table 3.4.8

| Vectors | | Bin. Rep. | Dec. Rep. |
|:---:|:---:|:---:|:---:|
| B | A | 00000101 | 5 |
| D | C | 00000101 | 5 |
| F | E | 00000101 | 5 |
| H | G | 00000101 | 5 |
| J | I | 00000101 | 5 |
| L | K | 00000101 | 5 |
| N | M | 00000101 | 5 |
| | O | 00000101 | 5 |

Table 3.4.9

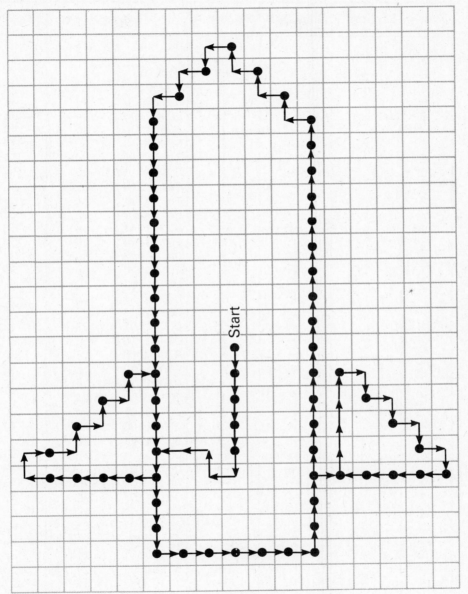

Start

Exhibit 3.4.8

## Byte Configuration of the Shape

| Byte # | Section C | Section B | Section A | Bin. Rep. | Hex. Rep. | Dec. Rep. |
|---|---|---|---|---|---|---|
| 1 |  | ← | ← | 00111111 | 3F | 63 |
| 2 |  | ← | ← | 00111111 | 3F | 63 |
| 3 | → | ↑ | ← | 01000111 | 4F | 71 |
| 4 | ← | ↑ | ↑ | 11000000 | C0 | 192 |
| 5 |  | ↕ | ↕ | 00100100 | 24 | 36 |
| 6 |  | ↕ | ↕ | 00100100 | 24 | 36 |
| 7 | ↓ | → | ↕ | 10001100 | 8C | 140 |
| 8 |  | → | ↓ | 00001110 | 0E | 14 |
| 9 |  | → | ↓ | 00001110 | 0E | 14 |
| 10 |  | → | ↓ | 00001110 | 0E | 14 |
| 11 |  | ← | ↓ | 00111110 | 3E | 62 |
| 12 |  | ← | ← | 00111111 | 3F | 63 |
| 13 |  | ← | ← | 00111111 | 3F | 63 |
| 14 |  | ← | ← | 00111111 | 3F | 63 |
| 15 |  | ↕ | ↕ | 00110110 | 36 | 54 |
| 16 |  | ↕ | ↕ | 00110110 | 36 | 54 |
| 17 |  | ↕ | ↕ | 00110110 | 36 | 54 |
| 18 |  | ↔ | ↔ | 00101101 | 2D | 45 |
| 19 |  | ↕ | ↔ | 00110101 | 35 | 53 |
| 20 |  | → | → | 00001001 | 09 | 9 |
| 21 |  | → | → | 00001001 | 09 | 9 |
| 22 |  | ← | ↓ | 01001110 | 1E | 30 |
| 23 |  | ← | ↓ | 01001110 | 1E | 30 |
| 24 |  | ← | ↓ | 01001110 | 1E | 30 |
| 25 |  | ← | ↓ | 01001110 | 1E | 30 |
| 26 |  | ↕ | ↕ | 00100100 | 24 | 36 |
| 27 |  | ↕ | ↕ | 00100100 | 24 | 36 |
| 28 |  | ↔ | ↕ | 00101100 | 2C | 44 |
| 29 |  | ↔ | ↔ | 00101101 | 2D | 45 |
| 30 |  | ↔ | ↔ | 00101101 | 2D | 45 |
| 31 |  | ↔ | ↔ | 00101101 | 2D | 45 |
| 32 |  | ↔ | ↔ | 00101101 | 2D | 45 |
| 33 |  | ↔ | ↔ | 00101101 | 2D | 45 |
| 34 |  | ↔ | ↔ | 00101101 | 2D | 45 |
| 35 |  | ↕ | ↔ | 00100101 | 25 | 37 |
| 36 |  | ↕ | → | 00100001 | 21 | 33 |
| 37 |  | ↕ | → | 00100001 | 21 | 33 |
| 38 |  | ↕ | → | 00100001 | 21 | 33 |
| 39 | ← | ↕ | ← | 11100011 | E3 | 227 |
| 40 |  | ← | ↕ | 00011100 | 1C | 28 |
| 41 |  | ← | ← | 00111111 | 3F | 63 |
| 42 |  | ← | ← | 00111111 | 3F | 63 |
| 43 |  | ← | ← | 00111111 | 3F | 63 |
| 44 |  | ← | ← | 00111111 | 3F | 63 |
| 45 |  | ← | ← | 00111111 | 3F | 63 |

Table 3.4.10

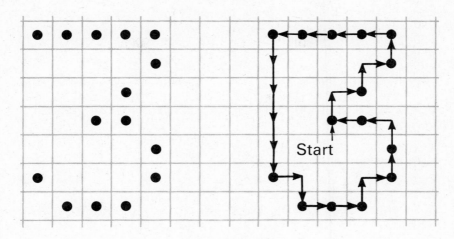

Exhibit 3.4.9

# ACTIVITY 3.5   Creating and Entering a Shape Table

**LEARNING BY DISCOVERY**   This activity introduces the design of a shape table directory and suggests possible memory areas for the entering of the shapes.

1.  Enter the following commands.

```
NEW
100    TEXT : HOME : GOTO 500
200    HIMEM : 37888 : REM ENTER TWO SHAPES
205    POKE 233, 148 : POKE 232, 0
210    FOR I = 37888 TO 37915
215    READ J : POKE I, J
220    NEXT : RETURN
300    DATA 2, 0, 6, 0, 20, 0
310    DATA 12, 37, 28, 63, 23, 54, 46, 30, 14, 45, 12, 36, 4,
       0 : REM 0
315    DATA 36, 188, 150, 18, 45, 28, 36, 0 : REM 1
500    GOSUB 200
510    HGR : HCOLOR = 3 : X = 140 : Y = 90
520    SCALE = 1 : ROT = 0
525    M = 2
530    FOR I = 1 TO M
535    DRAW I AT X, Y
```

```
540  FOR J = 1 TO 1000 : NEXT
545  HGR
550  NEXT
560  TEXT : HOME
RUN
```

Describe the screen display. _____

2. Retype lines 200, 205, 210, 300, and 525 and add lines 320, 325, and 330 as
   follows:

```
TEXT : HOME
200  REM ENTER FIVE SHAPES
205  POKE 233, 3 : POKE 232, 0
210  FOR I = 768 TO 833
300  DATA 5, 0, 12, 0, 26, 0, 34, 0, 44, 0, 56, 0
320  DATA 101, 228, 63, 23, 150, 241, 46, 45, 37, 0 : REM 2
325  DATA 12, 12, 60, 63, 183, 146, 21, 45, 12, 228, 7, 0 :
     REM 3
330  DATA 58, 39, 12, 12, 12, 54, 174, 55, 62, 0 : REM 4
525  M = 5
RUN
```

Describe the screen display. _____

3. Enter the following commands. Note: If you have the accompanying diskette, you
   can enter the program with the command, LOAD SEC3.5.3 and then LIST the
   program.

```
TEXT : HOME : NEW
100  REM *****************************************
101  REM *            SEC3.5.3                   *
102  REM *****************************************
105  TEXT : HOME : GOTO 505
197  REM ENTER SHAPE TABLE
198  REM N = NUMBER OF SHAPES IN TABLE
199  REM S = STARTING ADDRESS FOR STORING TABLE; BOTH N AND
     S ARE DEFINED IN MAIN PROGRAM
200  SH = INT (S / 256) : REM DETERMINE HIGH ORDER BYTE
220  SL = S - 256 * SH : REM DETERMINE LOW ORDER BYTE
225  POKE 232, SL : POKE 233, SH : REM ENTRY POINT FOR SHAPES
230  POKE S, N : POKE S + 1, 0 : REM ENTER NUMBER OF SHAPES
235  SL = S + 2 : REM INCREMENT LOW ORDER BYTE
240  FS = S + 2 * (N + 1) : REM DETERMINE LOCATION OF
     FIRST SHAPE
245  L = FS - S : REM DETERMINE LENGTH FROM STARTING
     ADDRESS TO NEXT SHAPE
250  IF L > 255 THEN 275 : REM TWO BYTES NEEDED FOR
     LENGTH OF SHAPE TABLE?
```

```
255  POKE SL, L : POKE SL + 1, 0 : REM ENTER LOCATION OF
     NEXT SHAPE
260  GOTO 275
265  LH = INT (L / 256) : LL = L - 256 * LH : REM
     DETERMINE HIGH/LOW ORDER BYTES
270  POKE SL, LL : POKE SL + 1, LH : REM ENTER LOCATION OF
     NEXT SHAPE
275  SL = SL + 2 : REM INCREMENT LOW ORDER BYTE
280  READ B : REM ENTER BYTE AS DECIMAL NUMBER
285  IF B = 0 THEN 305 : REM END OF SHAPE?
290  POKE FS, B : REM ENTER VALUE IN MEMORY
295  FS = FS + 1 : REM DETERMINE NEXT MEMORY ADDRESS
300  GOTO 280 : REM ENTER NEXT BYTE
305  POKE FS, 0 : REM END A SHAPE
310  FS = FS + 1 : REM DETERMINE NEXT MEMORY ADDRESS
315  N = N - 1 : REM REDUCE NUMBER OF SHAPES TO BE ENTERED
320  IF N = 0 THEN RETURN : REM ALL SHAPES ENTERED
325  GOTO 245
350  DATA 12, 37, 28, 63, 23, 54, 46, 30, 14, 45, 12, 36, 4,
     0 : REM 0
355  DATA 36, 188, 150, 18, 45, 28, 36, 0 : REM 1
360  DATA 101, 228, 63, 23, 150, 241, 46, 45, 37, 0 : REM 2
365  DATA 12, 12, 60, 63, 183, 146, 21, 45, 12, 228, 7, 0 :
     REM 3
370  DATA 58, 39, 12, 12, 12, 54, 174, 55, 62, 0 : REM 4
375  DATA 56, 39, 44, 45, 245, 170, 54, 23, 63, 28, 4, 0 :
     REM 5
380  DATA 117, 246, 63, 28, 36, 229, 12, 12, 45, 6, 0 : REM 6
385  DATA 12, 12, 60, 63, 183, 82, 30, 46, 0 : REM 7
390  DATA 231, 100, 45, 21, 246, 14, 246, 63, 28, 36, 0 : REM
     8
395  DATA 231, 100, 45, 21, 54, 119, 30, 30, 63, 4, 0 : REM 9
499  REM ESTABLISH CONDITIONS FOR LOADING SHAPE TABLE
505  N = 10 : K = N : S = 768 : GOSUB 200
510  HGR : HCOLOR = 3 : X = 140 : Y = 90
515  SCALE = 1 : ROT = 0
525  FOR I = 1 TO K
530  DRAW I AT X, Y
540  FOR Z = 1 TO 1000 : NEXT Z
542  HGR
545  NEXT
550  TEXT : HOME
RUN
```

Describe the screen display. _____

4. Save this program on your diskette (which is not write protected) by the name
   SHAPELOAD. Then reenter line 505 as follows:

```
TEXT : HOME
505  N = 10 : K = N : S = 2000 : GOSUB 200
RUN
```

Describe the screen display. _____

**DISCUSSION**   Several shapes can be collectively combined into a shape table by establishing a directory. The data in line 300 in Sections 1 and 2 is used to define the directory. The first number (byte 0) defines the number of shapes in the table. The second number (byte 1) is unused and is assigned the value zero (0).

In Section 1, two shapes are entered; in Section 2, five shapes are entered. The remaining numbers (bytes 2 through 2K + 1) are grouped in pairs and are pointers which define the relative position of each successive shape in relation to the beginning of the shape table.

The first number in the pair is the low order byte and the second is the high order byte. The high order byte will always be zero (0) unless the relative position exceeds 255, as with longer shape tables.

In Section 1, the 6 in line 300 indicates the first shape starts at the sixth byte. The first 12 in line 310 is the sixth byte in the data list (remember that the 2 in line 300 is defined to be byte 0, not byte 1). The 20 in line 300 of Section 1 indicates the second shape begins at the twentieth byte in the table.

Careful counting will reveal the first 36 in line 315 is located in byte 20 in relation to the beginning of the shape table. The trailing zeroes (0) at the end of lines 310 and 315 are used to end the definition of each shape.

In Section 2, the directory defined in line 300 becomes lengthier than in Section 1, since there are now five shapes rather than two. The numbers 12, 26, 34, 44, and 56 define the position (byte) where the first, second, third, fourth, and fifth shapes begin, respectively. Obviously, the directory becomes more difficult to define as more shapes are added to the table.

Section 3 introduces a routine (lines 100 through 325) which automatically defines the shape directory and enters the data for the shape. The interested reader may want to understand the well-documented code. To execute the subroutine, define N (the number of shapes) and S (the starting address) as in line 505. Here, N = 10 and S = 768. Table 3.5.1 summarizes the organization of a shape table.

The starting address can begin in any memory area which does not interfere with the APPLESOFT program. In Section 1, the shape is entered above HIMEM at location 37888 by executing line 200. Recall that after booting with DOS 3.3, HIMEM is set to 38400. By setting HIMEM to 37888, there is ample room for our shape table in Section 1 to be entered between 37888 and 38400, where DOS begins. The trailing number, 37915, in line 210 controls the length of the loop and is determined by the number of data items. This example has 28 pieces of data, giving 37915 = 37888 + 28 − 1.

Memory locations 232 and 233 coordinate as low order and high order bytes, respectively, to indicate where a shape table is to begin in memory. The strange numbers, 148 and 0, are determined by the formulas:

HB = High order byte (233) = INT (memory location/256) = 37888/256 = 148

LB = Low order byte (232) = memory location − 256 * HB = 37888 − 256 * 148 = 0

In Section 2, the shape table is entered at memory position 768, space specifically reserved for short shape tables (refer to Table 3.3.1). Notice the 3 in POKE 233, 3 is the result of INT (768/256) and the 0 in POKE 232, 0 is 768 − 256 * INT (768/256).

Section 4 results in an error message. Line 505 defines S to be 2000, which does not leave sufficient space for the loading of the shape table. The APPLESOFT program, which starts at location 2048, gets clobbered.

**COMPREHENSIVE EXAMPLE**   First LOAD SHAPELOAD. Next delete lines 350 through 395 (DEL 350, 395). Then add lines 350, 355, 360, and 365 and retype line 505 as follows. Finally, execute the program to observe the screen display. The example demonstrates how to use this subroutine when creating your shapes.

```
100   REM ****************************************
101   REM *            CE3.5                    *
102   REM ****************************************
350   DATA 12, 12, 12, 12, 12, 36, 35, 59, 23, 23, 28, 28, 63,
      58, 50, 14, 14, 14, 14, 6, 0 : REM HEART
355   DATA 12, 12, 12, 12, 12, 28, 28, 28, 28, 28, 23, 23, 23,
      23, 23, 14, 14, 14, 14, 6, 0 : REM DIAMOND
360   DATA 21, 21, 12, 12, 36, 28, 28, 28, 28, 23, 23, 23, 23,
      54, 14, 14, 12, 53, 54, 61, 63, 0 : REM SPADE
365   DATA 21, 21, 12, 12, 28, 28, 23, 39, 12, 12, 28, 28, 23,
      23, 14, 14, 62, 28, 23, 23, 14, 14, 12, 53, 54, 61, 63,
      0 : REM CLUB
505   N = 4 : K = N : S = 16384 : GOSUB 200
```

**Check Your Comprehension**

Why is a value of 4 assigned to N? _____

Why is a value of 16384 assigned to S? _____

**EXERCISE**   Write a program which uses SHAPELOAD to enter the 0, 4, 6, 8, 9, and spade shapes beginning at the top of high resolution Page 2.

**CHALLENGE**   Write a program which uses SHAPELOAD to enter the shapes of all ten digits, followed by the four shapes associated with a deck of cards, immediately below where DOS 3.3 resides.

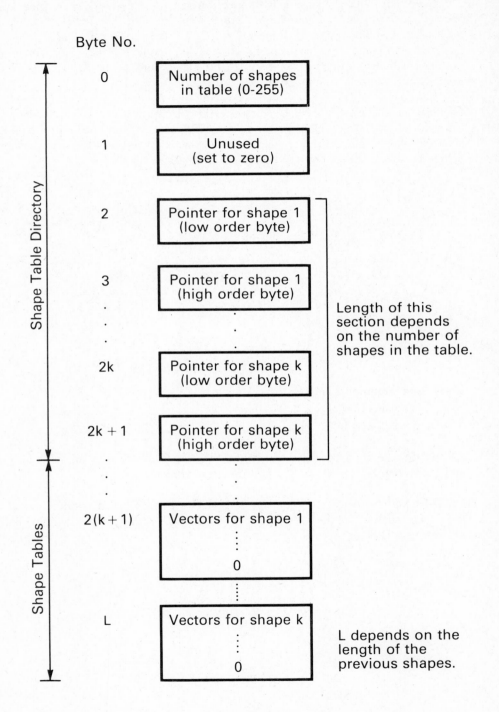

Table 3.5.1

# ACTIVITY 3.6  Displaying Shapes

**LEARNING BY DISCOVERY**   This activity examines the possibilities for drawing shapes on the display screen.

1. Load SHAPELOAD from your diskette. Modify this program by making deletions and additions as given below.

```
DEL 350, 395
DEL 505, 550
350   DATA 63, 63, 71, 192, 36, 36, 140, 14, 14, 14, 62, 63,
      63, 63, 54, 54, 54, 45, 53, 9, 9, 30, 30, 30, 30, 36,
      36, 44, 45, 45, 45, 45, 45, 45, 45, 40, 40, 36, 227,
      28, 63, 63, 63, 63, 63, 0
360   DATA 12, 12, 12, 12, 12, 36, 35, 59, 23, 23, 28, 28, 63,
      58, 50, 14, 14, 14, 14, 6, 0
505   N = 2 : S = 768 : GOSUB 200
510   HGR : HCOLOR = 3
520   SCALE = 1 : ROT = 0
530   DRAW 1 AT 230, 140
RUN
```

Observe the screen display.

What diagram appears on the screen? _____

Where is the diagram positioned? _____

2. Add line 540 and 550 as follows:

```
TEXT : HOME
540   DRAW 1 AT 41, 30
550   DRAW 2 AT 140, 90
RUN
```

Observe the screen display.

What new diagrams appear on the screen? _____

Where are the diagrams positioned? _____

3. Retype line 510 as follows:

```
TEXT : HOME
510   HGR : HCOLOR = 2
RUN
```

Observe the screen display.

Are the diagrams complete drawings? _____

Compare the completeness of the diagram in the upper left corner with the diagram in the lower right corner. _____

4. Delete lines 530 and 540 and retype lines 510 and 550 as follows:

```
TEXT : HOME
530
540
510  HGR : HCOLOR = 3
550  XDRAW 2 AT 140, 90
RUN
```

Observe the screen display.

Compare the diagram in the center of the screen with the diagram obtained in Section 2. _____

5. Retype line 550 and add lines 525 through 560 as follows:

```
TEXT : HOME
DEL  530, 550
525  FOR I = 1 TO 10
530  HCOLOR = 3
535  DRAW 1 AT 140, 90
540  FOR J = 1 TO 1000 : NEXT
545  HCOLOR = 0
550  DRAW 1 AT 140, 90
555  FOR J = 1 TO 1000 : NEXT
560  NEXT I
RUN
```

Describe the screen display. _____

6. Delete lines 530 and 545 and retype lines 535 and 550 as follows:

```
TEXT : HOME
530
545
535  XDRAW 1 AT 140, 90
550  XDRAW 1 AT 140, 90
RUN
```

Describe the screen display. _____

**DISCUSSION**   Shapes are drawn on the display screen by using either the DRAW or XDRAW command. Both commands require a high resolution page and color be established first, as well as values for a SCALE and ROT command. An examination of these latter two commands will occur in ACTIVITY 3.7. The parameters for DRAW and XDRAW include a number for the shape to be displayed and an (X, Y) coordinate for its location on the screen.

Shapes can be displayed in colors other than white, but two difficulties arise. First, as was the case when displaying images with HPLOT commands, coordination between the column coordinate and the color code numeral is essential. In Section 3, the rocket displayed in the upper left corner of the screen (drawn at 41, 30) is missing the vertical section of its tail but has wings. In contrast, the rocket displayed in the center of the screen (drawn at 140,90) includes the entire tail but the wings are not complete. The vertical part of the tail and wing are not an odd number of pixels apart, so they do not appear simultaneously at either an odd or even column coordinate. A second difficulty with coloring shapes is that oblique lines are unavoidably distorted because of the absence of some plotting vectors (or pixels).

The primary distinction between the DRAW and XDRAW commands is that DRAW plots the shape in the last defined color, while XDRAW plots the shape in the complement of the color found. Since white (3) and black (0) are complementary colors, the blinking of a white shape on a black background is most easily obtained by using successive XDRAW commands, as demonstrated in Section 6. The first XDRAW command plots the rocket in white, while the second XDRAW command has the effect of erasing the shape. ACTIVITY 3.8 will demonstrate the use of the XDRAW command to animate shapes.

**COMPREHENSIVE EXAMPLE**   Load SHAPELOAD, then delete lines 350 through 395 and lines 505 through 550. Study the following commands to determine the screen display. Check your answer by entering the program in the computer.

```
100   REM  ******************************************
101   REM  *              CE3.6                     *
102   REM  ******************************************
350   DATA 12, 12, 12, 12, 12, 36, 35, 59, 23, 23, 28, 28, 63,
      58, 50, 14, 14, 14, 14, 6, 0 : REM HEART
355   DATA 12, 12, 12, 12, 12, 28, 28, 28, 28, 28, 23, 23, 23,
      23, 23, 14, 14, 14, 14, 6, 0 : REM DIAMOND
360   DATA 21, 21, 12, 12, 36, 28, 28, 28, 28, 23, 23, 23, 23,
      54, 14, 14, 12, 53, 54, 61, 63, 0 : REM SPADE
365   DATA 21, 21, 12, 12, 28, 28, 23, 39, 12, 12, 28, 28, 23,
      23, 14, 14, 62, 28, 23, 23, 14, 14, 12, 53, 54, 61, 63,
      0 : REM CLUB
370   DATA 101, 228, 63, 23, 150, 241, 46, 45, 37, 0 : REM TWO
375   DATA 12, 12, 60, 63, 183, 146, 21, 45, 12, 228, 7, 0: REM
      THREE
380   DATA 58, 39, 12, 12, 12, 54, 174, 55, 62, 0 : REM FOUR
385   DATA 56, 39, 44, 45, 245, 170, 54, 23, 63, 28, 4, 0 : REM
      FIVE
505   N = 8 : S = 768 : GOSUB 200
510   HGR : HCOLOR = 1
515   HPLOT 21, 50 TO 81, 50 TO 81, 110 TO 21, 110 TO 21, 50
518   HCOLOR = 2
520   HPLOT 200, 50 TO 260, 50 TO 260, 110 TO 200, 110 TO 200,
      50
525   HCOLOR = 5
530   HPLOT 111, 10 TO 171, 10 TO 171, 70 TO 111, 70 TO 111, 10
532   HCOLOR = 6
535   HPLOT 110, 90 TO 170, 90 TO 170, 150 TO 110, 150 TO 110,
      90
```

```
540   HCOLOR = 3 : SCALE = 1 : ROT = 0
545   DRAW 5 AT 30, 60 : DRAW 5 AT 70, 100
547   DRAW 4 AT 50, 70 : DRAW 4 AT 50, 90
550   DRAW 8 AT 210, 60 : DRAW 8 AT 250, 100
552   DRAW 1 AT 130, 113 : DRAW 1 AT 150, 113 : DRAW 1 AT 130,
      134 : DRAW 1 AT 150, 134
555   DRAW 6 AT 120, 20 : DRAW 6 AT 160, 60
557   DRAW 2 AT 140, 30 : DRAW 2 AT 140, 45 : DRAW 2 AT 140, 60
560   DRAW 7 AT 120, 100 : DRAW 7 AT 160, 140
562   DRAW 3 AT 222, 68 : DRAW 3 AT 240, 68 : DRAW 3 AT 230, 80
      : DRAW 3 AT 222, 92 : DRAW 3 AT 240, 92
570   VTAB 22 : HTAB 12
575   PRINT "ANYONE FOR CARDS?";
580   GET Q$ : TEXT : HOME
```

**Check Your Comprehension**

Describe the screen display. _____

What shape does DRAW 8 display? _____

What effect does line 562 have on the screen display? _____

**EXERCISE**   Write a program that writes the numeral 45920 as a sequence of shapes in the center of the display screen. Load the shape table at the beginning of high resolution Page 2. Hint: load SHAPELOAD and continue from there.

**CHALLENGE**   Write a program that draws a shape of your choice at several different locations on high resolution Page 1. Use SHAPELOAD to enter the shape table beginning at memory location 768.

# ACTIVITY 3.7   Manipulating Shapes

**LEARNING BY DISCOVERY**   This activity demonstrates how shapes can be enlarged and rotated in a variety of positions.

1. Load SHAPELOAD from your diskette. Modify this program by making deletions and additions as given below.

```
DEL   350, 395
DEL   505, 550
350   DATA 63, 36, 63, 36, 45, 36, 45, 54, 45, 54, 63, 54, 0
360   DATA 63, 63, 71, 192, 36, 36, 140, 14, 14, 14, 62, 63, 63,
      63, 54, 54, 54, 45, 53, 9, 9, 30, 30, 30, 30, 36, 36, 44,
      45, 45, 45, 45, 45, 45, 37, 33, 33, 33, 227, 28, 63, 63,
      63, 63, 63, 0
505   N = 2 : S = 768 : GOSUB 200
510   HGR
```

```
520   HCOLOR = 3 : DRAW 1 AT 140, 90
RUN
```

Describe the screen display. _____

2. Retype line 520 and add lines 530 and 540 as follows:

```
TEXT : HOME
520   HCOLOR = 3 : SCALE = 1 : ROT = 0 : DRAW 1 AT 140, 90
530   HCOLOR = 2 : SCALE = 2 : DRAW 1 AT 50, 50
540   HCOLOR = 5 : SCALE = 3 : DRAW 1 AT 221, 120
RUN
```

Observe the screen display.

How does the size of the diagram in the upper left corner compare with the size of the diagram in the center of the screen? _____

What is its color? _____

How does the size of the diagram in the lower right corner compare with the sizes of the other two diagrams? _____

What is its color? _____

3. Retype lines 520, 530, and 540 and add lines 550 and 560 as follows:

```
TEXT : HOME
520   HCOLOR = 3 : SCALE = 1 : ROT = 0 : DRAW 2 AT 70, 70
530   ROT = 16 : DRAW 2 AT 200, 70
540   ROT = 32 : DRAW 2 AT 200, 120
550   ROT = 48 : DRAW 2 AT 70, 120
560   ROT = 8 : DRAW 2 AT 140, 90
RUN
```

Observe the screen display.

Describe the position of the rocket in the upper left corner. _____

Describe the position of the rocket in the upper right corner. _____

Describe the position of the rocket in the lower right corner. _____

Describe the position of the rocket in the lower left corner. _____

Describe the position of the rocket in the center of the screen. _____

4. Retype lines 520 through 560 as follows:

```
TEXT : HOME
520   HCOLOR = 3 : SCALE = 2 : ROT = 0 : XDRAW 2 AT 70, 70
530   ROT = 8 : XDRAW 2 AT 200, 70
540   ROT = 24 : XDRAW 2 AT 200, 120
550   ROT = 60 : XDRAW 2 AT 70, 120
560   ROT = 62 : XDRAW 2 AT 140, 90
RUN
```

Observe the screen display.

What direction is the shape in the upper left corner pointing? _____

What direction is the shape in the upper right corner pointing? _____

What direction is the shape in the lower right corner pointing? _____

What direction is the shape in the lower left corner pointing? _____

What direction is the shape in the center of the screen pointing? _____

5. Retype lines 520 through 560 as follows:

```
TEXT : HOME
520   HCOLOR = 3 : ROT = 0
530   FOR I = 1 TO 6
540   FOR X = 1 TO 8
550   SCALE = X : XDRAW 1 AT 140, 90
560   NEXT X : NEXT I
RUN
```

Describe the screen display. _____

6. Retype line 350 as follows:

```
TEXT : HOME
350   DATA 73, 60, 39, 60, 55, 62, 55, 46, 53, 46, 37, 44, 37,
      0
RUN
```

Describe the screen display. _____

**DISCUSSION**   The SCALE and ROT commands provide versatility in the display of shapes.

SCALE controls the size of the shape. SCALE = 1 draws the shape in the same size in which it was created. If SCALE = 2 is used, the size of the shape is doubled, because each defined vector is executed twice. Possible values for the SCALE command extend to 255. If SCALE = 0 (as occurs in Section 1 where the SCALE command is omitted), the shape is drawn 255 times the original size. This often has the effect of a random display of unexpected nonsense lines.

Section 2 demonstrates the cross-like shape could be drawn in color and in a variety of sizes. Drawing the shape in color is successful because the vertical lines in the cross remain, simultaneously, in odd or even column coordinates.

The ROT command has the effect of rotating the shape in a clockwise direction but usually distorts the shape to some degree. The acceptable values for ROT = depend upon the value used in the SCALE command.

Contrary to the APPLESOFT manual, when SCALE = 1 there are eight possible values for ROT: 0, 8, 16, 24, 32, 40, 48, and 56 (64 is equivalent to 0). ROT = 0 will always display the shape in the position in which it was created. ROT = 16 rotates the shape 90 degrees clockwise from its original position. ROT = 32 and ROT = 48 rotate the shape 180 and 270 degrees, respectively. The values 8, 24, 40 and 56 provide respective rotations of 45, 135, 225, and 315 degrees.

An unrecognizable value for ROT will execute using the next lowest acceptable value. For example, in Section 4, the ROT = 62 behaves as if it were ROT = 60. Also, in Section 4, values divisible by 4 (22 $^1/_2$ degree rotations) become allowable values for the ROT command when SCALE = 2. Smaller values of ROT can be used for larger values of SCALE following the number patterns described above for the SCALE values of 1 and 2. Table 3.7.1 lists the possible ROT values for various SCALE values.

Sections 5 and 6 demonstrate one last important concept for manipulating shapes: Both the SCALE and ROT commands are performed in relation to the starting point of the shape definition.

In Section 5, the data in line 350 pertains to the shape from Exhibit 3.4.2, where the starting point is at the lower right corner of the cross. Successive drawings with increasing SCALES result in an overlapping of the shapes.

In contrast, Section 6 uses the data determined by the shape definition from Exhibit 3.4.6, where the starting point is located at the center of the shape. Using this shape definition, concentric crosses can be drawn.

Sections 5 and 6 demonstrate the selection of a starting point for any shape should be carefully determined with anticipation as to future manipulation of the shape. The starting point becomes the pivot point for any rotations or scaling. General good advice is to select the starting point as close to the center of gravity of the shape as possible.

| SCALE = / ROT = | 0 | 4 | 8 | 12 | 16 | 20 | 24 | 28 | 32 | 36 | 40 | 44 | 48 | 52 | 56 | 60 | 64 |
|---|---|---|---|---|---|---|---|---|---|---|---|---|---|---|---|---|---|
| 1 | 0° | | 45° | | 90° | | 135° | | 180° | | 225° | | 270° | | 315° | | 360° |
| 2 | 0° | 22.5° | 45° | 67.5° | 90° | 112.5° | 135° | 157.5° | 180° | 202.5° | 225° | 247.5° | 270° | 292.5° | 315° | 337.5° | 360° |
| 3 | ROT can be assigned any value divisible by 2 | | | | | | | | | | | | | | | | |
| 4 | ROT can be assigned any integer value 0 through 64 | | | | | | | | | | | | | | | | |

Table 3.7.1

**COMPREHENSIVE EXAMPLE**   Load SHAPELOAD from your diskette then delete lines 350 through 395 and lines 505 through 550. Study the following commands to determine the screen display. Check your answer by entering the program into the computer.

```
100    REM ****************************************
101    REM *               CE3.7                    *
102    REM ****************************************
350    DATA 73, 60, 39, 60, 55, 62, 55, 46, 53, 46, 37, 44, 37, 0
505    N = 1 : S = 768 : GOSUB 200
510    HGR : HCOLOR = 3 : X = 140 : Y = 90
515    POKE -16302, 0
520    R = 0
525    FOR L = 1 TO 5
535    K = 3
540    FOR J = 1 TO 2
542    ROT = R
545    HCOLOR = K
550    FOR I = 1 TO 14
555    SCALE = 2 * I
560    DRAW 1 AT X, Y
565    FOR W = 1 TO 200 : NEXT
570    NEXT I
575    K = 0
580    NEXT J
585    R = R + 4
590    NEXT L
600    GET Q$ : TEXT : HOME
LIST
RUN
```

#### Check Your Comprehension
Describe the screen display. _____

What sizes are the crosses in terms of the SCALE command? _____

What degrees are the crosses rotated? _____

**EXERCISE**   Write a program that displays ten shapes anywhere on the high resolution screen between column values of 20 and 265 and row values of 20 and 145. The shapes are to be randomly selected from one of the four shapes (hearts, clubs, diamonds, or spades), randomly SCALEd with values of 1 or 2, and randomly ROTated with values which are multiples of 8.

**CHALLENGE**   Write a program that uses the ROT and SCALE commands to vary the display of a shape of your choice.

# ACTIVITY 3.8   Animating Shapes

**LEARNING BY DISCOVERY**   This activity demonstrates how the movement of shapes can be displayed on the video screen.

1. Load SHAPELOAD from your diskette. Modify this program by making deletions and additions as given below.

```
DEL   350, 395
DEL   505, 550
350   DATA 73, 60, 39, 60, 55, 62, 55, 46, 53, 46, 37, 44, 37,
      0
400   REM ANIMATION ROUTINE
405   HCOLOR = 3 : DRAW 1 AT X, Y
410   FOR Z = 1 TO 500 : NEXT Z
415   HCOLOR = 0 : DRAW 1 AT X, Y
420   FOR Z = 1 TO 500 : NEXT Z
425   RETURN
505   N = 1 : S = 768 : GOSUB 200
510   HGR
515   SCALE = 4 : ROT = 0 : Y = 140
520   FOR X = 80 TO 200 STEP 10
525   GOSUB 400
530   Y = Y — 10
535   NEXT X
540   GET Q$ : TEXT : HOME
RUN
```

Describe the appearance of the animated diagram. _____

2. Retype lines 405, 415 and 510 as follows:

```
TEXT : HOME
405   DRAW 1 AT X, Y
415   HGR
510   HGR : HCOLOR = 3
LIST
RUN
```

Describe the appearance of the animated diagram. _____

3. Retype line 415 as follows:

```
TEXT : HOME
415   XDRAW 1 AT X, Y
LIST
RUN
```

Describe the appearance of the animated diagram. _____

4. Retype line 515 as follows:

```
TEXT : HOME
515  SCALE = 4 : ROT = 8 : Y = 140
LIST
RUN
```

Describe the appearance of the animated diagram. _____

5. Retype lines 405 and 510 as follows:

```
TEXT : HOME
405  XDRAW 1 AT X, Y
510  HGR
LIST
RUN
```

Describe the appearance of the animated diagram. _____

**DISCUSSION**   In earlier activities you learned one method of animating a diagram on a black background screen is to first draw it in a color, then draw it again in black in the same position. Movement of the diagram is obtained by successively repeating this process while changing coordinate values. Section 1 demonstrates this animation technique is also successful when using shapes. However, animation can be achieved more efficiently by using the XDRAW command.

Recall from ACTIVITY 3.6 the XDRAW command draws the shape in the complement of the color found. Since black and white are complementary colors, two successive XDRAW commands at the same screen position will draw and undraw the diagram when the background color is black. Section 5 demonstrates this technique by using XDRAW commands in lines 405 and 415 of the Animation Routine (lines 400-425).

The conditions for displaying the animated diagram are established in lines 510 through 535. In particular, notice the HGR command in line 510 establishes black (0) as the value for HCOLOR. When XDRAW is encountered first on line 405, the diagram is drawn in the complementary color white. The XDRAW command on line 415 removes the appearance of the shape by plotting in the complement of white, which is black. The FOR-NEXT loop defined in lines 520 through 535 determines the positions for the animated diagram.

Section 4 demonstrates a peculiarity that occurs when combining DRAW and XDRAW commands to animate a diagram. The animation leaves a trail of pixels. Section 3, which uses the same combination of DRAW and XDRAW commands, does not leave this trail of dots. The difference is the shape in Section 3 is animated in its original rotation (ROT = 0), but in Section 4 ROT = 8 is used. Combining DRAW and XDRAW commands to animate a diagram will leave these strange dots if the value assigned to ROT is not zero.

The obvious way to avoid such occurrences is to utilize XDRAW commands only when creating animation, unless such an effect is desirable. This might be the case for displaying an accelerating automobile, illustrating the gradual disintegration of an object, or the like.

Section 2 also results in the animation of the cross, but not with the same smoothness. Using the HGR command to erase the diagram not only provides a displeasing visual effect but also erases the entire graphics page. Use of the XDRAW command for animation purposes removes only the diagram, leaving other screen displays intact.

**COMPREHENSIVE EXAMPLE**   Load SHAPELOAD from your diskette, then delete lines 350 through 395 and lines 505 through 550. Study the following commands to determine the screen display. Check your answer by entering the program into the computer.

```
100   REM ******************************************
101   REM *               CE3.8                    *
102   REM ******************************************
350   DATA 63, 63, 71, 192, 36, 36, 140, 14, 14, 14,
      62, 63, 63, 63, 54, 54, 54, 45, 53, 9, 9
360   DATA 30, 30, 30, 30, 36, 36, 44, 45, 45, 45, 45,
      45, 45, 37, 33, 33, 33, 227, 28, 63, 63, 63, 63,
      63, 0
399   REM  ROCKET MOVE WITHOUT TRAIL
400   XDRAW 1 AT X,Y
410   FOR Z = 1 TO 50: NEXT
415   XDRAW 1 AT X,Y
420   FOR Z = 1 TO 50: NEXT
425   RETURN
449   REM  ROCKET MOVE WITH TRAIL
450   DRAW 1 AT X,Y
460   FOR Z = 1 TO 50: NEXT
464   XDRAW 1 AT X,Y
468   FOR Z = 1 TO 50: NEXT
472   RETURN
474   REM  ROUTINE TO CONTROL PROGRAM
475   VTAB 24: HTAB 4
485   PRINT "PRESS THE SPACE BAR TO CONTINUE";
490   GET Q$: HOME : RETURN
500   REM  ESTABLISH CONDITIONS FOR LOADING SHAPE TABLE
505   N = 1: S = 768: GOSUB 200
510   HGR : HCOLOR =  3 : X = 140 : Y = 90
515   SCALE =   1: ROT =   0
520   DRAW 1 AT X,Y
525   VTAB 22: HTAB 11
530   PRINT "MEET KEITH'S ROCKET"
535   GOSUB 475
540   HGR : SCALE =  2
545   DRAW 1 AT X,Y
550   VTAB 22: HTAB 4
555   PRINT "GETTING CLOSER TO KEITH'S ROCKET"
```

```
560   GOSUB 475
565   HGR : SCALE =   4
570   DRAW 1 AT X,Y
575   VTAB 22: HTAB 4
580   PRINT "YOU ARE GETTING T O O  C L O S E"
585   GOSUB 475
590   HGR : SCALE =   1: ROT =   48
595   X = 50:Y = 140
600   DRAW 1 AT X,Y
605   VTAB 22: HTAB 7
610   PRINT "GETTING READY FOR BLAST OFF"
615   GOSUB 475
620   HGR : SCALE =   2: ROT =   48
625   VTAB 22: HTAB 12
630   PRINT "UP-UP-UP-AND-AWAY"
635   FOR Y = 140 TO 100 STEP  - 5
640   GOSUB 400
645   NEXT
650   SCALE =   1: ROT =   56
655   FOR X = 50 TO 100 STEP 10
660   GOSUB 400
665   Y = Y - 5
670   NEXT
675   ROT =   0
680   FOR X = 100 TO 250 STEP 10
685   GOSUB 400
690   NEXT
695   FOR X = 0 TO 50 STEP 10
700   GOSUB 400
705   NEXT
710   HOME : VTAB 22: HTAB 6
715   PRINT "OH! THE COMPUTER IS FAILING"
720   ROT =   8
725   FOR X = 50 TO 100 STEP 10
730   GOSUB 450
735   Y = Y + 7
740   NEXT
745   ROT =   16
750   FOR W = 1 TO 8
755   GOSUB 450
760   Y = Y + 5
770   NEXT
775   HOME : VTAB 22: HTAB 16
780   PRINT "C R A S H"
785   FOR L = 1 TO 40
790   X =   INT (40 *  RND (1)) + 90
795   Y = 159 -  INT (40 *  RND (1))
```

```
800   HPLOT X,Y
805   NEXT
810   GOSUB 475
815   GET Q$ : TEXT : HOME
LIST
RUN
```

**Check Your Comprehension**

Why does ROT = 48 in line 590? _____

What technique is used to animate the shape? _____

What is the purpose of lines 785 through 805? _____

**EXERCISE**   Write a program that animates the rolling of the cross shape along the bottom of the high resolution screen using successive ROT values which are multiples of 4 (0, 4, 8, 12, 16,....). Enlarge the cross by using a SCALE value of 6.

**CHALLENGE**   Write a program that animates a shape of your choice. Incorporate several different values for ROT and SCALE into the program.

# MODULE 3C   Text on the High Resolution Screen

## ACTIVITY 3.9   A High Resolution Character Generator

**LEARNING BY DISCOVERY**   In this activity you will install and investigate the use of a high resolution character generator. This will permit printing of text characters on either high resolution page.

1. If you have the diskette that supplements this book, do not complete this section. Instead, go to Section 2 since you already have the files HRCG$9280 and ASCII$9300 stored on your diskette. The BASIC program below will create and then BSAVE these binary files on disk.

    Be sure your system is booted with DOS, then enter the following program. Included in the program (lines 35, 57, and 70) is an error checking routine for assisting you in catching entry errors. Although the method is not foolproof (multiple errors could "cancel" each other out), it can be effective. The sum of the DATA values you enter for each of the two groups is stored in the variable T. This is compared with the value known to be the sum for correctly entered data. Any difference in values will result in program termination and an appropriate error message. Each DATA line contains 32 items. This is used to advantage in the second half of the program. Every 32nd item will be displayed, along with the line number to which it should belong. If the displayed value does not match the last item of the line number in the program listing, an error has occurred.

```
NEW
2   HIMEM : 37504 : REM  PROTECT UPPER MEMORY FROM STRINGS
5   HOME : PRINT "READ'N AND POKE'N ..."
10   FOR ADDR = 37504 TO 37614
15   READ VL
20   T = T + VL: REM  USED FOR ERROR CHECKING
25   POKE ADDR,VL
30   NEXT ADDR
35   IF T< >11691 THEN  PRINT "THERE IS AN ERROR IN YOUR
     HRCG DATA": PRINT "CHECK FOR ACCURACY IN LINES 100-130.":
     PRINT CHR$ (7): END
40   T = 0 : CNT = 0 : LN = 190
45   FOR ADDR = 37632 TO 38399
50   READ VL
55   T = T + VL: REM  USED FOR ERROR CHECKING
57   CNT = CNT + 1: IF CNT = 32 THEN LN = LN + 10: PRINT
     "LAST DATA VALUE IN LINE ";LN;": ";VL;" ?": CNT = 0
60   POKE ADDR,VL
```

```
65   NEXT ADDR
70   IF T< >15175 THEN  PRINT "THERE IS AN ERROR IN YOUR
     ASCII DATA.": PRINT "CHECK FOR ACCURACY IN LINES 200-430.":
     PRINT  CHR$ (7): END
75   PRINT : PRINT "SAVE THE BINARY FILES YOU CREATED";: INPUT
     A$: IF  LEFT$ (A$,1)< >"Y" THEN 95
80   PRINT  CHR$ (4);"BSAVE HRCG$9280,A37504,L111"
85   PRINT  CHR$ (4);"BSAVE ASCII$9300,A37632,L768"
90   PRINT "HRCG$9280 AND ASCII$9300 ARE SAVED ON ": PRINT "YOUR
     DISKETTE. GOOD WORK!"
95   END
97   REM
98   REM    ***** HRCG DATA *****
99   REM
100   DATA  169, 148, 133, 54, 169, 146, 133, 55, 76, 234, 3,
      169, 189, 133, 54, 169, 158, 133, 55, 96, 201, 160, 144,
      84, 72, 41, 127, 133, 60, 169, 0, 133
110   DATA  61, 152, 72, 56, 165, 60, 233, 32, 133, 60, 6, 60,
      6, 60, 38, 61, 6, 60, 38, 61, 24, 169, 0, 101, 60, 133,
      60, 169, 147, 101, 61, 133
120   DATA  61, 24, 165, 40, 101, 36, 133, 62, 165, 41, 101,
      230, 56, 233, 4, 133, 63, 160, 0, 177, 60, 145, 62, 200,
      24, 165, 62, 105, 255, 133, 62, 165
130   DATA  63, 105, 3, 133, 63, 192, 8, 144, 234, 104, 168,
      104, 76, 240, 253
131   REM    ***** END HRCG DATA *****
197   REM
198   REM    ***** ASCII DATA *****
199   REM
200   DATA  0, 0, 0, 0, 0, 0, 0, 0, 8, 8, 8, 8, 8, 0, 8, 0, 20,
      20, 20, 0, 0, 0, 0, 0, 20, 20, 62, 20, 62, 20, 20, 0    :
      REM SPACE, !, ", #
210   DATA  8, 60, 10, 28, 40, 30, 8, 0, 6, 38, 16, 8, 4, 50,
      48, 0, 4, 10, 10, 4, 42, 18, 44, 0, 8, 8, 8, 0, 0, 0, 0,
      0 : REM $, %, &, '
220   DATA  8, 4, 2, 2, 2, 4, 8, 0, 8, 16, 32, 32, 32, 16, 8, 0,
      8, 42, 28, 8, 28, 42, 8, 0, 0, 8, 8, 62, 8, 8, 0, 0    :
      REM (,), *, +
230   DATA  0, 0, 0, 0, 0, 8, 8, 4, 0, 0, 0, 62, 0, 0, 0, 0, 0,
      0, 0, 0, 0, 0, 8, 0, 0, 32, 16, 8, 4, 2, 0, 0    : REM ,,
      −,., /
240   DATA  28, 34, 50, 42, 38, 34, 28, 0, 8, 12, 8, 8, 8, 8,
      28, 0, 28, 34, 32, 24, 4, 2, 62, 0, 62, 32, 16, 24, 32,
      34, 28, 0    : REM 0, 1, 2, 3
250   DATA  16, 24, 20, 18, 62, 16, 16, 0, 62, 2, 30, 32, 32,
      34, 28, 0, 24, 4, 2, 30, 34, 34, 28, 0, 62, 32, 16, 8,
      4, 4, 4, 0    : REM 4, 5, 6, 7
```

```
260  DATA  28, 34, 34, 28, 34, 34, 28, 0, 28, 34, 34, 60, 32,
     16, 12, 0, 0, 0, 8, 0, 8, 0, 0, 0, 0, 0, 8, 0, 8, 8, 4,
     0 : REM 8, 9, :, ;
270  DATA  16, 8, 4, 2, 4, 8, 16, 0, 0, 0, 62, 0, 62, 0, 0, 0,
     4, 8, 16, 32, 16, 8, 4, 0, 28, 34, 16, 8, 8, 0, 8, 0    :
     REM <, =,>, ?
280  DATA  28, 34, 42, 58, 26, 2, 60, 0, 8, 20, 34, 34, 62, 34,
     34, 0, 30, 34, 34, 30, 34, 34, 30, 0, 28, 34, 2, 2, 2, 34,
     28, 0    : REM ', A, B, C
290  DATA  30, 34, 34, 34, 34, 34, 30, 0, 62, 2, 2, 30, 2, 2,
     62, 0, 62, 2, 2, 30, 2, 2, 2, 0, 60, 2, 2, 2, 50, 34, 60,
     0 : REM D, E, F, G
300  DATA  34, 34, 34, 62, 34, 34, 34, 0, 28, 8, 8, 8, 8, 8,
     28, 0, 32, 32, 32, 32, 32, 34, 28, 0, 34, 18, 10, 6, 10,
     18, 34, 0    : REM H, I, J, K
310  DATA  2, 2, 2, 2, 2, 2, 62, 0, 34, 54, 42, 42, 34, 34, 34,
     0, 34, 34, 38, 42, 50, 34, 34, 0, 28, 34, 34, 34, 34, 34,
     28, 0 : REM L, M, N, O
320  DATA  30, 34, 34, 30, 2, 2, 2, 0, 28, 34, 34, 34, 42, 18,
     44, 0, 30, 34, 34, 30, 10, 18, 34, 0, 28, 34, 2, 28, 32,
     34, 28, 0    : REM P, Q, R, S
330  DATA  62, 8, 8, 8, 8, 8, 8, 0, 34, 34, 34, 34, 34, 34, 28,
     0, 34, 34, 34, 34, 34, 20, 8, 0, 34, 34, 34, 42, 42, 54,
     34, 0 : REM T, U, V, W
340  DATA  34, 34, 20, 8, 20, 34, 34, 0, 34, 34, 34, 20, 8, 8,
     8, 0, 62, 32, 16, 8, 4, 2, 62, 0, 62, 6, 6, 6, 6, 6, 62,
     0    : REM X, Y, Z, [
350  DATA  0, 2, 4, 8, 16, 32, 0, 0, 62, 48, 48, 48, 48, 48,
     62, 0, 0, 0, 8, 20, 34, 0, 0, 0, 0, 0, 0, 0, 0, 0, 0,
     127    : REM \, ], ^, -
360  DATA  4, 8, 16, 0, 0, 0, 0, 0, 0, 0, 28, 32, 60, 34, 60,
     0, 2, 2, 30, 34, 34, 34, 30, 0, 0, 0, 60, 2, 2, 2, 60,
     0    : REM ', a, b, c
370  DATA  32, 32, 60, 34, 34, 34, 60, 0, 0, 0, 28, 34, 62, 2,
     60, 0, 24, 36, 4, 30, 4, 4, 4, 0, 0, 0, 28, 34, 34, 60,
     32, 28    : REM d, e, f, g
380  DATA  2, 2, 30, 34, 34, 34, 34, 0, 8, 0, 12, 8, 8, 8, 28,
     0, 16, 0, 24, 16, 16, 16, 18, 12, 2, 2, 34, 18, 14, 18,
     34, 0 : REM h, i, j, k
390  DATA  12, 8, 8, 8, 8, 8, 28, 0, 0, 0, 54, 42, 42, 42, 34,
     0, 0, 0, 30, 34, 34, 34, 34, 0, 0, 0, 28, 34, 34, 34, 28,
     0 : REM l, m, n, o
400  DATA  0, 0, 30, 34, 34, 30, 2, 2, 0, 0, 60, 34, 34, 60,
     32, 32, 0, 0, 58, 6, 2, 2, 2, 0, 0, 0, 60, 2, 28, 32, 30,
     0 : REM p, q, r, s
410  DATA  4, 4, 30, 4, 4, 36, 24, 0, 0, 0, 34, 34, 34, 50, 44,
     0, 0, 0, 34, 34, 34, 20, 8, 0, 0, 0, 34, 34, 42, 42, 54,
```

```
       0 : REM t, u, v, w
   420 DATA  0, 0, 34, 20, 8, 20, 34, 0, 0, 0, 34, 34, 20, 8, 8,
       6, 0, 0, 62, 16, 8, 4, 62, 0, 56, 12, 12, 6, 12, 12, 56,
       0 : REM x, y, z, {
   430 DATA  8, 8, 8, 8, 8, 8, 8, 8, 14, 24, 24, 48, 24, 24, 14,
       0, 44, 26, 0, 0, 0, 0, 0, 0, 127, 127, 127, 127, 127, 127,
       127, 127    : REM |, }, ~, █
   31  REM  ***** END ASCII DATA *****
   LIST
   RUN
```

It would be a wise idea to save the program above. Should you ever lose the files HRCG$9280 and ASCII$9300 created and saved on disk by this program, you can reconstruct them by reRUNing it. Aside from this purpose, there is no further use of the program.

2. As a result of a successful RUN of the program from Section 1, two binary files have been saved on your disk: HRCG$9280 and ASCII$9300. CATALOG your diskette and observe the file type parameter. The letter "B" to the left of these file names indicates these are binary files. This is why a BSAVE DOS command was used in lines 80 and 85.

To illustrate how you can load these files into memory, turn off your APPLE. Boot your system with DOS and be sure the diskette containing HRCG$9280 and AS-CII$9300 is in your disk drive. To load the files into memory, enter the DOS commands.

```
   BLOAD  HRCG$9280
   BLOAD  ASCII$9300
```

This permits BLOADing of the files from the immediate execution mode. In the deferred mode (within a program), you will simply enter

```
   line#  PRINT CHR$(4);"BLOAD HRCG$9280"
   line#  PRINT CHR$(4);"BLOAD ASCII$9300"
```

where CHR$(4) denotes CTRL-D.

The suffixes, $9280 and $9300, are the hexidecimal addresses of where each machine language program will initially reside in memory.   The decimal equivalents are:

$9280 = 9 * 16 \wedge 3 + 2 * 16 \wedge 2 + 8 * 16 = 37504
$9300 = 9 * 16 \wedge 3 + 3 * 16 \wedge 2 = 37632

It is emphasized these suffixes are merely parts of the file names and do not represent any form of DOS characteristic.

3. Enter the following program. It will assist in demonstrating the use of this machine language utility. Note: Be sure you have BLOADed the files HRCG$9280 and ASCII$9300 into memory prior to running the program below.

```
NEW
5    HIMEM : 37500 :REM PROTECT HRCG AND ASCII
10   CALL 37504: REM  INITIALIZE HRCG
20   HOME : HGR : HCOLOR=  3
30   HPLOT 49,64 TO 49,88 TO 216,88 TO 216,64 TO 49,64
40   VTAB 10: HTAB 9
50   PRINT "PRINTING ON HIRES PG 1"
60   VTAB 16: HTAB 9
70   PRINT "PRESS A KEY TO CONTINUE";: GET K$
80   HGR2
85   HPLOT 140,64 TO 14,90 TO 140,116 TO 255,90 TO 140,64
90   VTAB 12: HTAB 10
100  PRINT "NOW, PRINTING ON PG 2"
110  VTAB 18: HTAB 9
120  PRINT "PRESS A KEY TO CONTINUE";: GET K$
130  HOME
140  TEXT : END
LIST
RUN
```

Describe what happens. _____

On which high resolution page did the printing occur and where are the initial print positions? _____

DELete line 130 and reRUN the program. What differences do you observe between the prior RUN and the most recent RUN? _____

In the immediate execution mode enter the following statements.

```
CALL 37504
HGR : HOME : TEXT
VTAB 12 : HTAB 16 : PRINT "H E L L O"
```

Are you in TEXT mode or in high resolution mode? _____

Enter the POKEs necessary to view high resolution Page 1 without clearing the page:

```
POKE −16297,0 : POKE −16304,0
```

Remember, you cleared (HGR) high resolution Page 1. But what appears on the high resolution page now? _____

You are still viewing high resolution Page 1, but where is the cursor? _____

_____

Hit the RETURN key several times. Why do you think the cursor suddenly became visible about four lines from the bottom of the page? _____

4. RUN the program in Section 2 (with line 130 DELeted). Insert the following line and RUN the resulting program.

```
75   PRINT CHR$(13)+CHR$(4);"PR#0"
```

```
LIST
RUN
```

Now quickly reRUN the program with line 75 DELeted. What differences do you detect in the two RUNs? _____

DELete line 10 and enter PR#0 at your keyboard. ReRUN the program being sure to make at least two keypresses after it is running.

What happens now? _____

5. Finally, enter the following program.

```
NEW
10  HIMEM: 37500: REM  PROTECT HRCG AND ASCII
20  HRCG = 37504: REM  STARTING BYTE OF HRCG; HEX VAL =
    $9280
30  HGR2 : HCOLOR =  3
40  CALL HRCG: REM  INIT HRCG
50  VTAB 10: HTAB 8: PRINT "GET READY TO SEE THE FULL"
60  VTAB 12: HTAB 14: PRINT "ASCII SET ON"
70  VTAB 14: HTAB 9: PRINT "HIGH RESOLUTION PAGE 2"
80  GET K$: CALL 62450: REM  WAIT FOR KEYPRESS, THEN CLEAR
    SCREEN.
90  GOSUB 500: REM  GO TO GRID ROUTINE
100  ACV = 32: REM  1ST PRINTABLE ASCII VALUE
110  FOR VT = 2 TO 23 STEP 3
120  FOR HT = 3 TO 36 STEP 3
130  HTAB HT: VTAB VT
140  PRINT  CHR$ (ACV)
150  FOR K = 1 TO 250: NEXT : REM  DELAY
160  ACV = ACV + 1: REM  INCREMENT FOR NEXT ASCII VALUE
170  IF ACV > 127 THEN 190
180  NEXT HT,VT
190  PRINT  CHR$ (4);"PR#0": REM  DISCONNECT HRCG
200  GET Q$: TEXT : HOME : END
497  REM
498  REM  *****  GRID ROUTINE  *****
499  REM
500  FOR H = 7 TO 259 STEP 21
510  HPLOT H,0 TO H,191
520  NEXT H
530  FOR V = 0 TO 191 STEP 24
540  HPLOT 7,V TO 259,V
550  NEXT V
560  HPLOT 7,191 TO 259,191
570  RETURN
LIST
RUN
```

Which decimal value is indicated as the ASCII value of the first printable character and what is the character? _____

What is the range of ASCII values (ASC values) for the set of characters printed?

_____

**DISCUSSION**    The acronym HRCG is derived from the phrase "high resolution character generator." The file HRCG$9280 is a machine language program which permits text to be printed to either high resolution page. There are several high resolution character generator programs available on the commercial market. The APPLE TOOL KIT package contains an excellent high resolution character generator with many different styles of print available to the user. The file ASCII$9300 contains the standard set of ASCII characters including upper and lower case. The basic function of the driver program, HRCG$9280, is to intercept the normal flow of characters to the text page, and then byte map the approriate character defined in the table ASCII$9300 to the high resolution page. The appropriate high resolution page is determined by the value currently stored in the high resolution page byte located at $E6 (HEX) = 230.

The system is prepared for printing on the high resolution page by executing a CALL 37504. This sets up the appropriate hooks for monitoring character data as it is being sent to the text page. After interception, it is still printed on the text page. This explains why all printing on the high resolution page also occurs on the text page. This is one of the principle disadvantages of the generator included here.

The high resolution character generator is turned off by executing a PR#0. Using the statement

```
line#  PRINT  CHR$(4);"PR#0"
```

will permit a clean exit from within a program, and a return to normal text generation.

If a carriage return is needed prior to sending a DOS command, then it will be necessary to use CHR$(13) + CHR$(4) in place of CHR$(4) in the above statement. This was precisely what happened in Section 4. The GET statement in line 70 of that program supresses a carriage return. Without the CHR$(13) ( = RETURN), the PRINT statement would not be interpreted as a DOS command. Try it for yourself.

Finally, there is a word of caution to be noted. Unless the high resolution character generator is turned off, any text printed on the text page is also printed on the last high resolution page accessed and conversely; it's like an echo!

The print positions on the high resolution page correspond to those on the text page and are obtained by using HTABs and VTABs. However, the flashing cursor will not appear on the high resolution screen. Positioning the cursor with the commands HTAB C and VTAB R, will cause printing to begin at the pixel with coordinates:

$H = 7 * (C - 1)$
$V = (8 * R) - 1$

The coordinates H,V correspond to the lower left corner of the $7 \times 8$ grid in which the character is displayed. This means high resolution characters can be printed only at those positions of the high resolution screen where the lower left corner H,V has values:

H = 0, 7, 14, 21, 28, ... , 273

V = 7, 15, 23, 31, 39, ... , 191

It is at times convenient to be able to identify the print position on the screen where an arbitrary pixel will occur within the printed character. For example, let's determine the HTAB and VTAB values which will yield the 7 × 8 grid containing the point 131,94. You compute:

INT(131/7) = 18  and  INT(94/8) = 11

To compensate for the fact print positions range from 1 to 40 or 1 to 24 you must add one to each value obtained above. Thus the print positions HT and VT can be obtained using the formulas:

HT = INT(131/7) + 1 = 19

VT = INT( 94/8) + 1 = 12

Finally, the general statement needed to supply the print position containing the point H,V on the high resolution screen is given by the following "tabs":

HTAB  INT(H/7) + 1 : VTAB  INT(V/8) + 1

**COMPREHENSIVE EXAMPLE**    The program below combines high resolution character generation with page flipping to create an animated display. Enter the program below.

```
NEW
10  REM  ********************************
11  REM  *             CE3.9            *
12  REM  ********************************
13  REM
14  REM
15  HIMEM: 37500: GOTO 100: REM  BRANCH AROUND SUBRTS.
16  REM
27  REM  ********************************
28  REM  *      BLIMP/MESSG DRAW SBRT    *
29  REM  ********************************
30  HTAB HT%: VTAB VT%: REM  TAB TO PRNT POSITION.
32  PRINT  MID$ (MSG$(DSPL),35 — HT%,5) + BL$: REM  PRINT
    MESSAGE + TWO BLANKS.
34  HTAB HT% + 5: VTAB VT% + 2: PRINT BL$: REM  BLANK OUT
    'PROPELLER'.
36  HTAB HT% + 4: VTAB VT% + 2: PRINT P$(SW): REM  PRINT
    'PROPELLER' SHAPE DEPENDING ON DRAW PAGE.
37  REM  BLIMP DRAWING ROUTINE
38  HPLOT X% + H%(0),Y% + V%(0)
40  FOR K = 1 TO 11
42  HPLOT  TO X% + H%(K),Y% + V%(K)
44  NEXT K
46  HPLOT X% + H%(K),Y% + V%(K): REM  NOTE THAT K = 12 HERE
    AS A RESULT OF EXITING THE PREV LOOP; THIS IS START OF TAIL
    SECTION.
48  FOR K = 13 TO 15
```

```
50   HPLOT  TO X% + H%(K),Y% + V%(K)
52   NEXT K
54   RETURN
55   REM  **  END BLIMP/MSSG DRAW SBRT  **
97   REM  *******************************
98   REM  *          MAIN PROGRAM        *
99   REM  *******************************
100  GOSUB 1000: REM  GOTO DATA INITIALIZATION ROUTINE
110  PRINT  CHR$ (4);"BLOAD HRCG$9280"
120  PRINT  CHR$ (4);"BLOAD ASCII$9300"
130  CALL 37504: REM  INIT HRCG
140  HOME
150  HGR2 : HCOLOR=  0
160  HGR : POKE  - 16302,0: REM  FULL SCREEN PG 1
170  HTAB 9: VTAB 21
180  S$ = "HERE COME THE BLIMPS!!": PRINT S$
190  HTAB 9: VTAB 21
200  POKE BYT,64: PRINT S$: REM  PRINT MESSAGE ON PG 2 OF HIRES
     AS WELL.
210  FOR DSPL = 0 TO 1
220  X% = 223:Y% = 55 + 48 * DSPL: REM  SET BASE POSITION OF
     BLIMP DISPLAY.
230  VT% = 9 + 6 * DSPL:HT% = 34: REM  SET VTAB PRINT HEIGHT
     FOR DISPLAY # DSPL, AND SET INITIAL HTAB VALUE.
240  HCOLOR =  3: GOSUB 30: REM  DRAW BLIMP & MESSG ON PG 2.
250  POKE HPG(1),0: REM  VIEW PG 2 OF HIRES
260  POKE BYT,32: REM  SET BYTE FOR DRAWING ON PG 1
270  HT% = 33: REM  SET HORIZ (PRINT) HTAB VALUE
280  X% = 216: REM  HORIZ POSITION AT WHICH TO BASE BLIMP
     INTIALLY ON PG 1
290  GOSUB 30: REM  DRAW BLIMP
300  POKE HPG(0),0: REM  VIEW HIRES PG 1
310  SW = 1: REM  SET SW VAR FOR PG 2
320  FOR H = 209 TO 6 STEP  - 7
330  HT% = HT% - 1: REM  DECREMENT HTAB VALUE FOR NEW PRNT
     POSITION
340  POKE BYT,PG(SW): REM  SET BYTE FOR DRAWING ON PAGE SW+1
350  X% = H + 14: REM  SET HORIZ-BASE POSITION OF BLIMP TO
     POSITION OF TWO MOVES EARLIER.
360  HCOLOR =  0: GOSUB 38: REM  ERASE BLIMP ONLY; MESSAGE
     WILL BE ELIMINATED WHEN NEW POSITION IS DRAWN.
370  X% = H: REM  RESET TO CURRENT POSITION.
380  HCOLOR =  3: GOSUB 30: REM  PRINT NEW MESSAGE, ERASING
     LAST TWO CHARS OF OLD MESSG, AND, HPLOT BLIMP IN NEW
     POSITION.
390  POKE HPG(SW),0: REM  VIEW DRAW PAGE.
400  SW =  NOT SW: REM  SET FOR OPPOSITE HIRES PG
```

```
410   NEXT H
419   REM  NEXT THREE LINES ARE SAME AS IN LOOP ABOVE; ERASE OLD
      PICTURE FROM TWO MOVES AGO.
420   POKE BYT,PG(SW)
430   X% = H + 14
440   HCOLOR = 0: GOSUB 38
449   REM  SET NEW POSITION & MESSG OF BLIMP ON THIS HIRES PAGE
      TO MATCH POSITION & MESSG OF BLIMP ON OTHER PAGE.
450   X% = H + 7
460   HCOLOR = 3: GOSUB 30: REM  GO PRNT MESSG AND DRAW BLIMP
470   POKE HPG(0),0: REM  VIEW PAGE 1
480   POKE BYT,64: REM  SET BYTE FOR DRAWING ON HIRES PG 2
490   NEXT DSPL
500   HTAB 9: VTAB 21
510   S$ = "!! THAT'S ALL FOLKS !!": POKE BYT,32: PRINT S$: REM
      PRNT MESSG ON PG 1
520   HTAB 9: VTAB 21
530   POKE BYT,64: PRINT S$: REM  PRNT MESSG ON PG 2.
540   PRINT  CHR$ (4);"PR#0": REM  TURN OFF HRCG.
550   GET Q$: TEXT : HOME : END
551   REM  **      END MAIN PROGRAM      **
552   REM
997   REM  ******************************
998   REM  *    INITIALIZATION SUBRTN    *
999   REM  ******************************
1000  DIM H%(15),V%(15)
1010  FOR K = 0 TO 15
1020  READ H%(K),V%(K)
1030  NEXT K
1040  DIM MSG$(1)
1050  MSG$(0) = "......HI!....APPLE GRAPHICS.....BY......"
1060  MSG$(1) = "***** R.J. BRADY CO. *** & *** HB+EK ***"
1070  BL$ = "  ": REM  TWO SPACES
1080  BYT = 230: REM  HIRES DRAW BYTE
1090  DIM PG(1):PG(0) = 32:PG(1) = 64: REM  VALUES CORRESP TO
      HIRES PAGE; WILL BE POKED INTO BYTE BYT = 230.
1100  DIM HPG(1):HPG(0) = - 16300:HPG(1)= - 16299: REM  PG
      1 AND PG 2 SOFT SWITCHES.
1110  DIM P$(1):P$(0) = "X":P$(1) = "/": REM  'PROPELLER'
      CHARACTERS.
1120  RETURN
1121  REM  **      END INITIALIZATION    **
1122  REM
4997  REM  *****************************
4998  REM  *        DATA FOR BLIMP      *
4999  REM  *****************************
```

```
5000   DATA  55,10, 35,0, 7,0, 0,8, 0,16, 7,24, 34,24, 34,32,
       14,32, 14,24, 34,24, 55,14     : REM   BLIMP BODY
5010   DATA  49,6, 55,3, 55,21, 49,18      : REM   TAIL SECTION
5011   REM  **        END DATA FOR BLIMP     **
5012   REM
LIST
RUN
```

The DATA for the blimp construction is provided in lines 5000 and 5010. Since text is to appear within the body of the blimp, it is important to design the body large enough to contain the desired character string. The horizontal distance each blimp must be shifted must correspond exactly to the width of a single character. This is because character strings will be shifted one print position to the left for a new display.

Because page flipping is used, it is important to understand an old display on a high resolution page was created two moves earlier (not one move earlier). The message displayed on the screen is animated by simply using a five character wide window which views part of the fixed forty character strings MSG(0) and MSG(1). The minor problem to overcome here is the blimps are moving to the left while the character window must move to the right. Why?

## Check Your Comprehension

Why is it necessary to print the message "here come the ..." on both high resolution pages (lines 170-200)? Why not just print on Page 1? _____

After setting up the first frames of the display on Page 2 and then on Page 1, where does the loop begin for the erase-draw-view cycle typical of page flipping?

_____

For this particular display, why is it necessary to shift the blimp position by 7 pixels? Why not shift 6 or 8 pixels? _____

How is the erasure of a previously displayed blimp accomplished? _____

How is the erasure of a previously displayed message within a blimp accomplished? (Hint: see lines 30-32 and consider why two blanks are appended to the new message to be typed.) _____

When erasing an old frame, why must the blimp body be erased before the new message and "blanking out" of trailing old characters is executed? _____

Precisely what effect will the assignment SW = NOT SW produce on the variable SW? _____

In lines 420-460 the blimp (in an old frame) was forced to "catch up" to the same position as the blimp in the last frame when the loop was exited at line 410. Why?

_____

Is line 530 technically necessary?  Why or why not? _____

**EXERCISE**   Modify the COMPREHENSIVE EXAMPLE program so a third blimp appears at the bottom of the screen (DSPL = 2). You must add a third message (MSG$(2)); make up your own message being sure it is at least 36 characters in length. Be sure to reDIMension MSG$ in the process.

**EXERCISE** Modify the COMPREHENSIVE EXAMPLE program so the blimps move to the right. You must also change the blimp coordinates so the blimp is facing right. This is not a trivial exercise, but even from partial success, you will learn much about animation and page flipping.

**EXERCISE** Create the blimps as shapes and use the XDRAW-XDRAW feature to accomplish blimp creation and erasure.

**CHALLENGE** Modify the COMPREHENSIVE EXAMPLE program so the flight path of blimp across the screen is V-shaped or, more simply, diagonal.

# Two-Dimensional Graphics

## MODULE 4A   Fundamental 2-D Concepts

### ACTIVITY 4.1   Scaling in General

**LEARNING BY DISCOVERY**   This activity introduces the concept of scaling in high resolution graphics.

W A R N I N G

When entering the programs in the next two chapters, the following variables may lead to programming errors if not correctly transcribed from book to keyboard.

OH, OV : 1st character is the letter "O", not the number zero;

HO, VO : 2nd character is the number zero, not the letter "O";

H1, V1 : 2nd character is the number one, not the letter "I".

1. Enter the following program.

```
NEW
10   HGR2 : HCOLOR =  3
20   WD = 10:HT = 6: REM  SET WIDTH AND HEIGHT
30   SCL = 1
40   T = 0:L = 0: REM  SCREEN COORDS OF TOP/LEFT CORNER.
50   B = HT * SCL: REM  VERTICAL SCREEN COORD (AND HEIGHT)
     OF FIGURE.
60   R = WD * SCL: REM  HORIZ SCREEN COORD (AND WIDTH) OF
     FIGURE.
70   HPLOT L,T TO L,B TO R,B TO R,T TO L,T
90   GET Q$: TEXT : HOME : END
LIST
RUN
```

Describe what happened. _____

2. Change line 30 to the following.

```
30  SCL = 10
LIST
RUN
```

Describe what happened. _____

What do you think has happened to the width and height of the original rectangle?

_____

Retype line 30 as it appears below and add line 85.

```
30   FOR SCL = 1 TO 25
85   NEXT
LIST
RUN
```

Describe what happened. _____

3. Edit the necessary statements of the program in memory to reflect the following program.

```
10   HGR2 : HCOLOR=  3
20   WD = 23:HT = 14
25   REM  TOP COORD WILL INITIALLY BE 0.
30   FOR XSCL = 1 TO 10
40   L = 0
50   B = T + HT: REM  BOTTOM COORD IS TOP + HEIGHT
60   R = WD * XSCL: REM  SCALE ONLY IN HORIZ DIRECTION.
70   HPLOT L,T TO L,B TO R,B TO R,T TO L,T
80   T = B + 5: REM  SET TOP COORD OF NEXT RECTANGLE 5
     ROWS BELOW BOTTOM COORD OF PREVIOUS RECTANGLE.
85   NEXT
90   GET Q$: TEXT : HOME : END
LIST
RUN
```

Observe the screen display.

How do the width and height of each rectangle change? _____

How many times larger in width is each successive rectangle when compared to the width of the first rectangle? _____

4. Make the following changes in the program in Section 3.

```
30   FOR YSCL = 1 TO 10
40   T = 0
50   B = HT * YSCL: REM  SCALE IN VERT DIRECTION
60   R = L + WD
80   L = R + 5: REM  SET LEFT COORD OF NEXT RECTANGLE 5
     COLUMNS TO RIGHT OF PREVIOUS RECTANGLE.
LIST
```

```
RUN
```

Observe the screen display.

How do the width and height of each rectangle change? _____

How many times larger in height is each successive rectangle when compared to the height of the first rectangle? _____

**DISCUSSION**   The multiplying factors, SCL, XSCL, and YSCL used in the above programs are called scaling factors. In each case, the width and/or height is multiplied to produce an enlargement. By the same token, one can conceivably obtain a reduction in size by multiplication. This is accomplished by multiplying the appropriate dimension value by a scaling factor.

For example, if a rectangle is of width WD = 6, and of height HT = 10, then WD * SCL and HT * SCL are the width and height of a scaled rectangle. If SCL = 8, then the scaled width and height are 48 and 80, respectively. Now suppose the lower left corner of the rectangle is positioned at L,B (the screen coordinates). Then

```
R = L + WD * SCL   and   T = B − HT * SCL
```

are the right column and top row screen coordinates of the scaled rectangle.

In each of the programs presented, the dimensions and scaling factors have been very carefully selected so the coordinates of all points lie within the screen boundaries (otherwise you would have experienced the notorious ?ILLEGAL QUANTITY error message). In the next several sections, different scaling techniques and a clipping process will be investigated. They will help avoid this potential problem. These methods will also give you tremendous flexibility in creating two- and even three-dimensional graphics displays.

**COMPREHENSIVE EXAMPLE**   Study the following APPLESOFT program to determine the screen display. Check your answer by entering the program into the computer.

```
NEW
10   REM   ********************************
11   REM   *           CE4.1             *
12   REM   ********************************
50   GOTO 100
57   REM   ********************************
58   REM   *     STAR PLOT SUBROUTINE    *
59   REM   ********************************
60   HPLOT HC + X(0) * SCL,VC − Y(0) * SCL
62   FOR K = 1 TO 8
64   HPLOT  TO HC + X(K) * SCL,VC − Y(K) * SCL
66   NEXT K
68   RETURN
69   REM   ***    END STAR PLOT SUBRT   ***
97   REM   ********************************
```

```
98   REM  *         MAIN PROGRAM          *
99   REM  ********************************
100  A = 2:B = .0075:INCR = .5: REM  INITIALIZE PARAMETERS
     USED TO CONFIGURE SHIFTING CENTER OF STAR.
     A AND B ARE COEFFICIENTS OF THE FORMULA USED TO
     COMPUTE VERT COORD OF CENTER FROM THE HORIZ COORD.
110  HGR2
120  FOR K = 0 TO 8: READ X(K),Y(K): NEXT : REM  READ THE
     VERTEX COORDS OF A STAR CONSTRUCTED IN AN X—Y COORD
     PLANE. DATA VALUES OF COORDS LISTED IN X,Y FORM.
130  FOR I = 1 TO 2 STEP 0: REM  REPEAT FOREVER...
140  COLR =  INT(RND (1) * 3) + 1: REM  PICK A RANDOM COLR
     FROM HIRES COLORS 1,2 OR 3.
150  SCL = 0: REM  START SCALE VERY SMALL!
160  IF DSPLY THEN HC = 140:VC = 92: REM  IF DSPLY (IS 1)
     THEN FIX CENTER OF STAR.
170  FOR J = 1 TO 25
180  IF  PEEK ( − 16384) > 127 THEN 500: REM  (REPEAT
     FOREVER...) UNTIL A KEY IS PRESSED!
190  IF  NOT DSPLY THEN HC = J * 8:VC = (A − B * HC) * HC:
     REM IF DISPLAY (IS 0) THEN CALCULATE SHIFTING CENTER FOR
     EACH STAR. FORMULA IS BASICALLY Y = A*X − B*X^2,
     WHERE X = HC AND Y = VC.
200  SCL = SCL + INCR: REM  INCREMENT SCALE.
210  HCOLOR =  COLR: GOSUB 60: REM  DRAW SCALED STAR.
220  FOR L = 1 TO 400: NEXT : REM  DELAY LOOP
230  HCOLOR =  0: GOSUB 60: REM  ERASE STAR.
240  NEXT J
250  DSPLY =  NOT DSPLY: REM  SWITCH DISPLAY; FROM 0--> 1 OR
     1--> 0.
260  NEXT I
269  REM  DATA VALUES FOR STAR.
270  DATA  0,5,−1,1,−6,0,−1,−1,0,−5,1,−1,6,0,1,1,0,5
280  REM  ***    END OF MAIN PROG     ***
497  REM  ******************************
498  REM  *          EXIT PROG SUBRT      *
499  REM  ******************************
500  POKE  − 16368,0: REM  RESET KEYBOARD STROBE.
510  TEXT : HOME : END
511  REM  *         END EXIT PROG SUB     *
LIST
RUN
```

## Check Your Comprehension

Line 130 is the beginning of an infinite repetition of displays. The use of a zero step size will continue the loop as often as is desired. (Why will it continue indefinitely?) It is an unusual and interesting way to avoid the use of GOTOs (which are pet peeves of programmers who prefer structured programming languages). The variable

DSPLY (display) is used to flip between the type of display: a star with shifting center (DSPLY = 0) or fixed center (DSPLY = 1). The center coordinates of the star are determined in lines 160 or 190. In the case of the star with shifting center, the non-linear formula $Y = A * X - B * X^2$ is used to determine the vertical (Y) coordinate VC from the horizontal (X) coordinate HC. The formula provides for a path of centers which is curved (actually a parabolic arc). The A and B values used were found by simple experimentation.

Precisely how does the program select between a shifting star center or a fixed star center? _____

The major purpose in presenting the example is to illustrate the power of scaling. Observe all of the stars are created from one star, with coordinates of its eight vertices saved in the arrays X(K) and Y(K). The base star was designed on graph paper with the center of the star placed at the origin of an X,Y coordinate system. The reader should plot the vertex points on graph paper to see the design in its original and raw form. In the PLOT SUBROUTINE, the dimension values are scaled by the scaling factor SCL and then added to the center screen coordinates HC and VC. These ideas will be treated in greater detail in the succeeding sections.

The scaling factor SCL is successively incremented from .5 to 12.5 in line 200; the loop variable J determines how many times SCL is incremented (25 times). Each star is first HPLOTted using a randomly selected HCOLOR of 1, 2, or 3, and then by re-HPLOTting with HCOLOR = 0 (black).

Although there are clearly eight vertices (count them!), why is an array containing nine (K = 0,...,8) points used? _____
Why are the scaled Y(K) values subtracted from VC? _____

Finally, the exit routine is based upon checking byte −16384 to determine if a key has been pressed. If a keypress occurred, then this byte will contain, in the low order bits, the ASCII value of the character pressed, and the high order bit will be set to 1. This means the numerical value will be at least 128 or greater.

The check for a keypress is made in line 180. If no keypress is detected when the conditional test is made, then execution continues to the next line number. There will be no check again for a keypress until line 180 is again encountered on a pass within the J-loop. If a keypress is detected on a pass within the J-loop, then program control branches to the EXIT SUBROUTINE beginning at line 500. Line 500 contains the tandem statement to the keypress checking statement. If a keypress has occurred, then the keyboard strobe should be reset, permitting entry of another character from the keyboard. The POKE −16368,0 accomplishes this.

Although the POKE is not needed in this program, it is a matter of good programming style and therefore has been included. Consult your APPLESOFT manual for more details of this useful command. The main reason for using this method of program exit is it permits the program to continue execution without pause. The commonly used GET statement halts execution until a response is made.

Why is the keypress check statement placed in the particular position it now occurs? For example, why not place line 180 at say, line 135, instead? _____

An interesting graphics display results if the "erasing of old stars" is deleted. Eliminate lines 220 and 230, then add a line at 135 to clear the high resolution screen (either HGR2 or CALL 62450).

```
135  HGR2
```

Make the necessary changes and RUN the program to determine the display.

**EXERCISE**   Modify the COMPREHENSIVE EXAMPLE program so the blackout of each star does not occur until after one sequence of scaled stars is displayed. The stars will be erased in order of the smallest drawn to the largest.

**CHALLENGE**   Use the method of page flipping descibed in ACTIVITY 2.16 to obtain improved animation of the enlarging and shifting stars. In particular, this method will avoid the distracting appearance of star drawing and erasure.

# ACTIVITY 4.2   Scaling to Obtain Equivalent Scales Vertically & Horizontally

**LEARNING BY DISCOVERY**   In this activity you will discover how to select scaling factors so true squares, circles, etc., can be drawn on the high resolution screen. Note: For this activity you need a metric ruler. A pair of dividers or a circle drawing compass will be handy (but not absolutely necessary).

1. Enter the following APPLESOFT commands. (Note: the VTAB 21 statement in the first line below insures the cursor will appear in the text window.)

```
HGR : HCOLOR = 3 : VTAB 21
HPLOT 140 , 9  TO  140 , 159
HPLOT 65 , 80  TO  215 , 80
```

You see, of course, two intersecting lines ... one vertical and one horizontal. Let XP denote the number of pixel units used in drawing the horizontal line, and let YP denote the number of pixel units used in the vertical line. One vertical pixel unit is the distance vertically between two successive pixels; one horizontal pixel unit is similarly defined. By investigating the HPLOT statements you entered above, record below the values of XP and YP.

XP = _____ pixel units horizontally,

YP = _____ pixel units vertically.

You should have determined each line segment is 150 pixel units long.

2. Measure the lengths of the lines on the screen, expressing your measurements to the nearest millimeter (mm). If you have dividers, they can be helpful in obtaining better accuracy when you are measuring. Position the tips of the instrument at the ends of each line segment and then measure the distance between the tips using the ruler. Record your measurements below.

Length ( XP ) = _____ mm ,
Length ( YP ) = _____ mm .

The authors measured lengths of 124 mm in width and 149 mm in height on a 13″ Amdek Color-I monitor. Your measurements may be different for your particular monitor or TV. It is quite possible, so do not worry.

3. Using the immediate execution mode of your APPLE and the lengths you determined above, compute the ratio: Length( YP ) / Length( XP ). Record in the space provided below the value of the ratio rounded to the nearest hundredth. For example, 1.30731674 is rounded to 1.31 .

SFAC = Length( YP ) / Length( XP ) = _____

The authors' value for SFAC was determined to be 1.20 . Remember, it is quite possible your value may be different, and for the best results using your particular screen, it is important to use the value of SFAC, the Screen scale FACtor, you determined above.

4. Return to the TEXT mode, clear the workspace ( NEW ), and enter the following APPLESOFT program. The program is designed to draw true squares on the high resolution screen, alternately selecting between a random width or height and then scaling the other dimension to the proper value. Since screen coordinates are discrete values (and therefore fractional parts of a pixel unit cannot be actually plotted), the screen measurements you will take of the 'squares' may not yield exactly the same width and height. The smaller the square, the more likely the relative error will be large. The program will compute and output the relative error of deviation from a true square (line 150).

```
NEW
10   SFAC = 1.20: REM   ENTER YOUR SCREEN SCALE FACTOR IF
     DIFFERENT.
20   HC = 140:VC = 80: REM   CENTER COORDS OF HIRES
     MIXED-GRAPHICS SCREEN.
30   FOR I = 1 TO 2: REM   FOR FIRST THE HEIGHT DIMENSION (I
     = 1) AND THEN THE WIDTH DIMENSION (I = 2), ...
40   FOR J = 1 TO 2: REM   SELECT TWO 'SQUARES' IN WHICH THE
     SAME DIMENSION VALUE HAS BEEN RANDOMLY SELECTED.
50   HGR : HCOLOR =   3: HOME : VTAB 21
60   S = S + 1: REM   INCREMENT THE VARIABLE DESIGNATING THE
     NUMBER OF THE 'SQUARE'.
70   PRINT S;") RECORD THE HEIGHT AND WIDTH IN MM OF"
80   PRINT "THE 'SQUARE' DRAWN ABOVE...THEN INPUT"
90   ON I GOSUB 200,300: REM   IF I = 1 GO GET RANDOM HEIGHT;
     IF I = 2 GO GET RANDOM WIDTH.
100   HL = HC − XP / 2:HR = HL + XP: REM   COMPUTE LEFT AND
      RIGHT SCREEN COORDS OF CENTERED 'SQUARE'.
110   VB = VC + YP / 2:VT = VB − YP: REM   COMPUTE BOTTOM
      AND TOP SCREEN COORDS OF CENTERD 'SQUARE'.
120   HPLOT HL,VB TO HR,VB TO HR,VT TO HL,VT TO HL,VB: REM
```

```
       DRAW THE 'SQUARE'.
130    INPUT "THE OBSERVED HEIGHT, WIDTH?";HT,WD: REM  GET
       MEASURED VALUES OF HT AND WD OF 'SQUARE' ON SCREEN.
140    PRINT "THE RELATIVE ERROR IN DEVIATION FROM A"
150    PRINT "TRUE SQUARE IS "; INT (100 *  ABS (WD — HT) /
       HT);"%": REM  DETERMINE THE REL ERROR, ABS(WD—HT)/HT,
       AND THEN CONVERT TO % ROUNDED TO NEAREST WHOLE
       NUMBER.
160    PRINT "PRESS ANY KEY TO CONTINUE.";: GET K$
170    NEXT J,I
180    TEXT : HOME : END
197    REM  *******************************
198    REM  *   RANDOM HGT SELECT SUBRT   *
199    REM  *******************************
200    YP =   INT (100 *  RND (1)) + 50: REM  PICK A RANDOM
       HGT BETWEEN 50 AND 149.
210    XP = YP * SFAC: REM  DETERMINE EQUIVALENT WIDTH.
220    RETURN
221    REM  **  END RAND HGT SELECT SUBR **
297    REM  *******************************
298    REM  *   RANDOM WDTH SELECT SUBRT  *
299    REM  *******************************
300    XP =   INT (100 *  RND (1)) + 50: REM  SELECT A RANDOM
       WIDTH BETWEEN 50 AND 149.
310    YP = XP / SFAC: REM  DETERMINE EQUIVALENT HEIGHT.
320    RETURN
321    REM  **  END RAND WD SELECT SUBRT **
LIST
RUN
```

The program will give you an opportunity to test the screen scale factor, SFAC, determined in Section 3. Use the spaces below to record the measurements requested of you by the program.

### 'SQUARE' HEIGHT AND WIDTH IN mm

| | | |
|---|---|---|
| 1) vert. _____ mm | 2) vert. _____ mm | |
| horiz. _____ mm | horiz. _____ mm | |
| rel error _____ % | rel error _____ % | |
| 3) vert. _____ mm | 4) vert. _____ mm | |
| horiz. _____ mm | horiz. _____ mm | |
| rel error _____ % | rel error _____ % | |

The program will provide a measure of the relative error of each figure from a true square. Your error should remain within 10%. If you obtain larger errors, you may need to recheck the value of SFAC you determined in Sections 1-3. The reader should note the smaller figures may have a larger percentage of relative error. This is due primarily to truncation error in converting fractional coordinate values to integer screen coordinates.

Which set of squares has its width determined by random selection? its height by random selection? _____

**DISCUSSION**   The quantity SFAC determined in Section 3 represents a scaling factor for converting vertical distances to equivalent horizontal distances on the screen (1/ SFAC is used for the reverse process). SFAC is dependent on the type of video screen used in conjunction with the APPLE II; it may have a different value for different makes or sizes of video screen.

For example, if SFAC = 1.20, then 30 vertical pixel units will equal 30 * SFAC = 30 * 1.20 = 36 horizontal pixel units in length. Similarly, 50 horizontal pixel units will equal 50 / SFAC = 50 / 1.20 = 41.7 (approx.) vertical pixel units in length. To summarize this into easy to remember formulas:

### FORMULAS FOR OBTAINING EQUIVALENT SCREEN DISTANCES
HORIZ = VERT * SFAC  :  VERT = HORIZ / SFAC .

**COMPREHENSIVE EXAMPLE**   Study the following APPLESOFT program to determine the screen display. Check your answer by entering the program and then RUNning it. Don't be alarmed by its deceiving code length. It is well documented to permit the reader complete understanding of its instructions. The actual set of executable program commands is comparatively small. It serves a dual purpose as well. It supplies the reader with an example of the construction of a menu driven program.

Note the main body of the program consists of little more than printing the menu and then handling the user's response in line 210 with an ON . . . GOSUB command. Recall the command will branch execution to the Nth line number in the list following the GOSUB, if N is the value of the expression between the ON and GOSUB. If N is 0 or greater than the number of listed line numbers, then program execution proceeds to the next statement.

Lines 400 and 410 of the program use the functions SINe and COSine for plotting the circles. You encountered them earlier in another activity. A detailed discussion of the SINe and COSine will be treated in ACTIVITY 4.7. Therefore, if you are unfamiliar with these functions, do not labor to understand all of the circle construction routine in lines 390-410.

```
NEW
10   REM   *********************************
11   REM   *            CE4.2              *
12   REM   *********************************
13   REM
97   REM   *********************************
98   REM   *         MAIN PROGRAM          *
99   REM   *********************************
100  SFAC = 1.20: REM  USE YOUR SCREEN SCALE FACTOR IF
     DIFFERENT.
110  BLK = 0:WHT = 3: REM  INIT COLOR VARIABLES FOR BLACK1 AND
     WHITE1.
```

```
120   TEXT : HOME
130   VTAB 2: HTAB 5: PRINT "AN EQUIVALENT SCALING DEMO"
140   VTAB 5:T$ = "MENU": HTAB 20 —  LEN (T$) / 2: PRINT T$:
      REM PRINT TITLE CENTERED.
150   HTAB 5: FOR I = 1 TO 30: PRINT "—";: NEXT : REM  NOTE THE
      SEMICOLON AFTER PRINT "—".
160   VTAB 9: HTAB 5: PRINT "1. COMPARE PSEUDO AND": HTAB 9:
      PRINT "TRUE CIRCLES"
170   VTAB 13: HTAB 5: PRINT "2. COMPARE PSEUDO AND": HTAB 9:
      PRINT "TRUE EQUILATERAL TRIANGLES": REM  'EQUILATERAL'
      MEANS ALL SIDES ARE THE SAME LENGTH.
180   VTAB 17: HTAB 5: PRINT "3. EXIT PROGRAM"
190   VTAB 20: HTAB 10: PRINT "SELECT (1,2, OR 3) ";: GET K$
200   DSPLY =  VAL (K$): REM  CONVERT TO NUMERIC VALUE
210   ON DSPLY GOSUB 300,600,230
220   GOTO 120: REM  GO BACK AND REPRINT MENU AND SET UP FOR
      DISPLAY CHOICE. IF USER DOES NOT SELECT BETWEEN 1,2, OR 3
      THEN HE/SHE WILL BE REPROMPTED.
230   TEXT : HOME : END
231   REM  ***   END OF MAIN PROGRAM   ***
232   REM
297   REM  ********************************
298   REM  *   COMPARE CIRCLES ROUTINE   *
299   REM  ********************************
300   HGR : REM  CLEAR HIRES SCREEN PAGE1, MIXED GRAPHICS
310   HCOLOR =  WHT: REM  SET PLOT COLOR TO WHITE.
320   HOME : VTAB 21: PRINT "INPUT THE RADIUS OF THE CIRCLE. I
      WILL": PRINT "DRAW THE PSEUDO AND TRUE CIRCLES."
330   INPUT "INPUT THE RADIUS (< = 60)? ";R
340   IF R < 0 OR R > 60 THEN  PRINT "INVALID SIZE! TRY
      AGAIN.": GOTO 330
350   HOME : VTAB 21
360   FOR CIRC = 1 TO 2: REM  FOR TWO CIRCLES DO...
370   IF CIRC = 1 THEN HC = 68:VC = 80:SCL = 1: REM  IF 1ST
      CIRCLE THEN SET CENTER NEAR LEFT AND SET SCALE FACTOR
      = 1.
380   IF CIRC = 2 THEN HC = 206:VC = 80:SCL = SFAC: REM  IF
      2ND CIRCLE THEN SET CENTER NEAR RIGHT AND SET SCALE
      FACTOR = SFAC FOR OBTAINING HORIZ DIST EQUIVALENT
      TO VERT DIST.
390   FOR THETA = 0 TO 6.30 STEP .05: REM  PLOT CIRCLE PTS FOR
      EACH RADIAN VALUE FROM 0 TO 2*PI. SINES AND COSINES AND
      THEIR PRECISE RELATIONSHIP TO CIRCLES ARE TREATED IN
      DETAIL IN ACTIVITY 4.7.
400   Y% = R *  SIN (THETA) + .5: REM  COMPUTE Y-COORD, ROUND
      AND TRUNCATE TO INTEGER VALUE.
410   X = R *  COS (THETA):X% = X * SCL + .5: REM  COMPUTE
```

```
      X-COORD AND SCALE HORIZONTALLY. THEN ROUND AND TRUNCATE TO
      INTEGER VALUE.
420   HPLOT HC + X%,VC - Y%: REM  PLOT PT ON CIRCLE.
430   NEXT THETA
440   IF CIRC = 1 THEN  PRINT "PSEUDO CIRCLE": PRINT 2 * R;"
      WIDE, ";2 * R;" HIGH": REM  PRINT LABEL AND HORZ AND VERT
      PIXEL DIAMETERS FOR 1ST CIRCLE.
450   IF CIRC = 2 THEN  VTAB 21: HTAB 25: PRINT "TRUE CIRCLE":
      HTAB 22: PRINT 2 * R * SFAC;" WIDE, ";2 * R;" HIGH"
460   NEXT CIRC
470   FOR I = 1 TO 1000: NEXT : REM  DELAY
480   INPUT "TRY ANOTHER RADIUS? ";Q$
490   IF  LEFT$ (Q$,1) = "Y" THEN 300
500   RETURN : REM  IF ANY RESPONSE OTHER THAN "Y..." THEN
      RETURN TO MAIN PROG.
501   REM  **    END CIRCLE COMPARE SUB  **
502   REM
597   REM  *******************************
598   REM  * COMPARE EQUILAT. TRIANGLES  *
599   REM  *******************************
600   HGR : REM  CLEAR HIRES SCREEN PAGE1, MIXED GRAPHICS
610   HCOLOR =  WHT: REM  SET PLOT COLOR TO WHITE1.
620   HOME : VTAB 21: PRINT "INPUT A LENGTH FOR THE BASE. I
      WILL": PRINT "DRAW THE PSEUDO AND TRUE EQUILATERAL": PRINT
      "TRIANGLES (ALL SIDES THE SAME LENGTH)."
630   INPUT "INPUT THE BASE LENGTH ( < =130) ?";B
640   IF B > 130 THEN  PRINT "INVALID SIZE. TRY AGAIN!": GOTO
      630
650   HOME : VTAB 21
660   HT = B *  SQR (3) / 2: REM  DETERMINE HEIGHT OF
      EQUILATERAL TRIANGLE HAVING BASE LENGTH B. SQR( ) IS THE
      SQUARE ROOT FUNCTION.
670   VB = 80 + HT / 2: REM  DETERM BOTTOM VERT COORD SO
      TRIANGLES ARE APPROX. CENTERED VERTICALLY.
680   FOR TRNG = 1 TO 2: REM  FOR EACH OF TWO TRIANGLES DO...
690   IF TRNG = 1 THEN SCL = 1:HC = 70: REM  IF 1ST TRIANGLE
      THEN DON'T SCALE AND SET LEFT CENTER HORIZ COORD.
700   IF TRNG = 2 THEN SCL = 1 / SFAC:HC = 210: REM  IF 2ND
      TRIANGLE THEN SET VERT SCALE FOR OBTAINING VERT DISTANCES
      EQUIV TO HORIZ DISTANCES.
710   V(TRNG) = HT * SCL: REM  DETERMINE SCALED HEIGHT.
720   VT = VB - V(TRNG): REM  SET VERT COORD OF TOP VERTEX V
      UNITS FROM BASE.
730   HL = HC - B / 2:HR = HL + B: REM  DETERMINE HORIZ
      COORDS OF BASE VERTICES ON THE LEFT AND RIGHT. RECALL THAT
      HORIZ COORD HC OF TOP VERTEX SHOULD BE THE MIDPT OF THE
      BASE VERTICES, HENCE... THE FORMULAS USED HERE.
```

```
740   HPLOT HR,VB TO HL,VB TO HC,VT TO HR,VB: REM  PLOT
      TRIANGLE.
750   EDG(TRNG) =  SQR ((B / 2) ^ 2 + V(TRNG) ^ 2): REM
      DETERMINE LENGTH OF THE OTHER 2 SIDES OF THE TRIANGLE
      USING PYTHAGORAS; C^2 = A^2 + B^2. USED FOR LABELING
      ONLY.
760   EDG(TRNG) =  INT (10 * EDG(TRNG) + .5) / 10: REM  ROUND
      EDGE LENGTH TO NEAREST TENTH.
770   NEXT TRNG
780   PRINT "PSEUDO EQUILATERAL"; TAB( 22);"TRUE EQUILATERAL":
      PRINT  TAB( 5);"TRIANGLE"; TAB( 26);"TRIANGLE"
790   PRINT "SIDES: "B","EDG(1)","EDG(1);: PRINT  TAB(
      22);B","EDG(2)","EDG(2): REM  PRINT SIDE LENGTHS.
800   FOR I = 1 TO 1000: NEXT : REM  DELAY
810   INPUT "TRY ANOTHER TRIANGLE? ";Q$
820   IF  LEFT$ (Q$,1) = "Y" THEN 600
830   RETURN : REM  IF RESPONSE IS OTHER THAN "Y..." THEN GO
      BACK TO MAIN PROG.
831   REM  **  END EQUILAT TRNGLE DSPLY **
LIST
RUN
```

When RUNning the program, be sure to test the circle and equilateral triangle constructions with a wide range of input values. It is even advisable to retrieve your ruler and check some of the displays for accuracy of claimed results. In this regard, some explanation of the numeric values printed below each circle label is definitely required. The width and height values supplied beneath the circle labels are much easier to explain and will be undertaken first.

When a radius value for the circle is input (into the variable R), the X and Y coordinates of points on a circle of radius R, assumed to be centered at the origin, are calculated using well established methods (the COSine and SINe methods already alluded to). Theoretically, when these values are added to the center coordinates, a set of points on a circle of radius R will result. This result occurs under the implied assumption the unit of length in each direction is the same. The scales in both directions on the screen are not necessarily equivalent. If one applies the standard formulas directly, the result is the PSEUDO CIRCLE (SCL = 1). When the adjustment to equivalent scales is made (SCL = SFAC), the TRUE CIRCLE results. Thus, the width and height displayed beneath each circle represent the horizontal and vertical pixel lengths of diameters through the circle center. Lines 440 and 450 control the display of these values. If one single unit of length is chosen, for example the vertical pixel unit, then the TRUE CIRCLE will measure R units in diametric width and height. The PSEUDO CIRCLE will measure R units in diametric height and R / SFAC units in diametric width.

For example, if R = 60, then the PSEUDO CIRCLE will be 60 (horiz) pixels wide and 60 (vert) pixels high. In vertical pixel units, it is 60 high, but 60 / SFAC = 60 / 1.20 = 50 wide! The TRUE CIRCLE is 60 (vert) pixel units high and approximately 60 (vert) pixel units wide. But it is 60 * SFAC = 60 * 1.20 = 72 pixels wide horizontally.

The values appearing beneath the label on each triangle represent the input base width and the lengths of the remaining two sides. These lengths are determined by application of the theorem of Pythagoras on right triangles: The square of the hypotenuse length is the sum of the squares of the two arm lengths (see Figure 4.2.1).

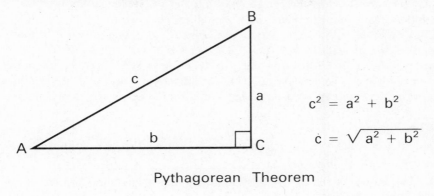

Pythagorean  Theorem

Figure 4.2.1

The problem again is the Pythagorean theorem makes an implied assumption the units of length in all directions are equivalent. From the theorem, one can ascertain the altitude of an equilateral triangle is one half the base width times the square root of 3. This is applied in line 660. In line 710 the altitude is either unchanged (result = PSEUDO EQUIL. TRIANGLE) or is scaled by 1/SFAC (result = TRUE EQUIL. TRIANGLE).

In using the formula, different units of length are being mixed. This occurred in line 750; line 760 merely rounded the result to the nearest tenth. If one single unit of length is used, say the horizontal pixel unit, then the TRUE EQUIL. TRIANGLE has side lengths of B, B, and B units. The PSEUDO EQUIL. TRIANGLE has side lengths of b = B, c, and c units for a = B/2 * SQR (3) * SFAC units.

For example, suppose a base width of B = 100 is input. For each triangle the base width is 100 (horiz) pixels. Mathematically, the altitude is 100 * SQR(3) / 2 = 85.5 high where SQR(3) is the square root of three (i.e., approximately 1.732). If this value is used to position the top vertex of the triangle, then the PSEUDO EQUIL. TRIANGLE results.

The problem is 85.5 VERT pixel units and 100/2 HORIZ pixel units are used concurrently in the Pythagorean formula. If arm lengths of 100/2 and 85.5 are substituted into the formula, then a value of 100 is returned. This is done in line 150, and the result displayed in line 790. Unfortunately, what seems natural leads to an incorrect result because units of length are being mixed within the formula.

To construct the TRUE EQUIL. TRIANGLE, the altitude is scaled by 1 / SFAC, converting 85.5 (horiz pixel units) to the equivalent number of vertical pixels: 85.5 / SFAC = 85.5 / 1.2 = 71.25 (vert) pixels. The TRUE EQUIL. TRIANGLE results.

When arm lengths of 100/2 and 71.25 are substituted into the Pythagorean formula, one obtains deceiving results for the lengths of the other two sides. The triangle appears equilateral but the numbers don't indicate it. The problem again is different units of length are being used in the formula. The correct interpretation is a base width of 100 and altitude of 85.5 (horiz pixel) units is displayed, resulting in an edge length of approximately 100 (horiz pixel) units; the 85.5 (horiz pixel) units is equivalent to 71.25 (vert pixel) units.

The reader is invited to make the necessary corrections in lines 440, 450, and 790 to display the correct values. Of course, lines 750 and 760 no longer are necessary. The less ambitious reader can eliminate these lines altogether.

If the preceding discussion seems confusing to you, don't worry. It took the authors a while make sense out of it too! The point is if you want to accurately reflect proportionate distances on the screen: 1) the scale factor SFAC must be used and; 2) caution should be invoked when applying formulas which use both horizontal and vertical distances. Blind adherence in using such formulas can lead to deceiving results.

### Check Your Comprehension

To obtain a true circle on the screen with a horizontal diameter of 60 pixel units, what is the vertical diameter? _____

What precautions should be taken when attempting to apply any distance formulas to the "screen coordinate" system? _____

**EXERCISE**   Write a program to draw a sequence of ten concentric truly square diamonds on high resolution screen Page 2 having horizontal diagonal widths of 20, 40, 60, ..., 200 pixels. Center the diamonds at the point 140, 96.

**CHALLENGE**   Write a program which will permit the user to input two values, representing the horizontal and vertical offsets between two points on the screen. Insist on positive values to be entered. Now, imagining these two points to be adjacent vertices on the edge of a square on the screen, draw the true square centered on the screen. If input values are kept within 0 to 95 you should experience no difficulty in fitting the square on the screen.

## ACTIVITY 4.3   Scaling to Achieve a Full Viewport

**LEARNING BY DISCOVERY**   This activity will show you how to transform a rectangular region and any figures within it onto a rectangular region of the APPLE screen. Scaling techniques are used.

1. On a sheet of paper draw a rectangle of any size (eg., lengths of approximately 10 - 20 cm will be satisfactory). List below the width and height of your rectangle.

RW(idth) = _____   RH(eight) = _____

Draw a triangle inside your rectangle. Let A, B, and C denote the vertices of your triangle. Measuring from the lower left-hand corner of your rectangle, determine the distances horizontally, $X(I)$, and vertically, $Y(I)$, the point A (cf., I = 0) is from this corner. (See Figure 4.3.1.) Record your values below. Repeat taking the measurements for vertices B and C (cf., I = 1 and I = 2).

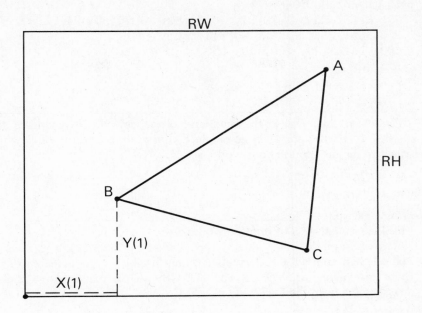

Figure 4.3.1

| Vertex A | Vertex B | Vertex C |
|---|---|---|
| X(0) = _____ | X(1) = _____ | X(2) = _____ |
| Y(0) = _____ | Y(1) = _____ | Y(2) = _____ |

2. The problem to be resolved is one of "transporting" the rectangle and the corresponding triangle within to a specified but arbitrary rectangular region on the APPLE high resolution screen. This restricted region on the screen is called the viewport. The objective is to preserve the relative position of points within the original rectangle, mapping the boundaries of the rectangle onto the boundaries of the viewport.

The reader is cautioned about possibly misunderstanding the image to be obtained on the high resolution screen. It will not in general represent a photographic enlargement or reduction of the given rectangle and points within it. Rather, there may be distortion of the original figure after the transfer process. The effect can compared to what would be obtained using a "rubber sheet." Imagine your rectangle and the included area to be a sheet of perfectly elastic material with the triangle drawn on it. By stretching or compressing the corners of the rubber sheet to meet those of the viewport, we obtain the transported image of the rectangle and its internal points.

3. Let's consider the viewport to be bounded between columns 20 and 260, and between rows 10 and 150. These have been chosen arbitrarily; any column or row values can be used. Enter the following APPLESOFT program.

```
NEW
50  READ HO, H1, V1, VO
```

```
60   HGR : HCOLOR = 3
70   HPLOT H0, V0 TO H1, V0 TO H1, V1 TO H0, V1 TO H0, V0
200  GET Q$ : TEXT : HOME : END
600  DATA  20, 260, 10, 150
LIST
RUN
```

Describe the display. _____

The screen display shows the boundaries of the viewport. By changing the DATA in line 600, other viewports can be obtained. For example, add the following DATA statement to the program in your workspace.

```
590  DATA  0, 100, 0, 90
RUN
```

Describe what you see. _____

DELete statement 590 from the workspace.

4. Let WDSCR and HTSCR denote width and height in pixel units of the viewport. Enter the values for WDSCR and HTSCR used in the program in Section 3, determinable from the DATA in line 600.

WDSCR = H1 − H0 = _____ and HTSCR = V0 − V1 = _____
To accomplish the desired transformation of points one must have (the symbol "~" used below may be read "corresponds to" or "is proportional to")

RW cm horiz ~ WDSCR pixels horiz,

so

1 cm horiz ~ WDSCR / RW pixels horiz.
Similarly,

RH cm vert ~ HTSCR pixels vert,
so that

1 cm vert ~ HTSCR/RH pixels vert.

Compute the scale ratios determined above using the immediate execution mode of your APPLE and record the values below.

XSCL = WDSCR/RW = _____ : YSCL = HTSCR/RH = _____

The formulas developed above show how to convert horizontal and vertical distances in your rectangle to corresponding distances within the viewport. For example, if a point P is 3 cm and 2.2 cm to the right and up, respectively, from the lower left corner of the rectangle, then the corresponding point SP (screen point) in the viewport will be

3 * XSCL horiz pixels and 2.2 * YSCL vert pixels
from the lower left corner of the viewport, that is, from the point H0, V0. Compute the values indicated in the above expression and write them below.

3 * XSCL = _____
and 2.2 * YSCL = _____

The coordinates of the point SP in the viewport will be
H0 + 3 * XSCL,    V0 − 2.2 * YSCL

Note: It is necessary to subtract from V0 because of the way rows are numbered on the high resolution screen.

Compute the coordinates of the point SP where H0 = 20 and V0 = 150, and enter below.

Screen coordinates of SP = _____ , _____

Note: If the values of the screen coordinates are fractional, then truncate the values when listing them above. This is exactly how the APPLE will handle the coordinates when actually HPLOTting the point SP. For example, if the coordinate computations yield the values 233.8, 74.23 then SP will be HPLOTted at 233, 74.

5. Add the following statements to the program in memory.

```
10   READ RW , RH
20   FOR I = 0 TO 2
30   READ X(I) , Y(I)
40   NEXT I
400  DATA < enter RW , RH from section 1. >
500  DATA < enter X(0) , Y(0) , X(1) , Y(1) , X(2) , Y(2)
     from section 1. >
LIST
```

The statements just entered will store the pertinent information about the rectangle and the interior points of interest.

Add the following block of lines to obtain the scaling factors XSCL and YSCL previously discussed.

```
80    GOSUB 1000
1000 WDSCR = H1 - H0 : HTSCR = V0 - V1
1010 XSCL = WDSCR / RW : YSCL = HTSCR / RH
1030 RETURN
LIST
```

Finally, the triangle itself is obtained by adding the following lines.

```
90    X(3) = X(0) : Y(3) = Y(0) : REM LAST PT = FIRST PT
100  HPLOT H0 + X(0) * XSCL , V0 - Y(0) * YSCL
110  FOR I = 1 TO 3
120  HPLOT TO H0 + X(I) * XSCL , V0 - Y(I) * YSCL
130  NEXT
LIST
```

Check to be sure all lines of code are correct and then RUN the program. At last, our triangle. It may seem like a lot of trouble for such trivial results, but the techniques discussed here serve as a foundation for a collection of exciting and powerful programs to be developed. One immediate application is that the method will permit transference of almost any picture to the APPLE screen.

The general process can be described as follows. Frame the picture to be copied with a rectangle and overlay with a sheet of transparent graph paper. Select a collection of discrete points in the order in which they are to be drawn, determining the graph paper coordinates as you proceed. Dummy coordinate values may be used to indicate when a contiguous curve is to be stopped and a new one is to begin. The picture can now be transferred to the high resolution screen using scaling techniques.

6. To observe the effect of changing the viewport, enter the following lines of code.

```
600  DATA 50 , 150 , 50 , 150
RUN
```

Describe what you see. _____

```
600  DATA 140 , 279 , 0 , 80
RUN
```

Describe what you see. _____

**DISCUSSION**   Reviewing the major points of this activity, suppose a collection of points, figures, etc., is contained within a specified rectangle of width RW and height RH. Suppose further a specified rectangular region of the high resolution screen, the viewport, is of width WDSCR and height HTSCR. The scale factors for converting horizontal and vertical distances within the rectangle to relative distances within the viewport are given by

XSCL = WDSCR / RW : YSCL = HTSCR / RH .

Let (P,Q) denote the coordinates of a fixed point relative to the rectangle, and (HP,VQ) denote the screen coordinates of the corresponding point relative to the viewport. Then

H = HP + (X − P) * XSCL , V = VQ − (Y − Q) * YSCL ,

are the formulas for converting a point (X,Y) in the rectangle to a point (H,V) on the screen. It is assumed here the positive sense of directions in determining the coordinates are to the right and up, respectively. X − P and Y − Q represent the signed or directed distances between (X,Y) and (P,Q), parallel to the sides of the rectangle.

There are several ways the point (P,Q) can be selected. The method used in the prior sections of this activity is to let (P,Q) denote the lower left corner of the rectangle. In this case, the lower left coordinate of the viewport, (H0,V0), is chosen as the corresponding point (HP,VQ) on the screen. If the rectangle is a rectangular region of a coordinate plane, then one can choose (P,Q) as the origin (0,0) regardless of whether it is in the rectangular region or not.

The calculation of the screen coordinates of the corresponding point (OH,OV) on (in reality, it may be off) the screen requires explanation. Suppose (A,C) are the coordinates of the lower left corner of the rectangle, and (H0,V0) are the screen coordinates of the lower left corner of the viewport. Taking X = 0 and Y = 0 in the formula above, one obtains

OH = H0 + (0 − A) * XSCL = H0 − A * XSCL

OV = V0 − (0 − C) * YSCL = V0 + C * YSCL

These expressions can be used to find OH and OV. Once this is done, then the transformation formulas simplify to

H = OH + X * XSCL : V = OV − Y * YSCL

It is instructive to work through one more example. Consider the following collection of points in a coordinate plane.

(8,12), (20,4), (10,14), (14,−1), (16,11)

Consider the smallest rectangle with sides parallel to the coordinate axes containing these points. Specifically, what are the left, right, top, and bottom coordinates? Calculating

$$\min X = \min(8,20,10,14,16) = 8 = A$$
$$\max X = \max(8,20,10,14,16) = 20 = B$$
$$\min Y = \min(12,4,14,-1,11) = -1 = C$$
$$\max Y = \max(12,4,14,-1,11) = 14 = D$$

$$RW = B - A = 20 - 8 = 12, \quad RH = D - C = 14 - (-1) = 15$$

Now suppose the viewport is taken to be the mixed graphics high resolution screen: $(H0,H1,V1,V0) = (0,279,0,159)$. Then

$$WDSCR = H1 - H0 = 279, \quad HTSCR = V0 - V1 = 159$$

and

$$XSCL = WDSCR/RW = 279/12 = 23.25$$
$$YSCL = HTSCR/RH = 159/15 = 10.6$$

The screen coordinates of the point on the screen corresponding to the origin $(0,0)$ are given by

$$OH = H0 - A * XSCL = 0 - 8 * 23.25 \quad = -166$$
$$OV = V0 + C * YSCL = 159 + (-1) * 10.6 = 148.4$$

Using the transformation formula above, the screen coordinates, say, of $(X,Y) = (10,14)$, are given by

$$H = OH + X * XSCL = -166 + 10 * 23.25 = 64.5$$
$$V = OV - Y * YSCL = 148.4 - 14 * 10.6 = 0$$

What are the screen coordinates $(H,V)$ of the point $(X,Y) = (8,12)$ ? of $(16,11)$ ?

**WARNING:** Although the transformation formulas are mathematically correct for any viewport and any rectangle, computer round-off error can possibly effect run-time errors when a viewport boundary is either the left or top screen edge. Specifically, there is the chance that a point, very near the boundary of the original rectangle, can transform (by virtue of round-off error) to a screen point with corresponding screen coordinate very near zero in value, but negative. For example, the number $-1E-38$ (or $-0. < 37$ zeros $> 1$) is extremely small in absolute value, but nonetheless, it is a negative number. Because the HPLOT command truncates each coordinate to the greatest integer less than or equal to the (coordinate) value, the HPLOT is equivalently performed on the point with the integer coordinate value equal to $-1$. This will appropriately result in an ?ILLEGAL QUANTITY error message.

A solution to the malady is to simply choose V0 and H1 greater than or equal to one. If this restriction is imposed on V0 and H1, then all transformed points will be legitimate screen points. Another solution is to round coordinate values to the nearest integer.

This warning is not meant to discourage you from using the full screen as the viewport, but rather to inform you of a possible (but highly unusual) situation. If a scaled display results in execution problems and one of the viewport boundary values is zero, remembering this discussion may resolve the "bug."

**COMPREHENSIVE EXAMPLE**   On a sheet of $8.5 \times 11$ paper (positioned in front of you so the longest side is horizontal), draw the points P(X,Y) defined below, where X and Y are the distances in inches horizontally and vertically from the lower left hand corner of the paper. The points are at (6,6.5), (4,2), (9,5), (3,5), and (8,2). Let P1, P2, P3, P4, and P5 denote the points as listed. Connect the points by straight lines in the sequence

P1 — > P2 — > P3 — > P4 — > P5 — > P1

The objective is to write a program which will:

1) Read the points as data;
2) Determine the minimum rectangle containing the given set of points and permit entry of any rectangle containing the minimum rectangle;
3) Permit the user to select any viewport of their choice; and
4) Transform the points from the rectangle to the viewport and connect them by straight lines in the sequence described.

With only slightly more effort, the program can be designed to handle any set of coordinate data for points which may or may not be connected by straight lines. The assumption is the majority of the points will be connected by straight lines in a continuous fashion. The use of HPLOT TO statements is an approach conducive to such collections of points; of course, the beginning point in the group must be HPLOT-ted.

In order to identify the beginning of a block of points sequentially connected by straight lines, and to identify the termination of a similar block, a dummy data pair such as $-9,-9$ will be inserted between the blocks of data. Two dummy values are inserted since data will be read in pairs X,Y. The value $-9$ is referred to as an End-of-PLot-to value and is stored in the variable EPL.

In order to test this feature, add the following points on your paper Q1(9.5,6.5), Q2(9.5,2), Q3(11,2), Q4(11,6.5); and R1(2.5,6.5), R2(2.5,2), R3(1,2), R4(1,6.5). Connect them by straight lines in the sequences

Q1 — > Q2 — > Q3 — > Q4 — > Q1
R1 — > R2 — > R3 — > R4 — > R1

Since the number of actual data points may be unknown, some way is needed to determine when the data has been completely read. One solution is to use the ONERR GOTO statement. If the number of data items is very large, this approach can eliminate the execution time involved in constantly checking for the end of file. The use of a dummy pair of values at the end of the data is the approach used in the COMPREHENSIVE EXAMPLE. As data is read in pairs, one of the values is tested for equality with EOF, the end-of-file variable. The value −99 is used in the program below to designate the end-of-file and is assigned to EOF.

In using such end-of-file or end-of-plot values, the user must make sure they are completely different from any of the data values. Otherwise, erroneous or incomplete displays can result. In line 110 in the program below, the EOF and EPL variables are assigned appropriate values for the DATA supplied. It is the user's responsibility to make the necessary adjustments for new DATA.

Finally, although in most cases the minimum rectangle will be the rectangle you want to transform to the viewport, the program will permit entry of any larger rectangle. The values XL, XR, YL, and YR denote the coordinates of minimum rectangle, and A, B, C, and D denote the coordinates of the rectangle to be transformed.

The length of the program below (about 12 sectors without REMarks) is due primarily to the input routines and error checking of input. The actual computation statements and plotting statements constitute a very small portion of the program.

```
NEW
10   REM   ********************************
11   REM   *          CE4.3              *
12   REM   ********************************
13   REM
97   REM   ********************************
98   REM   *        MAIN PROGRAM         *
99   REM   ********************************
100  GOSUB 7000: REM  GO TO INITIALIZATION ROUTINE.
110  EOF = −99 : EPL = −9: REM  EOF = END-OF-FILE VALUE;
     EPL = END-OF-HPLOT TO VALUE. THE USER MUST CHANGE THESE
     DEFINITIONS IF DIFFERENT VALUES ARE USED IN THE
     DISPLAY DATA.
120  HOME
130  PRINT : PRINT  TAB( 10);"*** READING DATA ***"
140  GOSUB 2000: REM  GO GET MAX AND MIN VALUES OF X- AND
     Y-COORDS. VALUES RETURNED IN VARIABLES XL = MIN X, XR =
     MAX X, YL = MIN Y, YR = MAX Y.
150  A = XL:B = XR:C = YL:D = YR: REM  INITIALLY SET
     ENCLOSING RECTANGLE TO MINIMUM RECTANGLE.
160  HGR : HCOLOR =  3: REM  INIT HIRES SCREEN AND HCOLOR.
170  H0 = 0:H1 = 279:V0 = 191:V1 = 0: REM  INITIALIZE
     VIEWPORT PARAMETERS TO FULL SCREEN.
```

```
180   GOSUB 3000: REM  GO TO ROUTINE TO PERMIT USER TO SELECT
      DIFF RECTANGLE BOUNDS IF WANTED.
190   RW = B — A:RH = D — C: REM  SET THE WIDTH AND HEIGHT OF
      RECTANGLE CONTAINING PTS X,Y.
200   GOSUB 4000: REM  GO TO VIEWPORT SELECT SUBRT.
210   WDSCR = H1 — HO:HTSCR = VO — V1: REM  SET VIEWPORT
      WIDTH AND HEIGHT.
220   HOME : VTAB 22
230   POKE  — 16304,0: POKE  — 16297,0: POKE  — 16301,0: REM
      TOGGLE HIRES GRAPHICS SWITCHES; MIXED MODE.
240   PRINT "CLEAR THE SCREEN? < Y/N > ";
250   GET K$: PRINT K$
260   IF K$ = "Y" THEN  CALL 62450
270   POKE  — 16302,0: REM  SET FULL SCREEN GRAPHICS SWITCH
      'ON'.
280   RESTORE : REM  RESTORE DATA POINTERS SO THAT DATA CAN BE
      REREAD FOR PLOTTING.
290   GOSUB 5000: REM  GO TO PLOTTING SUBRT.
300   POKE  — 16301,0: REM  SET MIXED GRAPHICS SWITCH 'ON'.
310   PRINT " < F > :FULL SCREEN"; TAB( 20);" < D > :DISPLAY
      VIEWPORT"
320   PRINT " < V > :NEW VIEWPORT"; TAB( 20);" < Q > :QUIT"
330   PRINT " < R > :NEW RECTANGLE"
340   VTAB 24: HTAB 25: INVERSE : PRINT "SELECT KEY:";: NORMAL :
      PRINT " ";: GET K$: REM  PRINT PROMPT MESSG AND WAIT FOR
      KEYPRESS.
350   IF K$ = "R" THEN 180: REM  IF NEW RECT BOUNDS ARE WANTED
      THEN BRANCH TO RECT INPUT SUBRT.
360   IF K$ = "V" THEN 200: REM   IF NEW VIEWPORT IS WANTED
      THEN BRANCH.
370   IF K$ = "Q" THEN 410
380   IF K$ = "F" THEN  POKE  — 16302,0: GET K$: POKE
      — 16301, 0: REM  IF FULL SCRN IS WANTED THEN TOGGLE FULL
      PG SWITCH AND WAIT FOR ANOTHER KEYPRESS TO GO BACK TO
      MIXED MODE.
390   IF K$ = "D" THEN  HPLOT HO,VO TO H1,VO TO H1,V1 TO HO,V1
      TO HO,VO
400   GOTO 340: REM  GO BACK FOR KEY SELECTION.
410   TEXT : HOME : END
411   REM  **   END OF MAIN PROGRAM     **
412   REM
1997  REM  ******************************
1998  REM  *   MAX/MIN SEARCH X,Y SUBRT  *
1999  REM  ******************************
2000  READ XL,YL:XR = XL:YR = YL: REM  INIT MIN AND MAX FOR
      EACH VARIABLE.
```

```
2010  FOR I = 0 TO 1 STEP 0: REM  REPEAT THE LOOP STEPS
      INDEFINITELY...
2020  READ X,Y
2030  IF Y = EOF THEN  RETURN
2040  IF Y = EPL THEN  NEXT I: REM  IF END OF PLOT MARKER,
      THEN SKIP TO NEXT PAIR.
2050  IF XL > X THEN XL = X: REM  RESET MIN X TO X IF LESS
      THAN CURRENT MIN X.
2060  IF XR < X THEN XR = X: REM  RESET MAX X TO X IF GREATER
      THAN CURRENT MAX X.
2070  IF YL > Y THEN YL = Y
2080  IF YR < Y THEN YR = Y
2090  NEXT I
2091  REM  ***  END MAX/MIN SEARCH X,Y ***
2092  REM
2997  REM  ******************************
2998  REM  *    INPUT RECT BOUNDS SUBRT  *
2999  REM  ******************************
3000  TEXT : HOME
3010  VTAB 2: PRINT "ENCLOSING RECTANGLE CURRENT SETTINGS":
      PRINT " MINIMUM SETTINGS TO CONTAIN POINTS"
3020  VTAB 5: HTAB 10: PRINT " < D > TOP = ";D
3030  HTAB 10: PRINT "MIN POSSBL:";YR
3040  VTAB 8: HTAB 1: PRINT " < A > LEFT = ";A
3050  PRINT "MAX POSSBL:";XL
3060  VTAB 8: HTAB 20: PRINT " < B > RIGHT = ";B
3070  HTAB 20: PRINT "MIN POSSBL:";XR
3080  VTAB 11: HTAB 10: PRINT " < C > BOTTOM = ";C
3090  HTAB 10: PRINT "MAX POSSBL:";YL
3100  VTAB 14: PRINT "CHANGE A VALUE(S) < Y/N >? ";
3110  GET K$: PRINT K$
3120  IF K$ < > "Y" THEN  RETURN
3130  B(0) = XL:B(1) = XR:B(2) = YL:B(3) = YR: REM  SET
      MINIMUM BOUNDS FOR CHECKING INPUT DATA IN ARRAYS.
3140  R(0) = A:R(1) = B:R(2) = C:R(3) = D: REM  SAVE CURRENT
      ENCLOSING RECT BOUNDS IN ARRAYS FOR DATA INPUT.
3150  FOR I = 0 TO 3
3160  PRINT : PRINT "CHANGE ' "R$(I)" ' <Y/N>? ";
3170  GET K$: PRINT K$" ";
3180  IF K$ < > "Y" THEN 3230
3190  INPUT "CHANGE TO WHAT ";Z
3200  IF I = 0 OR I = 2 THEN  IF Z > B(I) THEN  PRINT  CHR$
      (7);"INVALID! "R$(I)" MUST BE < =  "B(I): GOTO 3160:
      REM CHR$(7) IS 'BELL'.
3210  IF I = 1 OR I = 3 THEN  IF Z < B(I) THEN  PRINT  CHR$
      (7);"INVALID! "R$(I)" MUST BE > =  "B(I): GOTO 3160
3220  R(I) = Z: REM  Z IS VALID; STORE IT AWAY.
```

```
3230   NEXT I
3240   A = R(0):B = R(1):C = R(2):D = R(3): REM  RESET
       ENCLOSING RECTANGLE PARAMS.
3250   GOTO 3000
3251   REM  **   END INPUT RECT BOUNDS   **
3252   REM
3997   REM  *******************************
3998   REM  *   INPUT VIEWPORT ROUTINE   *
3999   REM  *******************************
4000   TEXT : HOME
4010   VTAB 3: HTAB 6: PRINT "CURRENT VIEWPORT PARAMETERS"
4020   VTAB 6: HTAB 12: PRINT " < V1 > TOP = ";V1
4030   VTAB 8: HTAB 1: PRINT " < H0 > LEFT = ";H0
4040   VTAB 8: HTAB 20: PRINT " < H1 > RIGHT = ";H1
4050   VTAB 10: HTAB 12: PRINT " < V0 > BOTTOM = ";V0
4060   VTAB 13: PRINT "CHANGE VIEWPORT VALUE(S)? < Y/N >";
4070   GET K$: PRINT K$
4080   IF K$ <> "Y" THEN  RETURN
4090   VTAB 15: PRINT "INPUT VIEWPORT PARAMETERS:"
4100   HTAB 5: INPUT "H0,H1,V1,V0: ?";V%(0),V%(1),V%(2),V%(3)
4110   IF V%(0) < 0 OR V%(1) > 279 OR V%(0) > V%(1) OR
       V%(2) < 0 OR V%(3) > 191 OR V%(3) < V%(2) THEN  PRINT
       CHR$ (7);"INVALID PARAMETERS!": FOR J = 1 TO 2500: NEXT
       J; GOTO 4000; REM  IF INVALID PARAMS THEN FLAG IT AND
       GO BACK TO BEGINNING OF ROUTINE AFTER A DELAY.
4120   H0 = V%(0):H1 = V%(1):V1 = V%(2):V0 = V%(3): REM
       INPUT VALUES OK; STORE PARAMS.
4130   GOTO 4000: REM  GO BACK AND REDISPLAY VIEWPORT PARAMS.
4131   REM  **   END VIEWPORT SELECTION   **
4132   REM
4997   REM  *******************************
4998   REM  *     PLOT X,Y PTS SUBRT     *
4999   REM  *******************************
5000   XSCL = WDSCR / RW:YSCL = HTSCR / RH
5010   OH = H0 - A * XSCL:OV = V0 + C * YSCL
5020   FL = 1: REM  SET 'START PLOT FLAG' (BOOLEAN) VARIABLE TO
       VAL 1. FL = 0 WILL INDICATE PROGRM IN 'HPLOT TO' PLOT
       CYCLE.
5030   FOR I = 0 TO 1 STEP 0
5040   READ X,Y
5050   IF Y = EOF THEN  RETURN
5060   IF Y = EPL THEN FL = 1: NEXT I: REM  IF END OF 'HPLOT
       TO'  PLOT CYCLE, THEN SET 'START OVER' FLAG TO 1; GO BACK
       AND READ ANOTHER PAIR.
5070   IF FL THEN  HPLOT OH + X * XSCL,OV - Y * YSCL:FL = 0:
       NEXT I: REM  IF 'START OVER' FLAG IS 'TRUE' THEN HPLOT
       PT; SET FL TO 'FALSE' AND GO BACK TO READ ANOTHER
```

```
       PAIR.
5080   HPLOT  TO OH + X * XSCL,OV - Y * YSCL: REM  IN 'HPLOT
       TO' PLOT CYCLE...
5090   NEXT I
5091   REM  ***   END X,Y PLOT SUBRT   ***
5092   REM
6997   REM  *******************************
6998   REM  *    INITIALIZATION SUBRT   *
6999   REM  *******************************
7000   DIM R$(3),R(3),B(3): REM  RECTANGLE BOUND PARAMETERS.
7010   R$(0) = "A":R$(1) = "B":R$(2) = "C":R$(3) = "D"
7020   DIM V%(3): REM  USED FOR VIEWPORT INPUT.
7030   RETURN
7031   REM  **    END INITIALIZATION   **
7032   REM
7997   REM  *******************************
7998   REM  *     DATA FOR PLOTTING     *
7999   REM  *******************************
8000   DATA  6,6.5, 4,2,9, 5,3, 5,8, 2,6, 6.5, -9,-9
8010   DATA  9.5,6.5, 9.5,2, 11,2, 11,6.5, 9.5,6.5, -9,-9
8020   DATA  2.5,6.5, 2.5,2, 1,2, 1,6.5, 2.5,6.5, -99,-99
LIST
```

**Check Your Comprehension**

If you have purchased the diskette which accompanies this book, then you will need to change the DATA on the diskette program to reflect the above DATA. The DATA supplied with the diskette program is listed a few paragraphs below. The DATA is for a picture representing combination of two of the five Platonic regular solids, a cube and an octahedron. (An octahedron is basically two pyramids base-to-base).

Using the minimum rectangle first, RUN the program supplying the following input data for the viewport.

```
      0, 279,  0, 191
      0, 279,  0, 159
      0,  50, 60, 100
     90, 120,  0, 159
    200, 270, 20, 100
    160, 220, 30,  70
    160, 220,  0, 191
```

Describe what you have seen. _____

Using the dimensions of your 8.5×11 paper, reRUN the program to test the program's ability to permit a change in the enclosing rectangle dimensions. The new dimension values will be A = 0, B = 11, C = 0, D = 8.5. Reuse the viewport data above.

Note how changing the viewport changes the shape, but still maintains its position within the viewport and its size in proportion to the size of the viewport. In order to test the error checking condition in line 4100, try INPUTing viewport parameters you know can not possibly exist on the screen. Are you satisfied it works?

In the MAX/MIN SEARCH SUBROUTINE, why is the first data pair read and assigned to XL and YL, and then subsequently assigned to XR and YR? _____

_____

Why can't one simply start with the loop beginning at line 2010? What will happen without it? _____

As you perceive it, what purpose do the lines at 190, 210, 5000, 5010, 5070, and 5080 serve in this program? Would you say they are the heart of the whole program?

_____

What will happen without the line at 280? _____

 Now, as indicated above, the CE4.3 program on the diskette available with this book contains the DATA needed to display an unusual combination of a cube and octahedron. Here is a list of the DATA for those of you who do not own the diskette.

```
8000   DATA   12,24, 6,18, 4,17, 4,5, 16,5, 16,17, 4,17, -9,-9
8010   DATA   24,12, 12,24, 8,10, 12,0, 24,12, 8,10, 4,11, 10,5,
       16,11, 10,17, 4,11, 0,12, 4,8, -9,-9
8020   DATA   16,5, 18,6, 16,11, 18,18, 10,17, 6,18, -9,-9
8030   DATA   0,12, 4,16, -9,-9, 7,5, 12,0, -9,-9
8040   DATA   18,6, 20,7, 20,8, -9,-9, 16,17, 20,19, 20,16,
       20,19, 17,19, -99,-99
```

Experiment with different parameters for the viewport. Using the viewport data 25,228,0, and 190, will provide you with an accurately scaled display.

 For a real treat and a display of the power of this program, use the DATA for generating the koala in the EXERCISE of ACTIVITY 2.18. The Koala DATA is on the diskette supplied with this book.

 Here is the way to combine the DATA of that program with the COMPREHEN-SIVE EXAMPLE, using the RENUMBER program from your DOS 3.3 SYSTEM MASTER diskette. There is the added twist that the CE4.3 program and the Koala DATA are too long to permit loading the combined program into memory beginning at location 2048. The problem is, during execution program variable storage is clobbered by clearing Page 1. Since the mixed graphics screen is to be used, it is not convenient to switch to high resolution Page 2. The simplest solution is to reset the pointers telling APPLESOFT where to begin loading the programs. Refer to ACTIVITY 3.3 if it is necessary to refresh your memory of this method.

1. Insert the SYSTEM MASTER into your disk drive.

2. Enter the following command.

```
RUN RENUMBER
```

3. Reset program loading pointers to just above high resolution Page one, ie., 16385 = $4001, and poke required zero into 16384.

```
POKE 104,64
POKE 103,1
POKE 16384,0
```

4. Insert your diskette with the program containing the Koala DATA.

    ```
    LOAD KOALA DATA
    ```

5. Now LIST the program to detemine the non-DATA lines. DELete all lines but the DATA lines. Disregard any lines beginning with REMarks.

6. The next instruction will renumber the DATA lines beginning with 8000 (incrementing by 10).

    ```
    &F8000
    ```

7. The next instruction will place your program (ie., data) on hold.

    ```
    &H
    ```

You should have received a message indicating your program is on hold.

8. Load the COMPREHENSIVE EXAMPLE program.

    ```
    LOAD CE4.3
    ```

9. Delete all DATA from CE4.3.

    ```
    DEL 8000,9000
    ```

10. The next instruction will merge the 'DATA' program on hold with CE4.3.

    ```
    &M
    ```

11. To verify it's there, LIST the program.

12. Check to see what values were used as end-of-file and end-of-plot values in the Koala DATA. You should obtain the values: EOF$=-1$ and EPL$=-2$. Make the required adjustment in the program.

    ```
    110  EOF = −1 : EPL = −2 :REM EOF AND EPL VALUES FOR
         KOALA DATA.
    ```

Now RUN the program once using all the default values of the program. What is the problem? Why do you think it is upside down? _____

The problem is the Koala DATA was designed using the screen coordinate system; the positive sense of direction is down! Fortunately it is not a serious problem, but it did give an unusual effect.

The simplest solution is the following. Instead of subtracting the transformed screen displacement Y $*$ YSCL from OV, you merely add it! Rather than go through and change the appropriate lines, there is an easier way. Simply redefine YSCL to be − YSCL; the effect will be equivalent.

There is one final correction to be made. Measurements in the original DATA were made from the upper left corner in the enclosing rectangle (actually the APPLE screen). The corresponding point in the viewport is located at (H0,V1). The formula for OV must be adjusted correspondingly.

13. Therefore, make the following changes and additions to the program, adding two more steps to those outlined above.

```
5005 YSCL = - YSCL
5010 OH = HO - A * XSCL : OV = V1 + C * YSCL : REM ONLY
     OV IS TECHNICALLY BEING CHANGED. THE '+' SIGN IS
     CORRECT SINCE YSCL HAS ALREADY BEEN CHANGED.
```

14. SAVE the merged programs for later use.

```
SAVE CE4.3+KOALA DATA
```

Now RUN the program using several different viewport sizes; use the sizes you ran for the other data and figure. Use the ability of the program to bypass, without erasing the screen in order to fill the screen with koalas. For example, you might draw one relatively large koala in the center and four smaller koalas in the four corners of the screen. Use your imagination, and above all, have fun!

**EXERCISE**   Alter the COMPREHENSIVE EXAMPLE program so the data is read into arrays and, as it is being read, the maximum X and Y values are determined. The use of arrays will avoid the RESTORE statement, but will have the disadvantage of requiring you to reserve adequate memory space to accommodate all the data. Since, in general, you will not know (nor really care to know) how many DATA points are to be READ, arrays X(*) and Y(*) will need to be dimensioned in advance. Dimension them for 1000 elements. Test to see if more than 1000 elements are needed; if so, inform the user that adequate space must be reserved and abort the program. Finally, to guarantee your arrays are not clobbered by initializing the high resolution page, set LOMEM above Page one to protect your variables.

**EXERCISE**   Alter the COMPREHENSIVE EXAMPLE program so that at the beginning of each block of data values connected by straight lines an HCOLOR value can be read and used to HPLOT the lines. Use the X-position of the of EPL DATA pair to signal whether or not the next DATA item is a new HCOLOR or there is to be no change.

**CHALLENGE**   Alter the COMPREHENSIVE EXAMPLE program so several sets of data corresponding to different pictures appearing within different viewports can all appear simultaneously on the screen. For example, you may have 3 different sets of data corresponding to pictures to be displayed on the screen in different viewports (of user choice). Allow the user to develop the subdisplays one at a time rather than having to provide the necessary parameters all at once.

# ACTIVITY 4.4   Scaling to Achieve Equivalent Scales & a Full Viewport

**LEARNING BY DISCOVERY**   In this section, we will unite the techniques of scaling discussed in the two previous sections. Namely, you will investigate how to combine equivalent scaling and scaling for maximum use of the viewport.

1. Enter and RUN the following APPLESOFT program.

```
NEW
100   READ H0,H1,V0,V1
110   DATA  40,240,130,40
120   HGR : HCOLOR =  3: HOME : VTAB 21
130   GOSUB 500: REM  GOTO VIEWPORT DISPLAY SUBRT.
350   GET Q$: TEXT : HOME : END
500   FOR H = H0 TO H1 STEP 6
510   HPLOT H,V0: REM  PLOT 'BOTTOM SIDE'
520   HPLOT H,V1: REM  PLOT 'TOP SIDE'
530   NEXT H
540   FOR V = V1 TO V0 STEP 5
550   HPLOT H0,V: REM  PLOT 'LEFT SIDE'
560   HPLOT H1,V: REM  PLOT 'RIGHT SIDE'
570   NEXT V
580   HOME : VTAB 21: HTAB 14
590   PRINT "THE VIEWPORT"
600   FOR J = 1 TO 2000: NEXT : REM  DELAY
610   RETURN
LIST
```

Describe the display. _____
(The authors observed a rectangular region bounded by approximately equally spaced dots, evidently representing the viewport region.)

By inspecting the program code, determine the viewport dimensions and write the values in the spaces below.

$$WDSCR = \text{_____} \text{ pixels horiz.}$$
$$HTSCR = \text{_____} \text{ pixels vert.}$$

(See ACTIVITY 4.2 for clarification if necessary. The correct values are 200 and 90, respectively.)

2. Consider the problem of drawing exactly proportioned rectangles, $12 \times 4$ and $3 \times 8$, on the high resolution screen using as much of the viewport as possible. In order to obtain a solution answer a few simple questions.

   a) What is the minimum width needed to contain both figures?
   $$\max(3, 12) = \text{_____} = RW.$$

   b) What is the minimum height needed to contain both figures?
   $$\max(8, 4) = \text{_____} = RH.$$

   Evidently, at least a $12 \times 8$ region is needed to contain both rectangles. Now determine the scaling factors needed to transform a $12 \times 8$ region onto the viewport. Based on the discussion in ACTIVITY 4.3, you compute

$$\text{XSCL} = \text{WDSCR} / \text{RW} = \underline{\hspace{2cm}} \text{ pixels horiz./unit,}$$
$$\text{YSCL} = \text{HTSCR} / \text{RH} = \underline{\hspace{2cm}} \text{ pixels vert./unit.}$$

(You should have obtained values of 16.6666667 and 11.25, respectively.)

XSCL and YSCL represent the scaling factors needed to map the minimum enclosing rectangle onto the viewport. However, recall the problem is to draw exactly proportioned rectangles using as much of the viewport as possible. The second condition is fulfilled using these scales, but what about the requirement of exactly proportioned rectangles? Clearly this calls for equivalent scales.

The observant reader will wonder how one can simultaneously use equivalent scales and achieve a "full" viewport. The answer is, you can't in general. By proper scale selection, you can make maximum use of the viewport. Since equivalent scales are needed, once a scale is chosen in one direction, the equivalent scale in the other direction is (necessarily) defined.

Because the $12 \times 8$ rectangle is the minimum rectangle enclosing the original two rectangles, the solution of the problem is tantamount to selecting the equivalent scales which permit the image of the minimum enclosing rectangle to fill as much of the viewport as possible.

3. A solution of how to select the proper scaling is obtained below.
   a) Using the XSCL value of 16.67 (rounded for convenience), determine the corresponding EYSCL value needed for an equivalent vertical scale. Note the choice of XSCL guarantees a maximum use of the viewport horizontally.
   XSCL = 16.67 pix horiz./unit,

   $$\text{EYSCL} = \text{XSCL} / \text{SFAC} = \underline{\hspace{2cm}} \text{ pix vert./unit.}$$

(The authors obtained an EYSCL value of 13.9 based on an SFAC value of 1.20. Remember, your value will differ if your screen display requires a different SFAC value. Determination of the value of SFAC was obtained in ACTIVITY 4.2.)

   b) Using the YSCL value of 11.25 determined above, compute the corresponding EXSCL value needed to obtain an equivalent scale horizontally. Again note the choice of YSCL will guarantee maximum use of the viewport vertically.
   YSCL = 11.25 pix vert/unit,

   $$\text{EXSCL} = \text{YSCL} * \text{SFAC} = \underline{\hspace{3.5cm}} \text{ pix horiz./unit.}$$

(The authors obtained an EXSCL value of 13.5 based on an SFAC value of 1.20.)

The problem now is to determine which set of scaling factors (from a) or b) above) permits display of the minimum rectangle entirely within in the viewport. The solution is rather simple, but "a picture is worth a thousand words." Add the following lines to the program in section 1 of this activity.

```
<Adding to the program from section 1 and changing lines 130
  and 350, enter ...>
130  PRINT "INPUT THE WIDTH AND HEIGHT OF A": PRINT "RECTANGLE
     TO TRANSFORM: ";: INPUT RW,RH
140  WDSCR = H1 - H0:HTSCR = V0 - V1
150  SFAC = 1.20: REM  USE YOUR SCREEN SCALE FACTOR IF
     DIFFERENT.
```

```
160   DEF  FN T(Z) =  INT (100 * Z) / 100: REM  TRUNCATE TO 2
      DECIMAL PLACES FUNCTION.
170   XSCL(1) = WDSCR / RW:YSCL(1) = XSCL(1) / SFAC: REM  THE
      EQUIV SCALES XSCL AND XSCL/SFAC.
180   SC$(1) = "XSCL & XSCL/SFAC"
190   YSCL(2) = HTSCR / RH:XSCL(2) = YSCL(2) * SFAC: REM  THE
      SCALES YSCL*SFAC AND YSCL.
200   SC$(2) = "YSCL*SFAC & YSCL"
210   FOR K = 1 TO 2: REM  FOR EACH SET OF SCALES DO ...
220   CALL 62450: GOSUB 500: REM  CLEAR SCREEN; MAP VIEWPORT.
230   XSCL = XSCL(K):YSCL = YSCL(K): REM  SET KTH SCALE PAIR
      FOR PLOTTING
240   HOME : VTAB 21: HTAB 6: PRINT "NOW USING THE EQUIVALENT
      SCALES:"
250   PRINT SC$(K)" = "; FN T(XSCL);" & "; FN T(YSCL)
260   GOSUB 800: REM  GO DRAW THE RECTANGLE FOR THIS PAIR OF
      EQUIV SCALES.
270   VTAB 24: HTAB 1: CALL  − 868: PRINT "PRESS A KEY TO
      CONTINUE:";: GET Q$
280   NEXT K
290   HOME : VTAB 21: PRINT "INPUT ANOTHER RECTANGLE? ";: GET
      K$: PRINT K$
300   IF K$ = "Y" THEN 120
350   HOME : TEXT : END
800   OH = HO:OV = VO: REM  THE SCREEN IMAGE OF THE ORIGIN IS
      HO,VO; THE RECT BNDRIES ARE: A = 0, B = RW, C = 0 AND D
      = RH.
810   HR = OH + RW * XSCL: REM  COMPUTE RIGHT HORZ COORD OF
      SCREEN IMAGE; LEFT COORD IS HO.
820   VT = OV − RH * YSCL: REM  COMPUTE TOP VERT COORD OF
      SCREEN IMAGE; BOTTOM COORD IS VO.
830   PRINT "RECTANGLE DIMENSIONS: ";RW;" X ";RH
840   IF HR > 279 THEN  HPLOT 279,VT TO OH,VT TO OH,OV TO
      279,OV: REM  RIGHT SIDE NOT VISIBLE BUT TOP IS; PLOT
      VISIBLE PART.
850   IF VT < 0 THEN  HPLOT OH,0 TO OH,OV TO HR,OV TO HR,0:
      REM  TOP NOT VISIBLE BUT RIGHT SIDE IS. PLOT VISIBLE PART.
860   IF HR < = 279 AND VT > = 0 THEN  HPLOT OH,OV TO HR,OV
      TO HR,VT TO OH,VT TO OH,OV: REM  IF TOP AND RT SIDES
      VISIBLE THEN PLOT ENTIRE RECTANGLE.
870   FOR J = 1 TO 2000: NEXT J: REM  DELAY
880   RETURN
LIST
```

Listed below are several examples of (minimum enclosing) rectangles with their width and height provided. Use the given dimensions as input into the program. For each rectangle supplied, screen images will be displayed for each of the two possible sets of equivalent scales. Record each set of scale values in the table below and note which of the two sets of scales has rectangle image entirely within the viewport.

The program itself is relatively simple. The image of a rectangle has its lower left corner based at (H0,V0). In some cases, one of the scales will map the upper right corner of the minimum enclosing rectangle to a point off the screen. In essence, the image rectangle must be clipped at the screen boundary. Lines 840-850 handle the necessary clipping. In the next activity you will study a much more general clipping problem and its solution. Matters are very simple here because the rectangle sides are parallel to the screen boundaries.

RUN the program and complete the spaces below. In the spaces provided, list the scale values for each set of equivalent scales and the set of factors for which the image appears to be entirely within the viewport.

| RECT DIM WD, HT | VALUES OF XSCL & THE EQUIV YSCL | VALUES OF YSCL & THE EQUIV XSCL | IMAGE WITHIN VIEWPORT FOR WHICH SCALE PAIR |
|---|---|---|---|
| 12, 8 | _____ | _____ | _____ |
| 13, 7 | _____ | _____ | _____ |
| 5, 6 | _____ | _____ | _____ |
| 5, 5 | _____ | _____ | _____ |
| 30,50 | _____ | _____ | _____ |
| 20,15 | _____ | _____ | _____ |
| 14,4 | _____ | _____ | _____ |

4. Note the rectangles remained within the viewport for the smaller set of scaling factors. (In one case, vz., 13,7, the scales are so close to one another both images appear to be enclosed within the viewport.)  The smaller set of scale factors will always display the image within the viewport. One can easily let the computer make the proper choice of scaling factors by deleting and adding the following lines of code to the existing program. You may wish to SAVE the program presently in memory before making changes.

```
DEL 170,210
DEL 230,230
DEL 280,280
170  XSCL = WDSCR / RW:YSCL = HTSCR / RH : REM  DETERMINE
     BASE SCALES.
180  EXSCL = YSCL * SFAC : REM DETERMINE EQUIV HORIZ SCALE
     TO YSCL.
190  IF EXSCL > XSCL THEN YSCL = XSCL / SFAC:EXSCL = XSCL
     : REM IF IT IS A LARGER SCALE THEN SWITCH TO OTHER
     EQUIV SCALES.
200  XSCL = EXSCL : REM XSCL AND YSCL NOW REDEFINED TO BE
     THE PROPER EQUIV SCALES.
250  PRINT  FN T(XSCL)" & " FN T(YSCL)
LIST
RUN
```

Describe the display. _____

   Compare the results of computer selection of the proper scale with your observations in the table of Section 3.

**DISCUSSION**   In transforming a collection of points, figures, etc., onto a viewport on the screen, an appropriate choice of equivalent scales can be made which will preserve proportionate distances and make maximum use of the viewport. The selection of scales is reduced to choosing between either the scales (XSCL, XSCL/SFAC) or the scales (YSCL*SFAC, YSCL), where XSCL and YSCL are the basic scales given by

   XSCL = (H1−H0)/RW      YSCL = (V0−V1)/RH

where H0,H1,V1,V0 are the viewport parameters and RW,RH are the width and height of the rectangular region to be transformed.

   The correct choice is always the smaller set of scales and it is only necessary to compare, say, XSCL with YSCL * SFAC. If, for example, XSCL < YSCL*SFAC then XSCL/SFAC < YSCL. Thus, (XSCL, XSCL/SFAC) represents a smaller set of scale factors than (YSCL*SFAC, YSCL). Since the factor XSCL has the effect of filling the viewport horizontally, and YSCL has the effect of filling it vertically, the smaller set of scales will display the image entirely within the viewport. Correspondingly, the larger set of scales will create an image which extends horizontally beyond the viewport limits.

   As you have already seen, the use of equivalent scales is necessary to make circles appear as true circles and to preserve proportionate distances or lengths in general. Specification of a viewport and the appropriate choice of scales gives the user complete control over where and how large screen images will appear. These concepts will be very useful in obtaining accurate curve plots. In CHAPTER 5, these concepts will be used to display 3-dimensional graphs.

   As a final point, there may arise occasions when it is desirable to center the image within the viewport. This can be accomplished by redefining the left and right coordinates or the top and bottom coordinates of the rectangular region to be mapped.

   Specifically, suppose A, B, C, and D are these coordinates. Suppose XSCL and YSCL have been redefined to be the proper equivalent scales. Then WDSCR/XSCL and HTSCR/YSCL are the width and height of a rectangle whose image is the viewport under the equivalent scales XSCL and YSCL. One can now center the original rectangle within this rectangle by subtracting one half the width WDSCR/XSCL from the center (A + B)*.5 of the original rectangle. The precise formulas are

$$A = (A + B − WDSCR/XSCL) * .5$$
$$C = (C + D − HTSCR/YSCL) * .5$$
$$B = A + WDSCR/XSCL : D = C + HTSCR/YSCL$$

**WARNING!**   If you decide to center, the values of RW and RH used to denote the width and length of the original rectangle should no longer be equated with the values of B − A and D − C.

   In order to test the centering formulas, add the following lines to the program in section 4.

```
800  A = 0:B = RW:C = 0:D = RH: REM  COORD PARAMETERS FOR
     ENCLOSING RECT.
804  A = (A + B - WDSCR / XSCL) * .5:C = (C + D - HTSCR /
     YSCL) * .5: REM  REDEFINE A AND C FOR CENTERING RECT
```

```
          IMAGE WITHIN VIEWPORT.
  808   OH = HO − A * XSCL:OV = VO + C * YSCL: REM   NEW SCREEN
          COORDS OF (0,0).
  LIST
  RUN
```

Use several different rectangle dimensions as input to test the centering formulas. In the program additions above, why isn't necessary to redefine B and D? _____

_____

Centering can be used in the programs of Sections 1 and 3. However, an additional set of clipping statements will need to be added. Why? _____
    The lead-in problem for this activity was to draw exactly proportioned 12×4 and 3×8 retangles on the screen using as much of the viewport as possible. You have the necessary tools in your repertoire to accomplish the task yourself.

**COMPREHENSIVE EXAMPLE**   The following program illustrates the use of the topics on scaling presented in this section. A discussion of its content follows the listing.

```
NEW
10    REM   ********************************
11    REM   *            CE4.4             *
12    REM   ********************************
13    REM
97    REM   ********************************
98    REM   *        MAIN PROGRAM          *
99    REM   ********************************
100   GOSUB 1000: REM  GO TO INIT ROUTINE.
110   SFAC = 1.20: REM  SCREEN SCALE FACTOR. USE YOUR FACTOR IF
      DIFFERENT.
120   EOF = − 99:EPL = − 9: REM  END-OF-FILE AND END-OF-PLOT
      VALUES USED IN DATA.
130   HGR2 : REM  INIT FULL SCREEN GRAPHICS PAGE.
140   TEXT : HOME
150   VTAB 12: HTAB 7
160   SPEED =  100: REM  SLOW DOWN PRT SPEED FOR SPECIAL
      EFFECT.
170   PRINT "READY-Y-Y-Y...OH-H-H";
180   T = 300: GOSUB 2000: REM  DELAY 300.
190   SPEED =  255: PRINT "....K !!!!"
200   T = 1000: GOSUB 2000: REM  DELAY 1000.
210   FOR K = 1 TO 5: REM  FOR EACH OF 5 LETTERS ...
220   WDSCR = 30 +  INT (240 *  RND (1)):HTSCR = 30 +  INT
      (150 * RND (1)): REM  SELECT RANDOM VIEWPORT DIMS
      > = 30
230   HO =  INT (140 − .5 * WDSCR):H1 = HO + WDSCR:VO =  INT
      (95 + .5 * HTSCR):V1 = VO − HTSCR: REM
      APPROXIMATELY CENTER VIEWPORT.
240   TEXT : VTAB 12: CALL  − 868: REM  SET TEXT MODE, CLEAR
```

```
          CENTER SCRN LINE.
250   HTAB 13
260   SPEED =  100: PRINT "GIVE ME "A$(K)" ..."
270   READ RW,RH: REM  READ WIDTH AND HEIGHT OF RECT ENCLOSING
      BLOCK LETTER.
280   GOSUB 3000: REM  GO TO SCALE SELECTION ROUTINE.
290   GOSUB 4000: REM  GO TO RECT BNDRY AND CENTERING ROUTINE.
300   HCOLOR =  K − 1: HPLOT 0,0: CALL 62454: REM  SET BACKGRND
      COLOR TO HCOLOR = K−1.
310   HCOLOR =  CC(K − 1): REM  SELECT COMPLEMENT HCOLOR FOR
      PLOTTING LINES.
320   GOSUB 5000: REM  GO TO PLOTTING ROUTINE.
330   POKE  − 16304,0: POKE  − 16299,0: POKE  − 16297,0: REM
      DISPLAY HIRES GRAPHICS PAGE 2.
340   T = 500: GOSUB 2000: REM  DELAY 500.
350   NEXT K
360   FOR K = 1 TO 5: REM  READ VIEWPORT DATA FOR NEXT DISPLAY.
370   READ HO(K),H1(K),VO(K),V1(K)
380   NEXT K
390   TEXT : VTAB 12: CALL  − 868
400   HTAB 3
410   SPEED =  150: PRINT "WHAT'S OUR FAVORITE COMPUTER-R-R-R
      ??"
420   SPEED =  255: REM  RESET PRT SPEED TO MAX VALUE.
430   T = 1000: GOSUB 2000: REM  DELAY 1000.
440   HOME
450   FOR N = 1 TO 3: REM  DO THREE TIMES ...
460   TEXT
470   HCOLOR =  4 + N: HPLOT 0,0: CALL 62454: REM  SET BACKGRND
      COLOR TO HCOLOR = 4+N, IE. 5,6,7.
480   RESTORE : REM  RESTORE PLOT DATA FOR REUSE.
490   HCOLOR =  CC(4 + N): REM  COMPLEMENT COLOR OF C(4+N).
500   POKE  − 16304,0: POKE  − 16299,0: POKE  − 16297,0: REM
      VIEW HIRES GRAPHICS PAGE 2.
510   FOR K = 1 TO 5
520   HO = HO(K):H1 = H1(K):VO = VO(K):V1 = V1(K): REM  PICK
      K-TH VIEWPORT PARAMETERS OBTAINED EARLIER FROM SUB 1000.
530   WDSCR = H1 − HO:HTSCR = VO − V1
540   READ RW,RH: REM  READ ENCLOSING RECT WITH AND HEIGHT OF
      BLOCK LETTER.
550   GOSUB 3000: REM  GO TO SCALE ROUTINE.
560   GOSUB 4000: REM  GO TO RECT BNDRY ROUTINE.
570   GOSUB 5000: REM  GO TO PLOT ROUTINE.
580   NEXT K
590   T = 500: GOSUB 2000: REM  DELAY 500.
600   NEXT N
610   RESTORE
```

```
620  FOR K = 1 TO 5: REM  PRINT SAME MESSG, SAME PAGE, DIFF
     VIEWPORTS.
630  HO = HO(K):H1 = H1(K):V1 = 191 - VO(K):VO = 191 -
     V1(K): REM SHIFT VIEWPORTS TO START FROM LOWER LEFT
     INCREASING TO TOP RIGHT.
640  WDSCR = H1 - HO:HTSCR = VO - V1
650  READ RW,RH
660  GOSUB 3000: GOSUB 4000: GOSUB 5000
670  NEXT K
680  GET Q$: TEXT : HOME : END
681  REM  **      END OF MAIN PROGRAM      **
682  REM
997  REM  ******************************
998  REM  *     INITIALIZATION ROUTINE    *
999  REM  ******************************
1000 DIM CC(8): REM  HCOLORS USED AND COMPLEMENT HCOLORS IN
     1ST DISPLAY.
1010 FOR I = 0 TO 7
1020 IF I < = 3 THEN CC(I) = 3 - I
1030 IF I > 3 THEN CC(I) = 11 - I
1040 NEXT I
1050 DIM HO(5),H1(5),VO(5),V1(5): REM  USED FOR DIFFERENT
     VIEWPORTS, SAME SCREEN.
1060 DIM A$(5)
1070 A$(1) = "AN":A$(4) = A$(1):A$(5) = A$(1)
1080 A$(2) = "A":A$(3) = A$(2)
1090 RETURN
1091 REM  **   END INITIALIZATON ROUT  **
1092 REM
1997 REM  ******************************
1998 REM  *       DELAY SUBROUTINE        *
1999 REM  ******************************
2000 FOR I = 1 TO T: NEXT I
2010 RETURN
2011 REM  **      END DELAY ROUTINE      **
2012 REM
2997 REM  ******************************
2998 REM  *  EQUIV SCALE SELECT SUBRT  *
2999 REM  ******************************
3000 XSCL = WDSCR / RW:YSCL = HTSCR / RH
3010 EXSCL = YSCL * SFAC
3020 IF EXSCL > XSCL THEN YSCL = XSCL / SFAC:EXSCL = XSCL
3030 XSCL = EXSCL
3040 RETURN : REM  RETURNED VALUES OF XSCL AND YSCL ARE
     EQUIVALENT SCALES PROVIDING MAX USE OF THE VIEWPORT.
3041 REM  **   END EQUV SCL SELECT    **
3042 REM
```

```
3997 REM ******************************
3998 REM *   CENTERING SUBROUTINE   *
3999 REM ******************************
4000 A = 0:B = RW:C = 0:D = RH: REM  PARAMETERS FOR MINIMUM
     ENCLOSING RECT.
4010 A = (A + B - WDSCR / XSCL) * .5: REM  SELECT LEFT BNDRY
     COORD SO MIN RECT IS CENTERED IN VIEWPORT.
4020 C = (C + D - HTSCR / YSCL) * .5: REM  SELECT BOTTOM
     BNDRY COORD SO MIN RECT IS CENTERED IN VIEWPORT.
4030 RETURN : REM  ALTHOUGH TECHNICALLY B AND D SHOULD BE
     REDEFINED, THEY ARE NOT NEEDED.
4031 REM **   END CENTERING SUBRT   **
4032 REM
4997 REM ******************************
4998 REM *     PLOTTING SUBROUTINE    *
4999 REM ******************************
5000 OH = HO - A * XSCL:OV = VO + C * YSCL
5010 REM  USING SAME PLOT ROUTINE AS IN CE4.3.
5020 FL = 1
5030 FOR I = 0 TO 1 STEP 0
5040 READ X,Y
5050 IF Y = EOF THEN  RETURN
5060 IF Y = EPL THEN FL = 1: NEXT I
5070 IF FL THEN  HPLOT OH + X * XSCL,OV - Y * YSCL:FL = 0:
     NEXT I
5080 HPLOT  TO OH + X * XSCL,OV - Y * YSCL
5090 NEXT I
5091 REM **    END PLOTTING SUBRT    **
5092 REM
7997 REM ******************************
7998 REM * BLK LETTERS /VWPRT DATA   *
7999 REM ******************************
8000 DATA  6,7 : REM  RW, RH; LETTER 'A'
8010 DATA  0, 0, 1, 0, 2, 3, 3, 3, 4, 0, 5, 0, 3, 6, 2, 6, 0,
     0, -9, -9, 2, 6, 3, 7, 4, 7, 3, 6, 4, 7, 6, 1, 5, 0,
     -9, -9, 1, 0, 2, 1, 2.667, 3, -9, -9, 2, 4, 3, 5; 2,
     5, 2, 4, 3, 4, 3, 5, -99, -99
8020 DATA  4, 7 : REM  RW, RH; LETTER 'P'
8030 DATA  0, 0, 1, 0, 1, 3, 2, 3, 3, 4, 3, 5, 2, 6, 0, 6, 0,
     0, -9, -9, 3, 7, 2, 6, 0, 6, 1, 7, 3, 7, 4, 6, 4, 5, 3,
     4, 3, 5, 4, 6, -9, -9, 1, 4, 2, 5, 1, 5, 1, 4, 2, 4, 2,
     5, -9, -9, 1, 0, 2, 1, 2, 3, -99, -99
8040 DATA  4, 7 : REM  RW, RH; LETTER 'P'
8050 DATA  0, 0, 1, 0, 1, 3, 2, 3, 3, 4, 3, 5, 2, 6, 0, 6, 0,
     0, -9, -9, 3, 7, 2, 6, 0, 6, 1, 7, 3, 7, 4, 6, 4, 5, 3,
     4, 3, 5, 4, 6, -9, -9, 1, 4, 2, 5, 1, 5, 1, 4, 2, 4, 2,
     5, -9, -9, 1, 0, 2, 1, 2, 3, -99, -99
```

```
8060   DATA   5, 7 : REM   RW, RH; LETTER 'L'
8070   DATA   0, 6, 0, 0, 4, 0, 4, 1, 1, 1, 1, 6, 0, 6, 1, 7, 2,
              7, 1, 6, 2, 7, 2, 2, 1, 1, 2, 2, 5, 2, 4, 1, 5, 2, 5, 1,
              4, 0, −99, −99
8080   DATA   5, 6 : REM   RW, RH; LETTER 'E'
8090   DATA   0, 5, 0, 0, 4, 0, 4, 1, 1, 1, 1, 2, 2, 2, 2, 3, 1,
              3, 1, 4, 4, 4, 4, 5, 0, 5, 1, 6, 5, 6, 4, 5, 5, 6, 5, 5,
              4, 4, −9, −9, 1, 1, 2, 2, 5, 2, 5, 1, 4, 0, 4, 1, 5, 2,
              2, 2, 3, 3, 3, 4, 2, 3, 1, 3, 2, 4, −99, −99
8099   REM   VIEWPORT DATA FOR DIAGONAL DISPLAY.
8100   DATA     0, 54, 60, 0
8110   DATA    58, 112, 93, 23
8120   DATA   112, 166, 130, 60
8130   DATA   168, 222, 159, 99
8140   DATA   224, 278, 191, 131
LIST
RUN
```

Lines 8000-8140 contain the data for constructing the block letters. The letters were formed initially by drawing them on a grid of size RW × RH (the values of RW and RH are provided in the DATA statements preceding each letter). The data points simply represent how the line segments which make up each letter are connected. Coordinate pair values −99, −99 are used to denote the end-of-file EOF for each set of letter data. The values −9, −9 are used to denote the end-of-plot EOP signal (ie., an HPLOT should be performed, rather than an HPLOT TO).

Lines 210-350 display the letters using a centered viewport with randomly generated dimensions. To avoid distortion of the image letters, minimum dimensions of 30×30 are used for the viewports. To obtain the diagonal display, the full screen width is divided into 5 roughly equal subintervals with some space allowed in between for adjacent letters. The vertical dimension of each viewport is approximately the same, but vertical overlap is permitted. The selection of the center viewport is critical to permit reprinting of the 2nd letter P in the same location. An alternative possibility is to simply skip to the next letter, but the transition is not as clean as one might prefer. Why? (Hint: The letters are READ!).

The background color and the plot color in each display are complementary colors. The creation of each letter on the screen basically proceeds through the same cycle of events: 1) The viewport dimensions are either created randomly or are READ as DATA (lines 360-380); 2) The grid size (RW, RH) of each letter is READ; 3) the grid size is passed to the scaling subroutine for obtaining equivalent scales (equivalent scales are used to preserve the original shape of each block letter); 4) Control is next passed to the routine to determine equivalent scales and 5) Control is passed to the centering and boundary re-definition routine; 6) Finally, the plotting subroutine is called.

## Check Your Comprehension

What problem can you imagine occurring if the viewport is permitted to be of very small size? _____

(You should experiment with this possibility by changing the viewport dimensions to very small values.)

What is the exact sequence of background and plot colors used in the program (list the colors by color number)? _____

"Hand crank" the loop in lines 1010-1040 to convince yourself the complementary color generation formulas really work. What do you determine? _____

The program demonstrates the tremendous flexibility and control scaling gives the user. The letters are created on simple grids, and it is only necessary to specify where on the screen (the viewport) the letter is wanted. The original grids and letters are displayed in Figure 4.4.1.

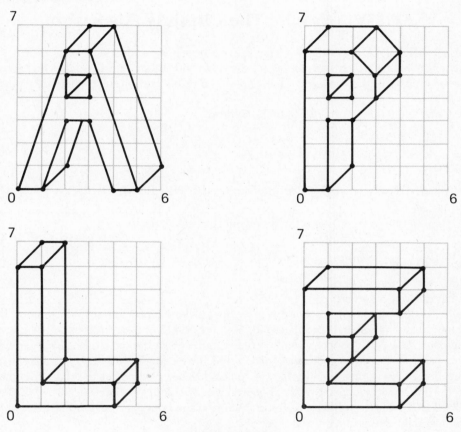

Figure 4.4.1

**EXERCISE**   Write a program which will transform coordinate data for four separate figures onto the second high resolution Page separating the screen into four separate regions of approximately the same dimensions. Place one figure per region, using equivalent scaling and making maximum use of each region. To test your program, use the data for the four distinct block letters supplied in the COMPREHENSIVE EXAMPLE.

**EXERCISE**   Create block letters for the word "HELLO" and then use the data in the program above.

**EXERCISE**   Modify the COMPREHENSIVE EXAMPLE so each letter appears on the left half of the screen using half the full screen as viewport and then the "mirror" image is created on the right half. If you are clever enough in your approach, this can be done without creating new DATA. Hint: Think negative!

**CHALLENGE**   Modify the COMPREHENSIVE EXAMPLE program of ACTIVITY 4.3 to permit the user to select equivalent scales and center the image in the viewport.

# ACTIVITY 4.5   The Clipping Algorithm

**LEARNING BY DISCOVERY**   This activity develops an algorithm used to clip the sections of a line which normally will extend beyond the screen boundaries or beyond the boundaries of the viewport. That is, only the visible portions of the line are plotted.

1. Enter the following APPLESOFT statements.

```
10   HGR : HCOLOR = 3
20   HPLOT 50, 30 TO 284, 74
RUN
```

What did you observe?  Did you receive the ?ILLEGAL QUANTITY ERROR message? _____
Replace statement 20 with the following corrected version.

```
20   SLOPE = (74 - 30)/(284 - 50)
30   HPLOT 50,30 TO 279,30 + (279 - 50)*SLOPE
```

Now reRUN the program.
What did you observe? _____
   The line displayed on the screen represents the clipped line segment joining the points located at screen coordinates (50, 30) and (284, 74). Note: Although technically the point (284, 74) does not visually represent a point on the screen, it is considered to be a point of the screen coordinate system which we consider to extend infinitely in all directions. The segment joining the two points has been clipped at the right boundary of the screen at the point with H-coordinate 279 and V-coordinate 30 + (279 - 50)*SLOPE. The coordinates of the endpoint on the boundary have been determined from straight line geometry and algebra.
   Recall the slope of a line passing through the points (X1,Y1) and (X2,Y2) is the ratio of the Y-change to the X-change, or SLOPE = (Y2 - Y1)/(X2 - X1). This quantity indicates how many units the Y-coordinate must change for each one unit of change in the X-coordinate.
   In the situation above, (X1,Y1) = (50,30) and (X2,Y2) = (284,74). The slope of the line through these two points is computed in the new line 20. The coordinates (X,Y) of any point on the line are given by the equation
   Y = Y1 + (X - X1) * SLOPE
In the example above, you determined the Y-value from the X-value (X = 279) in line 30, ie., you found the coordinates of the intersection of the line with the left screen boundary.

In the previous activity you dealt with a similar clipping problem when the edges of a rectangle extended beyond the boundaries of the screen. You clipped the edges at the screen boundary. The difference in that ACTIVITY is it was easier to determine where the edges need to be clipped because the edges were parallel to the screen boundaries.

In this section, you will consider the more general problem of clipping any line at the boundaries of the screen. With only a little more effort, one can deal with the problem of clipping lines at the boundaries of any viewport. From a programming standpoint, a procedure must be developed which will systematically clip line segments at the boundaries of the viewport regardless of the location of its two endpoints.

2. Clear the workspace (NEW) and enter the following APPLESOFT statements. Use the same line numbers as appear here. The numerically small line numbers are used in this case since the subroutine should be placed very early in your programs for increased access speed. Whenever you perform a GOSUB or GOTO, APPLESOFT must search through each line number, starting at the beginning, until it locates the line you directed it to find. By keeping such subroutines early in a program, you will speed up your program execution.

Note: By using the APPLE editing features the reader can use line 28 to efficiently produce lines 30-34. For example, after entering line 28, LIST 28. By pressing the ESC key (to enter the edit mode) and then using I (up), J (left), K (right), and M (down), position the cursor at the beginning of line 28 (ie., over the "2"). Press the space bar to exit the edit mode. Type the new line number, say 30, over the old line number 28. Use the copy key (the right arrow key) to copy over each character to be repeated in both lines. Change those characters which are different by simply typing over the old unwanted characters. You must copy completely to the end of the line. Don't forget to change the line number (28) to the new line number desired (eg., 30) when using this process.

```
NEW
13   REM  USER PASSES PTS TO BE PLOTTED THRU THE ARRAY
     VARIABLES: XP(I%),YP(I%) : I% = 0,1. HO,H1,VO,V1 SPECIFY
     THE VIEWPORT.
14   REM
15   REM  ACCESS TO THE SUBROUTINE IS MADE THROUGH A GOSUB 20 IN
     MAIN.
16   REM
17   REM  ******************************
18   REM  *        CLIPPING ALGORITHM       *
19   REM  ******************************
20   T%(0) = YP(0) < V1:B%(0) = YP(0) > VO:L%(0) = XP(0) <
     HO:R%(0) = XP(0) > H1:I% = 1
22   FOR TRY = 0 TO 1 STEP 0:T%(I%) = YP(I%) < V1:B%(I%)
     = YP(I%) > VO:L%(I%) = XP(I%) < HO:R%(I%) =
     XP(I%) > H1
24   IF T%(0) AND T%(1) OR B%(0) AND B%(1) OR L%(0) AND L%(1) OR
     R%(0) AND R%(1) THEN  RETURN
26   I% = 0: IF T%(I%) + B%(I%) + L%(I%) + R%(I%) = 0 THEN
```

```
         I% = 1: IF T%(I%) + B%(I%) + L%(I%) + R%(I%) = 0 THEN
         HPLOT XP(0), YP(0) TO XP(1),YP(1): RETURN
28       IF T%(I%) THEN XP(I%) = XP(0) + (V1 - YP(0)) * (XP(1) -
         XP(0)) / (YP(1) - YP(0)):YP(I%) = V1: NEXT
30       IF B%(I%) THEN XP(I%) = XP(0) + (V0 - YP(0)) * (XP(1) -
         XP(0)) / (YP(1) - YP(0)):YP(I%) = V0: NEXT
32       IF L%(I%) THEN YP(I%) = YP(0) + (H0 - XP(0)) * (YP(1) -
         YP(0)) / (XP(1) - XP(0)):XP(I%) = H0: NEXT
34       IF R%(I%) THEN YP(I%) = YP(0) + (H1 - XP(0)) * (YP(1) -
         YP(0)) / (XP(1) - XP(0)):XP(I%) = H1: NEXT
35   REM  **          END CLIPPING          **
LIST
SAVE CLIPPING ALGORITHM
```

Check for errors and then SAVE this algorithm on disk. It is a subroutine you can merge with other programs when it is needed. In the rest of this activity, you will write a program which will implement the subroutine you just entered and also simulate its execution.

Don't be to concerned right now about precisely what the algorithm is doing. In general terms, its function is the following. A pair of points to be connected by a straight line are passed to the subroutine through the variables XP(I%),YP(I%), I% = 1,2 (that is, somewhere else in the program XP(I%),YP(I%) have been defined). Lines 20,22 classify the location of the points relative to the viewport. Line 24 instructs the computer to do nothing if both points are on the opposite side of a boundary line of the viewport. Line 26 successively checks to see if each point is within the viewport. If not, program control falls through to lines 28-34. In these lines, the point of intersection with the appropriate viewport boundary line is determined. The original endpoint is now redefined to be this point on the viewport boundary. The process is repeated until either no segment is visible (line 24), or a portion of the line segment is HPLOTted (line 26).

3. Add the following lines to the clipping algorithm in your workspace. REMarks have been added to the program for the convenience of the user. They should be omitted when entering the program yourself.

```
    < ADD TO THE EXISTING CODE >

10   GOTO 100: REM   BRANCH AROUND CLIPPING SUBROUTINE.
11   REM
97   REM   ********************************
98   REM   *  MAIN PROGRAM:LINES 100-300  *
99   REM   ********************************
100  N$(0) = "FIRST":N$(1) = "SECOND"
110  H0 = 80:H1 = 190:V0 = 120:V1 = 40: REM   SET VIEWPORT.
120  HGR : GOSUB 2000: REM   INIT HIRES SCREEN PAGE 1 AND GO
         DISPLAY VIEWPORT.
300  TEXT : HOME : END
301  REM  **          END MAIN PROGRAM      **
302  REM
```

```
997   REM   *****************************
998   REM   *     CLEAR TEXT WINDOW      *
999   REM   *****************************
1000  HOME : VTAB 21: RETURN
1001  REM   **     END CLR TEXT WINDOW    **
1002  REM
1497  REM   *****************************
1498  REM   *         DELAY LOOP         *
1499  REM   *****************************
1500  FOR J = 1 TO 3000: NEXT J: RETURN
1501  REM   **     END DELAY LOOP         **
1502  REM
1997  REM   *****************************
1998  REM   *       DISPLAY VIEWPORT     *
1999  REM   *****************************
2000  GOSUB 1000: REM   DELAY
2010  HTAB 14: PRINT "THE VIEWPORT"
2020  HCOLOR =  3: HPLOT H0,V0 TO H1,V0 TO H1,V1 TO H0,V1 TO
      H0,V0
2030  GOSUB 1500: REM   DELAY
2040  HTAB 10: PRINT "AND ...THE UNIVERSE"
2050  GOSUB 2500: REM   GO DISPLAY UNIVERSE.
2060  GOSUB 1500: REM   DELAY
2070  RETURN
2071  REM   **    END DISPLAY VIEWPORT    **
2072  REM
2497  REM   *****************************
2498  REM   *        DISPLAY UNIVERSE    *
2499  REM   *****************************
2500  HCOLOR =  3
2510  HPLOT 0,V0 TO 279,V0: HPLOT 0,V1 TO 279,V1: REM   DRAW
      HORIZ LINES.
2520  HPLOT H0,0 TO H0,159: HPLOT H1,0 TO H1,159: REM   DRAW
      VERT LINES.
2530  RETURN
2531  REM   **    END DISPLAY UNIVERSE    **
2532  REM
LIST
RUN
```

Describe the display. _____

What is your interpretation of the term "UNIVERSE" used in the display? _____
_____

By changing the values in line 110, the size and the position of the viewport can
be changed. You may wish to experiment with a few values of your own.

4. Now, enter the lines of code needed to: 1) input the endpoints of a line segment; 2)
plot them; and 3) representatively draw the line segment (in the universe) joining

them. Add the following lines of code to the program in memory.

```
<ADD TO THE EXISTING CODE.>
130   GOSUB 1000: REM  CLR TEXT SCRN.
140   FOR I = 0 TO 1: REM  FOR EACH OF TWO PTS DO ...
150   I% = I: REM  WANTED TO USE I% FOR INDEX BUT APPLESOFT
      DOES NOT ALLOW INTEGER DECLARED LOOP INDEX VARIABLES.
160   PRINT "INPUT THE COORDINATES OF THE "N$(I%)" PT": PRINT
      "TO BE PLOTTED: < H,V > ";: INPUT XP(I%),YP(I%)
170   GOSUB 3000: REM  GO DISPLAY INPUT POINT.
180   NEXT I
190   GOSUB 1000: REM  CLR TEXT SCRN.
200   PRINT "THE POINTS ARE: ("XP(0)", "YP(0)") AND ("XP(1)",
      "YP(1)")."
210   PRINT "PRESS THE BAR TO SEE THE LINE SEGMENT": PRINT
      "JOINING THE TWO POINTS (IN THE UNIVERSE).";: GET K$:
      PRINT
220   GOSUB 4000: REM  GO DISPLAY DOTTED LINE SEGMENT JOINING
      PTS.
230   PRINT  TAB( 13)"PRESS THE BAR";: GET K$
240   GOSUB 1000: REM  CLR TEXT SCRN.
280   PRINT "TRY ANOTHER PAIR OF POINTS?";: GET K$: PRINT K$
290   IF K$ = "Y" THEN 120
2997  REM  ******************************
2998  REM  *      ENDPT DISPLAY SUBRT     *
2999  REM  ******************************
3000  IF XP(I%) < 2 OR XP(I%) > 277 OR YP(I%) > 157 OR
      YP(I%) < 2 THEN 7000: REM  CHECK TO SEE IF PT CAN
      BE DISPLAYED WITH A 4X4 BOX CENTERED AT PT.; IF NOT, GO
      TO INPUT ERROR ROUTINE.
3010  HCOLOR =  3: HPLOT XP(I%) + 2,YP(I%) + 2 TO XP(I%) +
      2,YP(I%) - 2 TO XP(I%) - 2,YP(I%) - 2 TO XP(I%) -
      2,YP(I%) + 2 TO XP(I%) + 2,YP(I%) + 2
3020  RETURN
3021  REM  **  END ENDPT DISPLAY SUB  **
3022  REM
3997  REM  ******************************
3998  REM  *    DOTTED LINE SEG DISPLAY  *
3999  REM  ******************************
4000  HCOLOR =  3:DH = XP(1) - XP(0):DV = YP(1) - YP(0)
4010  IF  ABS (DH) < ABS (DV) THEN M = DH / DV: FOR V =
      YP(0) TO YP(1) STEP 3 *  SGN (DV): HPLOT XP(0) +
      (V - YP(0)) * M,V: NEXT : RETURN
4020  IF DH = 0 THEN  RETURN
4030  M = DV / DH: FOR H = XP(0) TO XP(1) STEP 3 *  SGN
      (DH): HPLOT H,YP(0) + (H - XP(0)) * M:
      NEXT : RETURN
4031  REM  **   END DOTTED LINE SEG   **
```

```
4032  REM
6997  REM  ******************************
6998  REM  *   INPUT ERROR HANDLING RTN  *
6999  REM  ******************************
7000  POP : REM  PULL 'RETURN' OFF STACK SINCE A DIRECT
      BRANCH BACK TO GET VALID INPUT WILL BE USED.
7010  GOSUB 1000: REM  CLR TEXT SRN.
7020  PRINT "THE PROGRAM WILL NOT VISIBLY DISPLAY": PRINT
      "THE POINT. IT MUST BE WITHIN 2 PIXELS": PRINT
      "OF THE SCREEN BOUNDARIES."
7030  PRINT  TAB( 8)"PRESS THE BAR TO REENTER";: GET A$
7040  GOSUB 1000: REM  CLR TEXT SCRN.
7050  GOTO 160: REM  BRANCH BACK TO REGET INPUT.
7051  REM  **   END INPUT ERROR RT     **
7052  REM
LIST
```

RUN the program using the following pairs of numbers as input data.

| FIRST POINT | SECOND POINT |
|---|---|
| 2 ,    2 | 140 ,  80 |
| 90 ,  90 | 270 , 150 |
| 260 , 100 | 5 , 140 |
| 85 ,  45 | 180 , 110 |
| 40 ,  10 | 90 ,  30 |
| 120 , 140 | 20 ,  10 |
| 140 ,  20 | 0 ,   0 |

What did you observe? _____

What happened when the last point was input? _____

Why did you receive the error message when the last point was input? (See the subroutine at 7000) _____

Why is a two pixel buffer zone needed near the screen edge? (See lines 3000-3010)

_____

In the dotted line display, the equation of a line is used to determine the points to HPLOT. However, the subroutine distinguishes between an almost vertical line (ABS(DH) < ABS(DV), ie., 1 < ABS(SLOPE) ; line 4010)  and an almost horizontal line (ABS(DH) > = ABS(DV), ie., 1 > = ABS(SLOPE)). By making this distinction, the dotted lines have a better appearance and, in the case of a vertical line for which the slope is not defined, the line generation is handled more easily. You should study these program lines to be sure you understand them. If you are not convinced of the advantage of distinguishing between "nearly vertical" and "nearly horizontal" lines, use the plotting routine in line 4010 all the time to observe the effect on nearly vertical lines.

Why is line 4020 needed? _____

_____

5. Finally, add the lines of code needed to actually simulate the clipping process. Combine the following statements with the program in memory.

```
< ADD THE LINES BELOW TO THE EXISTING PROGRAM. >
27  OXP = XP(I%):OYP = YP(I%)
250  PRINT "EACH SUCCESSIVE PRESS OF THE BAR WILL": PRINT
     "ADVANCE THE CLIPPING PROCESS UNTIL THE": PRINT
     "CLIPPED SEGMENT IS DISPLAYED.";: GET K$
260  GOSUB 20: REM  GO TO THE CLIPPING ALGORITHM (MODIFIED
     FOR THIS PROGRAM ONLY).
270  GOSUB 1000: REM  CLR TEXT SCRN.
3497  REM  ******************************
3498  REM  *   OLD ENDPT DISPLAY SUBRT  *
3499  REM  ******************************
3500  HCOLOR =  3: HPLOT OXP + 2,OYP + 2 TO OXP + 2,OYP -
      2 TO OXP - 2,OYP - 2 TO OXP - 2,OYP + 2 TO OXP +
      2,OYP + 2
3510  RETURN
3511  REM  **   END OLD ENDPT DISPLAY  **
3512  REM
4997  REM  ******************************
4998  REM  *     ERASE SEGMENT SUBRT    *
4999  REM  ******************************
5000  HCOLOR =  0: HPLOT OXP,OYP TO XP(I%),YP(I%) TO OXP,OYP
      TO OXP,OYP + 1 TO XP(I%),YP(I%) + 1 TO XP(I%),YP(I%)
      - 1 TO OXP,OYP - 1
5010  GOSUB 2500: REM  GO REDRAW UNIVERSE LINES.
5020  GOSUB 3010: REM  GO DRAW PT 'BOX' OF PT ON BNDRY LINE.
5030  GOSUB 3500: REM   GO REDRAW OLD ENDPT BOX.
5040  GOSUB 1000: PRINT  TAB( 8)"PRESS THE BAR TO CONTINUE";:
      GET A$: RETURN
5041  REM  **   END ERASE SEGMT SUBRT  **
5042  REM
5997  REM  ******************************
5998  REM  *  ERASE SEGMENT: SPEC CASE  *
5999  REM  ******************************
6000  OXP = XP(0):OYP = YP(0):I% = 1
6010  GOSUB 5000: REM  GO ERASE SEGMENT FROM OLD ENDPT TO PT
      ON BNDRY LINE.
6020  RETURN
6021  REM  **  END ERASE SPECIAL CASE  **
6022  REM
LIST
```

To complete the program one needs to insert a GOSUB 5000 into lines 28, 30, 32, and 34 before the NEXT appearing at the end of each line. Use the APPLE edit mode to make the insertions. If you are not familiar with this aspect of the editor, the step by step procedure is outlined below. For each line to be changed complete the following steps.

1. List the line to be changed.
2. Enter the edit mode (ESC key), and move the cursor (I, J, K, M keys) to the

beginning of the line. Exit the edit mode (space bar).

3. Copy (right arrow key) over the line until the cursor is just to the right of the colon (:) preceding NEXT.

4. Enter the edit mode (ESC key), and move to any area of the screen above the present line. Exit the edit mode (space bar) and type

```
GOSUB 5000:
```

5. Enter the edit mode (ESC key), move (I, J, K, M keys) to the right of the colon (:) preceding NEXT in the original line, and exit the edit mode (space bar).

6. Copy over (right arrow key) the remainder of the line and press RETURN.

7. LIST the line to make sure the insertion has been properly made.

Using the editor, insert a GOSUB 6000: following the THEN in line 24. These GOSUB's and line 27 are inserted into the CLIPPING ALGORITHM only for the purpose of simulating the clipping process. They normally should not be inserted in the algorithm when it is used in programs which require clipping.

The complete program, exclusive of REMarks, is listed below. Use it to compare with your own listing.

```
10   GOTO 100
20   T%(0) = YP(0) < V1:B%(0) = YP(0) > V0:L%(0) =
     XP(0) < H0:R%(0) = XP(0) > H1:I% = 1
22   FOR TRY = 0 TO 1 STEP 0:T%(I%) = YP(I%) < V1:B%(I%) =
     YP(I%) > V0:L%(I%) = XP(I%) < H0:R%(I%) = XP(I%)
     > H1
24   IF T%(0) AND T%(1) OR B%(0) AND B%(1) OR L%(0) AND L%(1) OR
     R%(0) AND R%(1) THEN  GOSUB 6000: RETURN
26   I% = 0: IF T%(I%) + B%(I%) + L%(I%) + R%(I%) = 0 THEN
     I% = 1: IF T%(I%) + B%(I%) + L%(I%) + R%(I%) = 0 THEN
     HPLOT XP(0),YP(0) TO XP(1),YP(1): RETURN
27   OXP = XP(I%):OYP = YP(I%)
28   IF T%(I%) THEN XP(I%) = XP(0) + (V1 - YP(0)) * (XP(1) -
     XP(0)) / (YP(1) - YP(0)):YP(I%) = V1: GOSUB 5000: NEXT
30   IF B%(I%) THEN XP(I%) = XP(0) + (V0 - YP(0)) * (XP(1) -
     XP(0)) / (YP(1) - YP(0)):YP(I%) = V0: GOSUB 5000: NEXT
32   IF L%(I%) THEN YP(I%) = YP(0) + (H0 - XP(0)) * (YP(1) -
     YP(0)) / (XP(1) - XP(0)):XP(I%) = H0: GOSUB 5000: NEXT
34   IF R%(I%) THEN YP(I%) = YP(0) + (H1 - XP(0)) * (YP(1) -
     YP(0)) / (XP(1) - XP(0)):XP(I%) = H1: GOSUB 5000: NEXT
100  N$(0) = "FIRST":N$(1) = "SECOND"
110  H0 = 80:H1 = 190:V0 = 120:V1 = 40
120  HGR : GOSUB 2000
130  GOSUB 1000
140  FOR I = 0 TO 1
150  I% = I
160  PRINT "INPUT THE COORDINATES OF THE "N$(I%)" PT": PRINT
     "TO BE PLOTTED: < H,V > ";: INPUT XP(I%),YP(I%)
170  GOSUB 3000
180  NEXT I
```

```
190    GOSUB 1000
200    PRINT "THE POINTS ARE: ("XP(0)", "YP(0)") AND ("XP(1)",
       "YP(1)")."
210    PRINT "PRESS THE BAR TO SEE THE LINE SEGMENT":  PRINT
       "JOINING THE TWO POINTS (IN THE UNIVERSE).";:
       GET K$: PRINT
220    GOSUB 4000
230    PRINT  TAB( 13)"PRESS THE BAR";: GET K$
240    GOSUB 1000
250    PRINT "EACH SUCCESSIVE PRESS OF THE BAR WILL": PRINT
       "ADVANCE THE CLIPPING PROCESS UNTIL THE": PRINT
       "CLIPPED SEGMENT IS DISPLAYED.";: GET K$
260    GOSUB 20
270    GOSUB 1000
280    PRINT "TRY ANOTHER PAIR OF POINTS?";: GET K$: PRINT K$
290    IF K$ = "Y" THEN 120
300    TEXT : HOME : END
1000   HOME : VTAB 21: RETURN
1500   FOR J = 1 TO 3000: NEXT J: RETURN
2000   GOSUB 1000
2010   HTAB 14: PRINT "THE VIEWPORT"
2020   HCOLOR =  3: HPLOT H0,V0 TO H1,V0 TO H1,V1 TO H0,V1 TO
       H0,V0
2030   GOSUB 1500
2040   HTAB 10: PRINT "AND ...THE UNIVERSE"
2050   GOSUB 2500
2060   GOSUB 1500
2070   RETURN
2500   HCOLOR =  3
2510   HPLOT 0,V0 TO 279,V0: HPLOT 0,V1 TO 279,V1
2520   HPLOT H0,0 TO H0,159: HPLOT H1,0 TO H1,159
2530   RETURN
3000   IF XP(I%) < 2 OR XP(I%) > 277 OR YP(I%) > 157 OR
       YP(I%) < 2 THEN 7000
3010   HCOLOR =  3: HPLOT XP(I%) + 2,YP(I%) + 2 TO XP(I%) +
       2,YP(I%) − 2 TO XP(I%) − 2,YP(I%) − 2 TO XP(I%) − 2,
       YP(I%) + 2 TO XP(I%) + 2,YP(I%) + 2
3020   RETURN
3500   HCOLOR =  3: HPLOT OXP + 2,OYP + 2 TO OXP + 2,OYP − 2
       TO OXP − 2,OYP − 2 TO OXP − 2,
       OYP + 2 TO OXP + 2,OYP + 2
3510   RETURN
4000   HCOLOR =  3:DH = XP(1) − XP(0):DV = YP(1) − YP(0)
4010   IF  ABS (DH) < ABS (DV) THEN M = DH / DV: FOR V =
       YP(0) TO YP(1) STEP 3 *  SGN (DV): HPLOT XP(0) +
       (V − YP(0)) * M,V: NEXT : RETURN
4020   IF DH = 0 THEN  RETURN
```

```
4030   M = DV / DH: FOR H = XP(0) TO XP(1) STEP 3 * SGN (DH):
       HPLOT H,YP(0) + (H - XP(0)) * M: NEXT :
       RETURN
5000   HCOLOR =  0: HPLOT OXP,OYP TO XP(I%),YP(I%) TO OXP,OYP
       TO OXP,OYP + 1 TO XP(I%),YP(I%) + 1 TO XP(I%),YP(I%)
       - 1 TO OXP,OYP - 1
5010   GOSUB 2500
5020   GOSUB 3010
5030   GOSUB 3500
5040   GOSUB 1000: PRINT  TAB( 8)"PRESS THE BAR TO CONTINUE";:
       GET A$: RETURN
6000   OXP = XP(0):OYP = YP(0):I% = 1
6010   GOSUB 5000
6020   RETURN
7000   POP
7010   GOSUB 1000
7020   PRINT "THE PROGRAM WILL NOT VISIBLY DISPLAY": PRINT "THE
       POINT. IT MUST BE WITHIN 2 PIXELS": PRINT "OF THE
       SCREEN BOUNDARIES."
7030   PRINT  TAB( 8)"PRESS THE BAR TO REENTER";: GET A$
7040   GOSUB 1000
7050   GOTO 160
```

RUN the program using the points listed at the end of Section 4.
What do you observe? _____

Using the data values 2, 30 and 140, 80 observe the location of the point (2,30). For which two bounding lines does (2,30) fall on the "wrong side" of the viewport?
_____ (Answer: Top and Left)

What values will be assigned to the classification variables $T\%(0)$, $B\%(0)$, $L\%(0)$, and $R\%(0)$? _____

(Answer: 1, 0, 1, 0)

The point (140,80) lies entirely in the viewport. What values will be assigned to the classification variables $T\%(1)$, $B\%(1)$, $L\%(1)$, and $L\%(1)$? _____

(Answer: 0, 0, 0, 0)

When the segment joining 2,30 and 140,80 is clipped, at which bounding line of the viewport is the segment first clipped? _____ (Top, Bottom, Left, Right)
_____ Second ? _____ Compare the order you obtained here with the order in which the lines in 28-34 should be executed for $I\% = 0$. Do you perceive agreement? _____ Which line (28-34) will be executed in the first phase of the clipping process? _____ in the second phase? _____

Reverse the order in which the points 2,30 and 140,80 are passed to the program. That is, enter them in the order 140,80 to 2,30. Is there any change in the order in which the segment is clipped at the boundaries? _____

Consider the data values 2, 30 and 277, 130. Observe their positions on the screen relative to the viewport and write the classification values which must be assigned.

(2,30)          :    T % (0) _____, B % (0) _____, L % (0) _____, R % (0) _____
(277,130)       :    T % (1) _____, B % (1) _____, L % (1) _____, R % (1) _____

When the joining line segment is clipped, what is the order in which the bounding lines are clipped (from first to last)? _____ Now repeat the procedure for same points but entered in reverse order, i.e., enter 277, 130 and 2, 30. What do you observe? _____ Is it a reversal of the actions exhibited earlier? _____ Why not? _____ What sequence of events was reversed? _____ Consider the order of values assigned to I % in line 26.

What is the only way for program control to get past line 26? _____

What does it mean in terms of the locations of the points XP(0),YP(0) and XP(1),YP(1)? _____

Suppose both points are on same side of a viewport bounding line but not on the side containing the viewport (Consider line number 24). Use the program to test your impressions of what will happen using data points such as 4, 10 and 21, 140; 19, 152 and 155, 145; 57, 12 and 275, 20.

What do you observe? _____

If both points are within the viewport then the segment should be plotted in its entirety. (Consider line 26.) Experiment with values such as 90, 60 and 198, 118; 140, 45 and 140, 115. What do you observe? _____

**DISCUSSION**   The position of the endpoints relative to each bounding line of the viewport is determined by the variables T % (Top), B % (Bottom), L % (Left), and R % (Right). The value one is assigned to a classification variable if the endpoint being tested is on the opposite side of the bounding line from the viewport.

For example, the logical condition XP(I) < H0 is assigned the value one if it is true and the value zero otherwise. This value is assigned to L % (I): L % (I) = XP(I) < H0. Nearly duplicate sets of classify segments appear in lines 20 and 22, sacrificing an insignificant amount of memory. In return, some time consuming but otherwise necessary GOTO statements have been avoided. An alternative scheme using only one set of classification assignments will require the use of GOTO or GOSUB statements to classify each endpoint.

Statement 24 checks to see if both endpoints fall on the same side of a bounding line, but outside the viewport. If the conditional check is true, then no segment is drawn and the subroutine returns to the main program.

Statement 26 successively checks each point to see it is within the viewport. If not, then statements 28-34 systematically determine the point of intersection of the joining line with any bounding line which falls between an endpoint and the viewport. The variables XP(I) and YP(I) are reassigned the coordinate values of the point of intersection. The reader is advised to pay particular attention to this aspect of the algorithm in order to avoid inadvertent misuse of XP(I) and YP(I) after returning from a call to the subroutine. If the original values of XP(I) and YP(I) are needed on return from the CLIPPING ALGORITHM, they should be saved prior to calling the subroutine.

The point of intersection of the given segment with a viewport bounding line is easily obtained by considering the equation of a line. Indeed, the equation of the line joining the points (XP(0),YP(0)) and (XP(1),YP(1)) is given by

$$(YP(1)-YP(0)) * (Y-Y1) = (X-X1) * (XP(1)-XP(0))$$

where (X1,Y1) is a known point on the line and (X,Y) is an arbitrary point on the line.

For example, suppose the endpoint under consideration (which lies outside the viewport) is (XP(I%),YP(I%)) and suppose the point of intersection with the top boundary line is needed. Let X1 = XP(0) and Y1 = YP(0). Now, since the Y-coordinate (vertical displacement) of the point of intersection must be V1, let Y = V1 in the line equation above and then solve for X. In this case, X = XP(0) + (V1-YP(0)) * (XP(1)-XP(0)) / (YP(1)-YP(0)). If XP(I%) and YP(I%) are redefined to be these new values X and Y, then the formulas described in line 28 of the CLIPPING ALGORITHM are obtained. The formulas in lines 30-34 are similarly obtained.

**COMPREHENSIVE EXAMPLE**  The following program uses a combination of changes in scaling and the CLIPPING ALGORITHM to produce an unusual graphics effect. A very small shape table (one single plot-move instruction) is also used.

The main purpose of the program is to give one illustration of the use of the CLIPPING ALGORITHM. The point to be emphasized is the exact same figure is repeatedly redrawn, but the scale factor changes from one display to the next. The CLIPPING ALGORITHM controls the HPLOTting in the display. The mobile animation was entered at a whimsical fancy of one of the authors. It will require some extra coding effort from you, but gives an unusual effect. Enter, RUN, and enjoy. When you run the program, step by increments of one through the magnification responses for the best effect.

```
NEW
10  REM  ********************************
11  REM  *           CE4.5             *
12  REM  ********************************
13  REM
14  REM
15  GOTO 100: REM  BRANCH AROUND SUBROUTINES.
16  REM
17  REM  ********************************
18  REM  *        CLIPPING ALGORITHM     *
19  REM  ********************************
20  T%(0) = YP(0) < V1:B%(0) = YP(0) > V0:L%(0) =
    XP(0) < H0:R%(0) = XP(0) > H1:I% = 1
22  FOR TRY = 0 TO 1 STEP 0:T%(I%) = YP(I%) < V1:B%(I%) =
    YP(I%) > V0:L%(I%) = XP(I%) < H0:R%(I%) = XP(I%) > H1
24  IF T%(0) AND T%(1) OR B%(0) AND B%(1) OR L%(0) AND L%(1) OR
    R%(0) AND R%(1) THEN  RETURN
26  I% = 0: IF T%(I%) + B%(I%) + L%(I%) + R%(I%) = 0 THEN
    I% = 1: IF T%(I%) + B%(I%) + L%(I%) + R%(I%) = 0
    THEN  HPLOT XP(0),YP(0) TO XP(1),YP(1): RETURN
28  IF T%(I%) THEN XP(I%) = XP(0) + (V1 - YP(0)) * (XP(1) -
    XP(0)) / (YP(1) - YP(0)):YP(I%) = V1: NEXT
30  IF B%(I%) THEN XP(I%) = XP(0) + (V0 - YP(0)) * (XP(1) -
    XP(0)) / (YP(1) - YP(0)):YP(I%) = V0: NEXT
```

```
32   IF L%(I%) THEN YP(I%) = YP(0) + (H0 - XP(0)) * (YP(1) -
     YP(0)) / (XP(1) - XP(0)):XP(I%) = H0: NEXT
34   IF R%(I%) THEN YP(I%) = YP(0) + (H1 - XP(0)) * (YP(1) -
     YP(0)) / (XP(1) - XP(0)):XP(I%) = H1: NEXT
35   REM  **          END CLIPPING        **
36   REM
47   REM  ********************************
48   REM  * MOBILE AND LETTER DRAW SUBRT *
49   REM  ********************************
50   HPLOT HC,TM TO LM(DSP),VC TO HC,BM TO RM(DSP),VC TO HC,TM:
     REM  PLOT BNDRY OF MOBILE IN SEQUENCE: TOP - LEFT - BOTT
     - RT - TOP, FOR DISPLAY # DSP.
52   HPLOT HC - S(2,DSP),TL TO HC - S(8,DSP),TL TO HC -
     S(8,DSP),BL TO HC - S(2,DSP),BL: HPLOT HC - S(8,DSP),
     VC TO HC - S(2,DSP),VC: REM  DRAW LETTER 'E' AS IT APPEARS
     FOR THIS DISPLAY # ( = DSP).
54   HPLOT HC + S(2,DSP),TL TO HC + S(8,DSP),TL: HPLOT HC +
     S(5,DSP),TL TO HC + S(5,DSP),BL: REM  DRAW LETTER
     'T'.
56   HPLOT HC - S(1,DSP),BL: HPLOT HC + S(6,DSP),BL: REM  PLACE
     PERIODS.
58   RETURN
59   REM  **  END MOBILE AND LETTER SUB **
60   REM
97   REM  ********************************
98   REM  *          MAIN PROGRAM        *
99   REM  ********************************
100   GOSUB 3000: REM  GOTO TEXT INTRODUCTION.
110   GOSUB 4000: REM  GOTO INITIALIZATION ROUTINE.
120   VTAB 23: HTAB 8: PRINT "PRESS THE BAR TO CONTINUE": GET A$
130   HGR : HCOLOR = 3: REM  SET MIXED HIRES GRAPHICS; PLOT
      COLOR = WHT.
140   M = 1: REM  M = POWER DISPLAYED ON SCREEN; SET INITIALLY
      TO 1.
150   FOR VIEW = 0 TO 1 STEP 0: REM  FOR AS MANY VIEWS AS THE
      USER WANTS, DO ...
160   SCL = M * M / 30: REM  SCL = SCALE FACTOR FOR ENLARGING
      IMAGE; INITIALLY, SCL = 1/30.
170   GOSUB 6000: REM  GOTO ROUTINE TO DETERMINE MOBILE
      PARAMETERS DEPENDENT ON THE SCALE = SCL.
180   HOME : VTAB 21
190   HTAB 3: PRINT "YOUR PRESENT MAGNIFICATION IS "M" X ."
200   HTAB 14: PRINT "..FOCUSING..";
210   CALL 62450: REM  CLEAR HIRES SCREEN.
220   GOSUB 2000: REM  GOTO PLOTTING ROUTINE.
230   HTAB 1: CALL  - 868: REM  CLEAR TEXT LINE.
240   HTAB 8: PRINT "PRESS A KEY TO CONTINUE";
250   GOSUB 1000: REM  GOTO SPINNING MOBILE ROUTINE. RETURN FROM
```

```
         SUBRT IS EFFECTED BY ANY KEYPRESS.
260    HTAB 1: CALL  - 868
270    PRINT "SELECT NEW POWER OR TYPE END TO STOP.":  PRINT
       "(POWER RANGE: 1X TO 10X)";: INPUT M$
280    HTAB 1: CALL  - 868: REM  CLR TEXT LINE.
290    IF  LEFT$ (M$,3) = "END" THEN  TEXT : HOME : END
300    IF  RIGHT$ (M$,1) = "X" THEN M$ =  LEFT$ (M$, LEN (M$) -
       1): REM  IF USER ATTACHES 'X' TO INPUT THEN STRIP
       IT.
310    MM =  VAL (M$): REM  CONVERT STRNG INPUT TO NUMERIC VALUE
       ... A TRIAL MAGNIF.
320    IF MM < 1 OR MM > 10 THEN  PRINT "ILLEGAL
       MAGNIFICATION..TRY AGAIN!": FOR J = 1 TO 1000: NEXT :
       HOME : VTAB 21: PRINT "PRESENT POWER "M"X .":
       GOTO 270
330    M = MM: REM  A VALID MAGNIFCTN WAS INPUT
340    NEXT VIEW: REM  BRANCH BACK TO DISPLAY NEW MAGNIFICATION.
341    REM  **        END MAIN PROGRAM      **
342    REM
997    REM  *******************************
998    REM  *      SPINNING MOBILE SUBRT    *
999    REM  *******************************
1000   SCALE =  10 * M: REM  CHOOSE (LIGHT FLASH) SHAPE SCALE
       10 * MAGNIFICATION.
1010   POKE  - 16368,0: REM  RESET KEYBOARD STROBE.
1020   FOR SPN = 0 TO 1 STEP 0: REM  FOR AN INDEFINITE # OF
       SPINS OF THE MOBILE DO ...
1030   KP =  PEEK ( - 16384)
1040   IF KP > 127 THEN  POKE  - 16368,0:DSP = 1: HCOLOR =
       3: GOSUB 50: RETURN : REM  IF KEY PRESS IS DETECTED THEN
       RESET KEYBOARD STROBE, DISPLAY FULL FACE MOBILE, AND
       RETURN TO MAIN PROG.
1050   HCOLOR =  3: HPLOT HC,TM TO HC,BM: REM  DRAW MOBILE AS
       APPEARING ON EDGE.
1060   FOR J = 1 TO 2: REM  FOR DSP 1 AND 2 ...
1070   FOR C = 1 TO 8:S(C,J)= - S(C,J): NEXT C: REM  NEGATE
       SCALED HORIZ WIDTHS OF 1,...,8. THE EFFECT IS TO FLIP
       LETTERS FOR A REVERSE DISPLAY.
1080   NEXT J
1090   HCOLOR =  0: HPLOT HC,TM TO HC,BM: REM  ERASE 'EDGE
       APPEARING TOWARDS YOU'.
1100   FOR K = 1 TO 3: REM  FOR THE NEXT THREE DISPLAYS ...
1110   DSP = 2 - (K = 2): REM  DSP WILL CYCLE THRU DISPLAY
       VALUES 2,1,2.
1120   HCOLOR =  3: GOSUB 50: REM  DRAW MOBILE BNDRY AND
       LETTERS FOR DISPLAY # DSP.
1130   IF DSP = 1 THEN  FOR J = 1 TO 2: ROT =  255 *  RND (1):
```

```
        XDRAW 1 AT HC,VC: XDRAW 1 AT HC,VC: NEXT : REM
        MAKE 2 'FLASHES' OF LIGHT FOR RANDOM ROT VALUES IF MOBILE
        IS FULL FACE (DSP = 1).
1140    HCOLOR =  0: GOSUB 50: REM  ERASE MOBILE BNDRY AND
        LETTERS FOR DISPLAY # DSP.
1150    NEXT K
1160    NEXT SPN
1161    REM  **      END SPINNING MOBILE   **
1162    REM
1997    REM  ******************************
1998    REM  *  PLOT SUBRT USING CLIPPING *
1999    REM  ******************************
2000    H = HC + X(0) * SCL:V = VC — Y(0) * SCL: REM  SET UP
        1ST PT TO PLOT FROM.
2010    FOR K = 1 TO N: REM  FOR EACH DATA PT ...
2020    IF Y(K) = EPL THEN K = K + 1:H = HC + X(K) * SCL:V =
        VC — Y(K) * SCL: NEXT K: REM  IF Y(K) IS THE EPL
        VAL THEN ADVANCE INDEX TO GET NEXT PAIR X,Y AND DETRM
        SCRN COORDS.
2030    XP(0) = H:YP(0) = V: REM  XP(0),YP(0) IS THE PT
        'PLOTTING FROM', WHICH EQUALS PT 'PLOTTED TO' FOR
        PREVIOUS TWO PTS. NOTE: XP,YP DENOTE PTS USED IN CLIP
        ALG.
2040    H = HC + X(K) * SCL:V = VC — Y(K) * SCL: REM  GET SCRN
        COORDS OF X(K),Y(K).
2050    XP(1) = H:YP(1) = V: REM  PUT INTO CLIP VARIABLES.
2060    GOSUB 20: REM  GOTO CLIPPING ALG.
2070    NEXT K: REM  GO BACK FOR ANOTHER PT.
2080    RETURN
2081    REM  **      END PLOT SUBRT       **
2082    REM
2997    REM  ******************************
2998    REM  *      TEXT INTRO SUBRT      *
2999    REM  ******************************
3000    HOME : VTAB 4
3010    SPEED =  150
3020    PRINT "YOUR NEW TELESCOPIC LENS FOR YOUR": PRINT "CAMERA
        WILL PERMIT YOU TO TAKE": PRINT "PICTURES FROM A WIDE
        RANGE OF"
3030    PRINT "DISTANCES. A BRILLIANT FULL MOON WILL": PRINT
        "PERMIT YOU TO TRY SOME NIGHTTIME SHOTS.":
        PRINT
3040    PRINT "AS YOU SIGHT THROUGH THE LENS YOU SEE": PRINT
        "SOMETHING....SOMETHING FLASHING THROUGH": PRINT
        "THE EERIE MIST AND DARKNESS. YES,"
3050    PRINT "MOST OF THE IMAGE IS CLEAR NOW, BUT..": PRINT
        "WHAT? WHAT IS CAUSING THAT STRANGE": PRINT
        "FLICKERING?"
```

```
3060 SPEED =  255
3070 RETURN
3071 REM **      END TEXT INTRO SUB   **
3072 REM
3997 REM *******************************
3998 REM *    INITIALIZATION RTNE   *
3999 REM *******************************
4000 N = 44: REM  THE # OF DATA PTS FOR HOUSE CONSTRCTN.
4010 DIM X(N),Y(N): REM  ESTABLISH ARRAYS FOR STORING COORD
     DATA.
4020 CX = 700:CY = 500: REM  CENTRAL VALUES OF COORD DATA
     FOR HOUSE.
4030 FOR K = 0 TO N
4040 READ X(K),Y(K)
4050 X(K) = X(K) - CX:Y(K) = Y(K) - CY: REM  CENTRALIZE
     DATA. DATA NOW RANGES: -700 < =  X < =  700; -500
     < =  Y < =  500.
4060 NEXT K
4070 READ MWD,MHT,LHT: REM  READ MOBILE WD,HT AND LETTER HT.
4080 EPL =  - 509: REM  END OF PLOT VALUE: (-9) - CY=-509
4090 H0 = 0:H1 = 279:V0 = 159:V1 = 0: REM  SET VIEWPORT
     PARAMETERS = MIXED SCRN.
4100 HC = 140:VC = 80: REM  MIXED SCRN CENTER COORDS.
4110 POKE 232,0: POKE 233,3: REM  SET POINTERS TO WHERE SHAPE
     IS LOADED ($300 = 768).
4120 POKE 768,1: POKE 769,0: POKE 770,4: POKE 771,0: POKE
     772,5: POKE 773,0: REM  INSTALL SHAPE TABLE; SHAPE =
     PLOT MOVE RIGHT.
4130 DIM T%(1),B%(1),L%(1),R%(1),XP(1),YP(1): REM  DIM ARRAY
     VARIABLES FOR CLIPPING ALG.
4140 RETURN
4141 REM **   END INITIALIZATION    **
4142 REM
5997 REM *******************************
5998 REM *   MOBILE PARAMETERS SUBRT   *
5999 REM *******************************
6000 FOR DSP = 1 TO 2: REM  FOR EACH OF THE 2 NON-TRIVIAL
     DISPLAYS OF THE MOBILE ...
6010 XSCL = SCL / DSP: REM  MOBILE HORIZ SCALE IS FULL SCL
     FOR DSP = 1 AND HALF SCL FOR DSP = 2.
6020 LM(DSP) = HC - MWD * XSCL: REM  LEFT HORIZ COORD OF
     MOBILE FOR DISPLAY DSP.
6030 RM(DSP) = HC + MWD * XSCL: REM  RIGHT HORIZ COORD OF
     MOBILE FOR DISPLAY DSP.
6040 FOR C = 1 TO 8:S(C,DSP) = C * XSCL: NEXT C: REM  SCALED
     VALUES OF 1,...,8 IN THE HORIZ DIRECTION FOR USE IN
     LETTER CONSTRUCTION IN DISPLAY # DSP.
6050 NEXT DSP
```

```
6060   TM = VC − MHT * SCL:BM = VC + MHT * SCL: REM   VERT
       COORDS OF TOP AND BOTTOM PT OF MOBILE.
6070   TL = VC − LHT * SCL:BL = VC + LHT * SCL: REM   VERT
       COORDS OF TOP AND BOTTOM OF LETTERS.
6080   RETURN
6081   REM  **      END MOBILE PARAM        **
6082   REM
7997   REM  *****************************
7998   REM  *        HOUSE DATA          *
7999   REM  *****************************
8000   REM   FRAME & ROOF
8010   DATA  60, 640, 60, 100, 1050, 100, 1250, 220, 1250, 760,
       1216, 803, −9, −9, 1050, 100, 1050, 640, −9,
       −9, 1240, 840, 1110, 640, 0, 640, 130, 840, 1240, 840,
       1320, 740, 1250, 740, −9, −9
8020   REM   DOOR & WALK
8030   DATA  300, 0, 370, 100, 370, 560, 170, 560, 170, 100, 80,
       0, −9, −9, 230, 370, 300, 370, 300, 430, 230, 430, 230,
       370, −9, −9
8040   REM   WINDOW
8050   DATA  550, 320, 750, 320, 750, 560, 550, 560, 550, 320,
       −9, −9, 550, 440, 750, 440, −9, −9, 650,
       560, 650, 320, −9, −9
8060   REM   MOBILE STRING
8070   DATA  700, 560, 700, 512
8080   REM   MOBILE WIDTH AND HEIGHT, LETTER HEIGHT.
8090   DATA  15, 12, 4
8091   REM  **       END HOUSE DATA       **
9092   REM
LIST
```

**Check Your Comprehension**

A few comments on the program construction are in order. After a brief text introduction (lines 3000-3070), control is passed to an initialization routine where the point data for the figure is read into the arrays X( ) and Y( ); DATA for the mobile is read; and a small shape table is installed. The house and its components were originally designed on a $1400 \times 1000$ grid with the central point located at the center of the mobile. The use of integral coordinates for even the smallest aspects of the original display and an attempt to maintain relative sizes of objects dictated the final size of the design grid.

The data values −9, −9 indicate when an old succession of line plots is to terminate and a new one begin. As the coordinate data is read, the values are translated (by $- CX = - 700$ and $- CY = - 500$) so coordinate values of the central data point will be 0, 0 rather than 700, 500. Note the flag value for termination and beginning of successive line plots becomes − 709; the variable EPL is used to denote this flag value.

Why is it necessary in line 2020 to forcibly increment K and then determine XP(0) and YP(0)? _____

There are two scales used in the program. The scale factor SCL controls the size of the entire display and is directly related to the magnification power selected; the larger the power, the greater the scale. The CLIPPING ALGORITHM clips those points which extend beyond the screen boundaries.

The second scale factor, XSCL, is used as a horizontal scale factor for the mobile display. The value of XSCL is either the value of SCL (when DSP = 1) or is half the value of SCL (when DSP = 2). The factor XSCL is used to either display the mobile full face or as if it has experienced a 45 degree (one-eighth) turn. The letters displayed within the mobile and the four edges of the mobile have their measurements scaled by XSCL.

The three phases of the mobile and the details of letter construction are shown in Figure 4.5.1. When the letters are constructed in their raw form on the 1400 × 1000 grid, coordinate displacements from the central point (700,500) vary in the range of one to eight units. This is the reason for the existence of the array S(C,DSP). This array contains the scaled values of the constants 1,...,8 for each of the two possible (lettered displays). Permitting the array S(C,DSP) to alternate between positive and negative values (line 1070) causes the letters to appear in natural order or in reversed order.

What technique is used to keep the mobile spinning and also allow the viewer to interrupt the program so a new magnification can be supplied? _____

The letter height ( = 4 ) must, of course, be scaled by the factor SCL for each display. However, it is not changed for the two displays of the mobile as are the horizontal dimensions. Why not? _____

**EXERCISE**   Consider a diamond with vertices at (2,1), (1,2), (0,1), and (1,0). Write a program which will draw on high resolution Page 2 a sequence of scaled diamonds all centered at 140, 96. Starting with a scale of one, step through scaling factors incremented by five until a scale of 180 is achieved. Use the CLIPPING ALGO-RITHM to plot the diamonds. Make your program general enough so other data can be used and very few changes in the main body of the program will need to be made. In particular, use DATA statements to read in the vertices of the initial diamond.

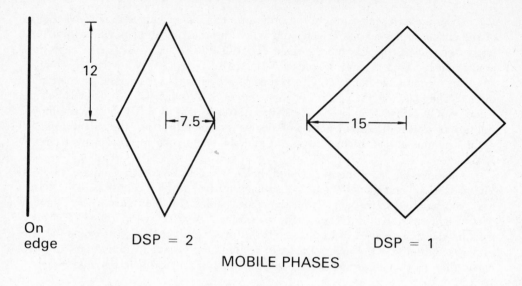

On
edge         DSP = 2                              DSP = 1

MOBILE PHASES

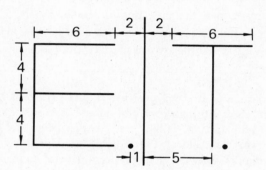

LETTER CONSTRUCTION DETAILS

Figure 4.5.1

**CHALLENGE**   A possible alternative to the CLIPPING ALGORITHM technique used in this section was submitted by one of the reviewers of this book. We are indebted to him for his suggestions and for including a listing of the alternative algorithm. In the listing below the points X0,Y0 and X1,Y1 denote the endpoints of the line segment to (possibly) be clipped.

```
20   IF X0 > X1 THEN TX = X1 : TY = Y1 : X1 = X0 : Y1 = Y0 :
     X0 = TX : Y0 = TY :REM SWAP X0,Y0 AND X1,Y1
22   IF X1 < H0 OR X0 > H1 THEN RETURN
24   IF X0 < H0 THEN Y0 = Y0 + (H0 - X0) * (Y1 - Y0) / (X1
     - X0) : X0 = H0
26   IF X1 > H1 THEN Y1 = Y0 + (H1 - X0) * (Y1 - Y0) / ( X1
     - X0) : X1 = H1
```

```
28   IF Y0 > Y1 THEN TX = X1 : TY = Y1 : X1 = X0 : Y1 = Y0 :
     X0 = TX : Y0 = TY : REM SWAP X0,Y0 AND X1,Y1
30   IF Y1 < V1 OR  Y0 > V0 THEN RETURN
32   IF Y0 < V1 THEN X0 = X0 + (V1 - Y0) * (X1 - X0) / (Y1
     - Y0) : Y0 = V1
34   IF Y1 > V0 THEN X1 = X0 + (V0 - Y0) * (X1 - X0) / (Y1
     - Y0) : Y0 = V0
36   HPLOT X0,Y0 TO X1,Y1 :RETURN
```

Investigate the effect of this alternative algorithm by incorporating it into the programs provided in this activity. Presumably, this algorithm is faster if there are not too many points X0,Y0 and X1,Y1 which are directly above or below the viewport.

# MODULE 4B   Graphics in Geometry

## ACTIVITY 4.6   Coordinate Graphs

**LEARNING BY DISCOVERY**   Ways to graphically create a "coordinate system" on the APPLE screen will be presented in this activity. The concepts of scaling and viewport will play a major role in the development.

1. Although it is assumed the reader is familiar with plane coordinate systems, a review of the crucial elements involved in a standard representation will clarify any misunderstandings. First of all, a pair of intersecting horizontal and vertical lines in a plane region represents the coordinate axes, with the origin corresponding to the point of intersection. The positive sense of directions are normally taken to the right and up, respectively.

   A unit of length (a scale) is chosen along each axis; the two scales may or may not be equivalent. Once a unit of length is chosen, each point on the coordinate axis corresponds to a unique real number; conversely, each real number corresponds to a unique point.

   Each point P in the plane corresponds to a unique ordered pair (X, Y) where X and Y represent the real numbers corresponding to the projection of P onto each coordinate axis. The X-axis is taken as the horizontal axis and the vertical axis corresponds to the Y-axis.

   The APPLE screen can be considered a coordinate system, but the designers of the APPLE decided to make the positive sense of direction downward and to the right. Indeed, (0,0) corresponds to the upper left-hand corner of the screen and any increase in second coordinate (or vertical coordinate) results in a displacement downward. This orientation requires the user to subtract vertical screen displacements while adding the corresponding displacement in a standard coordinate system. Another minor problem is the inequivalency of scales in the screen coordinate system (pixel distances horizontally are not the same as pixel distances vertically). This was treated in detail in ACTIVITY 4.2.

   Finally, the screen is an example of a discrete coordinate system. Specifically, each screen point corresponds to an ordered pair (X, Y) where X is an integer in the range 0 and 279 and Y is an integer in the range 0 and 191. There is technically no distinct point on the screen corresponding to say, (36.7, 21.09). For example, (36, 21) and (36.7, 21.09) correspond to the same point on the screen. In fact, as far as APPLE-SOFT BASIC is concerned there is no distinction between (36, 21) and (36.7, 21.09) or even (36.99, 21.99). To illustrate this situation, turn on your APPLE and enter the following commands in the immediate execution mode.

```
HGR : HCOLOR = 3
HPLOT   50, 0 TO 50, 29
HPLOT   50.9, 31 TO 50.9, 60
HPLOT   100, 50 TO 129, 50
HPLOT   131, 50.4 TO 160, 50.4
```

Note the vertical lines are in the same screen column and the horizontal lines are in the same screen row. Therefore, when HPLOTting a point, any fractional coordinate values are truncated to the integer part of the value.

2. A popular  mode of representing a coordinate system is with graph paper. The grid design aids in a more accurate placement of points and better readability of coordinate values of points. Although one can emulate exactly the grid-like design of horizontal and vertical lines, such a display might make it difficult to distinguish between portions of the grid lines and the actual curve or curves to be displayed on the screen. On the other hand, the use of a grid does make point coordinates easier to read.

An alternative approach is to use a grid of dots. These dots will correspond to the intersections of grid lines. This technique will be explored here further. One final point should be mentioned before proceeding. Just as the distance between two successive grid lines on graph paper may represent a fractional amount of one unit, like .5 or .1 or etc., a similar interpretation will be made for the distance between two successive "grid dots" or "ticks" on the APPLE screen. This scale will be referred to as the "grid density scale."

Boot your Apple with DOS and enter the following program.

```
NEW
100  HO = 1:H1 = 278:V0 = 190:V1 = 1: REM  SET THE VIEWPORT
110  READ OH,OV: REM  READ SCREEN ORIGIN COORDINATES
120  READ HTIC,VTIC: REM  READ SCREEN GRID DENSITY SCALES.
130  HGR2 : HCOLOR =  3
140  GOSUB 5000: REM  CALL COORD GRAPH ROUTINE
150  GET A$: TEXT : REM  PRESS A KEY TO RETURN TO TEXT MODE
160  END
170  DATA  150, 120: REM  SCREEN COORDS OF ORIGIN
180  DATA  12, 10 : REM  HORIZ AND VERT SCREEN GRID DENSITY
     SCALES.
4997 REM  *************************
4998 REM    COORD GRAPH SUBRT
4999 REM  *************************
5000 LH = OH - HTIC *  INT ((OH - HO) / HTIC): REM  SET
     LEFT MOST GRID MARK POSITIONS.
5010 TV = OV - VTIC *  INT ((OV - V1) / VTIC): REM  SET TOP
     MOST GRID MARK POSITIONS.
5020 IF (V1 < = OV) AND (OV < = V0) THEN  GOSUB 5100:
     REM  IF X-AXIS IS VISIBLE THEN SKETCH IT
5030 IF (HO < = OH) AND (OH < = H1) THEN  GOSUB 5180:
     REM  IF Y-AXIS IS VISIBLE THEN SKETCH IT
5040 IF (LH > H1) OR (RH > V0) THEN  RETURN : REM  IF
     GRID PTS ARE NOT VISIBLE THEN RETURN TO MAIN PROG
5050 FOR V = TV TO V0 STEP VTIC
5060 FOR H = LH TO H1 STEP HTIC
5070 HPLOT H,V: REM  PLOT GRID POINT
5080 NEXT H,V
```

```
5090  RETURN
5100  HPLOT HO,OV TO H1,OV: REM  DRAW HORIZ LINE = X-AXIS
5110  IF LH > H1 THEN  RETURN : REM  IF GRID MARKS ARE NOT
      VISIBLE THEN RETURN.
5120  PP% = 3: IF OV - PP% < V1 THEN PP% = OV - V1:
      REM  SET UPPER EXTENT OF GRID MARKS ON X-AXIS.
5130  MM% = 3: IF OV + MM% > VO THEN MM% = VO - OV:
      REM  SET LOWER EXTENT OF GRID MARKS ON X-AXIS.
5140  FOR H = LH TO H1 STEP HTIC
5150  HPLOT H,OV - PP% TO H,OV + MM%: REM  PLACE GRID MARK ON
      X-AXIS.
5160  NEXT H
5170  RETURN
5180  HPLOT OH,V1 TO OH,VO: REM  DRAW VERT LINE = Y-AXIS
5190  IF TV > VO THEN  RETURN : REM  IF GRID MARKS ARE NOT
      VISIBLE THEN RETURN.
5200  MM% = 3: IF OH - MM% < HO THEN MM% = OH - HO:
      REM  SET LEFT EXTENT OF GRID MARKS ON Y-AXIS.
5210  PP% = 3: IF OH + PP% > H1 THEN PP% = H1 - OH:
      REM  SET RIGHT EXTENT OF GRID MARKS ON Y-AXIS.
5220  FOR V = TV TO VO STEP VTIC
5230  HPLOT OH - MM%,V TO OH + PP%,V: REM  PLACE GRID MARK ON
      Y-AXIS.
5240  NEXT V
5250  RETURN
5251  REM  ************************
5252  REM  END OF COORD GRAPH SBRT
5253  REM  ************************
```

Check to be sure all program lines have been correctly entered and then RUN the program. You should observe a coordinate grid displaying the coordinate axes. Before proceeding further, SAVE this program on disk. The coordinate graph subroutine will be extracted later for incorporation into a program.

Let's experiment with changing the DATA statements in lines 170 and 180. Make the following changes and then RUN the program.

```
a)   170  DATA 20, 140
     RUN
b)   180  DATA 15, 15
     RUN
c)   170  DATA 0, 191
     180  DATA 10.7, 13.2
     RUN
d)   170  DATA -20, 100
     180  DATA 20, 24
     RUN
```

What effect did the OH value of $-20$ have in Example d) above?  What implications will an OH value outside of the range H0 to H1 have?  OV outside the range V1 to

V0? (Hint: Use DATA in line 170 such as 50, 192 or 280, −4.) _____
What do the variables LH and TV represent for a given viewport and a given grid density scale? _____
Under what circumstances might one have LH > H1 (or TV > V0)? _____
_____

It will generally not occur; but, to provide you with a hint, observe what happens with the data

```
170  DATA −1, 140
180  DATA 281, 10
```

What has happened to the "ticking?" _____
What effect will changing the viewport variables have? For example, make the following changes in the program and then RUN it.

```
100  HO = 90 : H1 = 230 : V1 = 20 : VO = 120
170  DATA 160, 70
180  DATA 10, 12
RUN
```

What do you observe? _____

**DISCUSSION**   Electronic graph paper? How do we effectively use it when the coordinate system is not the screen coordinate system? Scaling to the rescue!

Let's assume a rectangular region of the X-Y plane is to be represented on the APPLE screen. Suppose A and B are the left and right hand X-coordinate values and C and D are the lower and upper Y-coordinate values of the rectangular region. (See Figure 4.6.1.)

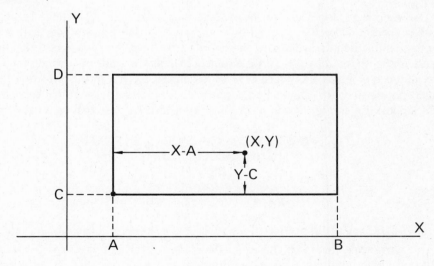

Figure 4.6.1

Applying the scaling techniques of Activity 3.2, the following formulas will convert the coordinates of a point (X, Y) to screen coordinates (SX, SY).

1. XSCL = (H1 − H0)/(B − A) : YSCL = (V0 − V1)/(D − C)
2. SX = H0 + (X − A) * XSCL : SY = V0 − (Y − C) * YSCL

The screen coordinate values OH and OV, which correspond to the screen coordinates of the origin, can be obtained by taking X = 0 and Y = 0 in formula 2 above.

OH = H0 − A * XSCL  : OV = V0 + C * YSCL

Using these expressions for OH and OV, one can simplify the formulas for SX and SY in 2. above.

SX = OH + X * XSCL  : SY = OV − Y * YSCL

These formulae will successfully transform the coordinates of points in the plane coordinate system to screen coordinates.

Now let's consider the grid density scale. There are two scales of concern: 1) the grid density scale for the coordinate axis, which is the distance between successive grid marks (ticking) on the coordinate axes; and 2) the screen grid density scale, which represents the screen distance between ticking on the coordinate axis.

There are several approaches which can be taken. One possibility is to use a preset (constant) screen grid density scale, and then determine the corresponding grid density scale for the coordinate region. The unattractiveness of this approach is the coordinate axis grid density scale will generally have unwieldy corresponding fractional values. Furthermore, the position of the coordinate axes may not correspond to grid positions.

Another possibility is to make the selection of grid density scales interactive. In this environment, the user must select the grid density scales on the coordinate axes. The advantage, of course, is the user can obtain exactly the effect desired. The disadvantage is the method generally requires a great deal of trial and error, or a very good perception of the coordinate region and how coordinate scale choices will appear on the screen. This possible method will be explored in an exercise at the end of this activity.

An alternative approach, which will be employed here, is to have acceptable predetermined grid densities selected by program. This will provide greater flexibility than the first method and eliminate guesswork by the user, but (you guessed it!) at the expense of slightly more work. Suppose some agreement is made concerning the minimum number of pixels PX which will be permitted for the screen grid density. (A smaller spacing may, for example, be aesthetically displeasing.) A sample value of PX is 12. Suppose it is further agreed a coordinate grid density scale will be a value of the form

TIC = COORD AXIS GRID DENSITY SCALE
.01, .02, .025,  .05, .075 ;
.1,  .2,  .25,   .5,  .75 ;
1,   2,   2.5,    5,  7.5 ;
10,  20,  25,    50,  75 ;
100, 200, 250,  500, 750 ;

TIC is a number of the form M * 10^P where M is 1, 2, 2.5, 5 or 7.5 times a power of 10. The above scale values are chosen for their simplicity, readability, and potential for easily calculating multiples. One can easily make additions, deletions, or substitutions.

With the above assumptions, one can now formulate a selection algorithm for choosing the grid density scale. If SCL is the number of pixels corresponding to one coordinate axis unit, then VL will denote the minimum value from the list of potential grid densities such that PX $<=$ SCL $*$ VL. An algorithm for the selection of VL proceeds as follows. Let VL be denoted by M $*$ 10^P, where M is one of the base factors (or mantissa values) 1, 2, 2.5, 5, or 7.5 . Since VL is the minimum value satisfying the inequality, we must have

SCL $*$ 10^P $<=$ PX $<=$ SCL $*$ VL $<=$ SCL $*$ 10^(P+1)

or, dividing by SCL

10^P $<=$ PX/SCL $<=$ VL $<=$ 10^(P+1)

To determine the power P needed, it is convenient, but not absolutely necessary (see the second EXERCISE at the end of this activity), to use a little mathematics. First, the base 10 logarithm of PX/SCL is (by definition) the power to which 10 must be raised to yield the value PX/SCL. For example, if PX/SCL = 8414, then the logarithm base 10 of 8414 is approximately 3.925 since 10^3.925 is 8414 (Note: 10^N is the Nth power of 10). Clearly, 10^3 $<=$ PX/SCL, whereas 10^4 $>$ PX/SCL; thus, P = 3. In general, P is the greatest integer less than or equal to the base 10 logarithm of PX/SCL.

APPLESOFT does not have an intrinsic base 10 logarithm function. However, from properties of logarithms, the base 10 logarithm can be found by computing the natural logarithm of the given number and then dividing by the natural logarithm of 10. Thus, one has

P = INT (LOG(PX/SCL)/LOG(10)),

where LOG( ) is the APPLESOFT natural logarithm function. Now, M (the mantissa value) is chosen as the smallest base factor for which PX $<=$ SCL $*$ M $*$ 10^P. If none of the factors M meet this condition then, since PX$<$ SCL $*$ 10^(P+1), we take M to be 1 and increment P by 1. Finally, set VL = M $*$ 10^P. The screen grid density scale now becomes TIC = SCL $*$ VL.

An example will be helpful. Suppose PX = 12 and SCL = 43.4. Enter the following program into your Apple.

```
NEW
10  PX = 12 : SCL = 43.4
20  PRINT "P =  "; INT (LOG (PX/SCL)/LOG (10))
RUN
```

Record your result here: P = _____

You should have obtained P = $-1$. Note

SCL $*$ 10^P = 43.4 $*$ .1 = 4.34 $<$ PX $<$ SCL $*$ 10^(P+1) = 43.4 $*$ 1

Now, starting with M = 1, and checking each successively larger value of M, we must compare SCL $*$ M $*$ 10^P with PX. Enter the following lines and then RUN. Remember, M = 1, 2, 2.5, 5, or 7.5.

```
NEW
10  PX = 12 : SCL = 43.4
20  TP = .1 : REM  TP = 10^-1 = 10^P WHERE THE VALUE OF
    P=-1 WAS DETERMINED EARLIER.
30  INPUT "INPUT M : "; M
40  IF PX <= SCL * M * TP THEN  60
50  PRINT "NO! TRY THE NEXT VALUE OF M." : GOTO 20
60  PRINT "GOT IT!"
```

```
70   PRINT "M = "; M
80   PRINT "VL = "; M * TP
90   PRINT "TIC = "; SCL * M * TP
100  END
LIST
RUN
```

Record the associated grid density scale values here.

M = _____ VL = _____ TIC = _____

(The authors obtained: M = 5, VL = .5, and TIC = 21.7 pixels.) With the values VL = .5 and TIC = 21.7, ticks will be placed on the coordinate axis on the screen 21.7 pixels apart with the coordinate grid density scale equal to +.5 units. (Technically, ticks will be placed either 21 or 22 pixels apart depending on the truncation values of integer multiples of 21.7.)

Before incorporating these ideas into the COMPREHENSIVE EXAMPLE, let's reflect for a moment on the coordinate graph algorithm in Section 2. In plotting the coordinate axes, one must first determine if each axis is visible. This was tested by comparing the axes' screen coordinates, OH and OV, with the viewport limits. Which lines of the program checked for this possibility? _____

In the case of the X-axis, the screen coordinate value LH represents the smallest screen tick coordinate to the right of H0. Under what circumstances can LH > H1? If the screen grid density scale HTIC is sufficiently large in comparison to the viewport width, H1 − H0, (in practice, a highly unlikely event), it is possible no grid will be visible; the validity of LH > H1 is the indicator that this circumstance has occurred. Of course, similar remarks will apply to the variables TV and VTIC relative to the Y-axis.

**COMPREHENSIVE EXAMPLE**   Be sure your system has been booted with DOS, and LOAD the coordinate graph subroutine you saved in Section 4.6.2. DELete the program lines 100 - 180 and then ADD the lines below. As always, the REMarks have been added for the purpose of understanding the program and may be omitted during entry of the program.

```
LOAD  Coordinate graph subroutine from Section 4.6.2 .
DEL  100,180
10   REM   ********************************
11   REM   *            CE4.6             *
12   REM   ********************************
13   REM
97   REM   ********************************
98   REM   *          MAIN PROGRAM        *
99   REM   ********************************
100  H0 = 1:H1 = 278:V0 = 190:V1 = 1: REM  SET VIEWPORT. IF
         DIMENSIONS ARE TO CHANGE, THEN USER SHOULD ALLOW FOR
         BORDER AROUND VIEWPORT...A 1 PIXEL DEDUCTION IN EACH
         DIRECTION.
110  DEF  FN DP(Z) =  INT (1000 * Z + .5) / 1000: REM  3
         DECIMAL DIGITS-OF-PRECISION FUNCTION.
120  XPX = 12:YPX = 10: REM   MINIMUM ALLOWABLE GRID
```

DENSITIES.

```
130   SFAC = 1.20: REM  EQUIV SCALE FACTOR. USE YOUR SFAC VALUE
      DETERMINED IN ACTIVITY 4.3.
140   HGR : HCOLOR =  3: HOME : VTAB 21
150   INPUT "INPUT THE X-LIMITS A,B: ";A,B
160   INPUT "INPUT THE Y-LIMITS C,D: ";C,D
170   INPUT "DO YOU WANT EQUIVALENT SCALES? ";EQ$:EQSCL = 0: IF
      EQ$ = "Y" THEN EQSCL = 1
180   HOME : VTAB 21: GOSUB 4000: REM  CALL 'GRAPH PAPER'
190   REM  PRINT OUT RANGE VALUES AND GRID DENSITY INFORMATION.
200   PRINT "X-RANGE:"; TAB( 20);"Y-RANGE:"
210   PRINT  FN DP(A);", "; FN DP(B); TAB( 20); FN DP(C);", ";
      FN DP(D)
220   PRINT "X-SCALE:"; XVL; TAB( 20);"Y-SCALE: ";YVL
230   VTAB 24: HTAB 15: PRINT "'F' = FULL PG  'E' = END PROG";
240   VTAB 24: HTAB 1: INVERSE : PRINT "SELECT KEY";: NORMAL :
      GET K$:K =  ASC (K$)
250   IF K = 69 THEN  TEXT : END : REM  IF KEY = 'E' THEN END
      PROGRAM
260   IF K = 70 THEN  POKE  - 16302,0: GET A$: POKE  -
      16301,0: GOTO 240: REM  IS KEY = F? IF YES, THEN TOGGLE
      FULL PG AND WAIT FOR KEYPRESS TO RETURN TO MIXED MODE
270   GOTO 240
271   REM  *          END MAIN PROGRAM        *
272   REM
3997  REM  ********************************
3998  REM  *        GRAPH PAPER SUBRT      *
3999  REM  ********************************
4000  XSCL = (H1 - H0) / (B - A):YSCL = (V0 - V1) /
      (D - C): REM  SET SCREEN SCALES
4010  IF EQSCL THEN  GOSUB 4300: REM  IF EQUIV SCALES ARE
      WANTED THEN MODIFY SCALES.
4020  OH = H0 - A * XSCL:OV = V0 + C * YSCL: REM  SET SCREEN
      COORDS OF COORDINATE AXES
4030  MM(0) = 1:MM(1) = 2:MM(2) = 2.5:MM(3) = 5:MM(4) =
      7.5: REM  MANTISSA VALUES OF GRID DENSITY SCALES. ACTUAL
      VALUE OF GRID DENSITY WILL BE A POWER OF 10 TIMES A
      MANTISSA VALUE.
4040  SCL = XSCL:PX = XPX: GOSUB 4200: REM  CALL GRID DENSITY
      SELECT SUBRT.
4050  HTIC = TIC:XVL = VL: REM  GET GRID DENSITY SCALES AND
      VALUES UPON RETURN FROM SUBRT. HTIC IS SCREEN GRID
      DENSITY SCALE AND XVL IS X-COORD GRID DENSITY SCALE.
4060  SCL = YSCL:PX = YPX: GOSUB 4200: REM  CALL GRID DENSITY
      SELECT SUBRT.
4070  VTIC = TIC:YVL = VL: REM  GET GRID DENSITY SCALES AND
      VALUES UPON RETURN FROM SUBRT. VTIC IS SCREEN GRID
```

```
             DENSITY SCALE AND YVL IS Y-COORD GRID DENSITY
             SCALE.
4080   GOSUB 5000: REM  CALL GRAPH PLOT SUBRT
4090   HPLOT HO - 1,V1 - 1 TO HO - 1,VO + 1 TO H1 + 1,VO + 1
             TO H1 + 1,V1 - 1 TO HO - 1,V1 - 1: REM  BORDER THE
             GRAPH
4100   RETURN : REM  RETURN TO MAIN PROG
4101   REM
4197   REM  *******************************
4198   REM  *  GRID DENSITY SELECT SUBRT  *
4199   REM  *******************************
4200   P =  INT ( LOG (PX / SCL) / LOG (10)): REM  DETERMINE
             THE EXPONENT OF GRID DENSITY SCALE VALUE. NOW CHOOSE A
             MANTISSA M SO THAT THE GRID DENSITY VALUE VL = M * 10^P
             SATISFIES PX < =  SCL*VL.
4210   IF P > = 0 THEN TP = 10 ^ P
4220   IF P < 0 THEN TP = 1: FOR NF = 1 TO  ABS (P):TP = .1
             * TP: NEXT NF: REM  A LOOP IS USED TO GENERATE 10^P FOR
             NEG  P TO AVOID ROUND OFF ERRORS.
4230   LBV = PX / (SCL * TP): REM   LOWER BOUND FOR MANTISSA OF
             GRID DENSITY SCALE.
4240   FOR K = 0 TO 4: REM  FOR EACH POTENTIAL MANTISSA VALUE
             OF GRID DENSTIY SCALE, CHECK...
4250   IF LBV < = MM(K) THEN M = MM(K):VL = M * TP:TIC =
             SCL * VL: RETURN : REM  IS MM(K) THE SMALLEST MANTISSA
             FOR GRID DENSITY? IF YES, THEN SET COORD AXIS GRID
             DENSITY SCALE AND SCREEN AXIS GRID DENSITY SCALE &
             RETURN.
4260   NEXT K: REM  TRY NEXT HIGHER MANTISSA VALUE.
4270   M = 1:P = P + 1:VL = 10 * TP:TIC = SCL * VL: RETURN :
             REM  MANTISSA VALUE MUST BE 1 AND EXPONENT OF GRID
             DENSITY IS P+1. SET GRID DENSITIES AND RETURN.
4297   REM  *******************************
4298   REM  *  SELECT EQUIV SCALE SUBRT   *
4299   REM  *******************************
4300   EXSCL = YSCL * SFAC: REM  ASSUME INITIALLY THAT THE
             EQUIV SCALES ARE TO BE YSCL AND YSCL*SFAC.
4310   IF EXSCL > XSCL THEN YSCL = XSCL / SFAC:EXSCL =
             XSCL: REM  IF XSCL IS LESS THAN YSCL THEN RESET YSCL TO
             EQUIV SCALE AND UPDATE THE EQUIV SCALE VALUE.
4320   XSCL = EXSCL: REM  LOCK IN THE EQUIV XSCL VALUE
4330   REM  IF USER DOES NOT WISH TO CENTER OLD RECTANGULAR
             REGION WITHIN VIEWPORT THEN NEXT STATEMENT SHOULD BE
             OMITTED.
4340   A = (A + B - (H1 - HO) / XSCL) * .5:C = (C + D -  (VO
             - V1) / YSCL) * .5: REM  REDEFINE X- AND Y- INTERVALS SO
             THAT OLD INTERVALS WILL BE CENTERED IN THE VIEWPORT.
```

```
4350  B = A + (H1 - HO) / XSCL:D = C + (VO - V1) / YSCL:
      REM  RESET B AND D. THIS SHOULD BE DONE REGARDLESS OF
      WHETHER OR NOT REGION IS CENTERED IN VIEWPORT.
4360  RETURN
4361  REM  **    END EQUIV SCALE SUBRT    **
4362  REM
4363  REM  **    END GRAPH PAPER SUBRT    **
4364  REM
4997  REM  ******************************
4998  REM  *       COORD GRAPH SUBRT      *
4999  REM  ******************************
5000  LH = OH - HTIC *  INT ((OH - HO) / HTIC): REM  SET LEFT
      MOST GRID MARK POSITIONS.
5010  TV = OV - VTIC *  INT ((OV - V1) / VTIC): REM  SET TOP
      MOST GRID MARK POSITIONS.
5020  IF (V1 < = OV) AND (OV < = VO) THEN  GOSUB 5100: REM  IF
      X-AXIS IS VISIBLE THEN SKETCH IT
5030  IF (HO < = OH) AND (OH < = H1) THEN  GOSUB 5180: REM  IF
      Y-AXIS IS VISIBLE THEN SKETCH IT
5040  IF (LH > H1) OR (RH > VO) THEN  RETURN : REM IF
      GRID PTS ARE NOT VISIBLE THEN RETURN TO MAIN PROG
5050  FOR V = TV TO VO STEP VTIC
5060  FOR H = LH TO H1 STEP HTIC
5070  HPLOT H,V: REM  PLOT GRID POINT
5080  NEXT H,V
5090  RETURN
5100  HPLOT HO,OV TO H1,OV: REM  DRAW HORIZ LINE = X-AXIS
5110  IF LH > H1 THEN  RETURN : REM  IF GRID MARKS ARE NOT
      VISIBLE THEN RETURN.
5120  PP% = 3: IF OV - PP% < V1 THEN PP% = OV - V1: REM
      SET UPPER EXTENT OF GRID MARKS ON X-AXIS.
5130  MM% = 3: IF OV + MM% > VO THEN MM% = VO - OV: REM
      SET LOWER EXTENT OF GRID MARKS ON X-AXIS.
5140  FOR H = LH TO H1 STEP HTIC
5150  HPLOT H,OV - PP% TO H,OV + MM%: REM PLACE GRID MARK ON
      X-AXIS.
5160  NEXT H
5170  RETURN
5180  HPLOT OH,V1 TO OH,VO: REM  DRAW VERT LINE = Y-AXIS
5190  IF TV > VO THEN  RETURN : REM  IF GRID MARKS ARE NOT
      VISIBLE THEN RETURN.
5200  MM% = 3: IF OH - MM% < HO THEN MM% = OH - HO: REM
      SET LEFT EXTENT OF GRID MARKS ON Y-AXIS.
5210  PP% = 3: IF OH + PP% > H1 THEN PP% = H1 - OH: REM
      SET RIGHT EXTENT OF GRID MARKS ON Y-AXIS.
5220  FOR V = TV TO VO STEP VTIC
5230  HPLOT OH - MM%,V TO OH + PP%,V: REM PLACE GRID MARK ON
```

```
       Y-AXIS.
5240   NEXT V
5250   RETURN
5251   REM  **  END OF COORD GRAPH SBRT  **
5252   REM
LIST
```

The program you have just entered is a subroutine which graphically emulates any rectangular region in an X-Y coordinate system and supplies an appropriate coordinate grid for informative readability and identification of point locations. It allows the user to select equivalent scales if desired. Test the program by using the following input data.

|     | X-LIMITS | Y-LIMITS | EQUIVALENT SCALES |
| --- | --- | --- | --- |
| 1. | −3, 4 | −2, 5 | Y & N |
| 2. | −.5, .5 | −100, 100 | N |
| 3. | 0, 20 | 10, 30 | Y & N |
| 4. | 10, 3000 | −2, 4 | N |
| 5. | −1, .1 | −3, −1 | Y & N |

**Check Your Comprehension**

After the endpoint values in each coordinate direction have been supplied by the user, control is passed to the graph paper subroutine beginning in line 4000. The primary transformation scales XSCL and YSCL are determined, with appropriate adjustments if equivalent scales are wanted (line 4010 and the subroutine at lines 4300-4380). The screen coordinates OH and OV of the transformed coordinate axes are determined in line 4020. Control is next passed to the subroutine determining the grid densities. On RETURN, appropriate values are saved for future use (lines 4040-4070). The COORD PLOT subroutine is accessed next (line 4080) in order to grid the screen. Equivalent scales should not be used when the values B - A and D - C differ greatly. Why? _____

For example, consider what would happen to figures within the coordinate regions using the entry limits in examples 2 or 5 above. How do you think the images would appear on the screen? _____

In determining the grid density scales, we used a loop for generating $10^P$ for negative P. Why not simply compute $10^P$? The reader should experiment with calculating $10^P$ for a wide range of values of negative P. Does one always get the exact value of $10^P$? Finally, the reader should note the order of multiplication of .1 and TP is significant. Reversal of the order above will permit round-off errors.

For a challenging problem, the reader can show the maximum possible value the screen grid density scale may be in our system is 2 * PX.

**EXERCISE**   In selecting the grid density scale, the exponent P can be determined by a non-logarithmic approach. The alternative method proceeds as follows.

1) If PX/SCL > = 1, then indexing by K and starting with T = 1, loop through values of K > = 0 until T > PX/SCL. When the condition is true, then P = K − 1. When the condition is false, redefine T to be 10 * T ; then try another K.

2) If PX/SCL < 1 then, indexing by K and starting with T = 10, loop through values of K > = 1 until 1 < T * PX/SCL . When the condition is true, then P=−K . When the condition is false, redefine M to be 10 * M ; then try another K. Write a subroutine to represent the algorithm above, then test and debug it.

**EXERCISE** Alter the comprehensive example program so the choice of grid density scaling becomes interactive. Specifically, the program should allow the user:

1) To input a possible coordinate grid density scale;

2) To modify the scale to suit preference; and

3) To select (if desired) a different reference point for grid placement other than the origin (which is the usual default point). For example, the user may wish to begin the scale at an endpoint of a coordinate axis.

With minor modifications the GRAPH PAPER SUBROUTINE can be used to create the grid. In fact, one is merely replacing the GRID DENSITY SELECTION ALGORITHM with a routine in which the user declares each grid density. That is, the user supplies the values of the coordinate grid density VL. The screen grid density TIC is given by TIC = SCL * VL. It is necessary for the user to select the coordinate grid density for each coordinate axes.

**CHALLENGE** Alter the comprehensive example program so high resolution Page 1 displays the coordinate graph over the specified intervals, while high resolution Page 2 displays the coordinate graph using equivalent scales. Use the "P" key as a "toggle switch" to allow the user to view Page 1 or Page 2, full screen.

# ACTIVITY 4.7   Sines & Cosines

**LEARNING BY DISCOVERY** In this section you will study the functions COSine and SINe, and the analytic and geometric properties they possess. These functions play an important role in the geometric aspects of computer graphics. The reader who is already familiar with these useful functions can briefly skim through most of the material presented in this section. However, it is recommended the reader carefully work through the COMPREHENSIVE EXAMPLE at the end of this section.

1. Insert a diskette with DOS on it, boot your system, and enter the following lines of code.

```
NEW
10    HOME
20    DEF  FN TR(V) =   INT (1000 * V + .5) / 1000: REM
      TRUNCATE AND ROUND TO 3 DECIMAL PLACES FUNCTION.
30    PI = 3.14159266: REM  'CIRCLE' CONSTANT.
40    FAC = PI / 180: REM  CONVERSION FACTOR FOR DEGREE TO
      RADIAN MEASURE.
50    PRINT "DEGREES"; TAB( 10);"RADIANS"
60    PRINT  TAB( 3);"DG"; TAB( 13);"TH"; TAB( 20);"COSINE";
      TAB( 30);"SINE"
70    FOR H = 1 TO 39: PRINT "−";: NEXT H: PRINT "−"
```

```
80   D0 = 0:D1 = 540:DT = 5
90   FOR DG = D0 TO D1 STEP DT
100  TH = DG * FAC: REM  CONVERT DEGREES TO RADIANS.
110  C =  COS (TH):S =  SIN (TH)
120  PRINT DG; TAB(10); FN TR(TH); TAB(20); FN TR(C);
     TAB(30); FN TR(S)
130  NUMLINES = NUMLINES + 1
140  IF NUMLINES > 18 THEN  VTAB 24: HTAB 8: PRINT "PRESS
     KEY FOR NEXT PAGE";: GET K$: HTAB 1: VTAB 4: CALL  -
     958:NUMLINES = 0:DG = DG - DT
141  REM  IF PAGE IS FULL THEN CLEAR SCREEN BELOW HEADING.
     RESET DG SO THAT LAST ENTRY OF PREVIOUS PAGE IS
     PRINTED AT TOP OF NEW PAGE.
150  NEXT DG
160  HOME : END
RUN
```

RUN the program (several times, perhaps). Observe the values in the COSine and SINe column and inspect for any possible patterns. The first page of output should appear as follows.

| DEGREES DG | RADIANS TH | COSINE | SINE |
|---|---|---|---|
| 0 | 0 | 1 | 0 |
| 5 | .087 | .996 | .087 |
| 10 | .175 | .985 | .174 |
| 15 | .262 | .966 | .259 |
| 20 | .349 | .94 | .342 |
| 25 | .436 | .906 | .423 |
| 30 | .524 | .866 | .5 |
| 35 | .611 | .819 | .574 |
| 40 | .698 | .766 | .643 |
| 45 | .785 | .707 | .707 |
| 50 | .873 | .643 | .766 |
| 55 | .96 | .574 | .819 |
| 60 | 1.047 | .5 | .866 |
| 65 | 1.134 | .423 | .906 |
| 70 | 1.222 | .342 | .94 |
| 75 | 1.309 | .259 | .966 |
| 80 | 1.396 | .174 | .985 |
| 85 | 1.484 | .087 | .996 |
| 90 | 1.571 | 0 | 1 |

```
PRESS KEY FOR NEXT PAGE
```

Once the program seems to be functioning properly, SAVE it on a disk to be recalled later and altered for use.

In responding to the questions below, it may be necessary to reRUN the program several times. For the convenience of the reader, most of the answers to the questions appear at the end of this section of the activity.

A) Evidently, the variable DG represents degrees. Recall from elementary geometry a degree is a measurement unit related to the size of an angle. The precise relationship of angles to COSines and SINes will be established in due time. Accept for the present some form of inter-relationship exists and respond to the questions below.

A1. What range of degree values is used in the computations? _____

The choice of degree values used in the program was made to illustrate the fact the values of COSine and SINe begin to repeat themselves after a certain interval of degree values.

A2. For which value of DG do the values of COSine and SINe begin to recycle the values following those beginning at DG = 0? _____

B) Note the COSine and SINe are evaluated in line 110. Also note they are treated as functions and not as arrays! The value of DG is converted to something called a radian value and stored in the variable THeta.

B1. In which program line does this conversion (to radians) occur and what is the conversion formula? _____

Note the conversion must be made for each value of the degree variable DG. In order for the returned value of the COSine or SINe to correctly correspond to the COSine or SINe of the degree measurement of an angle, this conversion must be made.

To illustrate there is indeed a significant difference between COS(DG) and COS(TH), where TH is the converted radian value of DG, enter the following line in the immediate execution mode.

```
DG = 30 : TH = DG * FAC : PRINT COS(DG), COS(TH)
```

< This statement requires that you have made a prior RUN of the program in this section in order for APPLESOFT to have the correct value of FAC stored in memory. >

Observe the values are very different! This indicates that in computing values of the COSine or SINe for a particular argument, one must be sure the argument is the radian value and not the degree value. Also note the value of COS(TH) printed above has 9 decimal digits of precision.

B2. Why didn't the program also print the values of COSine and SINe to 9 digits? ___

_____

B3. Within what interval of numerical values do COS(TH) and SIN(TH) appear to range? _____

B4. For which degree value(s) of DG does COS(TH) equal 0? SIN(TH) = 0 for which DG value(s)? _____

B5. For which degree value(s) of DG does COS(TH) equal +1 or −1? SIN(TH) = +1 or −1? _____

B6. What relationship seems to exist between the values of DG where one of the COSine or SINe is at an extreme value of −1 or +1, and those values of DG where the other function has value 0? _____

C) Let's look more closely at the conversion formula relating DG and TH.

C1. Consider the value DG = 180. By inspecting lines 40 and 100, what do you expect the radian value of TH to be? _____

C2. What is the radian value of TH for DG = 90 degrees ( =  one half of 180 degrees)? for DG = 45? for DG = 270? for DG = 360? _____

By condensing the expressions in lines 40 and 100, one can see the conversion formula is

TH = DG * PI / 180.

D) Inspect the list of SINe and COSine values which is a reproduction of the first page of the program output.

D1. How do the values of the COSine, when read from DG = 0 to DG = 90, compare to the values of the SINe read in reverse order? _____

Your comparison should suggest the following relationship

COSine of DG degrees = SINe of 90 − DG degrees.

E) Make the following changes in the program.

```
DEL 50,60
60   PRINT "DEG"; TAB(10); "DEG+360"; TAB(20); "COS(TH1)";
     TAB(30); "COS(TH2)"
100  TH1 = DG * FAC : TH2 = (DG + 360) * FAC
110  C = COS(TH1) : S = COS(TH2) :REM USE S VARIABLE FOR VALUE
     OF COSINE AT TH2. THIS AVOIDS HAVING TO ALTER THE
     PRINT STATEMENT BELOW.
RUN
```

What do you observe? _____

This illustrates the periodic relationship alluded to earlier. What do you expect to occur if line 100 is changed to permit TH2 to be (DG + 720) * FAC? _____

(Answers to selected questions: A1. From DG = 0 to DG = 540; A2. DG = 360; B1. line 100; B2. because values are printed out rounded to 3 decimal places; B3. between −1 and +1, inclusive; B4. COS(TH) = 0 for DG = 90, 270, 450, ...; SIN(TH) = 0 for DG = 0, 180, 360, ...; B5. COS(TH) = +1 for DG = 0, 360, 720,...; COS(TH) = −1 for DG = 180, 540,...; B6. COSine has value 0 precisely where SINe assumes an extreme value, and similarly the SINe has value 0 precisely where the COSine assumes an extreme value of −1 or +1; C1. PI = 3.14159266; C2. 90 deg = PI/2 rad, 45 deg = PI/4 rad, 270 deg = 3 PI/2, 360 deg = 2 PI; D1. the values are exactly the same when inspected in reverse order.)

2. Now you will consider the geometric aspects of the COSine and SINe functions. Load the original program from Section 1 you were asked to save, and make the following changes and additions.

```
LOAD < the program from Section 1 >
45   HGR : HCOLOR = 3 : VTAB 21
70   VTAB 24
75   HC = 140 : VC = 80 : R = 70 : REM CENTER COORDINATES
     AND RADIUS.
80   D0 = 0 : D1 = 360 : DT = 5
112  X = R * C : Y = R * S
118  HPLOT HC + X, VC − Y
```

< Add a semicolon to the end of line 120. The line should appear as

indicated below. >
```
120   PRINT DG; TAB(10); FN TR(TH); TAB(20); FN TR(C);
      TAB(30); FN TR(S);
125   FOR J = 1 TO 100 : NEXT J : REM DELAY LOOP.
140   HTAB 1 : CALL -958 : REM TAB BACK TO 1ST COLUMN AND
      CLEAR TO BOTTOM OF SCREEN.
160   GET Q$ : TEXT : HOME : END
RUN
```

What do you observe? _____

What are the screen coordinates of the center? _____

What is the radius? _____

Note the display is not a true circle. This is attributable to the inequivalency of screen scales. The scale correction factor can be made as indicated in ACTIVITY 4.3; this will be treated in detail in the next activity.
Observe that the order in which the points are HPLOTted is directly related to the increasing values of the degree variable DG. Which variables represent the horizontal and vertical offsets from the center? _____

To test the effect of changing the the value of R in the program, make the following changes.

```
85    FOR R = 30 TO 70 STEP 10
152   NEXT R
125   < Deleting line 125 will speed-up execution. >
RUN
```

What do you observe? Is it what you expected? _____

Restore the program to its original form by DELeting lines 85 and 152. Change the upper limit on the value of DG by changing line 80.

```
80    D0 = 0 : D1 = 180 : DT = 5
RUN
```

What effect did this have? _____
Recall what happened in Section 1 when the value of D1 was changed. What do you predict will happen if D1 is changed to D1 = 90? to D1 = 270? _____

Finally, to more clearly reflect the role the values of the COSine and SINe serve in determining the X-offset and Y-offset from the center (HC,VC) of the corresponding point on the circle, add the following lines which will HPLOT the X-offset and Y-offset as segments.

```
114   HPLOT HC,VC TO HC+X,VC TO HC+X,VC−Y
115   FOR J = 1 TO 100 : NEXT : REM DELAY.
116   HCOLOR = 0 : HPLOT HC,VC TO HC+X,VC TO HC+X,VC−Y :
      HCOLOR = 3 : REM ERASE SEGMENTS AND RESET HCOLOR TO
      WHITE.
RUN
```

Note how the direction of the offset segments is related to the sign of the COSine and SINe values. What sign does X have when the horizontal segment (X-offset) is

HPLOTted to the right of center? to the left of center? _____
The necessity to squeeze lines 114, 115 and 116 into this particular position within the
DG-loop is crucial. What would have happened if they had been placed after line 118?

---

**DISCUSSION**   The measure of an angle can be determined using one or more systems of units. The two most common systems use degree measure or radian measure. A
third system, which will not be discussed in this book, uses a unit of measure called a
gradian. In all systems of angular measurement, the positive sense of measurement
direction is counterclockwise, with measurement beginning along the initial side of the
angle and ending along the terminal side of the angle (Figure 4.7.1).

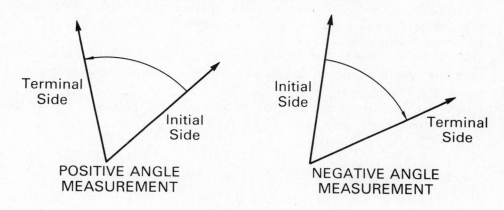

Figure 4.7.1

In the degree system, a straight angle (measured counterclockwise) is defined as
having measure 180 degrees. In the radian system, a straight angle (measured counterclockwise) is defined as having measure PI = 3.14159266 radians, which is precisely
one half the circumference length of a circle of radius one (called a unit circle). In fact,
the radian measure of any angle is simply the length of arc subtended by the angle
measured along the circle of radius one centered at the angle vertex (Figure 4.7.2).

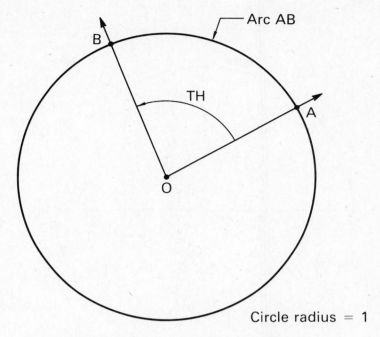

Circle radius = 1

TH = Radian measure = Length of Arc AB.

Figure 4.7.2

Consequently, one has the following correspondences.

    180 degrees = PI radians,

    1 degree  = PI / 180 radians,

    DG degrees = DG * PI / 180 radians.

Note the last formula is the conversion formula used in Section 1 of this ACTIVITY.

Given any angle AOB, there is a standard representation of the angle in the coordinate plane. Specifically, the initial side OA is placed along the positive X-axis with angle vertex at the origin. Suppose the point P is the intersection of the terminal side OB with the circle of radius one centered at the origin (Figure 4.7.3).

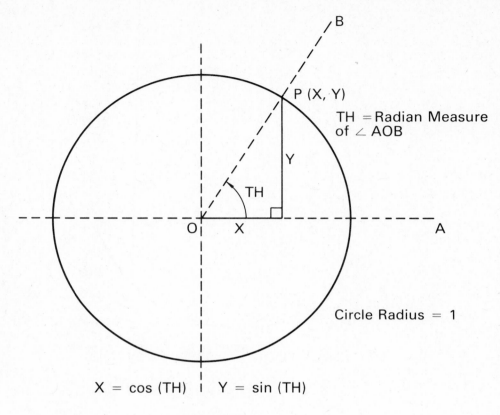

$$X = \cos (TH) \quad Y = \sin (TH)$$

Figure 4.7.3

The X-coordinate of the point P is defined as the COSine of the angle and the Y-coordinate is defined as the SINe of the angle.

In most computer languages the COSine and SINe must be evaluated for the radian measure of the angle. This is why the conversion process must be made from degree measure to radian measure. Degree measure is used here (as opposed to working solely with radian measure) because most people are more familiar with it, and it seems conceptually easier.

The above definition of the SINe and COSine as the Y- and X-coordinates of a point on the unit circle explains why, for example, the COSine has value 0 for DG = 90 degrees and the SINe has value +1. Indeed, the coordinates of the corresponding point P on the unit circle, for which OP is at 90 degrees from the positive X-axis, is (X,Y) = (0,1). Similarly, the COSine of 180 degrees is −1 and the SINe is 0 since P(−1,0) is the point of intersection of the unit circle and the terminal side of the 180 degree angle in standard position.

If an arbitrary circle of radius R is centered at the origin then, by considering this circle as magnification of the unit circle by the scale factor R, the point of intersection of it with the terminal side of an angle of TH radians has coordinates

   X = R * COS(TH)   :   Y = R * SIN(TH)

This explains the determination of values of the X- and Y-coordinates from the center (HC,VC) used to construct the circle in the program of Section 2. Observe the ratios X/R and Y/R are precisely COS(TH) and SIN(TH); ie., the ratio of the X-coordinate to the radius R is COS(TH), and the ratio of the Y-coordinate to the radius R is SIN(TH).

This observation concerning ratios is the manner by which these functions are first first introduced in grade school. Indeed, if T = ABC is a right triangle with arm lengths a and b and hypotenuse (the longest side) length c, then let D be the measure of the angle at the vertex B (Figure 4.7.4). One will then have the following: COS(D) = a/c and SIN(D) = b/c.

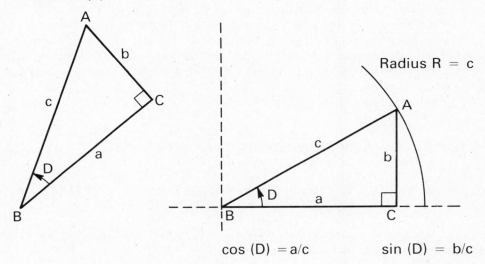

cos (D) = a/c                    sin (D) = b/c

Figure 4.7.4

These relationships are easy to see by merely considering the triangle T in the coordinate plane with the angle at B placed in standard position in the first quadrant. Consider the circle of radius R = c centered at the origin. Then X = a and Y = b are the X and Y coordinates of the point A on the circle. The ratios X/R and Y/R are clearly a/c and b/c. For example, consider the right triangle with sides a = 3, b = 4 and c = 5. The SINe of B is b/c = 4/5 = .8, and the COSine of B is a/c = 3/5 = .6.

To summarize the above discussion, COS(TH) and SIN(TH) represent the X- and Y-coordinates of a point P on the unit circle where the ray OP makes an angle TH radians with the positive X-axis. If DG is the degree measure of the angle, then TH = DG * PI / 180. As the angle increases in measure the point P traverses the circle counterclockwise. Multiplication of the COSine and SINe of TH by the factor R results in the coordinates of a point on the circle of radius R centered at the origin.

There are many remarkable properties of the COSine and SINe which will not be covered in this book. The properties used will be either developed or stated as fact as the need arises. One property already alluded to is

COSine of DG = SINe of 90 − DG

SINe of DG = COSine of 90 − DG

or

$$COS(TH) = SIN(PI/2 - TH)$$
$$SIN(TH) = COS(PI/2 - TH)$$

This particular property will be used to advantage in the next activity when circles and ellipses are treated in more detail.

**COMPREHENSIVE EXAMPLE**   In this example the information gathered about COSine and SINe will be combined with the concepts of the previous section on coordinate graphs to obtain an interesting graphics display. In particular, the objective is to obtain on the right half of the screen a graph of the values of the SINe function vs. angles measured in degrees. Simultaneously, a circle will be plotted in the left half of the screen. The idea is to coordinate the plotting of points on the circle with the plotting of points on the graph of the SINe function. To emphasize the SINe of an angle is the vertical offset (the Y-coordinate), this segment will be displayed on both graphs. The program itself is not particularly difficult; it simply requires close attention to coordination of events.

Enter the following lines of code.

```
NEW
```

< Load the COMPREHENSIVE EXAMPLE program from ACTIVITY 4.6 >

```
LOAD CE4.6
```

< DELete lines 100 to 270, leaving only the GRAPH PAPER SUBROUTINE. >

```
DEL 100,270
```

< Make changes in two lines of the GRAPH PAPER SUBROUTINE, but leave the remaining lines intact. >

```
4050 HTIC = 10:XVL = 30: REM  BYPASS GRAPH PAPER SELECTION
     SCALES AND DEFINE SPECIAL SCALES. X-COORD GRID DENSITY
     SCALE IS 30 DEGREES.
4070 VTIC = 8:YVL = .125: REM  BYPASS GRAPH PAPER SELECTION
     SCALES AND DEFINE SPECIAL SCALES. Y-COORD GRID DENSITY
     SCALE IS .125.
```

< Now add the following lines. >

```
10   REM  ********************************
11   REM  *           CE4.7             *
12   REM  ********************************
13   REM
40   HIMEM: 37503: REM  SET HIMEM TO PROTECT HRCG FROM STRING
     VARIABLE STORAGE. 37503 IS THE DECIMAL EQUIVALENT OF
     $9280 - 1.
50   GOSUB 1000: REM  GO TO ROUTINE TO LOAD HRCG AND ASCII SET.
     IF THE READER DOES NOT WISH TO USE HRCG THEN ELIMINATE THIS
     LINE AND ALL CALLS TO HRCG. HOWEVER, ITS USE IS
     ENCOURAGED FOR BEST EFFECT.
60   HO = 158:H1 = 278:V0 = 147:V1 = 19: REM  SET THE
     VIEWPORT FOR THE COORD GRAPH. VALUES ARE SELECTED SO
     THAT V0-V1 = DIAMETER OF CIRCLE AND H1-HO IS EVENLY
```

```
          DIVISIBLE BY XPX = 10 AND 4 = 360/90, AND THE SCREEN
          IS ROUGHLY DIVIDED IN HALF.
70        XPX = 10:YPX = 8: REM  SELECT SCREEN GRID DENSITIES.
80        HGR2 : HCOLOR =  3: REM  SET HIRES PAGE TWO, FULL SCREEN
          GRAPHICS.
90        A = 0:B = 360:C= − 1:D =  + 1: REM  SET HORIZ AND VERT
          AXIS RANGE LIMITS.
100       GOSUB 4000: REM  GO TO GRAPH PAPER SUBRT TO PLOT COORD
          GRAPH IN 'VIEWPORT'.NOTE THAT THE X-COORD GRID DENSITY
          SCALE IS SPECIFICALLY CHOSEN IN LINE 4050, INDEPENDENT OF
          THE GRAPH PAPER SELECTION ALGORITHM.
110       GOSUB 1500: REM  GO TO THE SPECIAL COORD GRAPH LABELING
          SUBRT.
120       SP = 0: GOSUB 2000: REM  GO TO THE PRIMARY SUBROUTINE. SP
          IS THE '2ND PASS THROUGH SUBRT' VARIABLE. ON 1ST PASS
          SP = 0.
130       SP = 1: GOSUB 2000: REM  GO FOR SECOND PASS
270       GET Q$: TEXT : HOME : END
271       REM  ******************************
272       REM  ***   END OF MAIN PROGRAM   ***
273       REM  ******************************
274       REM
997       REM  ******************************
998       REM  *  LOAD HRCG AND ASCII SET   *
999       REM  ******************************
1000      HOME : VTAB 3
1010      PRINT "     ONE MOMENT PLEASE WHILE I"
1020      PRINT "     LOAD HRCG AND THE ASCII SET."
1030      D$ =  CHR$ (13) +  CHR$ (4): REM  'RETURN'+'CTRL-D'
1040      P$ = "BLOAD HRCG$9280": PRINT : PRINT P$: PRINT D$;P$:
          REM  BLOAD HRCG. FIRST 'PRINT P$' IS FOR SCREEN
          DISPLAY ONLY.
1050      P$ = "BLOAD ASCII$9300": PRINT : PRINT P$: PRINT D$;P$:
          REM  BLOAD THE ASCII CHARACTER SET.
1070      HRCG = 37504: REM  BEGINNING BYTE LOCATION FOR HRCG
1080      RETURN
1081      REM  ***       END HRCG LOAD     ***
1082      REM
1497      REM  ******************************
1498      REM  *   COORD GRAPH LABEL SUBRT  *
1499      REM  ******************************
1500      CALL HRCG: REM  INITIALIZE 'HOOKS' FOR HRCG USE.
1510      T$ = "SINE GRAPH DEMONSTRATION": REM  TITLE LABEL.
1520      H = 20 −  INT ( LEN (T$) / 2): HTAB H: VTAB 1: PRINT T$:
          REM  PRINT TITLE LABEL AT TOP CENTER.
1525      HTAB 20: VTAB 4: PRINT "Y": REM  PRINT 'Y'-LABEL NEAR
          Y-AXIS.
```

```
1530   VT = 3: REM   STARTING VERT TAB POSITION FOR LABELING
       VERT COORD AXIS.
1540   FOR YV = 1 TO  − 1 STEP  − .5: REM   FOR EACH LABEL
       VALUE FROM 1 TO −1 DECREMENTING BY .5,...
1550   YV$ =  STR$ (YV): REM  GET STRING EQUIVALENT
1560   HTAB 23 −  LEN (YV$): VTAB VT: REM  TAB TO APPROPR PRINT
       POSITION.
1570   PRINT YV$
1580   VT = VT + 4: REM  INCREMENT VERT TAB POSITION.
1590   HPLOT HO − 3,OV − YV * YSCL TO HO,OV − YV * YSCL: REM
       EXTEND TIC MARK CORRESP TO LABEL VALUE.
1595   NEXT YV
1600   VT = 20:HT = 25: REM  SET VERT AND HORIZ TAB POSITIONS
       FOR FIRST PRINT POSTN OF HORIZ AXIS LABELS.
1610   FOR DG = 0 TO 360 STEP 90: REM  FOR EACH DEGREE LABEL
       VALUE FROM 0 TO 360 INCR BY 90 DEGREES,...
1620   DG$ =  STR$ (DG)
1630   VTAB VT: HTAB HT −  LEN (DG$): REM  TAB TO HORIZ PRINT
       POSTN FOR PRINT HORIZ LABEL VALUE.
1640   PRINT DG$
1650   HT = HT + 4: REM  INCRMNT HORIZ TAB POSTN.
1660   HPLOT OH + DG * XSCL,VO − 3 TO OH + DG * XSCL,VO + 3
1665   NEXT DG
1670   HTAB 29: VTAB 22: PRINT "DEGREES"
1675   HTAB 5: VTAB 22: PRINT "UNIT CIRCLE"
1680   HTAB 27: VTAB 2: PRINT "Y = SIN(DEG)"
1690   PRINT D$;"PR#0": REM  TURN OFF HRCG AND RESTORE NORMAL
       DOS 'HOOKS'.
1700   RETURN
1701   REM  *** END COORD GRAPH LABEL  ***
1702   REM
1997   REM  *****************************
1998   REM  * CIRCLE AND GRAPH PLOT SBRT *
1999   REM  *****************************
2000   FAC = 3.14159266 / 180: REM  CONVERSION CONSTANT.
2010   HC = 64:VC = 83:R = 64: REM  SET CIRCLE CENTER COORDS
       AND RADIUS OF CIRCLE.
2020   PH = OH:PV = OV −  SIN (0) * YSCL: REM  SET SCREEN
       COORDS OF INITIAL POINT ON GRAPH OF SINE FUNCTION.
       PT CORRESPONDS TO DEG = 0.
2030   PX = R *  COS (0):PY = R *  SIN (0): REM  SET X- AND
       Y-OFFSET VALUES OF INITIAL POINT ON CIRCLE CORRESP TO
       DEG = 0.
2035   CALL HRCG: REM  INIT HRCG
2040   FOR DG = 0 TO 360 STEP 3
2045   VTAB 20: HTAB 6: PRINT "DEG = ";DG: REM  PRINT DG VALUE
       BENEATH CIRCLE.
```

```
2050  TH = DG * FAC
2060  X = R *  COS (TH):Y = R *  SIN (TH)
2070  HCOLOR =  3: GOSUB 2500: REM  DRAW WITHIN THE CIRCLE THE
      'ARMS' OF THE RIGHT TRIANGLE REPRESENTING THE X- AND
      Y-OFFSET SEGMENTS FROM THE CENTER TO THE POINT P(X,Y) =
      (COS(TH),SIN(TH)).
2080  IF 1 — SP THEN  GOSUB 2600: REM  IF THIS IS NOT THE '2ND
      PASS' (IE., ITS THE 1ST), THEN GO TO PRINT "Y"
      ROUTINE.
2090  IF 1 — SP THEN  GOSUB 2600: REM  IF THIS IS NOT THE '2ND
      PASS' (IE., ITS THE 1ST), THEN GO TO THE ROUTINE TO PRINT
      "Y" NEXT TO THE Y-OFFSET SEGMENT.
2100  HPLOT HC + PX,VC — PY TO HC + X,VC — Y: REM  PLOT
      'ARC' OF CIRCLE FROM PREVIOUS POINT TO NEW POINT.
2110  H = OH + DG * XSCL:V = OV —  SIN (TH) * YSCL: REM
      COMPUTE SCREEN COORDS OF POINT ON GRAPH OF Y = SINE OF
      DG  = SIN(TH).
2120  HPLOT PH,PV TO H,V: REM  PLOT SEGMENT OF SINE GRAPH FROM
      PREVIOUS POINT TO NEW POINT.
2130  PH = H:PV = V: REM  SET COORDS OF THE PREVIOUS PT
      PLOTTED ON SINE GRAPH TO COORDS OF NEWEST PT.
2135  FOR T = 1 TO 100: NEXT T: REM  DELAY
2140  HCOLOR =  0: GOSUB 2500: REM  ERASE SEGMENTS DRAWN
      WITHIN CIRCLE.
2145  IF 1 — SP THEN  HTAB HT: VTAB VT: PRINT " ": REM  IF THE
      '1ST PASS' THEN ERASE "Y" LABEL.
2150  HCOLOR =  3: HPLOT HC + PX,VC — PY TO HC + X,VC — Y:
      REM  REDRAW 'ARC' OF CIRCLE TO REINSTATE POINTS POSSIBLY
      ERASED BY PREVIOUS STATEMENT.
2160  IF DG < = 6 THEN  HPLOT HC + R,VC TO HC + X,VC — Y:
      REM  THIS IS NECESSARY TO RESTORE NEARLY VERTICAL
      SECTIONS OF THE CIRCLE THAT ARE 'ERASED' BY ERASURE OF
      THE X-Y SEGMENTS.
2170  IF DG > = 180 AND DG < = 189 THEN  HPLOT HC —
      R,VC TO HC + X,VC — Y: REM  DITTO THE ABOVE REASON.
2175  IF SP THEN  HPLOT H,V TO H,OV: HPLOT HC + X,VC — Y TO
      HC + X,VC
2180  PX = X:PY = Y: REM  SET COORDS OF THE PREVIOUSLY
      PLOTTED PT ON CIRCLE TO COORDS OF NEWEST PT.
2185  NEXT DG
2190  VTAB 20: HTAB 6: PRINT "          ": REM  PRINT 9 BLANKS
      TO ERASE 'DEG = DG' FIELD BENEATH CIRCLE.
2195  PRINT D$;"PR#0": REM  TURN OFF HRCG
2200  RETURN
2201  REM  ** END OF CIRCLE/GRAPH PLOT **
2202  REM
```

```
2497  REM   ********************************
2498  REM   **   X-Y SEGMENT PLOT SUBRT  **
2499  REM   ********************************
2500  HPLOT HC,VC TO HC + X,VC TO HC + X,VC - Y
2510  RETURN
2511  REM   ***    END X-Y SEGMT PLOT   ***
2512  REM
2597  REM   ********************************
2598  REM   * PRNT 'Y' NEAR Y-SEG SUBRT  *
2599  REM   ********************************
2600  HT =  INT ((HC + X) / 7):VT = 1 +  INT ((VC - Y / 2)
      / 8): REM  DETERMINE BASIC PRINT POSITONS FOR "Y"
      LABEL.
2610  IF DG > 90 AND DG <= 270 THEN HT = HT + 2
2620  HTAB HT: VTAB VT
2630  PRINT "Y"
2640  RETURN
2641  REM   **   END PRNT 'Y' NEAR Y-SEG **
2642  REM
3997  REM   ********************************
3998  REM   *      GRAPH PAPER SUBRT      *
3999  REM   ********************************
```

< All lines of the GRAPH PAPER SUBRT should appear here. Lines 4050 and 4070 have been changed as indicated above. >

```
5251  REM   ** END OF GRAPH PAPER SUBRT **
```

RUN the program a few times, carefully noting the coordination of events, and then respond to the few questions below.

### Check Your Comprehension
How does the length of the Y-offset segment in the circle compare to the height (Y-coordinate) of the corresponding point on the SINe graph? _____

In the circle display, reference is made to an angle of DG degrees; the angle is not explicitly displayed. What angle is it? _____

A moment's reflection of the DISCUSSION section should convince you it is the angle formed by the radius to the point (X,Y) and the positive half of the X-axis. By adding the phrase TO HC,VC to the end of the HPLOT statement in line 2500, the radius vector will be displayed.

How can you correct the problem this addition presents on the second pass through the subroutine? _____

A discussion of the program development and logic is worthwhile. Considerable thought must go into the selection of the viewport for the coordinate graph if it is to be labeled with meaningful labels in a simple manner. This particularly applies to the horizontal coordinate axis. Since the unit on this axis is the degree unit and points of primary concern occur at multiples of 90 degrees, it is desirable to have grid ticking occur at these points. Furthermore, since roughly half of the screen is to be devoted to the coordinate graph and some space for labeling is needed to the left of the graph, approximately $140 - 2*7 = 126$ or fewer pixels are needed. After considering a few possibilities, a width of 120 pixels provides the following features: 1) it is divisible by 4, permitting convenient divisions corresponding to 90, 180, 270, and 360 degrees; 2) it is evenly divisible by a screen grid denstiy value of 10 pixels which will result in a coordinate grid density value of 30 degrees; and 3) it allows sufficient space on the left for labeling.

The height of the viewport for the coordinate graph must match the screen diameter of the circle. Since the Y-range of SINe values is from $-1$ to $+1$, it is desirable to select a screen height which provides for sensible label values such as .1, .2, .25, or .5 which are integer divisors of 1. The vertical screen grid density should be approximately near the horizontal grid density of 10 for best visual effect, and an integer multiple of this should provide the grid label density. A possible choice of grid density, VTIC = 10, will result in circle radius of 60 ( $7*10 = 70$ would be too large) with a grid density value of $1/6 = .166666667$ along the vertical coordinate axis. Actual label values will appear best only for $-1$, $-.5$, 0, .5 and 1.

The choice made in the program above is VTIC = 8. To meet the conditions of labeling, a radius of $8*8 = 64$ is best. This permits a grid density value of $1/8 = .125$ and the same set of label values. Although label values of $-.75$, $-.25$, .25 and .75 could also appear, their actual appearance seems to clutter the picture (try it for yourself, it's a good exercise in experimenting with the label process).

After setting the high resolution screen and defining the appropriate range parameters (lines 60-90), control is passed to the GRAPH PAPER SUBROUTINE for determining the appropriate scales and creating the coordinate graph. Although the routine actually computes default densities, the values returned are not used in light of the changes made in lines 4050 and 4070. The routine is obviously performing more computation than is necessary, but there is no need to make major alterations simply to save a few micro seconds of execution time.

In line 120 control is passed to the labeling subroutine which is fairly self-explanatory. However, the tic or hash marks corresponding to label values are emphasized by HPLOTting slightly longer segments at the appropriate points. The transformation formulas

H = OH + X * XSCL

V = OV − Y * YSCL,

presented in ACTIVITY 4.6 are used to determine the correct positioning of the hash marks. The reader should go back to that section to refresh his/her memory about the variable meanings. Although the actual positions could have been determined by other methods, it is more instructive and general to determine the positions in this fashion.

Following the labeling of the axes, control is passed to the major subroutine and heart of the program which begins at line 2000. The vertical coordinate of the circle center is the midvalue of the viewport vertical bounds: VC = (V0 + V1)/2 = (147 + 19)/2. In each graph, the construction process of the curve is to draw a line segment from the previously HPLOTted point to the newly determined point on the curve. Lines 2020 and 2030 initialize the variables used to remember the previously plotted points in each graph. These initial points will be plotted the first time through the DG-loop beginning at line 2040. Lines 2050, 2060, and 2100-2120 are the primary lines used to draw the circle arc and the SINe curve. Note the coordinate graph transformation formulas are used to convert the point (DG, COS(TH)) to the screen point (H,V). Lines 2130 and 2180 reset the coordinates of the previously plotted point to the coordinates of the most recently plotted point.

The remaining statements in the subroutine are merely icing on the cake. However, a few comments may be helpful. On the first pass through the subroutine (SP = 0), the X- and Y-offset segments are HPLOTted and then erased after a short delay. Unfortunately, for values of DG near DG = 0 and DG = 180, the Y-offset segments overlap portions of the circle already plotted. Mathematically the segments are disjoint from the circle, but because of truncation error (numerical values are truncated to the nearest integer value when plotting screen points), there is screen overlap. Lines 2160 and 2170 are designed to correct this situation. On the second pass through the subroutine (SP = 1), the Y-segments are HPLOTted on both graphs in line 2175. This is done to emphasize the common identity of the value in each graph. Indeed, in the circle graph a screen radius of R = 64 pixels corresponds to one unit in the circle graph, while in the coordinate graph, YSCL = (H0 − Y0)/(D − C) = 128/2 = 64 pixels/unit.

The graph of the SINe function in the coordinate plane is often referred to as a "sine wave." In the exercise which follows you can try your hand at creating a similar graph for the COSine.

**EXERCISE**   Make the necessary changes in the COMPREHENSIVE EXAMPLE to make a COSINE GRAPH DEMONSTRATION. Specifically, the coordinate graph should be for the COSine function and not the SINe function. All coordinate graph labeling should reflect graphing the function X = COS(DEG). In the circle graph, draw the X-offset and Y-offset segments in reverse order; ie., draw first the Y-offset segment and then the X-segment ( HPLOT HC,VC TO HC,VC − Y TO HC + X, VC − Y ). Position an "X" label near the X-segment. Make the necessary adjustments for overlapping of the X-offset segment with the circle near DG = 90 and DG = 270.

**CHALLENGE**   Integrate the two programs above so either program can be accessed from a menu. Rather than use COSine or SINe directly in the calculation of points on the graph, use a function such as FNF(DG) which has been previously defined (DEF FNF(Z) = COS(Z) or SIN(Z) depending upon the choice made from the menu). One can create string variables to hold the label values needed for each display. The use of ON...GOSUB statements will help in the peripheral routines needed which draw the offset segments and make adjustments and corrections in the display.

# ACTIVITY 4.8   Circles & Ellipses

**LEARNING BY DISCOVERY**   The focus of this activity is the construction of "true" circles and ellipses on the high resolution screen. The SINe and COSine are used extensively.

1. Enter the program below, then RUN it.

```
NEW
10  SFAC = 1.20: REM  ENTER YOUR OWN SCREEN SCALE FACTOR IF
    IT IS DIFFERENT, CF., ACTIVITY 4.2.
20  FAC = 3.14159266 / 180: REM  PI/180; DEG TO RAD
```

```
        CONVERSION FACTOR.
30      HC = 140:VC = 96: REM  CENTER SCREEN COORDS.
40      HGR2 : HCOLOR = 3
50      A = 90:B = 90
60      HPLOT HC + A,VC: REM  PLOT STARTING POINT OF 'CIRCLE'
        CORRESP TO DEG = 0.
70      FOR DEG = 0 TO 360 STEP 3
80      TH = DEG * FAC: REM  CONVERT DEGREES TO RADIANS.
90      X% = A * COS (TH):Y% = B * SIN (TH): REM  DETERMINE
        X AND Y COORDINATES OF POINT ON 'CIRCLE' CORRESP TO TH.
100     HPLOT  TO HC + X%,VC - Y%: REM  PLOT 'ARC'.
110     NEXT DEG
120     GET K$: TEXT : HOME : END
LIST
RUN
```

What do you observe? _____

Of course, a circle!  However, look carefully. Is it a "true" circle or merely suggestive of one? In ACTIVITY 4.2 we investigated this very point. To acheive a "true" circle, we must adjust one of the screen coordinate directions. Recall the following formulas involving SFAC, the screen scale factor.

**SCREEN EQUIVALENT SCALES**

HORIZ = VERT * SFAC      VERT = HORIZ / SFAC

To make the circle appear as a "true" circle, make the following change in the program.

```
50 A = 90 * SFAC : B = 90
LIST
RUN
```

Does this appear to be more of a circle now? _____

What is the circle radius? _____

This is open to interpretation; it all depends on which measurement scale you're using. If the measurement scale is based on vertical distance between pixels, then the radius is 90 vertical pixel units. If the horizontal distance between pixels is used, then the radius is 90 * SFAC horizontal pixel units.

2. Let's investigate what happens when different unrelated values are assigned to A and B in the program above. Make the following changes in line 50.

```
50  A = 135 : B = 80
LIST
RUN
```

What is happening to the circle? _____

On a grander scale, make the following changes which systematically vary the size of A from small to larger values.

```
50  B = 90
55  FOR A = 20 TO 130 STEP 10
```

```
115 NEXT A
RUN
```

What do you observe? _____

What would you expect to happen if say, A = 80 and the value of B is permitted to vary from B = 10 to B = 90 stepping by 10? Try changing lines 50, 50 and 115 to check your answer. _____

There is an obvious inefficiency about the program. Do you notice what it is? _____
_____

In fact, the values of COS (TH) and SIN (TH) are recalculated for each value of the loop variable A (or B). Let's rectify this situation.

3. Although much of the code is a repeat of that in the previous section, it will be less cumbersome to start from scratch. Enter the following lines of code.

```
NEW
10   SFAC = 1.20: REM  ENTER YOUR SCREEN SCALE FACTOR IF
     DIFFERENT.
20   FAC = 3.14159266 / 180
30   HC = 140:VC = 96
40   HGR2 : HCOLOR =  3
50   GOSUB 500: REM  GO CALCULATE SINES AND COSINES
60   B = 90
70   FOR A = 20 TO 130 STEP 10
80   HPLOT HC + A,VC
90   FOR I = 1 TO 120
100  X% = A * C(I) +  SGN (C(I)) * .5:Y% = B * S(I) +  SGN
     (S(I)) * .5: REM  ROUND TO NEAREST INTEGER THE X-
     AND Y-COORDS OF PT ON CURVE.
110  HPLOT  TO HC + X%,VC - Y%
120  NEXT I,A
130  GET K$: TEXT : HOME : END
497  REM  ******************************
498  REM  * COS & SIN VAL ARRAY CONSTR  *
499  REM  ******************************
500  DIM C(120),S(120): REM  DIMENSION ARRAYS FOR STORING
     COSINE AND SINE VALUES OF 120+1 = 360/3+1
     POINTS.
510  I = 0: REM  INITIALIZE INDEX COUNTER
520  FOR DEG = 0 TO 360 STEP 3
530  TH = DEG * FAC
540  C(I) =  COS (TH):S(I) =  SIN (TH)
550  I = I + 1: REM  INCREMENT INDEX COUNTER
560  NEXT DEG
570  RETURN
LIST
RUN
```

Do you notice any improvement in speed? _____

Those calculations of SINe and COSine can be very time consuming. Additional time can be saved by taking larger degree increments, or equivalently choosing fewer points to calculate SINe and COSine values. However, what problem can you foresee by taking larger increments of degrees between one angle and the next?

_____

Experiment!

4. The following program will provide you with the ultimate in speed and appearance for a circle or an ellipse.

```
NEW
100   DG = 3:NP = 30: REM   DG = DEGREE INCREMENT BETWEEN
      ANGLES FROM 0 TO 360; NP = # OF PTS AT WHICH COS AND
      SIN ARE DEFINED BETWEEN 0 AND 90.
110   DIM X%(NP),Y%(NP)
120   FAC = 3.14159266 / 180:SFAC = 1.20: REM   USE YOUR
      SCREEN SCALE FACTOR IF DIFFERENT.
130   A = 80:B = 80
140   A = A * SFAC: REM   SCALE HORIZ FOR EQUIV SCALES
150   HC = 140:VC = 96: REM   SCREEN COORDS OF CIRCLE CENTER.
160   HGR : HCOLOR = 3: POKE − 16302,0: REM FULL SCREEN
      PG1
170   GOSUB 500: REM   GO TO CIRCLE PLOTTING SUBRT.
180   GET Q$: TEXT : HOME : END
498   REM
499   REM   **   PERF CIRCLE PLOT SUBRT   **
500   I = 0:P5 = 0.5: REM   I IS THE INDEX FOR THE ARRAYS X%
      AND Y%; P5 IS USED TO ROUND TO THE NEAREST INTEGER
      WHEN GETTING CIRCLE SCREEN COORDS.
510   FOR D = 0 TO 45 STEP DG: REM   FOR ANGLES BETWEEN 0 AND
      45 DEGREES, DO ...
520   TH = D * FAC: REM   CONVERT DEG TO RADIANS
530   C =   COS (TH):S =   SIN (TH)
540   X%(I) = A * C + P5:Y%(I) = B * S + P5: REM   GET X-
      AND Y-OFFSETS FOR PTS ON CIRCLE.
550   X%(NP − I) = A * S + P5:Y%(NP − I) = B * C + P5:
      REM   GET X- AND Y- OFFSETS FOR PTS ON CIRCLE FOR
      ANGLES BETWEEN 90 AND 45 DEGREES.
560   I = I + 1: REM   INCREMENT INDEX VARIABLE FOR NEXT
      ANGLE.
570   NEXT D
580   HPLOT HC + X%(0),VC: FOR I = 1 TO NP: HPLOT  TO HC +
      X%(I),VC − Y%(I): NEXT
590   HPLOT HC + X%(0),VC: FOR I = 1 TO NP: HPLOT  TO HC +
      X%(I),VC + Y%(I): NEXT
600   HPLOT HC − X%(0),VC: FOR I = 1 TO NP: HPLOT  TO HC −
```

```
          X%(I),VC - Y%(I): NEXT
610       HPLOT HC - X%(0),VC: FOR I = 1 TO NP: HPLOT  TO HC -
          X%(I),VC + Y%(I): NEXT
620       RETURN
LIST
RUN
```

Do you notice a considerable improvement in speed?  Reflect on what you have learned about values of the SINe and COSine to justify line 550. _____

Reflect on the relationship between SINes and COSines and points on a circle to justify lines 580-610. _____

The program will easily adapt to the construction of ellipses as well. The user need only redefine the values of A and B in line 130. Finally, the number of points NP on the circle for which the SINe and COSine are determined can be greater or smaller, but corresponding adjustments must be made in the variable DG.

**DISCUSSION**   You learned in the previous activity that if a point P is on a circle of radius R, and if TH is the radian measure of the angle the ray OP makes with the positive x axis, then the horizontal and vertical offsets from O to P are given by

$$X = R * COS (TH)    Y = R * SIN (TH)$$

These formulas are the analytic formulas for the purist. The realist can see (the program in Section 1) a true circle does not result when attempting to directly apply these formulas to graphics on the Apple high resolution screen. Indeed, vertical and horizontal pixel distances are not necessarily equivalent. The problem and solution was discussed at length in ACTIVITY 4.2, and the conclusions of that section were applied at the end of Section 1 in this activity.

An ellipse is the closed curve obtained by magnification (or contraction) in one direction of all the points on a circle. In fact, if SCL represents some scale factor, then multiplication of each X-coordinate by SCL for each point (X, Y) on a circle of a radius R will result in an ellipse which is 2 * R units in diametric height and 2 * R * SCL units in diametric width (see Figure 4.8.1).

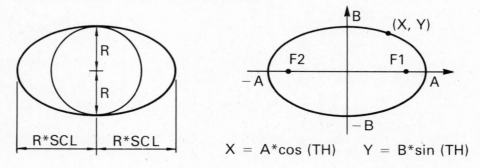

Figures  4.8.1 and 4.8.2

If the formulas for the X and Y coordinates of a point on the circle are considered, then by taking A = R * SCL and B = R one obtains

X = A * COS (TH)      Y = B * SIN (TH)

The collection of points (X, Y) will represent an ellipse in the X-Y plane (See Figure 4.8.2).

This scaling procedure was used in the program in Sections 2 and 3, where A was permitted to change in value and B was held fixed. The result was several ellipses with different widths but common height.

It is impossible to resist telling the reader something about the significance of these simple geometric curves. In 1609, Johannes Kepler discovered that the motion of the planets conforms to orbital paths in the form of ellipses. Furthermore, the sun is located at a focus of the ellipse.

An ellipse has two focii, which lie on the longer diametric axis at equal distances from the center. For those of you who are curious about such things, this distance is given by SQR(A*A − B*B) where A is the larger of the two diametric axis distances from the center.

In addition, an ellipse has the following unusual property. Consider an elliptically shaped pool table. It can be shown (theoretically) that any shot passing through one focus must, after a carom off the side of the table, necessarily pass through the other focus. If you ever have the occassion to stand in a whisper chamber, this simple related principle is used. The chamber is constructed with elliptically shaped walls. If you stand at one focus and whisper to a friend standing at the other focus, then all sound (be it ever so slight) is reflected off the walls and converges to the point where your friend is standing. Your partner will be able to hear you remarkably well.

**COMPREHENSIVE EXAMPLE**   The program below combines ellipses and circles to simulate the graphic image of a sphere. There are methods which work as well but typically involve the use of spherical coordinate formulas in addition to coordinate transformations from 3- to 2-dimensions. The second part of the program is a collection of randomly created displays which provide some very unusual graphics. Some of the patterns will put you to sleep while others are fantastic. With some, the interesting aspect is the development of the display. To halt execution of the displays, simply press a key.

```
NEW
10   REM   ********************************
11   REM   *            CE4.8             *
12   REM   ********************************
13   REM
14   REM
15   GOTO 100: REM   BRANCH AROUND SUBROUTINES.
16   REM
27   REM   ********************************
28   REM   *      CIRCLE PLOTTING SUBRT   *
29   REM   ********************************
30   HPLOT HC + X%(0),VC: FOR I = 1 TO NP: HPLOT   TO HC +
     X%(I),VC − Y%(I): NEXT
32   HPLOT HC + X%(0),VC: FOR I = 1 TO NP: HPLOT   TO HC +
```

```
     X%(I),VC + Y%(I): NEXT
34   HPLOT HC - X%(0),VC: FOR I = 1 TO NP: HPLOT  TO HC -
     X%(I),VC - Y%(I): NEXT
36   HPLOT HC - X%(0),VC: FOR I = 1 TO NP: HPLOT  TO HC -
     X%(I),VC + Y%(I): NEXT
38   RETURN
39   REM  **      END CIRCLE PLOT SBRT   **
40   REM
47   REM  *******************************
48   REM  *      CALC COS AND SIN VALS     *
49   REM  *******************************
50   I = 0
52   FOR D = 0 TO 45 STEP DG
54   TH = D * FAC
56   C(I) =  COS (TH):S(I) =  SIN (TH)
58   I = I + 1
60   NEXT
62   RETURN
63   REM  **      END CALC COS AND SIN    **
64   REM
97   REM  *******************************
98   REM  *           MAIN PROGRAM          *
99   REM  *******************************
100  DG = 3:NP = 30: REM  DG = DEGREE INCREMENT BETWEEN
     ANGLES FROM 0 TO 360; NP = # OF PTS AT WHICH COS AND
     SIN ARE DEFINED BETWEEN 0 AND 90.
110  DIM X%(NP),Y%(NP),C(15),S(15)
120  FAC = 3.14159266 / 180:SFAC = 1.20: REM  USE YOUR SCREEN
     SCALE FACTOR IF DIFFERENT.
130  GOSUB 50: REM  GO CALCULATE VALUES OF COS AND SIN AND
     STORE IN ARRAYS C() AND S().
140  HC = 140:VC = 96: REM  SCREEN COORDS OF CENTER OF CIRCLES
     AND ELLIPSES.
150  P5 = 0.5: REM  CONSTANT USED FOR ROUNDING TO NEAREST
     INTEGER VALUE.
160  HGR : HCOLOR =  3: POKE  - 16302,0: REM  FULL SCREEN
     GRAPHICS PAGE 1.
170  GOSUB 2000: REM  GOTO SUBRT SIMULATING SPHERE USING
     ELLIPSES WITH COMMON SEMI-AXIS LENGTH.
180  GET Q$: REM  WAIT FOR KEYPRESS
190  HOME : VTAB 21: POKE  - 16301,0: REM  SET UP FOR MIXED
     GRAPHICS.
200  PRINT "PRESS A KEY. WHEN YOU ARE READY TO STOP": PRINT
     "VIEWING RANDOMLY CREATED DISPLAYS,": PRINT "PRESS A
     KEY AGAIN."
210  GET Q$
220  POKE  - 16302,0: REM  RESET FULL SCREEN GRAPHICS.
230  GOSUB 3000: REM  GOTO SPECIAL DISPLAY IN WHICH THE VALUE
```

```
       OF THE VARIABLE FAC IS DELIBERATELY CHANGED TO PRODUCE
       UNUSUAL DISPLAYS.
240    TEXT : HOME : END
241    REM  **       END MAIN PROGRAM        **
242    REM
997    REM  *******************************
998    REM  *  ELLIPSE & CIRC PTS SUBRT   *
999    REM  *******************************
1000   FOR I = 0 TO 15
1010   C = C(I):S = S(I)
1020   X%(I) = A * C + P5:Y%(I) = B * S + P5: REM  GET X- AND
       Y-OFFSETS FOR PTS ON CIRCLE.
1030   X%(NP - I) = A * S + P5:Y%(NP - I) = B * C + P5: REM
       GET X- AND Y- OFFSETS FOR PTS ON CIRCLE FOR ANGLES
       BETWEEN 90 AND 45 DEGREES.
1040   NEXT
1050   GOSUB 30: REM  GOTO CIRCLE PLOTTING SUBRT.
1060   RETURN
1061   REM  **       END ELLIPSE & CIRC   **
1062   REM
1997   REM  *****************************
1998   REM  *     SPHERE SIMULATION SBRT  *
1999   REM  *****************************
2000   B = 80: REM  SET FIXED VERT SEMI-AXIS LENGTH FOR FIRST
       SET OF ELLIPSES.
2010   FOR A = 96 TO 0 STEP  - 12: REM  FOR HORIZ SEMI AXIS
       LENGTHS FROM 96 TO 0 DO ...
2020   GOSUB 1000: REM  GO DRAW ELLPISES WITH COMMON CENTER AND
       COMMON VERT SEMI-AXIS LENGTH.
2030   NEXT
2040   A = 96: REM  SET FIXED HORIZ SEMI-AXIS LENGTH FOR SECOND
       SET OF ELLIPSES.
2050   FOR B = 70 TO 0 STEP  - 10: REM  FOR  VERT SEMI-AXIS
       LENGTHS FROM 70 TO 0 DO ...
2060   GOSUB 1000: REM  DRAW ELLIPSES WITH COMMON HORIZ
       SEMI-AXIS LENGTH.
2070   NEXT
2080   RETURN
2081   REM  **       END SPHERE SIMULTN   **
2082   REM
2997   REM  *****************************
2998   REM  *       SPECIAL DISPLAY       *
2999   REM  *****************************
3000   B = 80:A = B * SFAC: REM  SET A AND B PARAMETERS FOR
       TRUE CIRCLE.
3010   POKE  - 16368,0: REM  CLEAR KEYBOARD STROBE
3020   FOR K = 0 TO 1 STEP 0: REM  REPEAT INDEFINITELY ...
```

```
3030  IF  PEEK ( − 16384) > 127 THEN  RETURN : POKE  −
      16368,0: REM  ... UNTIL A KEYPRESS IS DETECTED.
3040  FAC =  RND (1) * 10: REM  SELECT RANDOM FAC VALUE
      BETWEEN 0 AND 10
3050  GOSUB 50: REM  GO CALCULATE COS AND SIN VALUES.
3060  CALL 62450
3070  GOSUB 1000: REM  GOTO 'CIRCLE' PLOTTING ROUTINE.
3080  NEXT K
3081  REM  **      END SPECIAL DISP      **
LIST
RUN
```

**Check Your Comprehension**

In an ellipse, the semi-minor axis length is the shortest of distances from the center to points on the ellipse. The semi-major axis length is the longest of distances from the center to points on the ellipse.

What are the semi-minor and semi-major axis lengths for the set of ellipses used to simulate the sphere? _____

In the second half of the program, where randomly generated displays are created, there is one single instruction of difference between simply displaying circle-after-circle (ad nauseum) and the actual resulting display.

What is the difference? _____

**EXERCISE**   Write a program to construct a family of circles, each larger than the previous, which are all tangent at the same point and so each one contains all the previously drawn (and smaller) circles (see Figure 4.8.3). Locate the common point of tangency at the bottom of the screen at (140,185) and successively increase the (vertical) radius from 0 to 90 stepping by 10.

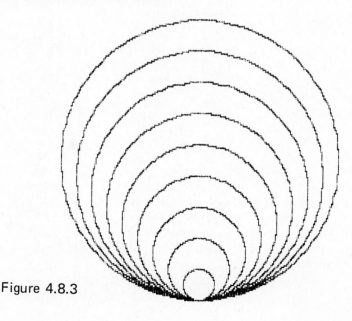

Figure 4.8.3

**CHALLENGE** The technique of Section 4.8.4 for plotting a circle used the symmetry of a circle about each of the coordinate axes to reduce computation time and improve display appearances. This also explains why it was plotted in four separate sections. One can also use to advantage its symmetry about the lines Y = X and Y = − X. This will result in plotting the circle in eight different sections, with two sections in each octant. Write a subroutine (like the one beginning in line 500 in the program of Section 4.8.4) which uses this idea. This technique will avoid the necessity of line 550 in that subroutine, and will consequently result in further execution speed. However, there will be a trade-off in program length when writing a plotting routine. Lines 580-610 cannot be used in their present form, but rather, will be replaced by twice as many statements.

# ACTIVITY 4.9   Pie Charts

**LEARNING BY DISCOVERY** In this activity you will learn how to generate pie chart displays.

1. Consider the following set of data for a home budget.

### HOME BUDGET

| ITEM | MONTHLY EXPENSE |
|---|---|
| Mortgage/rent | $ 350 |
| Food | $ 250 |
| Utilities | $ 100 |
| Automobile | $ 150 |
| Insurance | $ 90 |
| Charge accounts | $ 60 |
| Total | $1000 |

In order to construct a pie chart, a whole circle must be divided into wedges corresponding to the fractional part of each expense in the monthly budget. For a circle of fixed radius, the area of a wedge depends only on the central angle subtended by the wedge. It follows one need only know the size of each central angle; the sides of each angle will determine the precise positions at which to make each cut.

Complete the table below. In the table, the fractional part of the total   each subtotal represents is obtained by dividing the subtotal by the total expenses.

| Item | Subtotal of cumulative expense | Fraction of total | Angle (* 360) |
|---|---|---|---|
| Mort/rent | 350 | 350/1000 = .35 | 126 Deg |
| Food | 600 | 600/1000 = .60 | 216 Deg |
| Utilities | 700 | 700/1000 = .70 | 252 Deg |
| Automobile | 850 | _____ | _____ |
| Insurance | ____ | _____ | _____ |
| Charge acc | ____ | _____ | _____ |

Once a circle is constructed, it is only necessary to HPLOT line segments from the center to points on the circle. With the initial side being the positive X-axis, these segments will be the terminal sides of central angles corresponding to the sizes listed in the table above.

2. Enter the program provided below. It emulates the above process and displays the resulting pie chart.

```
NEW
10   HOME
20   FAC = 3.14159266 / 180:SFAC = 1.20: REM  USE YOUR
     SCREEN SCALE FACTOR IF DIFFERENT.
30   N = 6: REM  NUMBER OF EXPENSE ITEMS
40   FOR I = 1 TO N
50   READ VL(I): REM  READ VALUE OF I-TH EXPENSE
60   SBTL(I) = SBTL(I - 1) + VL(I): REM  ACCUMULATE
     SUBTOTALS
70   NEXT I
80   TL = SBTL(N): REM  TOTAL = NTH SUBTOTAL
90   HC = 140:VC = 80: REM  SCREEN COORDS OF CIRCLE CENTER.
100  B = 60:A = B * SFAC: REM  SET RADIUS PARAMETERS FOR
     TRUE CIRCLE.
110  HGR : HCOLOR =  3
120  GOSUB 1000: REM  GOTO CIRCLE PLOTTING ROUTINE
130  HPLOT HC,VC TO HC + A,VC: REM  PLOT INITIAL SIDE OF 1ST
     SLICE.
140  FOR I = 1 TO N
150  TH = SBTL(I) / TL * 360 * FAC: REM  COMPUTE THE ANGLE
     THAT THE I CUMMULATIVE SLICES REPRESENT, AND THEN
     CONVERT TO RADIANS.
160  HPLOT HC,VC TO HC + A *  COS (TH),VC - B *  SIN (TH):
     REM  'SLICE' PIE FOR CENTRAL ANGLE OF TH RADIANS.
170  HOME : VTAB 21
180  PRINT "SECTOR #";I;", REPRESENTING "; INT (1000 * VL(I)
     / TL) / 10;"%";" OF TOTAL."
190  GOSUB 2000
200  NEXT I
210  HOME : VTAB 21: HTAB 11: PRINT "HOME BUDGET PIE CHART"
220  GET Q$: TEXT : HOME : END
221  REM  ****  END MAIN PROG  ****
222  REM
998  REM  ***** CIRCLE PLOTTING SBRT *****
999  REM  SPECIFICALLY FROM SEC 4.8.5
1000  DIM X%(30),Y%(30)
1010  K = 0:P5 = 0.5
1020  FOR D = 0 TO 45 STEP 3
1030  TH = D * FAC
1040  C =  COS (TH):S =  SIN (TH)
1050  X%(K) = A * C + P5:Y%(K) = B * S + P5
```

```
1060   X%(30 - K) = A * S + P5:Y%(30 - K) = B * C + P5
1070   K = K + 1
1080   NEXT D
1090   HPLOT HC + X%(0),VC: FOR K = 1 TO 30: HPLOT  TO HC +
       X%(K),VC - Y%(K): NEXT
1100   HPLOT HC + X%(0),VC: FOR K = 1 TO 30: HPLOT  TO HC +
       X%(K),VC + Y%(K): NEXT
1110   HPLOT HC - X%(0),VC: FOR K = 1 TO 30: HPLOT  TO HC -
       X%(K),VC - Y%(K): NEXT
1120   HPLOT HC - X%(0),VC: FOR K = 1 TO 30: HPLOT  TO HC -
       X%(K),VC + Y%(K): NEXT
1130   RETURN
1999   REM  ***** DELAY SUBROUTINE *****
2000   FOR K = 1 TO 2000: NEXT
2010   RETURN
5999   REM  ***** DATA FOR HOME BUDGET *****
6000   DATA  350, 250, 100, 150, 90, 60
LIST
RUN
```

Which line(s) determine the subtotals? _____

Which line(s) compute the fractional part of the total represented by each subtotal
and then convert to the appropriate angle? _____

Which line(s) are used to "divide the pie?" _____

3. The addition of colors can greatly enhance a pie chart display. Since there are only
six distinct colors available on the APPLE, one is apparently limited to at most six
items in a pie chart representation. This is not necessarily the case. Alternatives exist
through the use of high resolution color filling programs which usually provide a
palette consisting of many distinct color shades. Other possibilities for coloring
consist of checker-boarding point plots within a sector using one's own programming, or through the use of labels for commonly colored regions.

   Add the following lines to the program to color-fill one sector of the chart
using one of the six colors (black, green, violet, white, orange, and blue) available
on the APPLE.

```
215   GOSUB 3000
3000   HCOLOR =  1
3010   FOR TH = 0 TO SBTL(1) / TL * 360 * FAC STEP .015
3020   HPLOT HC,VC TO HC + A *  COS (TH) + P5,VC - B *  SIN
       (TH) + P5 TO HC,VC
3030   NEXT TH
3040   RETURN
LIST
RUN
```

Describe the screen display. _____

How can one alter the subroutine beginning at line 3000 to accommodate color-filling all the sectors? This will be treated in the COMPREHENSIVE EXAMPLE.

_____

The color-filling subroutine plots from the center to a point on the circle and then back to the center. Investigate what results when the plot back to the center is omitted. What do you observe? _____

Set B equal to 60 and A equal to 25 in the program, then reRUN it. What do you observe? _____

**DISCUSSION**    The use of pie charts can be a very effective way of displaying relative proportions of data. One should refrain from using pie charts when the number of subdivisions becomes too great. The display will become cluttered and difficult to read. The addition of color and labeling can greatly enhance the overall display. There are two popular methods used to label a pie chart. In one method, each label name is placed outside the pie near its corresponding sector. The second method uses a label table in combination with a color scheme which identifies each sector. Commonly colored sectors will require an additional identifier. An example of the second method will be treated in the COMPREHENSIVE EXAMPLE section.

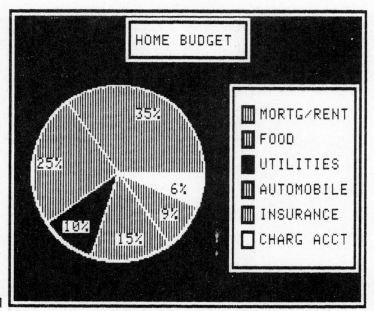

Figure 4.9.1

**COMPREHENSIVE EXAMPLE**    The program below is a general utility program for pie chart display. A maximum of six items (label fields) is permitted as input. The user supplies a title label, label fields, and entry values for each field. An example of the data entry is provided with this program. After creating the background display, the pie will be created by color-filling each sector using HPLOTs from the circle center to the boundary. These line segments are sufficiently close together to entirely fill the sectors. Following the pie construction, the table of label fields is created. The color corresponding to each field is repeated in a color swatch appearing next to the label.

```
NEW
10    REM   *********************************
11    REM   *            CE4.9             *
12    REM   *********************************
13    REM
14    REM
15    GOTO 100: REM   BRANCH AROUND SUBRTS.
16    REM
47    REM   *********************************
48    REM   *   DRAW DBL LINE BOX SUBROUTN  *
49    REM   *********************************
50    FOR JJ = 0 TO 1
52    HPLOT L,T TO L,B TO R,B TO R,T TO L,T
54    L = L + 1:R = R - 1:T = T + 1:B = B - 1
56    NEXT JJ: RETURN
57    REM   **     END DRAW BOX SUBRT      **
58    REM
97    REM   *********************************
98    REM   *          MAIN PROGRAM         *
99    REM   *********************************
100   HOME : HIMEM: 37500: REM   SET HIMEM BELOW STARTING ADDRESS
      OF HRCG (SEE BELOW).
110   PRINT "DO YOU NEED INSTRUCTIONS < Y,N >? ";:
      GET A$: PRINT A$
120   IF A$ = "Y" THEN  GOTO 5000
130   D$ =  CHR$ (13) +  CHR$ (4): REM  'RETURN' + CTRL-D.
140   PRINT "BLOAD HRCG$9280": PRINT D$;"BLOAD HRCG$9280": PRINT
150   PRINT "BLOAD ASCII$9300": PRINT D$;"BLOAD ASCII$9300"
160   HRCG = 37504: REM   STARTING BYTE OF HRCG: $9280.
170   FOR I = 1 TO 6
180   READ COLOR(I): REM   READ THE COLORS USED FOR FILLING IN
      THE ORDER PRESCRIBED; SEE LINE 370.
190   NEXT I
200   SFAC = 1.20: REM   USE YOUR SCREEN SCALE FACTOR IF
      DIFFERENT.
210   READ T$,N: REM   READ TITLE AND # OF DATA ENTRIES.
220   IF  LEN (T$) > 30 THEN T$ =  LEFT$ (T$,30)
230   IF N > 6 THEN  HOME : PRINT "AT MOST 6 ENTRY VALUES ARE
      PERMITTED.": PRINT "TRY AGAIN.": STOP
240   FOR I = 1 TO N: REM   FOR EACH DATA ENTRY ...
250   READ LB$(I),VL(I): REM   READ LABEL AND VALUE.
260   SBTL(I) = SBTL(I - 1) + VL(I): REM   KEEP CUMULATIVE
      SUBTOTALS OF VALUES.
270   NEXT I
```

```
280   TL = SBTL(N): REM   TL = TOTAL OF ENTRIES.
290   VTAB 12: HTAB 8: PRINT "... ONE MOMENT PLEASE ..."
300   HC = 85:VC = 105: REM   SCREEN COORDS OF CENTER OF PIE
      CHART.
310   B = 55:A = B * SFAC: REM   (VERT) RADIUS IS 55; ADJUST A
      FOR EQUIV SCALES AND TRUE CIRCLE.
320   GOSUB 2000: REM   GO TO SUBRT TO DETERMINE PTS ON CIRCLE
      AND STORE IN ARRAYS.
330   HGR2
340   GOSUB 3000: REM   GOTO SCREEN DISPLAY SUBRT WHICH PREPARES
      SCREEN FOR PIE CHART.
350   GOSUB 4000: REM   GOTO PIE CHART & LABEL DISPLAY SUBRT.
360   GET Q$: TEXT : HOME : END
370   DATA  1, 2, 3, 6, 5, 4   : REM   COLOR DATA.
371   REM  **           END MAIN PROG        **
372   REM
996   REM  ******************************
997   REM  * ENTRY DATA BEGN AT LN 1000  *
998   REM  ******************************
999   REM  ** TITLE, # ITEMS **
1000   DATA   HOME BUDGET, 6
1009   REM  ** LABELS, VALUES **
1010   DATA   MORTG/RENT, 350
1020   DATA   FOOD, 250
1030   DATA   UTILITIES, 100
1040   DATA   AUTOMOBILE, 150
1050   DATA   INSURANCE, 90
1060   DATA   CHARG ACCT, 60
1100   REM  **          END DATA SECTION       **
1101   REM
1997   REM  ******************************
1998   REM  *    CALC PTS ON CIRCLE SBRT   *
1999   REM  ******************************
2000   DIM X%(360),Y%(360): REM   ARRAYS USED TO HOLD COORDS OF
       PTS ON CIRCLE.
2010   FAC = 3.14159266 / 180: REM   CONVERSION FACTOR: DEG TO
       RADNS.
2020   FOR D = 0 TO 45: REM   FOR EACH ANGLE FROM 0 TO 45
       DEGS ...
2030   TH = D * FAC: REM   CONVERT TO RADNS.
2040   C =   COS (TH):S =   SIN (TH)
2050   X%(D) = .5 + A * C:Y%(D) = .5 + B * S: REM   COMPUTE
       COORDS ON CIRCLE (ROUNDING TO NEAREST INTEGER).
2060   X%(90 − D) = .5 + A * S:Y%(90 − D) = .5 + B * C: REM
       GET COORDS FOR ANGLES BETWEEN 90 AND 45 AS WELL.
2070   NEXT D
```

```
2080  FOR D = 0 TO 90: REM  GET COORDS FOR REMAINING ANGLES
      BETWEEN 90 AND 360 DEGREES.
2090  X%(180 - D) = - X%(D):Y%(180 - D) = Y%(D)
2100  X%(180 + D) = - X%(D):Y%(180 + D) = - Y%(D)
2110  X%(360 - D) = X%(D):Y%(360 - D) = - Y%(D)
2120  NEXT D
2130  RETURN
2131  REM  **      END CIRCLE PTS SUBR  **
2132  REM
2997  REM  ******************************
2998  REM  *    SCREEN DISPLAY SUBRT   *
2999  REM  ******************************
3000  HCOLOR =  3: HPLOT 0,0: CALL 62454: REM  COLOR HIRES
      SCREEN ALL WHITE1.
3010  HCOLOR =  0: REM  SET PLOTTING COLOR TO BLACK1.
3020  L = 2:R = 277:T = 2:B = 189: GOSUB 50: REM  PUT BORDER
      AROUND ENTIRE SCREEN.
3030  L = 140 - 7 * ( INT ( LEN (T$) / 2) + 2):R = 279 -
      L:T = 5:B = 33: GOSUB 50: REM  DRAW BORDER FOR TITLE
      BOX; LEFT AND RIGHT EDGES DEPEND ON TITLE LENGTH.
3040  L = L + 2:R = R - 2:T = T + 2:B = B - 2: REM  SET
      BOUNDARIES FOR INNER MOST SECTION OF TITLE BOX.
3050  FOR V = T TO B: REM  CLEAR OUT INSIDE OF TITLE BOX.
3060  HPLOT L,V TO R,V
3070  NEXT V
3080  CALL HRCG: REM  INITIALIZE HRCG.
3090  HTAB 20 -  INT ( LEN (T$) / 2): VTAB 3: REM  TAB TO
      APPROPRIATE PRINT POSITION IN TITLE BOX.
3100  PRINT T$: REM  PRINT TITLE.
3110  PRINT  CHR$ (4);"PR#0": REM  DISCONNECT HRCG.
3120  L = 173:R = 273: REM  LEFT & RIGHT BOUNDARIES FOR LABEL
      BOX.
3130  T = 112 - 8 * (N + 2):B = T + 16 * (N + 1) + 8: REM
      TOP & BOTTOM BOUNDARIES FOR LABEL BOX; THEY DEPEND ON
      THE NUMBER OF ENTRIES.
3140  GOSUB 50: REM  GO DRAW BORDER OF LABEL BOX.
3150  L = L + 2:R = R - 2:T = T + 2:B = B - 2: REM  SET
      BOUNDARIES FOR INNER MOST SECTION OF LABEL BOX.
3160  FOR V = T TO B: REM  CLEAR OUT INSIDE OF LABEL BOX.
3170  HPLOT L,V TO R,V
3180  NEXT V
3190  F = 1.03:P5 = .5: REM  F IS A SCALE FACTOR USED TO CLEAR
      OUT CIRCULAR AREA LARGER THAN PIE CIRCLE; P5 IS USED IN
      AVERAGING AND ROUNDING TO NEAREST INTEGER.
3200  PX% = F * X%(90):PY% = F * Y%(90): REM  STARTING WITH
      THE TOP PT ON THE EXPANDED CIRCLE AS THE PREVIOUS PT, ...
```

```
3210  FOR D = 90 TO 270: REM  FROM THE TOP TO THE BOTTOM OF
      THE EXPANDED CIRCLE, IE., AS THE ANGLES FROM 90 TO 270
      ARE CONSIDERED ...
3220  X% = F * X%(D):Y% = F * Y%(D): REM  GET THE NEXT LOWER
      CALCULATED PT, ...
3230  HX% = P5 * (PX% + X%) + P5:HY% = P5 * (PY% + Y%) +
      P5: REM  GET THE MIDPT BETWEEN PREV PT AND NEW PT, ...
3240  HPLOT HC + HX%,VC - HY% TO HC - HX%,VC - HY%: REM
      PLOT FROM ONE SIDE TO OTHER SIDE OF CIRCLE; MIDPTS MUST
      BE CONSIDERED TO BE SURE OF COMPLETE CLEARING.
3250  HPLOT HC + X%,VC - Y% TO HC - X%,VC -Y%: REM  PLOT
      FROM ONE SIDE TO OTHER FOR NEW PT AS WELL.
3260  PX% = X%:PY% = Y%: REM  RESET PREV PT AS (OLD) NEW PT.
3270  NEXT D
3280  RETURN
3281  REM  ** END SCREEN DISPLAY SBRT **
3282  REM
3997  REM  ******************************
3998  REM  * PIE CHRT & ENTRY LBL SBRT *
3999  REM  ******************************
4000  FOR I = 1 TO N: REM  FOR EACH DATA ENTRY, ...
4010  D%(I) = SBTL(I) / TL * 360: REM  DETERMINE ANGLE (DEG)
      OF TERMINAL SIDE OF SECTOR CORRESPONDING TO SECTOR I.
4020  NEXT I
4030  FOR I = 1 TO N: REM  FOR EACH SECTOR OF THE PIE, ...
4040  HCOLOR =  COLR(I): HPLOT HC + X%(D%(I - 1)),VC -
      Y%(D%(I - 1)): REM  START BY PLOTTING PT ON INITIAL
      EDGE OF SECTOR AND ON CIRCLE;
4050  FOR D = D%(I - 1) TO D%(I): REM  FOR THE REMAINING PTS
      ON CIRCLE CORRESP TO ANGLES (DEG) BETWEEN INITIAL AND
      TERMINAL SIDE OF I-TH SECTOR.
4060  HPLOT  TO HC,VC TO HC + X%(D),VC - Y%(D): REM  PLOT
      FROM CIRCLE EDGE TO CENTER AND THEN BACK TO NEW PT. THE
      DOUBLE PLOTTING INSURES COMPLETE FILLING.
4070  NEXT D
4080  NEXT I
4090  FOR I = 1 TO N: REM   PLOT IN APPROPRIATE COLOR OF BLACK
      THE SIDES OF EACH SECTOR. THIS IS FOR COSMETIC PURPOSES
      ONLY; IT PROVIDES A CLEAR IDENTITY FOR EACH SECTOR.
4100  HCOLOR =  0: IF I > 2 THEN  HCOLOR =  4
4110  HPLOT HC,VC TO HC + F * X%(D%(I)),VC - F * Y%(D%(I))
4120  NEXT I
4130  CALL HRCG: REM  INITIALIZE HRCG.
4140  VTB = 15 - N:HTB = 29: REM  SET TAB VARIABLES FOR 1ST
      PRINT POSITION IN LABEL BOX.
4150  FOR I = 1 TO N: REM  FOR EACH DATA ENTRY, DO ...
4160  HTAB HTB: VTAB VTB: PRINT  LEFT$ (LB$(I),10): REM  TAB TO
```

```
       PRINT POSITION AND PRINT I-TH ENTRY LABEL (AT MOST 10
       CHARS).
4170   L = 7 * (HTB - 3):R = L + 10:B = 8 * VTB + 1:T = B
       - 11: REM  DETERMINE BOUNDARIES FOR BOX TO CONTAIN
       COLOR SWATCH APPEARING NEXT TO PRINTED LABEL.
4180   HCOLOR =  3: REM  BOX BORDER COLOR SET TO WHITE.
4190   GOSUB 50: REM  DRAW BORDER OF BOX TO CONTAIN COLOR
       SWATCH.
4200   FOR V = T TO B: REM  COLOR INTERIOR OF COLOR SWATCH BOX
       WITH APPROPRIATE COLOR.
4210   HCOLOR =  COLR(I)
4220   HPLOT L,V TO R,V
4230   NEXT V
4240   VTB = VTB + 2: REM  INCREMENT VERT TAB VARIABLE
       DESIGNATING VTAB PRNT POSITION FOR LABELS IN LABEL BOX.
4250   NEXT I: REM  GET ANOTHER LABEL ENTRY
4260   FOR I = 1 TO N: REM  FOR EACH SECTOR OF PIE CHART, ...
4270   D = (D%(I - 1) + D%(I)) / 2: REM  GET MID ANGLE OF I-TH
       SECTOR.
4280   H% = HC + .8 * X%(D):V% = VC - .8 * Y%(D): REM  GET
       SCREEN COORDS OF PT ON MID RAY .8 * RADIUS UNITS
       FROM CENTER.
4290   HTB =  INT (H% / 7):VTB =  INT (V% / 8) + 1: REM
       DETERMINE PRINT TAB POSITIONS NEAR THIS POINT.
4300   HTAB HTB: VTAB VTB: REM  TAB TO PRINT POSITION.
4310   PRINT  INT (VL(I) / TL * 1000 + .5) / 10;"%": REM  PRINT
       PERCENTAGE ROUNDED TO NEAREST 1/10-TH PERCENT THAT I-TH
       SECTOR REPRESENTS OF ENTIRE PIE.
4320   NEXT I
4330   PRINT  CHR$ (4);"PR#0": REM  DISCONNECT HRCG.
4340   RETURN
4341   REM  **    END PIE CHRT & LBL SBR **
4342   REM
4997   REM  *****************************
4998   REM  *    INSTRUCTIONS SECTION    *
4999   REM  *****************************
5000   HOME
5010   VTAB 3: HTAB 12: PRINT "PIE CHART DISPLAY"
5020   VTAB 6: PRINT "  THE USER IS EXPECTED TO ENTER A TITLE"
5030   PRINT "LABEL IN A DATA STATEMENT IN LINE 1000,"
5040   PRINT "FOLLOWED BY THE NUMBER OF ENTRY VALUES."
5050   PRINT : PRINT "  THE ENTRY LABELS, FOLLOWED BY THEIR"
5060   PRINT "VALUES, ARE EXPECTED TO OCCUR IN DATA"
5070   PRINT "STATEMENTS IN SUCCEEDING LINES."
5080   PRINT : HTAB 5: PRINT "TO SEE AN EXAMPLE PRESS A KEY.";:
       GET A$
5090   PRINT : LIST 999,1060
```

```
5100   PRINT : PRINT "DEMONSTRATE PIE CHART < Y,N >?";:
       GET A$
5110   IF A$ = "Y" THEN  HOME : GOTO 130
5120   HOME : END
5121   REM **      END INSTRUCTIONS      **
LIST
RUN
```

**Check Your Comprehension**

What commands in the program result in coloring the background all white? \_\_\_\_

_____

How is the area for the pie originally blacked out and what method is used to create a slightly larger area? _____

Will the label table on the right (automatically) adjust its height dimension to accommodate fewer entries? _____

What is the only reason for limiting the number of DATA entries to be supplied by the user? _____

**EXERCISE**   Write a program which will permit the user to supply any number (be reasonable, less than or equal to 10) of DATA entries; will draw a corresponding pie chart; will label each sector with a letter (beginning with the letter A); and finally build a table with the label fields keyed by letters.

**CHALLENGE**   Write a program which will permit the user to supply any number of DATA entries, will draw a corresponding pie chart, and will label each sector with the appropiate label field. The labels should not overlap the pie. It will be necessary to make some restrictions on label field length.

# ACTIVITY 4.10   Rotations

**LEARNING BY DISCOVERY**   In this activity you will learn how to rotate objects to be displayed on the screen.

1. Enter the following program.

```
NEW
99   REM *****  MAIN PROGRAM  *****
100    EOF = − 99: EPL = − 9
110    FAC = 3.14159266 / 180
120    HC = 140:VC = 96
130    HGR2
170    HCOLOR =  3: GOSUB 500
240    GET Q$: TEXT : HOME : END
241    REM  *** END MAIN PROGRAM ***
499    REM  *****  PLOT SUBROUTINE *****
500    FL = 1
```

```
510   FOR I = 0 TO 1 STEP 0
520   READ X,Y
530   IF Y = EOF THEN  RETURN
540   H% = HC + X:V% = VC — Y
550   IF FL THEN  HPLOT H%,V%:FL = 0: NEXT I: RETURN
560   HPLOT  TO H%,V%
570   NEXT I
580   RETURN
581   REM  *** END PLOT SUBROUTINE ***
1000  DATA  0,0, 90,0, 70,5, 70,—5, 90,0, —99,—99
LIST
RUN
```

You should observe an arrow. In which direction does it point? _____

What is the value of the angle (in degrees) represented by the arrow if considered in standard position? _____

2. Add the subroutine and the lines below.

```
15    GOTO 100
49    REM ***** ROT SUBROUTINE *****
50    RX = C * X — S * Y
52    RY = S * X + C * Y
54    RETURN
55    REM ***** END ROT SUBROUTINE *****
140   D = 30
150   TH = D * FAC: REM  CONVERT TO RADIANS
160   C =  COS (TH):S =  SIN (TH)
540   GOSUB 50:H% = HC + RX:V% = VC — RY
LIST
RUN
```

What effect did the change in line 540 make on the display? _____

Make an educated guess of the angle size (in degrees) the arrow now points if considered in standard position? _____

3. Make the following changes.

```
140   FOR D = 0 TO 360 STEP 20
180   RESTORE
220   NEXT D
LIST
RUN
```

What effect did this have on the display? _____

What is the range of angle values of the arrow? _____

4. Make the change listed below.

```
140   FOR D = 0 TO −360 STEP −20
LIST
RUN
```

What effect did the change have on the arrow rotation? _____

5. Change the DATA beginning at line 1000 and add the following statements.

```
140   FOR D = 0 TO 360 STEP 20
190   FOR K = 1 TO 500: NEXT : REM   DELAY
200   HCOLOR =  0: GOSUB 500: REM   ERASE
210   RESTORE
230   HCOLOR =  3: GOSUB 500: REM   DRAW
535   IF Y = EPL THEN SF = 1: NEXT I
1000  DATA  0,10, 10,10, 10,20, 0,20, 0,30, 10,30, −9,−9
1010  DATA  20,10, 20,30, 30,30, 30,20, 20,20, −9,−9
1020  DATA  40,10, 40,30, −9,−9
1030  DATA  50,10, 50,30, 60,10, 60,30, −99,−99
LIST
RUN
```

**DISCUSSION**   The major focus of this activity is the effect the transformation formulas

$$RX = C * X - S * Y      RY = S * X + C * Y$$

have on the points (X,Y) in the coordinate plane, where $C = COS(TH)$ and $S = SIN(TH)$ for a fixed angle TH (in radians). Evidently, the effect is to rotate the points (X,Y) about the origin through the angle TH. This was observed in the programs of Sections 1-5. If TH is positive then the rotation is counterclockwise. If TH is negative then the rotation is clockwise.

Geometrically, the rotation formulas can be derived from inspecting Figure 4.10.1.

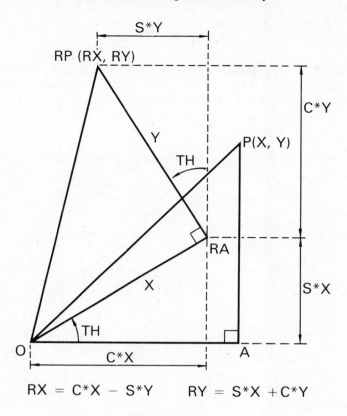

$$RX = C*X - S*Y \qquad RY = S*X + C*Y$$

Figure 4.10.1

Imagine the right triangle O-A-P (with hypotenuse OP) is rotated into the right triangle O-RA-RP (with hypotenuse O(RA). The vertical component of the point RP (cf., RY) can be decomposed into a sum of its components: S * X + C * Y. Similarly, the horizontal component RX can be decomposed into the difference between its components: C * X − S * Y. The expressions for each of the separate components are detemined by applying some right angle trigonometry to the triangles at hand as discussed in ACTIVITY 4.7.

When rotating an object about a point, particularly an object on the screen, the distance from the center of rotation to the object will have considerable impact on whether or not the rotated image will remain on the screen. Generally, it will be necessary to place the center of rotation within the object. For example, if (XC,YC) denotes the coordinates of the rotation center for the points (X,Y), then (X − XC, Y − YC) denotes the displacements from the rotation center. The point corresponding to (X − XC, Y − YC) should be rotated, not the point (X,Y). That is, X − XC and Y − YC denote the quantities that should be used in the rotation formulas instead of X and Y. Finally, it may be necessary to use scaling to insure the image of the rotated object remains within the screen boundaries. Alternatives exist by using the CLIPPING AL-GORITHM.

In CHAPTER 5, where topics in three-dimensional ghaphics are discussed, two-dimensional rotation techniques will be used extensively.

**COMPREHENSIVE EXAMPLE**   Some attractive graphics displays can result from rotating a regular N-gon about a fixed point, while simultaneously scaling the size. Recall a regular N-gon is an N-sided convex polygon with all sides of equal length and all vertex angles of equal measure (Figure 4.10.2).

Figure 4.10.2

Enter the program below.

```
NEW
10   REM   **********************************
11   REM   *            CE4.10            *
12   REM   **********************************
13   REM
14   REM
15   GOTO 100: REM   BRANCH AROUND SUBRT
16   REM
17   REM   *********************************
18   REM   *        CLIPPING ALGORITHM      *
19   REM   *********************************
20   T%(0) = YP(0) < V1:B%(0) = YP(0) > VO:L%(0) = XP(0)
     < HO:R%(0) = XP(0) > H1:I% = 1
22   FOR TRY = 0 TO 1 STEP 0:T%(I%) = YP(I%) < V1:B%(I%) =
```

```
     YP(I%) > VO:L%(I%) = XP(I%) < HO:R%(I%) = XP(I%)
     > H1
24   IF T%(0) AND T%(1) OR B%(0) AND B%(1) OR L%(0) AND L%(1) OR
     R%(0) AND R%(1) THEN  RETURN
26   I% = 0: IF T%(I%) + B%(I%) + L%(I%) + R%(I%) = 0 THEN
     I% = 1: IF T%(I%) + B%(I%) + L%(I%) + R%(I%) = 0
     THEN  HPLOT XP(0),YP(0) TO XP(1),YP(1): RETURN
28   IF T%(I%) THEN XP(I%) = XP(0) + (V1 - YP(0)) * (XP(1) -
     XP(0)) / (YP(1) - YP(0)):YP(I%) = V1: NEXT
30   IF B%(I%) THEN XP(I%) = XP(0) + (VO - YP(0)) * (XP(1) -
     XP(0)) / (YP(1) - YP(0)):YP(I%) = VO: NEXT
32   IF L%(I%) THEN YP(I%) = YP(0) + (HO - XP(0)) * (YP(1) -
     YP(0)) / (XP(1) - XP(0)):XP(I%) = HO: NEXT
34   IF R%(I%) THEN YP(I%) = YP(0) + (H1 - XP(0)) * (YP(1) -
     YP(0)) / (XP(1) - XP(0)):XP(I%) = H1: NEXT
35   REM  **        END CLIPPING        **
36   REM
97   REM  ********************************
98   REM  *        MAIN PROGRAM          *
99   REM  ********************************
100  HOME : PRINT "   A SEQUENCE OF UNIFORMLY ROTATED AND"
110  PRINT "MAGNIFIED REGULAR N-GONS WILL BE"
120  PRINT "DISPLAYED. THE CLIPPING ALGORITHM IS"
130  PRINT "USED TO CONTROL THE PLOTTING."
140  PRINT : PRINT "WHICH DISPLAY DO YOU WANT? ...."
150  INPUT "ENTER A VALUE OF N: ";N
160  N =  INT (N): IF N < = 0 THEN  PRINT  CHR$
     (7);"INVALID ENTRY!": GOTO 150
170  FAC = 3.14159266 / 180:SFAC = 1.20: REM  ENTER YOUR
     SCREEN SCALE FACTOR IF DIFFERENT.
180  DN = 360 / N: REM  INTERIOR ANGLE (DEGREES) OF REG N-GON.
190  DIM X(N),Y(N),XP(1),YP(1)
200  FOR K = 0 TO N
210  T = K * DN * FAC: REM  CONVERT K*DN DEG TO RADIANS.
220  X(K) =  COS (T):Y(K) =  SIN (T): REM  DETERMINE POINTS
     ON UNIT CIRCLE CORRESPONDING TO A REGULAR N-GON.
230  NEXT K
240  TH = .1: REM  TH IS THE FIXED ANGLE THROUGH WHICH EACH
     N-GON IS ROTATED.
250  C =  COS (TH):S =  SIN (TH): REM  GET COS AND SIN VALUES
     FOR ROTATION BY TH.
260  HO = 0:H1 = 279:VO = 191:V1 = 0: REM  SET VIEWPORT TO
     FULL SCREEN.
270  OH = 140:OV = 96: REM  SCREEN COORDS OF ORIGIN.
280  HGR2 : HCOLOR = 3
290  ENSC = 151 /  COS (DN / 2 * FAC): REM  LAST SCALE NEEDED
     TO GUARANTEE COMPLETE FILLING OF SCREEN.
300  FOR SCL = 0 TO ENSC STEP 4
```

```
310   XSCL = SCL * SFAC: REM  SET EQUIV XSCL IF YSCL IS TO BE
      SCL.
320   SX = OH + X(0) * XSCL:SY = OV - Y(0) * SCL: REM
      INITIALIZE PREV SCREEN PT PLOTTED AND OLD VALUE OF
      XP(1),YP(1).
330   FOR K = 1 TO N: REM  FOR EACH OF THE N-SIDES DO ...
340   XP(0) = SX:YP(0) = SY: REM  SET ONE ENDPT OF SEGMENT TO
      BE PLOTTED TO BE SCREEN COORD OF PREV X(K),Y(K)
350   SX = OH + X(K) * XSCL:SY = OV - Y(K) * SCL: REM  GET
      SCREEN COORD OF SCALED X(K),Y(K)
360   XP(1) = SX:YP(1) = SY: REM  SET 2ND ENDPT OF SEGMT TO BE
      PLOTTED.
370   GOSUB 20: REM  GOTO CLIPPING ALGORITHM.
380   NEXT K
390   FOR K = 0 TO N: REM  ROTATE EACH OF THE VERTICES OF THE
      N-GON BY TH = .1 RADIANS.
400   X = X(K) * C - Y(K) * S
410   Y(K) = X(K) * S + Y(K) * C
420   X(K) = X
430   NEXT K
440   NEXT SCL
450   HPLOT HO,V1 TO HO,VO TO H1,VO TO H1,V1 TO HO,V1: REM
      BORDER SCREEN; SERVES AS AN INDICATION WHEN PLOTTING
      IS COMPLETED.
460   GET Q$: TEXT : HOME : END
461   REM  **         END MAIN PROGRAM       **
LIST
RUN
```

## Check Your Comprehension

Which arrays are used to hold the coordinate values of the vertices of the regular N-gon? _____

Which lines of the program accomplish the rotation of the vertices and what is the angle of rotation (in radians)? _____

Why is it necessary in lines 400-420 to use a temporary storage variable for the rotated X-coordinate? Why not simply define X(K) to be the right-hand side of line 400? Hint: You must consider the quantities used in line 410. _____

To guarantee complete filling of the screen by all visible line segments, clipped or not, the distance from the center to the edge of the N-gon was calculated. Which line number do you think has, in effect, calculated this distance? _____

When you observe the display, how will you know when the picture has been completed? _____

**EXERCISE**  Write a program to read the KOALA DATA and rotate it through any angle requested by the user. Select the center of rotation to be the central or average X- and Y- values of the data.

**CHALLENGE**   Modify the COMPREHENSIVE EXAMPLE program of ACTIVITY 4.3 to permit the user to rotate the object through any angle. Select the rotation center to be the midpoint of the range of X-values and Y-values. Use scaling to insure the rotated image remains on the screen, or incorporate the CLIPPING ALGORITHM to handle off-screen points.

# ACTIVITY 4.11   Function Plotting

**LEARNING BY DISCOVERY**   In this activity you will learn how to plot graphs of functions of the form Y = F(X) over an interval A <=  X <=  B.

1. Enter the following program.

```
NEW
10   OH = 140:OV = 96
20   XSCL = 18:YSCL = 50
30   HGR2 : HCOLOR =  3
40   DEF  FN Y(X) =   COS (X)
50   A = − 7:B = 7:DX = .1
70   FOR X = A TO B STEP DX
80   HPLOT OH + X * XSCL,OV −  FN Y(X) * YSCL
90   NEXT X
100  GET Q$: TEXT : HOME : END
LIST
RUN
```

Describe the screen display. _____

What curve (ie., graph of what function) do you think is being displayed? _____

_____

What interval of X-values is being considered? _____

What purpose do the variables XSCL and YSCL serve in the above program? ____

_____

2. Make the following changes in the program in section 1.

```
60   HPLOT OH + A * XSCL,OV −  FN Y(A) * YSCL
80   HPLOT  TO OH + X * XSCL,OV −  FN Y(X) * YSCL
LIST
RUN
```

What effect did these changes have on the resulting display? _____

3. Change line 40 to the following:

```
40  DEF FN Y(X) = SIN(X)
LIST
RUN
```

What curve (ie., graph) is now displayed? _____

4. Change line 20 to the following:

```
20  XSCL = 10 : YSCL = 20
LIST
RUN
```

What effect did this produce on the display? _____

5. Change line 50 to the following:

```
50  FOR X = -12 TO 12 STEP .4
LIST
RUN
```

What effect did this produce on the display? _____

6. Change line 40 to the following:

```
40  DEF FN Y(X) = SIN(2 * X)
LIST
RUN
```

Describe the effect of this change. _____

7. Change line 40 to the following:

```
40  DEF FN Y(X) = SIN(3 * X)
LIST
RUN
```

Describe the effect. _____

**DISCUSSION**    In mathematics, a function is a correspondence between two sets of numbers. Generally a "rule" is provided which indicates how to determine the unique number in the second set given a number of the first set. Typically, a function is represented by a statement

F(X) = (an algebraic expression in X)

For example,  F(X) = 3 * X − 5 . In this form, each real value X is assigned the value Y = 3 * X − 5. The collection of admissible X-values is called the domain of the function, while the set of Y = F(X) values is called the range of the function.

APPLESOFT BASIC permits the user to programmatically define functions using a DEF statement. The syntax is

(line #)  DEF FN Y(X) = arithmetic expression in X

The variable X must be a real variable and the name Y assigned to the function must be a real variable name. When the function is accessed, as in the statement:

200  W = FN Y( value )

the value within the parentheses is used as a replacement value for X wherever it appears in the statement defining the function.

The graph of a function is defined as the collection of points (X,Y) in the X-Y plane, where X is in the domain of the function and Y is determined from the value of Y(X). For example, if FN Y(X) = X^2 (or X * X), then the point (4,16) is plotted since FN Y(4) = 4^2 = 16. Similarly, the point (−3,9) will be plotted since FN Y(X) = 9 if

X=−3.

In the example programs presented at the beginning of this activity, graphs of the COSine and SINe functions were obtained. There are two basic techniques used for plotting the graphs of functions. One method is to simply plot single points, sufficiently close to one another to obtain the general shape of the graph. The second method connects point plots (again sufficiently close to one another) using straight line segments. This gives the appearance of a continuous plot of points. The curve obtained in this fashion is sometimes called a spline. Technically, it represents an approximation to the true curve using piecewise linear curves. Finally, the use of scale factors will help control the size of the image on the screen.

**COMPREHENSIVE EXAMPLE**   In the program below, the graph paper subroutine of ACTIVITY 4.6 is combined with scaling techniques to permit the user to graph any definable function. With only slightly more effort the program will permit the user to plot several functions on the same coordinate graph, with each possibly defined on a different X-interval. This is a useful feature when one wants to compare the graphs of several functions.

Enter the program below.

```
NEW
10   REM   ********************************
11   REM   *          CE4.11            *
12   REM   ********************************
13   REM
14   REM
15   GOTO 1000: REM   BRANCH AROUND FUNCTION DEF SUBRTNS
16   REM
97   REM   ********************************
98   REM   *     FUNCTION DEFINITIONS     *
99   REM   ********************************
100  DEF  FN Y(X) = 3 *  EXP ( − .5 *  ABS (X)) *  COS (3 *
     X)
110  DATA   −5,5     : REM   DOMAIN INTERVAL
120  RETURN
200  :
220  RETURN
300  :
320  RETURN
400  :
420  RETURN
500  :
520  RETURN
600  :
620  RETURN
700  :
720  RETURN
800  :
820  RETURN
```

```
900    :
920    RETURN
995    REM  *      END FUNCTION DEFNTNS      *
996    REM
997    REM  ********************************
998    REM  *        MAIN PROGRAM BLOCK       *
999    REM  ********************************
1000   LOMEM: 16384: REM  SET LOMEM JUST ABOVE PG1.
1010   H0 = 1:H1 = 278:V0 = 190:V1 = 1: REM  SET VIEWPORT. IF
       DIMENSIONS ARE TO CHANGE, THEN USER SHOULD ALLOW FOR
       BORDER AROUND VIEWPORT...A 1 PIXEL DEDUCTION IN EACH
       DIRECTION.
1020   DEF  FN DP(Z) =  INT (1000 * Z + .5) / 1000: REM  3
       DECIMAL DIGITS-OF-PRECISION FUNCTION.
1030   XPX = 12:YPX = 10: REM  MINIMUM ALLOWABLE GRID
       DENSITIES.
1040   SFAC = 1.20: REM  EQUIV SCALE FACTOR. USE YOUR SFAC
       VALUE DETERMINED IN ACTIVITY 4.2.
1050   SPC = 3: REM  SPC = PIXEL SPACE BETWEEN POINT
       COMPUTATIONS OF FUNCTIONS.
1060   A = 1E38:B = − A: REM  INTIALIZE MINIMUM ENCLOSING
       X-INTERVAL ENDPT VALUES.
1070   ONERR  GOTO 1130: REM  USED BELOW TO DETECT WHEN THERE
       ARE NO MORE FUNCTIONS DEFINED. THIS WILL BE DETECTED
       BECAUSE DATA FOR DOMAIN INTERVAL WILL CEASE TO BE READ.
1080   FOR N = 0 TO 9
1090   READ A(N),B(N): REM  READ ENDPTS OF DOMAIN INTERVALS.
1100   IF A > A(N) THEN A = A(N): REM  FIND MINIMUM LEFT
       ENDPT
1110   IF B < B(N) THEN B = B(N): REM  ... AND MAXIMUM RIGHT
       ENDPT.
1120   NEXT N
1130   POKE 216,0: REM  DATA HAS BEEN READ; THERE ARE PRESUMABLY
       N FUNCTIONS DEFINED. RESET NORMAL ERROR CHECKING WITH
       THIS POKE.
1140   IF N = 0 THEN  HOME : PRINT "THERE IS NO DATA FOR
       FUNCTION DOMAINS!": END
1150   N = N − 1: REM  REDEFINE NUMBER OF FUNCTIONS TO BE N−1;
       THIS WILL PERMIT USE OF O-TH ELEMENT OF ARRAY CONTAINING
       FUNCTION VALUES OF EACH FUNCTION.
1160   NP =  INT ((H1 − H0) / SPC) + 1: REM  NP = MAX # PTS
       AT WHICH FUNCTION EVALUATIONS ARE TO BE MADE USING
       THE SPACING SPC BETWEEN SCREEN PTS.
1170   DX = (B − A) / NP: REM  X-INCR CORRESPONDING TO APPROX
       SPC PIXELS BETWEEN SUCCESSIVE X-PTS.
1180   FOR K = 0 TO N: REM  FOR EACH FUNCTION, ...
1190   NP(K) =  INT (ABS (B(K) − A(K)) / DX) + 1: REM  GET
```

```
         THE # OF PT EVALUATIONS USED FOR K-TH FUNCTION.
1200     IF NP(K) > NP THEN NP(K) = NP: REM  TAKE PRECAUTION
         AGAINST POTENTIAL ROUNDOFF ERRORS YIELDING MORE PTS THAN
         MAX # NEEDED.
1210     DX(K) = (B(K) — A(K)) / NP(K): REM  THE INCREMENT
         BETWEEN SUCCESSIVE PTS FOR K-TH DOMAIN INTERVAL.
1220     NEXT K
1230     GOSUB 1500: REM  GOTO ROUTINE TO SEE IF USER WISHES TO
         SELECT Y-RANGE OR LET THE PROGRAM SELECT IT. DECISION
         RETURNED IN VAR DSP: DSP = 1 IF PROG SELECTS; DSP
         = 2 IF USER SELECTS.
1240     IF DSP = 1 THEN  GOSUB 2000: REM  IF COMPUTER SHOULD
         SELECT RANGE THEN GOTO FUNCTION EVALUATION ROUTINE TO
         DETERMINE Y-RANGE.
1250     HGR : POKE  — 16302,0: HCOLOR = 3: REM  FULL SCREEN PG1
1260     GOSUB 4000: REM   CALL 'GRAPH PAPER' SUBRT.
1270     GOSUB 3000: REM  GOTO PLOTTING SUBROUTINE.
1280     GET Q$: REM  KEEP FULL SCREEN UNTIL KEYPRESS.
1290     HOME : VTAB 21: POKE  — 16301,0: REM  SET MIXED SCREEN
         GRAPHICS.
1300     PRINT "X-RANGE:"; TAB( 20);"Y-RANGE:"
1310     PRINT  FN DP(A);", "; FN DP(B); TAB( 20); FN DP(C);", ";
         FN DP(D)
1320     PRINT "X-SCALE: ";XVL; TAB( 20);"Y-SCALE: ";YVL
1330     VTAB 24: HTAB 15: PRINT "'F' = FULL PG  'E' = END
         PROG";
1340     VTAB 24: HTAB 1: INVERSE : PRINT "SELECT KEY";: NORMAL :
         GET K$:K =  ASC (K$)
1350     IF K = 69 THEN  TEXT : HOME : END : REM  IF KEY = 'E'
         THEN END PROGRAM
1360     IF K = 70 THEN  POKE  — 16302,0: GET A$: POKE
         —16301,0: GOTO 1340: REM  IS KEY = F? IF YES,
         THEN TOGGLE FULL PG AND WAIT FOR KEYPRESS TO RETURN TO
         MIXED MODE
1370     GOTO 1340
1380     REM  **        END MAIN PROG       **
1390     REM
1497     REM  ****************************
1498     REM  *   DISPLAY SELECTION SBRT   *
1499     REM  ****************************
1500     HOME : VTAB 5
1510     PRINT "YOU WILL BE PLOTTING "N + 1" FUNCTIONS IN"
1520     PRINT "THE X-INTERVAL: "A" <=  X <= "B"."
1530     PRINT : PRINT "MAKE A SELECTION:": PRINT
1540     HTAB 5: PRINT "< 1> PROGRAM SELECTS Y-RANGE"
1550     HTAB 5: PRINT "< 2 > USER SELECTS Y-RANGE"
1560     HTAB 5: PRINT "< 3 > QUIT"
1570     PRINT : PRINT "SELECT A NUMBER: ";: GET DSP$
```

```
1580   DSP = VAL (DSP$): PRINT DSP$
1590   ON DSP GOTO 1640,1620,1610
1600   GOTO 1570: REM  DSP WAS NOT 1,2, OR 3; SO GO BACK FOR
       ANOTHER CHOICE.
1610   HOME : END : REM  DSP = 3 SO QUIT.
1620   PRINT : INPUT "ENTER THE Y-RANGE C,D: ";C,D
1630   IF D < C THEN T = D:D = C:C = T: REM  IF ENTERED IN
       WRONG ORDER THEN SWAP.
1640   PRINT : INPUT "DO YOU WANT EQUIVALENT SCALES < Y,N >?
       ";EQ$:EQSCL = 0: IF EQ$ =  "Y" THEN EQSCL = 1
1650   RETURN
1651   REM  **     END DISPLAY SELECT     **
1652   REM
1997   REM  *****************************
1998   REM  *   CALC FUNCTION VALUES SBRT *
1999   REM  *****************************
2000   HOME : VTAB 12: HTAB 7: PRINT "... ONE MOMENT PLEASE ..."
2010   DIM Y(NP,N): REM  SET UP ARRAY TO CONTAIN FUNCTION
       VALUES.
2020   GOSUB 100:C =  FN Y(A(0)):D = C: REM  INITIALIZE
       MINIMUM AND MAXIMUM Y-VALUES FOR FINDING Y-RANGE. THE
       THE # OF PT EVALUATIONS USED FOR K-TH FUNCTION.
2030   FOR K = 0 TO N: REM  FOR EACH FUNCTION, ...
2040   ON K + 1 GOSUB 100,200,300,400,500,600,700,800,900: REM
       GOTO THE K+1-ST SUBROUTINE DEFINING K+1-ST FUNCTION.
2050   FOR I = 0 TO NP(K)
2060   Y(I,K) =  FN Y(A(K) + I * DX(K))
2070   IF C > Y(I,K) THEN C = Y(I,K): REM  GET MIN Y-VALUE.
2080   IF D < Y(I,K) THEN D = Y(I,K): REM  GET MAX Y-VALUE.
2090   NEXT I,K
2100   RETURN
2101   REM  **     END CALC FUNCT VALS     **
2102   REM
2997   REM  *****************************
2998   REM  *      PLOTTING SUBROUTINE    *
2999   REM  *****************************
3000   FOR K = 0 TO N: REM  FOR EACH FUNCTION, ...
3010   DX = DX(K):AK = A(K): REM  DX IS INCREMENT BETWEEN
       X-VALS IN KTH DOMAIN INTERVAL; AK IS LEFT ENDPT OF
       INTERVAL.
3020   ON DSP GOSUB 3200,3400
3030   NEXT K
3040   RETURN : REM  RETURN TO MAIN PROGRAM
3199   REM  **** PLOT SUBRT FOR DSP = 1 ****
3200   H% = OH + AK * XSCL:V% = OV - Y(0,K) * YSCL
3210   HPLOT H%,V%
```

```
3220  FOR I = 1 TO NP(K): REM  FOR EACH OF THE NP(K) PTS IN
      KTH DOMAIN INTERVAL, ...
3230  H% = OH + (AK + I * DX) * XSCL:V% = OV - Y(I,K) *
      YSCL: REM  FIND SCREEN COORDS OF X,Y VALUE CORRESP TO
      KTH FUNCTION.
3240  HPLOT  TO H%,V%
3250  NEXT I
3260  RETURN : REM  RETURN TO MAIN PLOT SUBRT
3261  REM  **** END PLOT SUB DSP = 1 ****
3399  REM  **** PLOT SUBRT FOR DSP = 2 ****
3400  ON K + 1 GOSUB 100,200,300,400,500,600,700,800,900: REM
      SINCE DSP = 2 WE NEED TO DEFINE EACH FUNCTION; GO GET
      K-TH FUNCTION DEFNTN.
3410  SF = 1: REM  SET BEGINNING OF PLOT FLAG.
3420  FOR I = 0 TO NP(K)
3430  X = AK + I * DX:H  = OH + X * XSCL: REM  GET HORIZ
      SCREEN COORD OF PT (X,FNY(X)).
3440  V  = OV -  FN Y(X) * YSCL: REM  COMPUTE VERT SCREEN
      COORD OF PT (X,FNY(X)).
3450  IF V  > VO OR V  < V1 THEN SF = 1: NEXT I: RETURN
      : REM  CHECK TO SEE IF PT IS WITHIN SCREEN BOUNDARIES. IF
      NOT THEN DON'T PLOT.
3460  IF SF THEN  HPLOT H ,V :SF = 0: NEXT I: RETURN
3470  HPLOT  TO H ,V
3480  NEXT I
3490  RETURN : REM  RETURN TO MAIN PLOT SUBRT.
3491  REM  **** END PLOT SUB DSP = 2 ****
3492  REM
3493  REM  **      END PLOTTING SUBRT    **
3494  REM
3997  REM  *****************************
3998  REM  *       GRAPH PAPER SUBRT       *
3999  REM  *****************************
```

< Insert the GRAPH PAPER SUBROUTINE from CE 4.6 in ACTIVITY 4.6. Use the
MERGE feature of RENUMBER on your SYSTEM MASTER DISKETTE. >

```
5251  REM  **      END GRAPH PAPER SUBRT    **
LIST
RUN
```

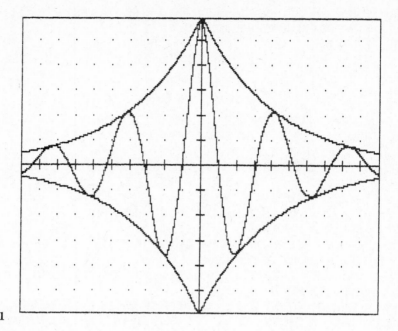

**Figure 4.11.1**

The quantity SPC represents the approximate number of horizontal pixels between screen images of successively generated graph points. The number of points at which the function is evaluated is given by the value of NP in line 1160. The purpose of using the variable SPC is to control the number of function evaluations required, to ensure curve smoothness, and to avoid "overlayment" of screen images corresponding to distinct points in the function domain. The user is at liberty to change the value of SPC, but there is little reason to select the value smaller than one pixel space.

The user enters the function definitions on lines 100, 200, 300, ..., 900. DATA for the domain interval is placed on the succeeding lines 110, 210, 310, ..., 910. Following some initialization of variables in lines 1000-1050, the number of functions to be graphed and the maximum X-interval needed to graph all the funcions are determined in lines 1060-1140. The number N is determined when an absence of DATA is detected; in this regard, the ONERR statement in line 1070 is used to detect an out-of-data condition. Line 1150 redefines N to $N - 1$ so the 0-th element of arrays of size N can be used.

In lines 1160-1220, the X-increment between successive point evaluations is calculated for each function and stored in the array DX(K). Line 1230 causes a branch to the subroutine which requests the user to select the Y-range or let the program select the Y-range. Determination of the Y-range is necessary for determining the appropriate scale factor YSCL, which is used in vertically scaling the display. The user also has an opportunity to select equivalent scales. This feature should be used with discretion. If a function has a large or very small range of Y-values compared to the domain interval, distortion of the display can occur.

If the user requests the program to select the Y-range (DSP = 1), then a branch to the subroutine beginning at line 2000 occurs (line 1240). This subroutine will calculate the points (X,Y) for all of the functions and store the values in the doubly subscripted array Y(I,K). Furthermore, the maximum and minimum Y-values are determined and stored in the variables D and C. These are needed for determination of the vertical scale factor YSCL.

Following the initialization of the high resolution screen (line 1250), control is passed to the GRAPH PAPER subroutine which determines the scale factors and displays the coordinate grid. Finally, in line 1270 the program calls the subroutine which plots the functions.

The method of plotting depends on whether the user selects the Y-range (DSP = 2) or the program selects it (DSP = 1). If DSP = 1 then all the function evaluations are computed and saved in the array Y(I,K). If DSP = 2, then the actual function evaluations are performed when the curve is HPLOTted. These two situations are handled with lines 3200-3260 and lines 3400-3490. In the case of user selection of the Y-range (DSP = 2), the screen image point H, V (corresponding to the point X,FN Y(X) on the function graph) must be checked for containment within the viewport (line 3450). If it is not visible, the point and any line segment from it or to it is not HPLOTted.

There is one final point which may clear up some confusion. When the user is actually defining the individual functions to be graphed, the syntax should always be:

n00 DEF FN Y(X) = expression in X

Specifically, use the same function name Y for each function you define. APPLESOFT will only remember the last function definition accessed. The use of ON K + 1 GOSUB statements in lines 2070 and 3400 controls which of the functions FN Y is the currently defined function.

If you wish to see some applications of the multiple function plotting ability, add the following functions to the one currently defined in the above program.

```
200  DEF FN Y(X) = 3 * EXP ( - .5 * ABS (X))
210  DATA -5, 5
300  DEF FN Y(X) =- 3 * EXP ( - .5 * ABS(X))
310  DATA -5, 5
LIST 100,320
RUN
```

Another example of the multiple function plotting ability is obtained by comparing the graphs of the first several terms of Taylor polynomial approximations of the SINe function. In fact, these polynomial approximations serve as a foundation for the technique by which numerical approximations of the SINe are determined. Test the following functions:

```
100  DEF FN Y(X) = SIN (X)
105  HCOLOR = 1 : REM  HPLOT SINE GRAPH IN GREEN; WILL PLOT
     IN GREEN ONLY IF USER SELECTS Y-RANGE.
110  DATA -4, 4
200  DEF FN Y(X) = X
205  HCOLOR = 3 : REM  HPLOT TAYLOR POLYS IN WHITE.
210  DATA -4, 4
300  DEF FN Y(X) = X - X^3 / 6
310  DATA -4, 4
400  DEF FN Y(X) = X - X^3 / 6 + X^5 / 120
```

```
410   DATA  −4, 4
500   DEF FN Y(X) = X − X^3 / 6 + X^5 / 120 − X^7 / 5040
510   DATA  −4, 4
LIST  100,520
RUN
```

When you are requested to either select the range or let the program select it, you select the Y-range. Set the range to −1.5, 1.5. Observe how the successive approximations approach the graph of the SINe function.

**Check Your Comprehension**

What purpose do the lines 1070-1140 serve? _____

Would you expect a more accurate graph on your screen if 400 points were chosen at which to determine function values on the interval A < = X < = B? Why or why not? _____

What purpose do the lines 2030-2120 serve? _____

If the user decides to select the Y-range, how does the program "instruct" the APPLE not to HPLOT points outside the vertical range of the viewport? _____

In which lines are the scale factors XSCL and YSCL determined and what quantities are used in their computation? _____

**EXERCISE**   Modify the COMPREHENSIVE EXAMPLE program so a different HCOLOR is used for different functions. A limitation of three functions for input should be imposed to avoid duplication of color choice and to avoid clashing of colors from the low and high color groups.

**EXERCISE**   Modify the COMPREHENSIVE EXAMPLE program so the graph paper subroutine is not used. Be careful!  You cannot simply delete lines.

**EXERCISE**   Modify the COMPREHENSIVE EXAMPLE program so a point plot graph is obtained rather than the "continuously" plotted graph.

**CHALLENGE**   Write a program to plot parametric equations of the form:
      X = F(T) , Y = G(T)   T1 < = T < = T2
Specifically, your program should:

1) Expect the user to enter the function definitions of FN X(T) and FN Y(T) to be entered in lines 100 and 110.

2) Expect the user to enter the T-domain as a DATA statement in line 120 which will supply the values of T1 and T2.

3) Expect the user to supply the number of points T at which the function evaluations are to be made in the interval T1 < =  T < =  T2 (100 points is a good starting number).

4) Permit the user to select the X- and Y- ranges or let the program select the range values. Selection by program should result in the entire graph displayed on the screen.

5) To make the programming easier, anticipate that only one pair of parametric functions will be supplied. You can get fancy later; get it to work properly for one pair first!

# 5

# Three-Dimensional Graphics

## MODULE 5A    Simple 3-D Graphics

### ACTIVITY 5.1    Orthogonal Projections

**LEARNING BY DISCOVERY**    In this activity you will investigate the most fundamental of ways to display three-dimensional objects in two-dimensions: via orthogonal projections.

1. Orthogonal? The word is longer than the concept is difficult. Before you investigate what the concept means, let's consider the basics of three-dimensional coordinate systems. A point in two-dimensional space (a plane) can be labeled using a pair of coordinates (X,Y). In three-dimensional space, a point is identified using a triple of coordinates (X,Y,Z). The third axis, the Z-axis, is considered to be perpendicular to the X-Y plane, passing through the origin in the plane. The origin in three-dimensional space is taken as the origin in the X-Y plane (see Figure 5.1.1).

   There are two possibilities for assigning a positive sense of direction to the Z-axis. If the positive sense of direction is chosen in the direction of the "Z" label in the picture below, then the X-Y-Z coordinate system is called a right-handed coordinate system; otherwise, it is called left-handed. There is a simple way to tell when a three-dimensional coordinate system is right-handed or left-handed. Using your right hand, curl your fingers as though you were attempting to rotate the positive X-axis through 90 degrees into the positive Y-axis; extend your thumb. If your thumb points in the direction of the positive Z-axis then you have a right-handed coordinate system; if not, it is left-handed. For example, lay a sheet of paper on the table in front of you. Draw a standard X-Y coordinate system (positive X-axis points right and positive Y-axis points away from you). In which direction (up or down) must the positive Z-axis point to yield a right-handed coordinate system?  If you answered "down" you had better reread this paragraph!

   Before proceeding to three-dimensional computer graphics, let's consider one final point. How does one locate a point in three-dimensional space given its coordinates? With your paper still in front of you, locate the point (X,Y) on the paper with coordinates (2,3). Imagine, if you can, moving one unit above the paper straight up from that point. The resultant point in three-dimensional space has coordinates (2,3,1)

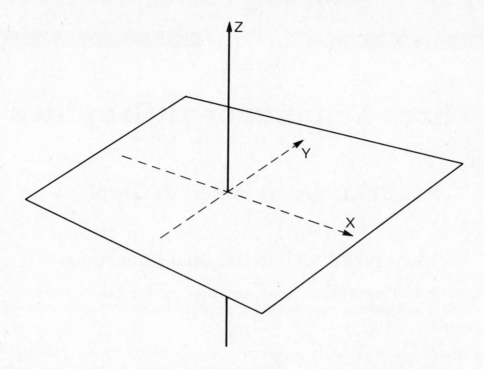

Figure 5.1.1

(see Figure 5.1.2). To test your understanding, think about how you would locate the point (1,4,-2). You move down two units below the paper from the point (X,Y) = (1,4).

It is also helpful to think about how the coordinates of a given point can be found. For example, consider an imaginary point above your paper. Now drop a line segment from the point perpendicular to the paper. The directed length of this segment is the Z-coordinate. The (X,Y) values are the coordinates of the projected point on your paper (see Figure 5.1.3).

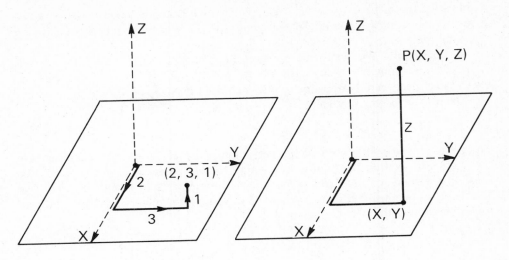

Figures 5.1.2 and 5.1.3

2.  In representing three-dimensional objects on the screen, the typical procedure is to transform to a two-dimensional display the points and edges of the object which seem to identify it: specifically, a wire-frame representation of the object. For example, in displaying a box, most people can identify it by simply observing the pattern of edges and vertices (corners) displayed. Specifically, the 8 vertices and 12 edges connecting them are usually sufficient to display a "box."

The problem confronting you now is how to take a point (X,Y,Z) in three-dimensional space and convert it (transform it) to a point (PX,PY) which can be displayed on the screen. We will consider (PX,PY) to be a point in a standard two-dimensional coordinate system. That is, the positive PX-direction extends to the right and the positive PY-direction extends upward. In actually displaying the point on the screen, a point with screen coordinates (OH, OV) will be selected to correspond to the origin, the value of PX will be added to OH, and PY will be subtracted from OV. In the first few activities of CHAPTER 5, extreme care will be taken to be sure the screen point corresponding to (PX,PY) is indeed a point on the screen. In subsequent activities, scaling and/or the CLIPPING ALGORITHM will accommodate the situations where the points (PX,PY) may be off the screen.

What is needed now is a way to determine the values (PX,PY) given (X,Y,Z). One of the simplest procedures is to project each corner point (X,Y,Z) to a coordinate plane. The projected images of lines will again be straight lines; consequently it is only a matter of connecting the projected vertices by line segments. In this section the projection direction will be considered to be perpendicular (orthogonal) to the coordinate plane, hence the term orthogonal projection.

For example, suppose you hold a small block of wood above your graph paper. Project the corners and edges straight down onto your paper. The resulting figure is the image of an orthogonal projection. Another interpretation is as follows. Imagine a flashlight is focused, high above both your paper and the block of wood, in a line perpendicular to the paper. The shadow cast on your paper is the projected image of the block. If the block is made of a transparent material, distinctive shadows of the edges will appear on your paper. Such an image is very close to what is obtained by an othogonal projecton.

In considering the perpendicular projection onto the X-Y plane, each point (X,Y,Z) in three-dimensional space is projected onto the point (X,Y) in the X-Y plane. Thus, if Oxy denotes the orthogonal projection onto the X-Y plane, then

Oxy : (X,Y,Z) --- > (X,Y) = (PX,PY)

i.e.,

PX = X    PY = Y

There are, of course, other orthogonal projections, Oyz: PX = Y , PY = Z, etc.

Let's put some of these ideas into action. In the program below, you will test them on a particular three-dimensional object. We are not going to tell you what it is. The hope is you will be able to decide for yourself by observing the orthogonal projections. Enter the following program.

```
NEW
10   OH = 120:OV = 96: REM  BASE THE ORIGIN OF PX-PY COORD
     SYSTEM AT OH,OV.
20   HGR : HOME : VTAB 21
30   HCOLOR =  3
40   EOF =   - 99:EPL =   - 9: REM  END-OF-FILE;
     END-OF-PLOT VALUES.
50   FL = 1: REM  SET BEG-OF-PLOT FLAG 'ON'.
60   FOR I = 0 TO 1 STEP 0: REM  DO INDEFINITELY, UNTIL ...
70   READ X,Y,Z
75   FOR J = 1 TO 500: NEXT : REM  DELAY TO PERMIT USER TO SEE
     EACH SEGMENT AS IT IS PLOTTED.
80   IF Z = EOF THEN 200: REM  ... UNTIL END-OF-FILE.
90   IF Z = EPL THEN FL = 1: NEXT I
100  GOSUB 500: REM  GO CALC PROJ COORDS.
110  IF FL THEN  HPLOT OH + PX,OV - PY:FL = 0: NEXT I: REM
     IF BEG-OF-PLOT FLAG IS 1, THEN 'HPLOT'; SET FLAG
     TO 0. OTHERWISE, ...
120  HPLOT  TO OH + PX,OV - PY
130  NEXT I
200  GET Q$: TEXT : HOME : END
497  REM  ******************************
498  REM  *     ORTHOGRAPHIC PROJ SUB    *
499  REM  ******************************
500  PX = X:PY = Y
510  RETURN
520  REM  **    END ORTHO PROJ SUBRT    **
600  DATA  0,0,0, 80,0,0, 80,80,0, 0,80,0, 0,0,0
610  DATA  40,40,80, 80,0,0, -9,-9,-9
620  DATA  80,80,0, 40,40,80, 0,80,0, -99,-99,-99
LIST
RUN
```

What do you observe? _____

To give you some idea of what you are seeing, here is the interpretation. Imagine you are on the Z-axis directly above the object, and you are viewing the object from a great distance. The important point is light rays, reflecting off the object and back to your eye, are (for all practical purposes) parallel and perpendicular to the X-Y plane. When we discuss perspective views, the "parallel light ray" assumption will be discarded. Imagine you are positioned so as you look down on the object, the positive X-axis points to the right and the positive Y-axis points upward. The image on your APPLE screen is a projected image of the object on the X-Y plane; it is equivalent to the view to be experienced from the indicated vantage point.

3. Let's experiment with other orthogonal projections. Change line 500 to the following.

```
500  PX = Y : PY = Z
LIST 500
RUN
```

What do you observe? _____
Which coordinate axis is parallel to your line-of-sight? _____
Which coordinate axis points to the right? upward? _____

You should imagine yourself viewing the object from the positive Y-axis with line-of-sight parallel to the X-axis. As you view the object, the Y-axis points to the right and the Z-axis points upward.

4. The next orthogonally projected view may seem slightly awkward at first. If you are accumstomed to considering the Z-axis as the vertical direction, then, as you view the object from the positive Y-axis, imagine lying on your left side looking toward the origin.
Make the following change in the program above.

```
500  PX = Z : PY = X
LIST 500
RUN
```

What do you observe? _____
What are the positions of the coordinate axes? _____

Finally, interchange the order of the variables assigned to PX and PY for each of the three previous orthogonal projections. For example, in the last projection Ozx: PX = Z, PY = X. Change assignment to the following:

```
500  PX = X : PY = Z
LIST 500
RUN
```

ReRUN the program for each change. Try to describe your position and the direction of all three coordinate axes. _____
_____

(For example, the projection above has the following interpretation. As you view the object from the negative Y-axis, the positive X-axis appears on your right and the positive Z-axis points upward.)

5. Can you describe the object now that you have seen orthographic views of it? If not, this is your last hint! In the early days of television there was a popular game show hosted by Groucho Marx called "You Bet Your Life." When a contestant failed to win any money, the person was afforded a reprieve by merely having to answer some ridiculous question like "Who was buried in King Tut's tomb?" The answer to your question is equivalent to the only slightly more difficult game show question "In what kind of tomb was King Tut buried?"

Didn't get it yet? Well, change line 500 to the following:

```
500  PX = Y - .4 * X : PY = Z - .5 * X
LIST 500
RUN
```

Is it what you expected? _____

Do not concern yourself with the formulas just entered in line 500. They will be discussed in the next activity. It is used here to provide you a "different view" of the object.

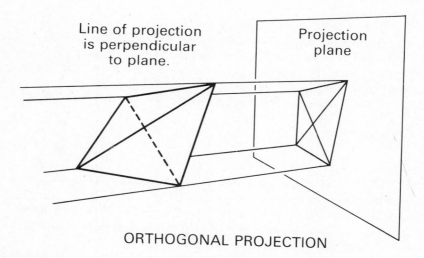

Line of projection is perpendicular to plane.

Projection plane

ORTHOGONAL PROJECTION

**DISCUSSION**   The different views of the pyramid you obtained in Sections 2-5 are the result of using orthogonal projections. Under the influence of an orthogonal projection, each point of the object is projected onto a coordinate plane along lines parallel to the third coordinate axis. In each of the first three cases considered Oxy, Oyz and Ozx, you imagine your position to be on the positive side of the third coordinate axis at a great distance from the object. The coordinate axis corresponding to the X, Y or Z variable assigned to PX appears on your right, and the coordinate axis corresponding to the variable assigned to PY points upward on the screen. In each of the succeeding three cases Oyx, Ozy and Oxz, where the order of assignment to PX and PY is reversed, your position is on the negative side of the third coordinate axis, looking toward the origin.

The orthographic views are crude but provide much information about the object. In the next activity, more general projections (vz.,  parallel projections) will be considered. These will permit you to position yourself virtually anywhere to view the object, but still at the expense of viewing it from a great distance. The transformation formulae used in Section 5, which give you a different (non-orthographic) view of the object, is an example of the projected image created by parallel projection.

**COMPREHENSIVE EXAMPLE**   In the program below, the user can simultaneously display on the screen three projected views of a three-dimensional object. The positions of the coordinate axes are displayed to help orient the viewer. The high resolution character generator HRCG$9280 is used to label the axes. A special view of the object, using the formulae in Section 5 of this activity, is provided on high resolution Page 2. The "S" key can be used as a toggle switch to permit the viewer to flip between pages. By quickly depressing the "S" key you will be able to easily compare the special display with the orthogonally projected images.

The DATA for three distinct objects is included at the end of the program. When you RUN the program, try to determine the object by studying its orthogonally projected images: an overhead view and two side views. Don't peek too soon at the special display. You'll get more out of the exercise by studying the orthogonal images for awhile.

```
NEW
10   REM   ********************************
11   REM   *           CE5.1            *
12   REM   ********************************
13   REM
14   REM
15   GOTO 100: REM   BRANCH AROUND SUBROUTINES.
16   REM
17   REM
47   REM   ********************************
48   REM   *  ORTHOGRAPHIC & SPEC SUBRTS   *
49   REM   ********************************
50   PX = X:PY = Y: RETURN
52   PX = Y:PY = Z: RETURN
54   PX = X:PY = Z: RETURN
56   PX = Y - .4 * X:PY = Z - .5 * X: RETURN
57   REM   **      END ORTHO AND SPECL     **
58   REM
97   REM   ********************************
98   REM   *          MAIN PROGRAM         *
99   REM   ********************************
100  HIMEM: 37500: REM   PROTECT HRCG FROM STRG VARS.
110  PRINT  CHR$ (4)"BLOAD HRCG$9280"
```

```
120    PRINT   CHR$ (4)"BLOAD ASCII$9300"
130    EOF =  - 99:EPL =  - 9
140    VW$(1) = "FROM POSTV":VW$(2) = "FROM POSTV":VW$(3) =
       "FROM NEGTV"
150    AX$(1) = " Z-AXIS":AX$(2) = " X-AXIS":AX$(3) = " Y-AXIS"
160    LB$ = "YZXZXYZYX": REM  STRG USED TO HOLD LABELS FOR AXES
       FOR DIFF VIEWS.
170    DIM X(50),Y(50),Z(50)
180    FOR OBJ = 1 TO 3
190    OH = 0:OV = 96: REM  PUT PT CORRESP TO ORG AT EXTREME
       LEFT.
200    GOSUB 2000: REM  GOTO SUBRT TO READ DATA POINTS.
210    HGR : HCOLOR =  7: HOME : VTAB 21
220    VTAB 24: HTAB 3: PRINT "EACH KEYPRESS DISPLAYS A VIEW";
230    FOR VIEW = 1 TO 3
240    GET K$
250    TB = 1 + 13 * (VIEW - 1)
260    VTAB 21: HTAB TB: PRINT VW$(VIEW)
270    HTAB TB: PRINT AX$(VIEW)
280    GOSUB 1500: REM  GOTO SUBRT TO DSPL AXES
290    VTAB 24: HTAB 35: REM  RETURN CURSOR TO BOTTOM OF PAGE
       AFTER HRCG USE.
300    GOSUB 1000: REM  GOTO PLOTTING ROUTINE.
310    OH = OH + 93: REM  SHIFT PT CORRESP TO ORG 1/3 SCRN WDTH.
320    NEXT VIEW
330    VTAB 24: HTAB 3: PRINT "PRESS A KEY FOR SPECIAL VIEW
       ";: GET K$
340    VTAB 24: HTAB 1: CALL  - 868
350    HGR2 : REM  USE PG2 FOR SPEC DSPLY.
360    OH = 120:OV = 96
370    GOSUB 1600: REM  GOTO SPEC SUBRT FOR DISPLAYING COORD
       AXES.
380    VIEW = 4: GOSUB 1000: REM  GOTO PLOT ROUTINE; SPEC DSPLY.
390    FOR J = 1 TO 1000: NEXT : REM  DELAY
400    POKE  - 16300,0: POKE  - 16301,0:SW = 0: REM  DISPLAY
       PG1, MIXED; SET TOGGLE SWITCH VAR TO 0.
410    VTAB 23: HTAB 1: PRINT "TOGGLE 'S' KEY TO SWITCH BETWEEN
       PAGES"
420    PRINT "ANY OTHER KEY FOR NEXT OBJECT";
430    GET K$
440    IF K$ = "S" THEN SW = 1 - SW: POKE  - 16300 + SW,0:
       POKE - 16301 - SW,0: GOTO 430
450    NEXT OBJ
460    TEXT : HOME : END
461    REM  **    END MAIN PROGRAM        **
462    REM
997    REM  ******************************
```

```
998   REM  *        PLOT SUBROUTINE        *
999   REM  ******************************
1000  FL = 1
1010  FOR K = 0 TO N
1020  IF Z(K) = EPL THEN FL = 1: NEXT K
1030  X = X(K):Y = Y(K):Z = Z(K)
1040  FOR J = 1 TO 500: NEXT
1050  ON VIEW GOSUB 50,52,54,56
1060  IF FL THEN  HPLOT OH + PX,OV - PY:FL = 0: NEXT K
1070  HPLOT  TO OH + PX,OV - PY
1080  NEXT K
1090  RETURN
1091  REM  **        END PLOT SUBRT        **
1092  REM
1497  REM  ******************************
1498  REM  * COORD AXES DSPLY & LABELS  *
1499  REM  ******************************
1500  CALL 37504: REM  INIT HRCG
1510  HPLOT OH,110 TO OH,140 TO OH + 36,140
1520  VTAB 15: HTAB  INT (OH / 7) + 2: PRINT  MID$ (LB$,3 *
      VIEW - 2,1)
1530  VTAB 19: HTAB  INT (OH / 7) + 1: PRINT  MID$ (LB$,3 *
      VIEW - 1,1)
1540  VTAB 18: HTAB  INT ((OH + 36) / 7) + 2: PRINT  MID$
      (LB$,3 * VIEW,1)
1550  PRINT  CHR$ (4)"PR#0": REM  TURN OFF HRCG
1560  RETURN
1599  REM  **  SPECIAL AXES DSPLY        **
1600  CALL 37504: REM  INIT HRCG
1610  X = 100:Y = 0:Z = 0: GOSUB 56
1620  HPLOT OH,OV TO OH + PX,OV - PY: REM  DISPLAY X-AXIS
1630  VTAB  INT ((OV - PY) / 8): HTAB  INT ((OH + PX) / 7):
      PRINT "X"
1640  X = 0:Y = 100: GOSUB 56
1650  HPLOT OH,OV TO OH + PX,OV - PY: REM  DISPLAY Y-AXIS
1660  VTAB  INT (OV / 8): HTAB  INT ((OH + PX) / 7) + 2: PRINT
      "Y"
1670  Y = 0:Z = 90: GOSUB 56
1680  HPLOT OH,OV TO OH + PX,OV - PY: REM  DISPLAY Z-AXIS
1690  VTAB  INT ((OV - PY) / 8) + 1: HTAB  INT (OH / 7) + 2:
      PRINT "Z"
1700  PRINT  CHR$ (4)"PR#0": REM  TURN OFF HRCG
1710  RETURN
1711  REM  **  END DSPLY AXES & LABEL  **
1712  REM
1997  REM  ******************************
1998  REM  *    READ DATA SUBROUTINE    *
```

```
1999  REM   ******************************
2000  N = 0
2010  FOR I = 0 TO 1 STEP 0
2020  READ X(N),Y(N),Z(N)
2030  IF Z(N) = EOF THEN N = N - 1: RETURN
2040  N = N + 1
2050  NEXT I
2051  REM   **     END READ DATA SUBRT    **
2052  REM
2999  REM   OBJ #1
3000  DATA   0,0,0, 80,0,0, 0,80,0, 0,0,0, 0,0,80, 80,0,80,
       0,80,80, 0,0,80, -9,-9,-9
3010  DATA   80,0,80, 80,0,0, -9,-9,-9, 0,80,80, 0,80,0,
       -99,-99,-99
3019  REM   OBJ #2
3020  DATA   0,0,0, 80,0,0, 80,80,0, 0,80,0, 0,0,0, 0,0,80,
       0,80,80, 0,80,0, -9,-9,-9
3030  DATA   80,0,0, 80,0,20, 80,80,20, 80,80,0, -9,-9,-9,
       0,0,80, 80,0,20, -9,-9,-9, 0,80,80, 80,80,20,
       -99,-99,-99
3039  REM   OBJ #3
3040  DATA   0,0,0, 50,0,0, 50,50,0, 0,50,0, 0,0,0, 0,0,80,
       50,0,80, 50,50,80, 0,50,80, 0,0,80, -9,-9,-9
3050  DATA   50,0,80, 50,0,0, -9,-9,-9, 50,50,80, 50,50,0,
       -9,-9,-9, 0,50,80, 0,50,0, -9,-9,-9
3060  DATA   25,50,0, 25,75,0, 0,75,0, 0,50,0, -9,-9,-9,
       0,50,40, 25,50,40, 25,75,40, 0,75,40, 0,50,40, -9,-9,-9
3080  DATA   25,50,40, 25,50,0, -9,-9,-9, 25,75,40, 25,75,0,
       -9,-9,-9, 0,75,40, 0,75,0, -99,-99,-99
LIST
RUN
```

If a three-dimensional object is to be used in this program, the points (X,Y,Z) supplied as DATA should have coordinates in the range 0 to 80. Values outside this range may lead to points beyond the screen boundaries or overlap with the next figure.

**Check Your Comprehension**

Consider the three positions of the base point (OH,OV) as defined in the program. Assume all coordinate DATA values are nonnegative and assume displays will not overlap.

What is the maximum possible range of values in each of the two coordinate directions for an orthogonally projected view? _____

A delay loop is inserted in the plotting subroutine to slow down the drawing and make it easier to view each segment of the figure as it is drawn. Remove the delay loop and observe the speed of drawing. With the delay loop reinserted, notice there seem to be periods where there is no apparent drawing. This is particularly evident in the first view of object 3.

What is causing the "false" appearance of no activity? _____

You are encouraged to create your own set of DATA for three-dimensional objects. Try using this on someone you know to test his or her perception of three-dimensional objects. Rather than using a coordinate scheme, we suggest you use the terms "overhead view," "side view 1," etc.

**EXERCISE**   Create the DATA necessary to display two pyramids base to base. For example, the tops of the pyramids can be located at (40, 40, 0) and (40, 40, 80). Use the COMPREHENSIVE EXAMPLE program to display your object.

**EXERCISE**   Create the DATA necessary to display a stack of three boxes, each box successively smaller as the level increases. Use the COMPREHENSIVE EXAMPLE program to display your picture.

**EXERCISE**   Alter the COMPREHENSIVE EXAMPLE so one can also see the other three orthogonally projected images. The drawing of the three remaining views can be made on high resolution Page two. Instead of three views, you have the potential of displaying six views. The special view routine can be still be used, but when accessed, the three new views will be lost.

**CHALLENGE**   Display all six projected views on one page. To provide sufficient screen space, overlay each projected view and the coordinate axes. Use the full screen for display. A toggle switch arrangement will permit you to view either the full or mixed screens.

# ACTIVITY 5.2   Parallel Projections

**LEARNING BY DISCOVERY**   In this activity you will learn how to display three-dimensional objects on the screen using parallel projections. In theory these projections can provide you with a view of an object from almost any position in three-dimensional space.

1. In the previous activity you substituted the following expressions for PX and PY: PX = Y − .4 * X, PY = Z − .5 * X (line 56 of CE5.1). Consider the more general expressions

    (I)  PX = Y − A * X  :  PY = Z − B * X

where A and B are any numerical constants. The primary objective of this activity is to investigate the effect these transformation formulas have on the display when different values are substituted for the constants A and B. Initially, your investigation will be in the form of experimentation followed by observation. The mathematical foundations will be covered in the DISCUSSION section.

   If A and B are set to zero in the formulas in (I) above, then to which orthogonal projection do the formulas correspond? _____

   Under the assumption the formulas represent some way of projecting an image onto the PX-PY coordinate system, how do you put the image on the screen? The method is identical to the approach used in the previous activity. Let (OH,OV) denote the screen coordinates of the screen point corresponding to the origin in the PX-PY coordinate system. The screen point corresponding to (PX,PY) is obtained by moving PX units horizontally and −PY units vertically from the point (OH,OV). The formulas become:

$$H\% = OH + PX = OH + Y - A * X$$
$$V\% = OV - PY = OV - (Z - B * X)$$
$$= OV - Z + B * X$$

The point H%,V% to be HPLOTted on the screen corresponds to the screen image of (X,Y,Z).

2. You are asked below to enter a program to demonstrate the effect of changing the A and B values. When the program is executed, you are prompted to enter a value for A. For each value of A you supply, a series of images is displayed. Each image corresponds to a different value of B which ranges from B = 0 to 1.8, STEPping by +.2. The constraint of 1.8 on the upper limit of B is to insure the image remains within the screen boundaries. The object to be displayed is similar to the wedge with truncated front face you observed in the COMPREHENSIVE EXAMPLE of ACTIVITY 5.1 (cf., object #3). For each value of B, the object is "projected" onto the screen using the formulas in (I) (cf., lines 180, 190 below).

Enter the program below using precisely the line numbering indicated.

```
NEW
10   N = 19:EPL =  − 9: REM  N = # OF PTS X,Y,Z; EPL =
     END-OF-PLOT VAL
20   DIM X(N),Y(N),Z(N)
30   FOR K = 0 TO N
40   READ X(K),Y(K),Z(K)
50   X(K) = X(K) − 20:Y(K) = Y(K) − 20:Z(K) = Z(K) − 20:
     REM  CENTRALIZE DATA ABOUT THE POINT (20,20,20). THE NET
     EFFECT NOW IS AS IF THE ORIGIN HAS BEEN MOVED TO
     (20,20,20).
60   NEXT K
70   EPL = EPL − 20: REM  RESET END-OF-PLOT VAR ACCORDINGLY;
     NOW EQU −29.
80   OH = 140:OV = 80: REM  CENTER OF MIX SCRN
90   HGR : HCOLOR =  3
100  FOR VIEW = 0 TO 1 STEP 0: REM  FOR AS MANY VIEWS AS THE
     USER WANTS ...
110  HOME : VTAB 21
120  INPUT "INPUT A? ";A
130  FOR B = 0 TO 1.81 STEP .2
140  HOME : VTAB 21
150  PRINT  TAB( 12);"A = "A" B = "B
160  REM  ***** PROJECT AND PLOT OBJ *****
170  FOR K = 0 TO N
180  IF Z(K) = EPL THEN K = K + 1:H% = OH + Y(K) − A *
     X(K):V% = OV −Z(K) + B * X(K): HPLOT H%,V%:
     NEXT K
```

```
190  H% = OH + Y(K) − A * X(K):V% = OV − Z(K) + B * X(K)
200  HPLOT   TO H%,V%
210  NEXT K
220  REM  ***** END PROJECT AND PLOT *****
320  FOR J = 1 TO 1000: NEXT : REM  DELAY
330  CALL 62450: REM  CLEAR HIRES SCREEN
340  NEXT B
350  PRINT "TRY ANOTHER VIEW?";: GET K$
360  IF K$ = "Y" THEN  NEXT VIEW
370  TEXT : HOME : END
380  REM  SETTING 1ST X,Y,Z IN DATA EQUAL TO EPL VAL WILL
     PERMIT 1ST OFFICIAL PT, (0,0,0), TO BE HPLOTTED.
390  DATA  −9,−9,−9, 0,0,0, 40,0,0, 40,40,0, 0,40,0,
     0,0,0, 0,0,40, 0,40,40, 0,40,0, −9,−9,−9
400  DATA  0,0,40, 40,0,10, −9,−9,−9, 0,40,40, 40,40,10,
     −9,−9,−9
410  DATA  40,0,0, 40,0,10, 40,40,10, 40,40,0
LIST
```

Starting with the value A = .2 as INPUT, RUN the program. The value of A = .2 is recommended since the image may be difficult to discern for A = 0. As you observe the display, try to concentrate on how your apparent viewing position is changing relative to the object. Where are you viewing the object from initially? Where do you appear to be moving? Further overhead? It is suggested you repeat the display several times using A = .2.

Beginning with A = 0, successively input values of A, incrementing by +.2 until A = 1.8. As you observe each display, concentrate on how your viewing position appears to change. Watch each frame with an eye on the values of B as they change from 0 to 1.8. Formulate a hypothesis concerning the changing values of B and your apparent view position.

For each value of A, how do you perceive your position to change relative to the object, as B increases in value (rough descriptions only)? _____

3. There is a simple technique you can use which will enhance the display and make it easier to perceive depth in the image; it will also help you in orienting your position relative to the object. All of the three-dimensional objects displayed so far have been transparent views. (You didn't know you had x-ray vision, did you?) The idea now is to shade the short front face of the object with a solid color. The effect will be to hide some of the edges behind the face which would not be seen if the object were truly solid.

This process is a relative of more general methods known as a "hidden line" techniques. In the general case, hidden lines are removed from the display when they fall behind surfaces closer to the viewer. The method to be employed here is referred to as a "blackout method," in which faces of the object are shaded to hide lines behind them. In the display, not all lines will be hidden; the amount of programming necessary to remove them will detract from the major objective of this activity.

Add the following lines to the program in memory.

```
230   REM  ***** FILL-IN 'FRONT FACE' *****
240   REM  FRONT FACE DETERMINED BY CORNERS AT X,Y,Z(F1) AND
      X,Y,Z(F2).
250   F1 = 16:F2 = 18: REM  INDICES PROVIDING DIAG CORNERS OF
      FRONT FACE; F1 CORRESP TO LOWER LEFT, F2 TO UPPER RIGHT
      CORNER.
260   HL% = OH + Y(F1) - A * X(F1):HR% = OH + Y(F2) - A *
      X(F2)
270   VB% = OV - Z(F1) + B * X(F1):VT% = OV - Z(F2) + B *
      X(F2): REM  GET LOWER AND UPPER VERT EXTENT OF FRONT
      FACE ON SCREEN.
280   FOR V = VT% + 1 TO VB% - 1
290   HPLOT HL% + 1,V TO HR% - 1,V
300   NEXT V
310   REM  ***** END FILL-IN FRNT FC *****
LIST
```

RUN the expanded version of the program using several of the values for A you input before. Do you perceive more depth in the two-dimensional display of the object? Are you better able to identify the faces closer to you and those further away? _____

---

Try making the following addition to the program in memory.

```
155   HCOLOR = 3 : REM  DRAW FRAME IN WHITE
235   HCOLOR = 0 : REM  SHADE FACE IN BLACK
LIST
```

ReRUN the display. What do you think is happening? _____

By inserting the color assignments at these points in the program, the facial frame is drawn in white while the interior is filled with black to hide the lines behind the front face.

4. Let's proceed with the investigation of how the changing values of A and B affect the display and your perception of your position as you view the object. The hidden line display should be helpful. What happens when B is permitted to assume negative values? To observe the effect, change the beginning of the B-loop.

```
130   FOR B = 0 TO -1.81 STEP -.2
RUN
```

Use values of A varying from 0 to 1.8 incrementing by +.2. Again, concentrate on your apparent viewing position as B decreases in value.

In what manner do you perceive your viewing position to change as B decreases in value? _____

5. If you have considered the question "What happens when I let B increase in value?" then you're following the material very well. If you already know the answer then PASS GO...COLLECT $200!

In either case, make the following changes to the program currently in memory.

```
120   INPUT "INPUT B?"; B
130   FOR A = 0 TO 1.81 STEP .2
340   NEXT A
LIST
```

When you RUN the program, input values of B ranging from $-1.8$ to $+1.8$. Describe your viewing position relative to the object as A increases in value from 0 to 1.8. _____

Change line 130 to permit A to vary from 0 to $-1.81$, stepping by $-.2$. Describe your viewing position relative to the object when you input different values of B, and A ranges in value from 0 to $-1.8$. _____

6. So far most of the action has been one-sided (forgive us for the pun). Your viewpoint has been from the positive side of the Y-Z plane, that is, from the side containing the positive X-axis. To view the "other side," it is necessary to make the following change in the formulas in (I). Specifically, let PX = $-Y + A * X$ and PY = $Z + B * X$.

But wait! There is an easier way than going through the program and changing each line to reflect the new formulas. Simply turn the object around to face you! Technically, you will be rotating the object about the Z-axis through an angle of 180 degrees. How is it done?  Change each (X,Y) value to $(-X, -Y)$ before applying the projection formulas. This is equivalent to the rotation indicated. Therefore, make the following addition to the program.

```
55   X(K) =− X(K) : Y(K) =− Y(K)
LIST 55
```

There is one more thing to do. First, answer the following question. Since the object is being turned so you can view the opposite side, which face will be closest to you after the rotation? _____

Of course, the answer is the large face with original coordinates at (0,0,0), (0,0,40), (0,40,40) and (0,40,0). Since this face is now closest to you, let's use the "blackout method" to hide lines behind it. Inspect the DATA statements at the end of the program listing. Beginning with the first point listed and starting your count at zero, count points (triples of numbers) until you find the first of the four points describing the face. If you counted correctly, these four points are indexed from K = 5 to K = 8. Now, the rectangle itself is completely determined by the diagonally opposite vertices at (0,0,0) (where K = 5) and (0,40,40) (where K = 7). Therefore, in the blackout routine make the following changes:

```
250   F1 = 5 : F2 = 7
260   HL% = OH + Y(F2) − A * X(F2) : HR% = OH + Y(F1) − A *
      X(F1) : REM  WITH THE LARGEST FACE CLOSEST TO THE VIEWER,
      THE POINT (X(F2),Y(F2),Z(F2)) CORRESPONDS TO THE LOWER
      RIGHT CORNER OF THE FACE.
LIST 250,260
```

RUN the program with the modifications and vary the values of A and B as you did in the previous sections. Is your perception of how your viewing position changes as A and B vary the same as before? _____

**DISCUSSION**   Before explaining what the formulas in (I) truly represent, let's summarize the viewing positions of an observer as A and B change values.

$$PX = Y - A * X \; : \; PY = Z - B ** X$$

### VARIABLE A SUMMARY

| A VALUE | VIEW POSITION | CHANGE IN A VALUE | CHANGE IN POSITION |
|---|---|---|---|
| + | Y > 0 SIDE OF X-Z PLANE | INCREASING | MOVE RIGHT |
| − | Y < 0 SIDE OF X-Z PLANE | DECREASING | MOVE LEFT |
| 0 | ON X-Z PLANE | | |

### VARIABLE B SUMMARY

| B VALUE | VIEW POSITION | CHANGE IN B VALUE | CHANGE IN POSITION |
|---|---|---|---|
| + | Z > 0 SIDE OF X-Y PLANE | INCREASING | MOVE UP |
| − | Z < 0 SIDE OF X-Y PLANE | DECREASING | MOVE DOWN |
| 0 | ON X-Y PLANE | | |

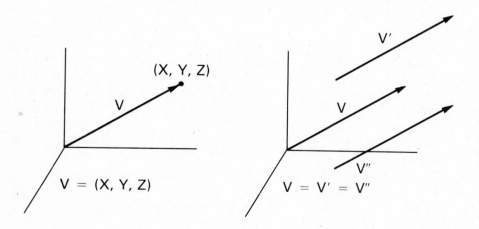

Figure 5.2.1

Each point (X,Y,Z) in three-dimensional space, different from (0,0,0), determines a direction and magnitude by considering the directed segment from (0,0,0) to (X,Y,Z). The magnitude of the point is the length of the segment. This quantity having magnitude and direction is called a vector. The end at (0,0,0) is referred to as the "tail" and the end at (X,Y,Z) is referred to as the "head" of the vector. The point of application of the tail is not significant. Specifically, this means the directed segment from (0,0,0) to (X,Y,Z) has magnitude and direction only. If the directed segment is based at some other point by simple translation, it is the same vector since it has the same direction and same magnitude (length).

When vectors are "multiplied" by numbers, the effect is to lengthen (or shorten) the vector by that factor, and the direction is either the same or reversed depending upon whether the number is positive or negative. For example, if V = (2, 3, 1) then 1.5*V = (1.5*2, 1.5*3, 1.5*1) = (3, 4.5, 1.5); the result points in the same direction but is 1.5 times greater in magnitude than the magnitude of V.

When two different vectors are added, the resulting sum can be found by the parallelogram law. Specifically, the tail of the second vector is positioned at the head of the first vector. The sum vector is the directed segment from the tail of the first vector to the head of the second when positioned as indicated (See Figure 5.2.2). Note the sum vector is the diagonal of the parallelogram determined by the two vectors.

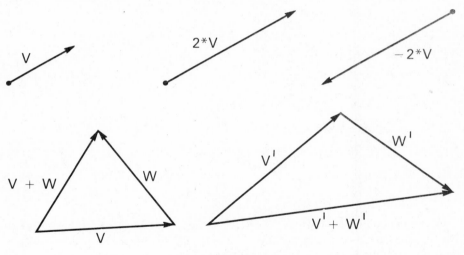

Figure 5.2.2

In terms of coordinates, if V = (2,3,1) and W = (1,2,−3) then V + W = (2+1, 3+2, 1+(−3)) = (3,5,−2).

A straight line in three-dimensional space can be completely determined by two points. A line has a direction, i.e., a vector which provides the-line-of sight along the line. By considering multiples of vectors, you can see the line-of-sight vector is not unique. Parallel lines have a common direction vector. One parallel line is distinguished from another by knowing a particular point the line passes through.

For example, suppose a line is to pass through the points (1,2,4) and (2,5,6). (It may be helpful for you to lay this out on paper). The directed segment (vector) from

(1,2,4) to (2,5,6) is a direction (vector) for the line. In Figure 5.2.2, imagine (1,2,4) to be V and (2,5,6) to be V + W. The vector W is the directed segment between the two given points. With this point of view, what vector W needs to be added to V = (1,2,4) to obtain V + W = (2,5,6)?

After a little reflection, you will see W = (1,3,2). Indeed, V + W = (1,2,4) + (1,3,2) = (2,5,6). By generating multiples t*W of the direction vector W for different numerical values t, the "head" of the resulting vector will correspond to other points on the line through (1,2,4) and (2,5,6). To obtain these other points and the coordinates as well, one can add the vector V = (1,2,4) to the multiple t*W. Thus, every point on the line through (1,2,4) and (2,5,6) can be generated by

$$V + t*W = (1, 2, 4) + t*(2, 5, 6)$$
$$= (1 + 2*t, 2 + 5*t, 4 + 6*t)$$

where t is a real number. For example, if t = 3, then V + 3*W = (1 + 2*3, 2 + 5*3, 4 + 6*3) = (7, 17, 22) is also on the line.

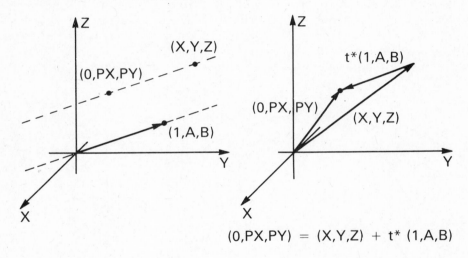

$$(0,PX,PY) = (X,Y,Z) + t* (1,A,B)$$

Figure 5.2.3

What does all of this have to do with the images you have created on the screen? Well, suppose (X,Y,Z) is a point in three-dimensional space to be projected onto the Y-Z plane. To find the projected point, you sight through the point (X,Y,Z) along the direction given by the fixed vector (1,A,B). That is, (1,A,B) is a direction vector for the line-of-sight or projection onto the plane. (See Figure 5.2.3).

Since the projected point is in the Y-Z plane, its X-coordinate is zero. Let (0,PX,PY) denote the coordinates of the projected point. It was shown previously that every point on the line through (X,Y,Z) with direction (1,A,B) can be written in the form (X,Y,Z) + t*(1,A,B). In this case, there must be some value of t which permits the point (0, PX, PY) on the line to be described in this form. Thus,

$$(0,PX,PY) = (X,Y,Z) + t*(1,A,B),$$

or

$$0 = X + t$$
$$PX = Y + t*A$$

PY = Z + t*B

Since the first equation indicates t = −X, one has by substitution

PX = Y − A*X , PY = Z − B*X

The formulas in (I) result.

In summary, the projection formulas (I) in Section 5.2.1 are equivalent to the following geometric interpretation. Each point (X,Y,Z) is projected onto the Y-Z plane along a line with direction vector (1,A,B). The Y-Z coordinates of the projected point are given by PX, PY using the formulas: PX = Y − A * X, PY = Z − B * X. Since the projection of all points onto the Y-Z plane is in the direction of (1,A,B), the projections are along parallel lines. As a result the term parallel projection is used.

There is one final observation. Let (E,F,G) denote a vector (and therefore a direction) in three-dimensional space. Assume E is non-zero. Then (1/E) * (E,F,G) represents a direction parallel to the direction determined by (E,F,G). Computing the product, one obtains the vector (1,F/E,G/E). Thus, an arbitrary direction (E,F,G) with E < > 0 will yield the same parallel projection as the one with projection parameters A and B given by A = F/E and B = G/E.

For those of you who do not fully understand the mathematics above, here is another interpretation. Imagine you are shining a flashlight on an object near to and in front of a wall. You are at a considerable distance from the object, so light rays which strike the object are (for all practical purposes) parallel to those just missing the edges. A shadow is cast on the wall. If the object is moved closer to you in the direction of the light, the shadow size on the wall will show no detectable change. (Remember, the light rays are parallel!) The shadow on the wall corresponds to the projected image by parallel lines. As you move about shining the light on the object, you create different shadows on the wall. The changes of direction you make correspond to changes in the A and B values. As you move further to the right (increasing A), the shadow on the wall lengthens. This corresponds precisely to what happened to the screen display as the value of A was increased. Similar interpretations can be made for changing the value of B. Figure 5.2.4 clearly exhibits the lengthening effect of the screen image as A or B is increased.

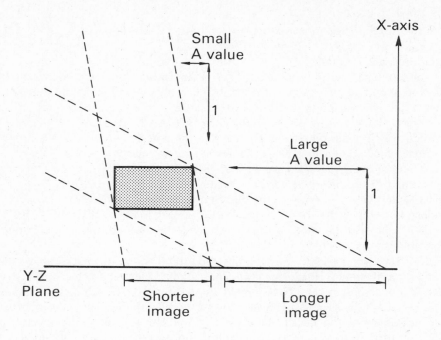

Figure 5.2.4

A true-to-life example of the parallel projection process and its effect is the casting of an object's shadow on the ground by sunlight. All shadows are created by "parallel" rays of light. As the sun lowers in the horizon (corresponding to larger A or B) the shadows become longer.

**COMPREHENSIVE EXAMPLE**    As you have probably noticed, certain values of A and B seem to yield better results than others. For example, values of A = .4 and B = .5 provide a pleasing display for the wedge in the program of Section 5.2.1 and the other objects displayed in the COMPREHENSIVE EXAMPLE of ACTIVITY 5.1. As the values of A and B are changed, the image becomes distorted using parallel projections. On the other hand, it is desirable to have the freedom to see the object from different points of view.

Rather than make you move to obtain a different view, why not rotate the object instead?  In CHAPTER 4 you learned how to rotate figures in the X-Y plane. The idea here is similar. Simply rotate the X-Y coordinates but do not change the vertical coordinates at all!  Each original point (X,Y,Z) will now have new (rotated) coordinates (RX,RY,Z). The plan will be to (1) rotate, and then (2) project.

Suppose A and B have been selected, i.e., a direction for parallel projection has been determined. Suppose you want to rotate the object DG degrees about the Z-axis in the counterclockwise direction. From ACTIVITY 4.10, you list the following formulas.

TH = DG * PI / 180 : C = COS(TH)  : S = SIN(TH)
RX = X * C − Y * S : RY = X * S + Y * C

The original point (X,Y,Z) is rotated DG degrees counterclockwise about the Z-axis, into the point (RX,RY,Z). If you parallel project this point onto the Y-Z plane (equivalently, the PX-PY coordinate plane), you obtain

PX = RY − A * RX : PY = Z − B * RX

Finally, HPLOT the point (H%,V%) on the screen where

H% = OH + PX : V% = OV − PY

These ideas are put to use in the program below. The subroutine which reflects the computations above is performed in lines 50 − 58. This is placed early in the program to speed execution since it may be accessed many times.

The program below will permit the display of three-dimensional objects using parallel projections and rotations about the Z-axis. The object to be displayed is defined using DATA statements, which provide the (X,Y,Z) coordinates of its vertices. The edges are displayed by connecting the vertices in the order of appearance in the DATA statements. The use of an end-of-plot EPL value will identify when a set of contiguously connected points terminates and a new set is to begin. The EPL value used for the DATA supplied with the program is −9 and can be changed at the user's discretion. The end-of-file value EOF currently used is −99 and can be changed at the user's discretion as well.

When the program is RUN, the user is directed to a menu. At this point the user has the opportunity to input new parallel projection parameters A and B, and can input the angle DG of rotation about the Z-axis (the vertical axis).

Displaying your own images on the screen using parallel projections and without major programming modifications will require attention to where and how large the object should be in its three dimensional state. The problem of where it should be constructed is easier to deal with.

Because the projection process is by parallel lines, the projected image onto the Y-Z plane will, aside from a translated image, be the same regardless of where the object is positioned in three-dimensional space. Therefore, the object can be placed near the origin with no fear of affecting the final image. In fact, "centralizing" the object about the origin will give the user the greatest latitude in different view parameters and rotation values.

There is a simple way to accomplish this. Describe your object by accumulating the necessary (X,Y,Z) coordinates of vertices. Now, make an estimate of the location of the "central" point in your object. Let (XC,YC,ZC) denote the coordinates of this point. Subtract XC, YC, and ZC from the respective coordinates of each point in your data list. The new set of coordinate data will be the "centralized" data. It is not necessary for you to find the exact "geometric center" of the object; rough approximations will generally be acceptable. In fact, in the data provided with the program below, the data is "centralized" about (0,0,0) and this point is at one of the extreme corners of the object!

With regard to the problem of the "size" of the object, there are many factors which affect the final display: the viewing parameters A, B; the minimum and maximum values of X, Y, and Z for the coordinate data; the position of the origin (0,0,0) relative to the coordinate data; the screen coordinates (OH,OV), which correspond to the origin (0,0,0); etc. Use the coordinate bounds in the examples presented here to serve as a guide. Experiment!

Try designing some sample objects of your own. For instance, three-dimensional letters, like a block "T," "F," "V," or "Z" are relatively easy to design in three-dimensional space. But remember, you are constructing the letters in three-dimensional space; use three-dimensional coordinates to describe them! Construct some simple geometric objects like a small box on top of a large box, or a one room house. Let your imagination run free. When we cover perspective projections in the next section, you can reuse your data there. For now, you need to develop your three-dimensional thinking, and practice constructing three-dimensional objects. All the intriguing but conceptually more difficult displays will require your familiarity and experience with these basic concepts.

```
NEW
10   REM   ********************************
11   REM   *            CE5.2            *
12   REM   ********************************
13   REM
14   REM   BRANCH AROUND SUBRTS
15   GOTO 100
16   REM
47   REM   ********************************
48   REM   *      ROTATE AND PROJ SUBRT     *
49   REM   ********************************
50   RX = X * C - Y * S:RY = X * S + Y * C:RZ = Z
52   PX = RY - A * RX:PY = RZ - B * RX
54   H% = OH + PX:V% = OV - PY
56   RETURN
57   REM   **     END ROT AND PROJ SUBRT     **
58   REM
97   REM   ********************************
98   REM   *          MAIN PROGRAM          *
99   REM   ********************************
100  DIM C(16),S(16): REM  SET ARRAYS FOR SAVING SINE AND
     COSINE VALUES EVERY 22.5 DEGREES; NOTE: 16*22.5 = 360.
110  GOSUB 3000: REM  GO CALC SINES AND COSINES.
120  EOF =  - 99:EPL =  - 9: REM  END OF FILE AND END OF
     PLOT TO VALUES IN DATA.
130  OH = 140:OV = 96: REM  CENTER OF FULL SCRN
140  GOSUB 4000: REM  GO TO MENU ROUTINE.
150  HGR : POKE  - 16302,0: HCOLOR =  3: REM  FULL SCREEN PG
     1; COLOR WHITE.
160  ON DSPL GOSUB 1000,2000: REM  DSPL = 1 THEN GOTO SINGLE
     FRAME; DSPL = 2 THEN GOTO 360 ROTATION.
170  GET K$: REM  ALLOW USER TO VIEW DSPLY; WAIT FOR KEYPRESS.
180  GOTO 140: REM  GO BACK FOR ANOTHER MENU SELECTION.
181  REM   **       END MAIN PROGRAM       **
182  REM
997  REM   ********************************
998  REM   *       PLOTTING SUBROUTINE      *
999  REM   ********************************
1000 RESTORE :FL = 1: REM  RESTORE DATA AND SET FLAG FOR
     BEGINNING OF PLOT TO 1.
```

```
1010   FOR I = 0 TO 1 STEP 0
1020   READ X,Y,Z
1030   IF Z = EOF THEN  RETURN
1040   IF Z = EPL THEN FL = 1: NEXT I
1050   GOSUB 50: REM  GO CALC PROJ AND SCREEN COORDS; SCREEN
       COORDS RETURNED IN H%,V%
1060   IF H% < 0 OR H% > 279 OR V% < 0 OR V% > 191
       THEN FL = 1: NEXT I: REM  IF PT NOT ON SCREEN THEN
       FORGET IT! GET ANOTHER PT., BUT RESET START OF
       PLOT FLAG.
1070   IF FL THEN  HPLOT H%,V%:FL = 0: NEXT I
1080   HPLOT  TO H%,V%
1090   NEXT I
1091   REM  **     END PLOTTING SUBRT     **
1092   REM
1997   REM  ******************************
1998   REM  *     ROTATE 360 SUBROUTINE    *
1999   REM  ******************************
2000   FOR K = 0 TO 15: REM  FOR 0*22.5 TO 15*22.5 = 337.5
       DEGREES, DO ...
2010   C = C(K):S = S(K): REM  SET COS AND SIN VALS FOR KTH
       FRAME FOR USE IN DETERMINING PROJ IMAGE (AND THEN
       PLOTTING).
2020   HCOLOR =  3: GOSUB 1000: REM  GO TO PLOT ROUTINE FOR
       ROTATED FRAME.
2030   FOR J = 1 TO 500: NEXT : REM  DELAY
2040   X =  PEEK ( - 16384): IF X > 127 THEN  POKE  -
       16368,0: GET K$: POKE  - 16368,0: REM  IF KEYPRESS IS
       MADE TO STOP TO SEE FRAME THEN WAIT TIL NEXT
       KEYPRESS.
2050   CALL 62450: REM  CLEAR HIRES SCREEN
2060   NEXT K
2070   C = C(0):S = S(0): REM  ROT 0 = ROT 360.
2080   HCOLOR =  3: GOSUB 1000: REM  DRAW LAST FRAME ROTATED
       360 = ROT 0
2090   RETURN
2091   REM  **     END ROT 360 SUBRT      **
2092   REM
2997   REM  ******************************
2998   REM  *   CALC COSINES AND SINES    *
2999   REM  ******************************
3000   FAC = 3.14159266 / 180: REM  CONVERSION FACTOR: DEG TO
       RADIANS.
3010   K = 0
3020   FOR D = 0 TO 360 STEP 22.5
3030   TH = D * FAC
3040   C(K) =  COS (TH):S(K) =  SIN (TH)
```

```
3050   K = K + 1
3060   NEXT D
3070   RETURN
3071   REM  **     END CAL COS AND SIN   **
3072   REM
3997   REM  ******************************
3998   REM  *        MENU SUBROUTINE       *
3999   REM  ******************************
4000   TEXT : HOME
4010   HTAB 7: PRINT "A DEMONSTRATION OF ROTATIONS"
4020   HTAB 9: PRINT "AND PARALLEL PROJECTIONS"
4030   VTAB 5: PRINT "1) SET NEW VIEW PARAMS A & B": HTAB 5:
       PRINT "CURRENT VALUES: ";A","B
4040   VTAB 8: PRINT "2) SET NEW ROTATION VIEW": HTAB 5: PRINT
       "CURRENT ANGLE: ";DG" DEG"
4050   VTAB 11: PRINT "3) VIEW SINGLE FRAME DISPLAY"
4060   VTAB 13: PRINT "4) VIEW OBJ ROTATED 360 DEG"
4070   VTAB 15: PRINT "5) QUIT"
4080   VTAB 17: HTAB 10: INVERSE : PRINT "SELECT #: ";: NORMAL :
       GET K$:KV =  VAL (K$)
4090   IF KV = 1 THEN  PRINT : INPUT "INPUT A,B: ";A,B: IF  ABS
       (A) > = 1 OR  ABS (B) > = 1 THEN  PRINT  CHR$ (7);"**
       WARNING ** : FOR SOME ROTATIONS PIC" :PRINT "MAY NOT BE
       COMPLETE. PRESS A KEY:";: GET K$
4100   IF KV = 2 THEN  VTAB 19: HTAB 1: INPUT "INPUT THE # OF
       DEGREES: ";DG
4110   IF KV = 3 THEN DSPLY = 1:C =  COS (DG * FAC):S =  SIN
       (DG * FAC): RETURN
4120   IF KV = 4 THEN DSPLY = 2: POKE  − 16368,0: RETURN
4130   IF KV = 5 THEN  HOME : END
4140   GOTO 4000
4141   REM  **     END MENU SUBROUTINE    **
4142   REM
5997   REM  **********  DATA  **********
6000   DATA  0,0,0, 20,0,0, 20,20,0, 60,20,0, 60,50,0, 0,50,0,
       0,0,0, −9,−9,−9   : REM  BOTTOM FACE
6010   DATA  0,0,20, 20,0,20, 20,20,20, 60,20,20, 60,50,20,
       0,50,20, 0,0,20, −9,−9,−9   : REM  TOP FACE
6020   DATA  0,0,0, 0,0,20, −9,−9,−9, 20,0,0, 20,0,20,
       −9,−9, −9, 20,20,0, 20,20,20, −9,−9,−9, 60,
       20,0, 60,20,20, −9,−9,−9, 60,50,0, 60,50,20,
       −9, −9,−9, 0,50,0, 0,50,20, −99,−99,−99
       : REM  BOTT-TOP CONNECTIONS
LIST
RUN
```

**Check Your Comprehension**

Which line in the program effects the rotation about the Z-axis? _____

What is the (fixed) angular increment between displays using the 360 degree view option? _____

What numerical values are represented by the arrays C(K) and S(K)? _____
_____

How does the program avoid attempting to plot off screen points? _____

A few comments are in order. After the user supplies values for A and B, they are checked to determine if either value is outside the interval −1 to 1. If one of them is outside the interval, then a warning is printed that an incomplete image may appear on the screen. However, there is no guarantee this range will be sufficient for obtaining complete images for different objects. Since considerable distortion results for values of A and B outside this range, this represents a reasonable range for parallel projection parameters.

Regardless of the values supplied, the plotting routine will not attempt to plot any points or segments which extend beyond the screen boundaries. This is why incomplete images may result. You might even try values like A = 1.5 and B = 2 to see what happens. However, since an object can be rotated through any angle about the Z-axis, there is little need to use large values of A and B. Simply select values for A and B which provide satisfying projected images (such as A = .4 and B = .5), then rotate the object!

The reader is encouraged to study the plotting subroutine and ascertain the need for each conditional check and assignment of flag values. For example, if a projected point is visible on the screen and the next point isn't, what happens? Is there a more efficient way to plot the example object using arrays?

Using arrays, one only needs to read in the coordinates of the bottom face. The coordinates of the top face merely have the Z-coordinate incremented by 20. A more efficient plotting algorithm could be developed, but it will be object specific. On the other hand, the use of arrays, special data definition blocks, and special plotting routines, can decrease the amount of actual data you must supply and speed program execution.

**EXERCISE**   Create the coordinate DATA for a three-dimensional block "T" and use the COMPREHENSIVE EXAMPLE program to display it. Keep (X,Y,Z) values within the range from 0 to 70, and centralize your data after gathering it in raw form.

**EXERCISE**   Alter the COMPREHENSIVE EXAMPLE program so the rotation is about the Y-axis, instead of the Z-axis. This will require changing the statement defining the rotated coordinates (Hint: the Y-coordinate will not change with this rotation).

**CHALLENGE**   Alter the COMPREHENSIVE EXAMPLE program so the user can rotate the object about any of the three coordinate axes from its initial position. Permit the user to select the axis of rotation and the amount of rotation (the angle in degrees). Do not attempt at this time to try to combine rotations into a succession of events. Be content to allow one rotation about a selected axis.

# MODULE 5B     General 3-D Graphics

## ACTIVITY 5.3     Perspective Projections

**LEARNING BY DISCOVERY**     In this activity you will learn how to display three-dimensional objects on the screen using perspective projections. These transformations will, in general, result in projected images which improve viewer perception of object depth, size and position.

1.  In considering parallel projections in the previous activity, it was emphasized that a parallel projection will provide the same projected image on the Y-Z plane regardless of the position of the object (assuming no rotations have been performed on it). You know this situation does not prevail in much of the real world.

    In reality, objects of the same size appear larger when they are closer to you than when they are further away. When you gaze down a long highway, the edges of the road appear to converge to a point in the distance, and those edges closest to you surpass the limits of your field of vision. The two-dimensional representation of this type of view is called a perspective view. The effect is that the impression of depth and position has been added to one's perception of objects in three-dimensional space.

    Perspective projections, which provide perspective views, are different from parallel projections because the line-of-sight (i.e., the direction of the projecting line) varies for each point to be projected. Moreover, the distance the viewer is from the object plays a significant role in how the total image appears. On the other hand, locally, the projected image is nearly a parallel projection. In fact, this is the basis by which the formulas providing the projected coordinates (PX,PY) of a point (X,Y,Z) will be developed.

    In a parallel projection, every point in the object is projected onto the plane using the same projection direction, that is, along parallel lines.

    In a perspective projection, the line of projection is from a fixed point (normally regarded as the position of the viewer's eye) through the point (X,Y,Z) to the projection plane. As the point (X,Y,Z) changes, the line-of-sight changes. If the fixed point (the position of the viewer's eye) changes, the line-of-sight is different for the point (X,Y,Z).

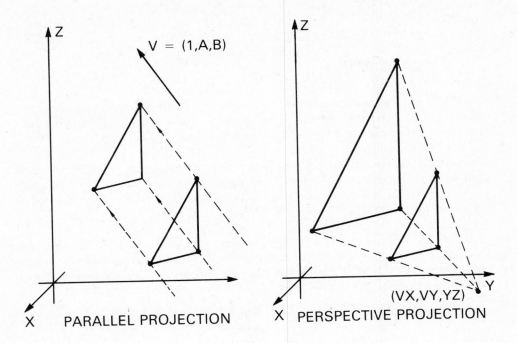

Figure 5.3.1

2. How does one obtain the projected coordinates (PX,PY) for a given point (X,Y,Z)? What new computations are involved and what is the reasoning behind them? Well, fear not! You need no new mathematical concepts beyond those already introduced in the previous activity. The only additional computation necessary is the determination of the viewing parameters A and B. These values depend on the viewing coordinates (VX,VY,VZ) (or where your eye is located), and on the point (X,Y,Z) to be projected. Specifically, to perspective project the point (X,Y,Z), one must calculate

$$A = (Y - VY)/(X - VX) \quad : B = (Z - VZ)/(X - VX)$$

Using these A and B values, one can calculate the projected coordinates (PX,PY) in the same way as for parallel projections. A complete explanation of where the expressions for A and B originate will be covered in the DISCUSSION section of this activity.

For now, let's investigate the effect of a perspective projection. LOAD the COMPREHENSIVE EXAMPLE program CE5.2 from the previous activity. You will alter that program to permit perspective views. Make the following changes and additions.

```
LOAD CE5.2
```

< Make the following changes and additions to CE5.2 . >

```
54   A = (RY - VY) / (RX - VX):B = (RZ - VZ) / (RX - VX)
135  VX = 200 : VY = 75 : VZ = 100 : REM  SET DEFAULT VALUES
     FOR VIEWPOINT
```

```
4020   HTAB 7: PRINT "AND PERSPECTIVE PROJECTIONS"
4030   VTAB 5: PRINT "1) SET VIEWING POINT: VX,VY,VZ": HTAB 5:
       PRINT "CURRENT VALUES: ";VX","VY","VZ
4090   IF KV = 1 THEN  PRINT : INPUT "INPUT VX,VY,VZ:
       ";VX,VY,VZ
LIST
```

When the program is executed, you are supplied with a menu from which you can change the viewing position (VX,VY,VZ) or the rotation angle. To obtain a complete image, some care must be taken in selecting the viewing parameters (VX,VY,VZ) and the rotation angle.

One final point needs mentioning before you investigate the effect of these changes. In defining A and B in line 51, the ratios $A = (RY - VY)/(RX - VX)$ and $B = (RZ - VZ)/(RX - VX)$ are used because the perspective projection is performed on the rotated point (RX,RY,RZ) rather than the original point (X,Y,Z). When the rotation angle is zero, $(RX,RY,RZ) = (X,Y,Z)$.

Here are some suggested input parameters to use when you RUN the program. For the particular object supplied in the program, it will best to select a viewing position with VX $> = $ 100. For very distant views notice the similarity with the image created by a parallel projection.

| VX, VY, VZ | ROT ANGLE | VIEW |
|---|---|---|
| 400, 100, 200 | 0 | SINGLE FRAME |
| 120, 30, 40 | 0 | SINGLE FRAME |
| 160, 30, 40 | 0 | ROTATE 360 |
| 160, 40, 20 | 45 | SINGLE FRAME |
| 140, 40, 20 | −10 | SINGLE FRAME |
| 160, 20, 20 | 170 | SINGLE FRAME |
| 300, 80, 50 | 0 | ROTATE 360 |
| 140, −60, −40 | 0 | ROTATE 360 |

EXPERIMENT ON YOUR OWN!

Maintain a constant VX value and move further from the X-axis. What kind of distortions do you observe? _____

3. The ability to view the object as it is rotated a full 360 degrees is instructive and enlightening, but the draw-erase cycle currently used can be distracting. The use of page flipping can eliminate the distraction. Displaying successively rotated images as quickly as possible requires advance calculation of the projected images for each rotation angle. Of course, one must pay the penalty of an inactive display for the period of time during which the calculations are made. As you increase the complexity of the object and make greater demands on the quality of display (parallel versus perspective view), the amount of computation time increases. In our biased opinion, the results are worth the wait.

Modifications, made below, to the program of Section 2 will permit a more pleasing animation of the object rotation through 360 degrees. When option 4 is selected, the screen coordinates of each perspective view for each angle of rotation are calculated. The values are stored in a doubly indexed array H%(I,K). K is the index variable corresponding to the K-th rotation position and I is an index variable for the vertices of the object. To speed up the calculations and the plotting, special subroutines have been written which are specific to the "L" shaped object used in the program. Aside from these special routines, the page flipping subroutine can be used, virtually without change, for your own displays.

< With the program of Section 5.3.2 in memory, make the following changes and additions. >

```
15   LOMEM: 24576: GOTO 100
67   REM  *********************************
68   REM  *    PLOT SUBRT FOR 'L' OBJCT    *
69   REM  *********************************
70   FOR J = 0 TO 7 STEP 7
72   HPLOT H%(J,KK),V%(J,KK)
74   FOR I = 1 TO 6
76   HPLOT  TO H%(I + J,KK),V%(I + J,KK)
78   NEXT I,J
80   FOR I = 0 TO 6
82   HPLOT H%(I + 7,KK),V%(I + 7,KK) TO H%(I,KK),V%(I,KK)
84   NEXT I
86   RETURN
87   REM  **    END SPEC PLOT SUBRT        **
105  DIM H%(13,16),V%(13,16)
107  H0 = 0:H1 = 279:V0 = 191:V1 = 0
1997 REM  ******************************
1998 REM  *  ROTATION 360 W PG FLPPNG  *
1999 REM  ******************************
2000 POKE  - 16301,0: REM  SET MIXED GRAPHICS TO DELIVER
     MESSAGE.
2010 HOME : VTAB 21
2020 HTAB 10: PRINT "... CALCULATING ..."
2030 FOR K = 0 TO 15: REM  FOR EACH ANGLE 0*22.5 TO 15*22.5
     DEG DO ...
2040 C = C(K):S = S(K): REM  GET COS AND SIN OF K*22.5 DEG.
2050 RESTORE
2060 FOR I = 0 TO 6: REM  GET THE COORDS OF THE 7 VERTICES ON
     BOTTOM FACE.
2070 READ X,Y,Z
2080 GOSUB 50
2090 IF H% < H0 OR H% > H1 OR V% < V1 OR V% > V0
     THEN 2500
2100 H%(I,K) = H%:V%(I,K) = V%
2110 Z = Z + 20: GOSUB 50: REM  NOW GET THOSE FOR THE TOP
     FACE WHICH IS 20 UNITS UP FROM BOTTOM FACE.
2120 IF H% < H0 OR H% > H1 OR V% < V1 OR V% > V0
     THEN 2500
```

```
2130  H%(I + 7,K) = H%:V%(I + 7,K) = V%
2140  NEXT I,K
2150  FOR I = 0 TO 13: REM  LAST POSITION (K = 16) IS THE SAME
      AS 0-TH POSITION.
2160  H%(I,K) = H%(I,0):V%(I,K) = V%(I,0)
2170  NEXT I
2180  HGR : HGR2
2190  POKE  - 16300,0: POKE 230,32: REM  VIEW PG 1 AND SET
      MEMORY DRAW-PG BYTE ACCORDINGLY.
2200  KK = 0: HCOLOR =  3: GOSUB 70: REM  GO DRAW 0-TH ROT
      POSITION ON PG 1.
2210  POKE 230,64: REM  SET DRAW-PG POINTER FOR PG 2, WHILE
      STILL VIEWING PG 1.
2220  KK = 1: GOSUB 70: REM  GO DRAW 1-TH ROT POSITION (ON PG
      2).
2230  POKE  - 16299,0: REM  PICTURE DONE SO DSPLY PG 2.
2240  PG = 64:SW = 1: REM  SET PG INDICATOR VAR AND DSPLY
      SWITCH VAR. PG = 32, SW = 0 IS PG 1; PG = 64, SW =
      1 IS PG 2.
2250  FOR K = 2 TO 16: REM  FOR EACH OF THE REMAINING ROTATION
      POSITIONS ...
2260  PG = 96 - PG: POKE 230,PG: REM  SWITCH PAGE ON WHICH TO
      DRAW; NOTE: 96-32 = 64; 96-64 = 32.
2270  KK = K - 2: HCOLOR =  0: GOSUB 70: REM  ERASE DSPLY
      CREATED ON CURRENT DRAW-PG FROM TWO ROTATION INCRMNTS
      EARLIER.
2280  X =  PEEK ( - 16384): IF X > 127 THEN  POKE  -
      16368,0: GET K$: POKE  - 16368,0
2290  KK = K: HCOLOR =  3: GOSUB 70: REM  DRAW K-TH ROTATION
      DSPLY.
2300  SW =  NOT SW: REM  FLIP DSPLY SWITCH VAR TO PREPARE FOR
      NEW DSPLY.
2310  POKE  - 16300 + SW,0: REM  FLIP DSPLY SWITCH TO SEE
      COMPLETED PAGE.
2320  NEXT K
2330  POKE  - 16301,0: HOME : VTAB 21: REM  SET MIXED MODE
      GRAPHICS.
2340  PRINT "AGAIN<Y,N>?": GET K$: PRINT K$
2350  IF K$ = "Y" THEN 2180
2360  VTAB 23: HTAB 10: PRINT "PRESS A KEY TO CONT."
2370  RETURN
2499  REM  ***** ERROR HANDLING SUB *****
2500  TEXT : HOME
2510  PRINT  CHR$ (7);"SORRY, SELECT A MORE DISTANT VIEWPOINT!"
2520  VTAB 3: PRINT "THE PRESENT VALUES DO NOT PERMIT A COM-"
2530  PRINT "PLETE IMAGE FOR EVERY ROTATION ANGLE."
2540  PRINT : PRINT "PRESS A KEY TO RETURN TO THE MENU."
```

```
2550  RETURN
2551  REM  **      END PG FLIPPNG        **
LIST
SAVE SEC5.3.3
```

RUN the program selecting option 4 and using different perspective views. Some experimentation with the viewpoint will be required to obtain complete images.

What is the function of lines 2030-2170 in the program? _____

**DISCUSSION**  Let's review the basic formulas needed to convert a point $(X,Y,Z)$ to screen coordinates $H\%, V\%$ via a perspective projection. They are:

$A = (Y - VY)/(X - VX)$  $: B = (Z - VZ)/(X - VX)$

$PX = Y - A * X$  $: PY = Z - B * X$

$H\% = OH + PX$  $: V\% = OV - PY$

Recall OH and OV denote the screen coordinates of the point corresponding to the origin in the PX-PY (or Y-Z ) coordinate system.

Evidently, if $A$ and $B$ are defined as above, the line through the viewing points $(VX,VY,VZ)$ and $(X,Y,Z)$ meets the Y-Z plane in the point $(0,PX,PY)$. Let's see why.

Consider the vector V with direction and magnitude corresponding to the directed segment from $(VX,VY,VZ)$ toward $(X,Y,Z)$; that is, V is the vector which must be added to $(VX,VY,VZ)$ to yield $(X,Y,Z)$. Thus, $V = (X-VX, Y-VY, Z-VZ)$ since $(VX, VY, VZ) + (X-VX, Y-VY, Z-VZ) = (X,Y,Z)$. The straight line through $(VX,VY,VZ)$ and $(X,Y,Z)$ has $V = (X-VX, Y-VY, Z-VZ)$ as a direction vector.

According to the DISCUSSION section of the previous activity, the vector $(1/(X - VX)) * V$ serves as a direction vector for the same line. This vector has the components $(1, (Y-VY)/(X-VX), (Z-VZ)/(X-VX))$. If $A$ and $B$ denote the second and third component values of this vector, then $(1,A,B)$ is a direction vector for the line through $(X,Y,Z)$ and $(VX,VY,VZ)$. But, in the DISCUSSION of ACTIVITY 5.2 it was shown the coordinates of the intersection of such a line with the Y−Z plane are given by $(0,PX,PY)$, where $PX = Y - A * X$ and $PY = Z - B * X$. This explains why the values of $A$ and $B$ are defined as they are for a perspective projection.

In effect, a perspective projection applied to a single point behaves exactly like the parallel projection having direction $(X-VX, Y-VY, Z-VZ)$. In normalized form, this is the vector $(1,A,B)$ where $A = (Y-VY)/(X-VX)$ and $B = (Z-VZ)/(X-VX)$.

As you move closer to a group of objects, perspective projections give the impression that nearer objects appear larger than those farther away, when in fact they may all be the same size. The primary viewpoint variable to increase or decrease to effect the greatest change in the display size is the VX-value. This is because the VX-value is the directed distance from the viewpoint to the projection plane.

The point $(0,VY,VZ)$ in the projection plane has a classical significance. It is often referred to as the vanishing point because all lines perpendicular (normal) to the projection plane result in projected images which converge at this one point. (From a mathematical standpoint, we say the vanishing point is the limit point of projections of points tending to infinity which are on these lines.) In the COMPREHENSIVE EXAMPLE program which follows, you will observe this situation. Look for the vanishing point in the example of Section 5.3.2.

When $VY = 0$ and $VZ = 0$, the projection is termed a normalized perspective projection. This means the viewpoint is chosen on the X-axis; equivalently, the vanishing point is at the origin. In the next section the process of combining rotations about different coordinate axes will be used to obtain normalized perspective views of an object from any position in three-dimensional space.

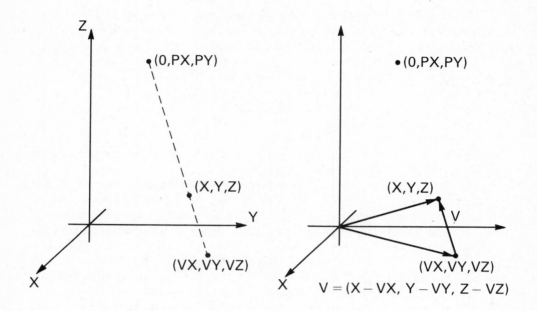

Figure 5.3.2

**COMPREHENSIVE EXAMPLE**    The program below simulates a common roadway scene. Telephone poles border the sides of a road and striped lines divide the highway. In designing the scene, it was estimated a telephone pole is approximately 30 feet (or 9 meters) high with cross pieces approximately 6 feet (or 1.8 meters) long. A suitably wide road was estimated to have shoulder boundaries approximately 24 feet (or 7.3 meters) to either side of center. As a result, the poles were placed 30 feet from center on each side of the road. Finally, it was decided to place the poles every 500 feet (or 160 meters). (Upon reflection, we recognized this to be a ridiculous estimate, but it gave satisfactory results; it was decided to leave well enough alone).

After deciding the viewer would be permitted to view the display within the road width (−24 to 24), the lower limit on the value of VX was obtained by experimentation. Of course, greater latitude with VY can be taken; but to keep the display within the screen boundaries, the value of VX will need to be increased.

```
NEW
10   REM   ********************************
11   REM   *            CE5.3             *
12   REM   ********************************
13   REM
```

```
14   REM
15   GOTO 100: REM   BRANCH AROUND SUBROUTINES.
16   REM
47   REM   ********************************
48   REM   *     PERSP PROJ CALC SUBRT     *
49   REM   ********************************
50   A = (VY - Y) / (VX - X):B = (VZ - Z) / (VX - X)
52   PX = Y - A * X:PY = Z - B * X
54   H% = OH + PX:V% = OV - PY
56   RETURN
57   REM   **       END PERSP PROJ SUB      **
58   REM
67   REM   ********************************
68   REM   *         PLOTTING SUBROUTINE    *
69   REM   ********************************
70   FL = 1: REM   SET BEGINNING OF PLOT FLAG 'ON'.
72   FOR I = 0 TO NP
76   IF Z(I) = EPL THEN FL = 1: NEXT I
78   X = M + X(I):Y = S + Y(I):Z = Z(I): REM   TRANSLATE DATA
     TO PUT POLE AT POINT (M,S,0).
80   GOSUB 50: REM   GO CALC PERSPECTIVE PROJ
     COORD AND SCREEN COORD H%,V%.
82   IF FL THEN   HPLOT H%,V%:FL = 0: NEXT I
84   HPLOT   TO H%,V%
86   NEXT I
88   RETURN
89   REM   **       END PLOTTING SUBRT      **
90   REM
97   REM   ********************************
98   REM   *         MAIN PROGRAM           *
99   REM   ********************************
100  HOME
110  GOSUB 1000: REM   GO READ DATA FOR ONE TELEPHONE POLE AND
     POKE SHAPE FOR SPEC DSPLY INTO MEMORY.
120  OH = 140:OV = 105: REM   SCRN COORD CORRESP TO ORIGIN IN
     PX-PY COORD SYSTEM.
130  VX = 1000:VY = 0:VZ = 6: REM   VIEW POSITION FOR INITIAL
     DISPLAY.
140  HGR : HCOLOR = 3
150  GOSUB 2000: REM   GOTO TELEPH AND ROAD DSPLY SUBRT.
160  POKE  - 16301,0: REM   THROW MIXED GRAPHICS SWTCH.
170  HOME : VTAB 21
180  PRINT "SELECT: 1. CHANGE VIEWING PARAMETERS"
190  PRINT "        2. QUIT & VIEW SPECIAL DISPLAY"
200  GET Q$: IF  VAL (Q$) = 2 THEN 290
210  IF  VAL (Q$) < > 1 THEN 170
220  HOME : VTAB 21
```

```
230   PRINT "INPUT VIEWING PARAMETERS VX,VY,VZ:"
240   PRINT "VX > = 1170, -24 < = VY < = 24,
      0 < = VZ < = 50"
250   INPUT "VX,VY,VZ: ";VX,VY,VZ
260   IF VX < 1170 OR VY < - 24 OR VY > 24 OR VZ <
      0 OR VZ > 50 THEN 170
270   OV = 105 - VZ: REM  SETTING OV SLIGHTLY HIGHER PERMITS
      GREATER LATITUDE OF INPUT VALUES FOR VZ, OTHERWISE PLOT
      VALUES WILL BE BELOW SCREEN.
280   GOTO 140: REM  GO BACK TO DISPLAY A PICTURE USING NEW VIEW
      PARAMS.
290   CALL 62450: HCOLOR = 3: REM  IF USER 'QUITS' THEN PROG
      BRANCHES TO HERE. CLEAR SCREEN.
300   VX = 1100:VY = 12:VZ = 10: REM  SET VIEW POSITION FOR
      SPEC DISPLY.
310   OH = 140:OV = 100: REM  SET SCRN COORD CORRESP TO ORIGIN
      OF PX-PY SYSTM.
320   GOSUB 2000: REM  GOTO TELE & ROAD DSPLY.
330   GOSUB 5000: REM  GOTO SPEC DISPLAY SUBRT.
340   HOME : VTAB 21
350   POKE  - 16301,0: REM  SET MIXED MODE.
360   PRINT "AGAIN ?";: GET Q$
370   IF Q$ = "Y" THEN 290
380   TEXT : HOME : END
381   REM  **          END MAIN PROG          **
382   REM
997   REM  ********************************
998   REM  * READ DATA & POKE SHAPE TBLE *
999   REM  ********************************
1000  EPL= - 9: REM  END OF PLOT VALUE.
1010  NP = 10: REM  NUMBER OF PTS NEEDED IN GENERATING ONE
      TELEPH POLE INCLUDING EPL VALS.
1020  FOR I = 0 TO NP
1030  READ X(I),Y(I),Z(I)
1040  NEXT I
1060  POKE 232,0: POKE 233,3: REM  TELL APPLE WHERE SHAPE TABLE
      BEGINS; HEX 300 = 768.
1070  ADDR = 768:N = 20
1080  FOR K = 1 TO N: REM  READ AND POKE IN SHAPE TABLE; ONLY
      ONE SHAPE.
1090  READ V
1100  POKE ADDR,V
1110  ADDR = ADDR + 1
1120  NEXT K
1130  RETURN
1131  REM  **     END READ AND POKE      **
1132  REM
```

```
1997 REM *******************************
1998 REM *  DSPLY TELEPH & ROAD SUBR  *
1999 REM *******************************
2000 M0 = 750:M1 = − 4250: REM  INITIAL X-POSITION AND FINAL
     X-POSITION OF POLES WHICH ARE PLACED 500 (FT) APART.
2010 POKE − 16302,0: REM  THROW FULL SCRN GRAPHICS SWTCH.
2020 FOR M = M0 TO M1 STEP − 500: REM  AT 500 (FT) INTERVALS
     PLACE ...
2030 FOR S = − 30 TO 30 STEP 60: REM  AT 30 (FT) FROM CENTER
     ON EACH SIDE OF ROAD ...
2040 GOSUB 70: REM  ... PUT POLE, IE., GOTO INDIV POLE
     GRAPHING SUBRT.
2050 NEXT S,M
2060 Z = 0: REM  EDGES AND CENTER STRIPE OF ROAD ARE AT
     'GROUND-ZERO.'
2070 FOR Y = − 24 TO 24 STEP 48: REM  AT 24 (FT) EACH SIDE
     OF CENTER ...
2080 X = M0 + 75: GOSUB 50: HPLOT H%,V%: REM  PLOT CLOSEST PT
     OF ROAD EDGE ...
2090 X = M1: GOSUB 50: HPLOT  TO H%,V%: REM  ... TO FARTHEST
     PT OF ROAD EDGE.
2100 NEXT Y
2110 Y = 0:Z = 0: REM  CENTER STRIPE OF ROAD CORRESP TO
     X-AXIS.
2120 FOR M = M0 + 100 TO M1 STEP − 100: REM  AT 100 (FT)
     INTERVALS ... (AND BEGINNING SLIGHTLY CLOSER)
2130 X = M: GOSUB 50: HPLOT H%,V%
2140 X = M − 20: GOSUB 50: HPLOT  TO H%,V%: REM  ... PAINT A
     STRIPE 20 (FT) LONG.
2150 NEXT M
2160 RETURN
2161 REM ** END DSPLY TELEPH & ROAD **
2162 REM
4997 REM ******************************
4998 REM *  SPECIAL DISPLAY SUBRT  *
4999 REM ******************************
5000 HPLOT 140,0 TO 140,20 TO 135,20 TO 130,25 TO 130,50 TO
     135,55 TO 145,55 TO 150,50 TO 150,25 TO 145,20 TO 140,20:
     REM OUTLINE STOPLIGHT.
5010 FOR V = 27 TO 41 STEP 14: REM  DRAW BOUNDARIES FOR TOP &
     BOTTOM LIGHTS.
5020 HPLOT 136,V TO 136,V + 7 TO 144,V + 7 TO 144,V TO 136,V
5030 NEXT V
5040 HCOLOR = 1: REM  GREEN
5050 FOR V = 42 TO 47: REM  COLOR TOP LIGHT AREA GREEN.
5060 HPLOT 137,V TO 143,V
5070 NEXT V
```

```
5080   FOR J = 1 TO 1000: NEXT J: REM  DELAY TO DRAW VIEWER'S
       ATTENTION WHEN CHANGING FROM GREEN TO RED.
5090   FOR C = 0 TO 1: REM  FOR FIRST THE BOTTOM LIGHT AREA AND
       THEN THE TOP ...
5100   TV = 42 - C * 14: REM  TV IS TOP VERT COORD OF LIGHT
       AREAS IN STOPLIGHT. C = 0 CORRESP TO BOTTOM AREA; C = 1
       TO TOP AREA.
5110   HCOLOR =  5 * C: REM  C = 0 YIELDS BLACK; C = 1 YIELDS
       ORANGE ('RED').
5120   FOR V = TV TO TV + 5: REM  COLOR IN LIGHT AREA. FIRST
       PASS (C = 0) IS TO ERASE GREEN; SECND PASS (C = 1)
       IS TO COLOR 'RED'.
5130   HPLOT 137,V TO 143,V: REM  COLOR HORIZ SEGMENT.
5140   NEXT V
5150   NEXT C
5160   ROT =  0: REM  SET ROTATION FOR SHAPE.
5170   SP= - 16336:N1 = 1: REM  SP IS THE SPEAKER MEM
       LOCATION; N1 IS VAR USED TO HOLD CONSTANT 1.
5180   H = 150:V1 = 92:V0 = 140:F = 10 / (V0 - V1): REM
       (H,V1) IS BEGINNING PT FOR SHAPE; PT IS NEAR VANISHING PT
       AT (152,88). (H,V0) IS FINAL PT FOR BEGINNING SHAPE WHEN
       AT LARGEST SCALE. F IS A FACTOR USED TO OBTAIN
       INCREASING SCALE.
5190   FOR V = V1 TO V0: REM  FROM THE BEGNG PT TO FINAL PT ...
5200   X =  PEEK (SP) -  PEEK (SP): REM  TWEAK SPKR FOR MOTOR
       NOISE.
5210   SCALE =  N1 + F * (V - V1): REM  UNIFORMLY SCALE SHAPE
       FROM SCALE  = 1 (V = V1) TO 11 (V = V0).
5220   XDRAW N1 AT H,V: REM  DISPLAY SHAPE.
5230   X =  PEEK (SP) -  PEEK (SP): REM  TWEAK SPKR FOR MOTOR
       NOISE.
5240   XDRAW N1 AT H,V: REM  ERASE SHAPE.
5250   NEXT V
5260   XDRAW N1 AT H,V0: REM  DISPLAY SHAPE; STATIONARY AND
       SCALE = 11.
5270   SW = 1
5280   FOR K = 1 TO 6: REM  DO THE FOLLOWING SIX TIMES TO
       SIMULATE WAITING AT STOPLIGHT ...
5289   REM  MAKE REVVING NOISE OF MOTOR BY PUTTING SHORTER AND
       SHORTER DELAYS BETWEEN TWEAKS OF SPEAKER.
5290   FOR I = 1 TO 40
5300   X =  PEEK (SP) -  PEEK (SP) +  PEEK (SP)
5310   FOR J = 40 - I TO 1 STEP  - 2
5320   NEXT J,I
5330   ROT =  0: XDRAW N1 AT H,V0: REM  ERASE 'STATIONARY'
       SHAPE.
5339   REM  IN NEXT SEVEN STATEMENTS ROTATE SHAPE IN REVERSE
```

```
            DIRECTIONS TO SIMULATE IDLING CAR. NOTE: YOU MUST DRAW
            AND THEN ERASE EACH ROTATED VIEW.
5340   ROT =  SW: XDRAW N1 AT H,VO
5350   XDRAW N1 AT H,VO
5360   X =  PEEK (SP)
5370   SW = 255 - SW
5380   ROT =  SW: XDRAW N1 AT H,VO
5390   XDRAW N1 AT H,VO
5400   X =  PEEK (SP)
5410   ROT =  0: XDRAW N1 AT H,VO: REM  REDRAW IN '0-ROT'
            POSITION.
5420   NEXT K
5430   FOR C = 0 TO 1: REM  FIRST ERASE 'RED' (C = 0) AND THEN
            COLOR TOP LIGHT AREA GREEN.
5440   HCOLOR =  C
5450   TV = 28 + C * 14
5460   FOR V = TV TO TV + 5
5470   HPLOT 137,V TO 143,V
5480   NEXT V
5490   X =  PEEK (SP): REM  KEEP MOTOR RUNNING.
5500   NEXT C
5510   FOR J = 1 TO 50: NEXT J: REM  PAUSE A MOMENT. YOU LOOK
            BOTH WAYS FIRST TOO, DON'T YOU?
5520   FOR J = 1 TO 2: REM  MAKE TWO HONKS OF HORN, BEFORE
            LEAVING LIGHT. MULTIPLE PEEKS BELOW ARE FOR MAKING HIGHER
            PITCHED SOUND.
5530   FOR I = 1 TO 10:X =  PEEK (SP)
            -  PEEK (SP) +  PEEK (SP) -  PEEK
            (SP) +  PEEK (SP) -  PEEK (SP) +  PEEK
            (SP) -  PEEK (SP) +  PEEK (SP) -  PEEK (SP)
5540   NEXT I
5549   REM  DRAW AND ERASE BELOW ARE NOT NECESSARY BUT SLIGHT
            FLICKER SEEMS TO KEEP A SENSE OF CONTINUED ACTIVITY.
5550   XDRAW N1 AT H,VO
5560   XDRAW N1 AT H,VO
5570   NEXT J
5580   FOR K = 1 TO 100: NEXT K: REM  DELAY; MAKE SURE NO CARS
            COMING!
5590   XDRAW N1 AT H,VO: REM  ERASE CAR IN 'STATIONARY' POSITION
            TO PREPARE TO LEAVE.
5599   REM  LEAVE SAME WAY SHAPE CAME, JUST REVERSE DIRECTION.
5600   FOR V = VO TO V1 STEP  - 1
5610   X =  PEEK (SP) -  PEEK (SP)
5620   SCALE =  N1 + F * (V - V1)
5630   XDRAW N1 AT H,V
5640   X =  PEEK (SP) -  PEEK (SP)
5650   XDRAW N1 AT H,V
```

```
5660   NEXT V
5670   RETURN
5671   REM  **      END SPEC DSPLY SUBR     **
5672   REM
5997   REM  *****************************
5998   REM  * DATA FOR POLE & SHAPE TABL *
5999   REM  *****************************
6000   DATA  0,0,0, 0,0,30, -9,-9,-9   : REM   VERT SECTION OF
       POLE.
6010   DATA  0,-3,24, 0,3,24, -9,-9,-9    : REM   BOTT CROSS
       PIECE.
6020   DATA  0,-3,26, 0,3,26, -9,-9,-9    : REM   MIDD CROSS
       PIECE.
6030   DATA  0,-3,28, 0,3,28    : REM   TOP CROSS PIECE.
6190   REM  ***** SHAPE TABLE DATA  ******
6200   DATA  1, 0, 4, 0, 55, 45, 45, 37, 63, 63, 36, 45, 53, 22,
       46, 220, 27, 62, 4, 0
LIST
```

When you RUN the program, try different viewing positions. Try to estimate where the vanishing point is on the screen. Finally, enjoy the special display. And please, no letters about driving down the wrong side of the road; at least we're correct half of the time. Besides, it depends on which continent the scene resides!

**Check Your Comprehension**
What are the (X,Y,Z) coordinates of the base of each telephone pole? _____
Are rotations used in the perspective projection subroutine? _____
Where is the vanishing point on the screen for the special display? _____
What causes the car shape to change size? _____

**EXERCISE**   Make the necessary changes in the COMPREHENSIVE EXAMPLE so the telephone poles are placed 200 feet apart beginning with M0 = 400 and ending with M1 = – 1600. Find ranges for the viewing parameters VX and VZ which will permit VY values between –50 and 50. Set the X-values for the closest points of the road edge and center stripe to the new value of M0 (see the subroutine beginning at 2000, cf., lines 2080 and 2120).

**EXERCISE**   Use the modified programs in Sections 5.3.2 and 5.3.3 to obtain perspective views of some of the three-dimensional objects you created in the other activities. Remember, there are limitations on the sizes of the objects and their positions in X-Y-Z space.

**CHALLENGE**   Modify the COMPREHENSIVE EXAMPLE program so that "half way down the road" there is a right angle turn. Design your picture so there are four telephone poles on each side of the road with each pole being approximately 100 feet apart. You will need to experiment with viewing parameters in order to obtain a complete image.

# ACTIVITY 5.4   Rotations

**LEARNING BY DISCOVERY**   In this section you will learn how to obtain rotations about all the coordinate axes, and how to obtain composite rotations. One application is the viewer can select a normalized perspective view of an object from any position in three-dimensional space.

1. In the previous activities, you experimented with rotations about the Z-axis. The formulas necessary to rotate three-dimensional space DG degrees about the Z-axis are given by

$$RX = X * C - Y * S$$
Rot-Z:   $$RY = X * S + Y * C$$
$$RZ = Z$$

where TH = DG * PI/180, C = COS(TH), S = SIN(TH), and where (RX,RY,RZ) denotes the coordinates of the point (X,Y,Z) rotated about the Z-axis. It is now time to consider other rotation possibilities: rotations about the X-axis, the Y-axis, and composites of such rotations.

　　LOAD the program from Section 5.3.3 in ACTIVITY 5.3 and make the indicated changes.

```
LOAD SEC5.3.3
50 RX = X : RY = Y * C - Z * S : RZ = Y * S + Z * C
LIST 50
```

　　RUN the program using different values for the viewpoint and different rotation angles. Some care must be taken in selecting the viewpoint. If you are not sure where to start, begin with the viewpoint at (180, 20, 30). Experiment with the 360 degree rotation option.

About which coordinate axis does the rotation occur? _____

What happens when negative angles are used? _____

　　Change line 50 to the following:

50 RX = Z * S + X * C : RY = Y : RZ = Z * C - X * S

LIST 50

　　Repeat the procedure of testing the effect of these transformation formulas.

About which coordinate axis does the rotation occur? _____

What is the direction of rotation? _____

2. Make the following changes in the program.

```
50   TX = X * CO - Y * SO:TY = X * SO + Y * CO: REM  TZ =
     Z ; WE OMIT THIS REDUNDANT FORMULA.
51   RX = Z * S + TX * C:RY = TY:RZ = Z * C - TX * S
4040  VTAB 8: PRINT "2) SET NEW ROTATION VIEW": HTAB 5:
      PRINT "CURRENT ANGLES DZ,DY: ";DZ","DY" DEG"
4060  VTAB 13: PRINT "4) ROTATE DZ AND THEN 360 ABOUT
      Y-AXIS"
4100  IF KV = 2 THEN  VTAB 19: HTAB 1: INPUT "INPUT DZ,DY IN
      DEGREES: ";DZ,DY
```

```
4110  IF KV = 3 THEN DSPLY = 1:CO =  COS (DZ
      * FAC):SO =  SIN (DZ * FAC):C =  COS (DY * FAC):S
      =  SIN (DY * FAC): RETURN
4120  IF KV = 4 THEN DSPLY = 2: POKE  - 16368,0:CO =  COS
      (DZ * FAC):SO =  SIN (DZ * FAC): RETURN
LIST
```

To which of the three fundamental rotations does the set of formulas in line 50 correspond? in line 51? _____

The first set of rotation formulas corresponds to Rot-Z; the redundant TZ = Z formula was omitted. The second set of rotation formulas corresponds to Rot-Y. The effect of combining the rotations in this fashion is points are first rotated DZ degrees about the Z-axis, then rotated DY-degrees about the Y-axis. RUN the program using the following input values.

| Viewpoint | Rotation Angles | Option # |
|-----------|-----------------|----------|
| 150, 0, 0 | 30, 0 | 3 |
| 150, 0, 0 | 0, 50 | 3 |
| 150, 0, 0 | 30, 50 | 3 |
| 190, 0, 0 | 30, immaterial | 4 |

Experiment with your own values. Option #4 can be useful in helping you to visualize rotations about the Y-axis. Experiment with negative angles.

Which rotation angle values can be input to "stand up the block L", and have it face forward? backward? right? left? _____

What values of DZ and DY will position the "L" in the "sleeping position," on its "back" with "feet" pointing upward? _____

3. Finally, make the following changes in the program. These will give the viewer the potential for rotation about any line.

   < Be sure the program of SEC5.4.2 is in memory. >

```
50    TX = X * CO  -  Y * SO:TY = X * SO +  Y * CO: REM  TZ =
      Z
51    SX = Z * S1 +  TX * C1:SZ = Z * C1  -  TX * S1: REM  SY
      = TY
52    RX = SX:RY = TY * C  -  SZ * S:RZ = TY * S +  SZ * C
4040  VTAB 8: PRINT "2) SET NEW ROTATION VIEW": HTAB 5: PRINT
      "CURRENT ANGLES DZ,DY,DX: ";DZ","DY","DX" DEG"
4060  VTAB 13: PRINT "4) COMPOSITE: ROT-Z:ROT-Y:ROT-X(360)"
4100  IF KV = 2 THEN  VTAB 19: HTAB 1: INPUT "INPUT DZ,DY,DX
      IN DEGREES: ";DZ,DY,DX
4110  IF KV = 3 THEN DSPLY = 1:CO =  COS (DZ * FAC):SO
      =  SIN (DZ * FAC):C1 =  COS (DY * FAC):S1
      =  SIN (DY * FAC):C =  COS (DX * FAC):S =  SIN (DX *
      FAC): RETURN
4120  IF KV = 4 THEN DSPLY = 2: POKE  - 16368,0:CO =  COS
      (DZ * FAC):SO =  SIN (DZ * FAC):C1 =  COS
      (DY * FAC):S1 =  SIN (DY * FAC): RETURN
LIST
```

When RUNning the program, experiment with different viewpoints and different angles of rotation. Setting the viewpoint at (200, 0, 0) should permit you complete freedom of input for rotation angles. Either mentally or with an "L" shaped object in hand, try to work through the process of each rotation to obtain the final result. Use option #4 to rotate the object about the X-axis.

What rotation angle values should be entered to equivalently obtain a simple rotation about the X-axis? _____

Compare the final positions of the object when the following two sets of rotation angles are input: DZ,DY,DX = 270,20,−90 ; or 90,160,90. What is your conclusion regarding any suggestion there may be a one-to-one relationship between the rotation angles DZ,DY,DX and the final position? _____

**DISCUSSION**   Consider the rotation formulas for rotating points about the Z-axis.
$$RX = X * C - Y * S$$
$$RY = X * S + Y * C$$
$$RZ = Z$$
where C and S are the COSine and SINe values of the angle of rotation. The formulas for rotation about the X-axis and the Y-axis can be obtained by a simple renaming process. That is, suppose Z is renamed "X." How should X and Y be renamed to maintain a right-handed coordinate system?  See Figure 5.4.1 which shows the labeled axes.

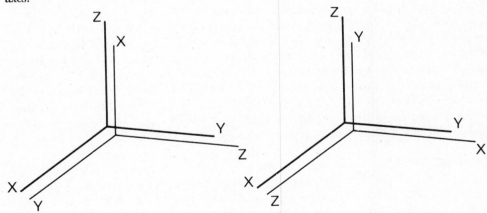

Figure 5.4.1

If the following replacements are made (literally)
$$Z <--- X ; \quad X <--- Y ; \quad Y <--- Z$$
then the formulas for Rot-X will be obtained.
$$RY = Y * C - Z * S$$
$$RZ = Y * S + Z * C$$
$$RX = X$$
Similarly, literal replacement of "X" by "Z," "Z" by "Y," "Y" by "X" will result in the rotation formulas

$$RZ = Z * C - X * S$$
$$RX = Z * S + X * C$$
$$RY = Y$$

These rotation formulas were applied in Section 1 of this activity.

In Sections 2 and 3, axis rotations were combined by successive applications of the formulas to obtain a composite transformation of the object. The programmatic changes in Section 2 have the following effect. First, the object is rotated DZ degrees about the Z-axis, then it is rotated DY degrees about the Y-axis. In Section 3, this sequence of two rotations was followed by a third rotation: rotation about the X-axis. The net effect of composite rotations is they permit the viewer to (essentially) remain stationary and yet view the object from any direction. The different view directions are obtained by rotating the object through composite axis rotations. A major advantage of this technique is one can obtain normalized projective views of an object from any direction. This will be explored in the next activity.

In forming composites of rotations in Section 3, the order was specifically: Rot-Z - Rot-Y - Rot-X. There are other order possibilities for combining the three fundamental rotations (in fact, 6 = 3*2*1 permutations altogether). The reader is encouraged to experiment with other composite possibilities. However, there is no need to study the other possibilities at length. It can be proven that any order and number of rotation composites can be duplicated with an appropriate Rot-Z - Rot-Y - Rot-X composition.

The following exercise can be used to help you see the effect of forming composites of rotations. Take an object such as a book or coffee cup and hold it at eye level. Imagine your eye to be positioned on the X-axis; the Z-axis points upward and the Y-axis extends to your right. Now, rotate the object about the Z-axis through a certain angle, for example, 45 degrees. Remember, if you look from the positive Z-axis, the rotation is counterclockwise. Now rotate the object counterclockwise about the Y-axis, say 45 degrees. The top of the object will appear to move down and closer to you. Finally, rotate the object about the X-axis through an angle of 30 degrees. The top position will move from a twelve noon position to an eleven o'clock position. The final position is the result of a composite of three rotations. As you look at the object, the projected image is a normalized perspective view.

**COMPREHENSIVE EXAMPLE**   In the program below, a rocket is constructed using a three-dimensional wire-frame design to outline its shape. The rocket has two stages: the top which is cylindrically shaped, and the much larger bottom stage which is elliptically shaped lengthwise. Cross sections perpendicular to the Z-axis (or rocket length) are circles (see Figure 5.4.2).

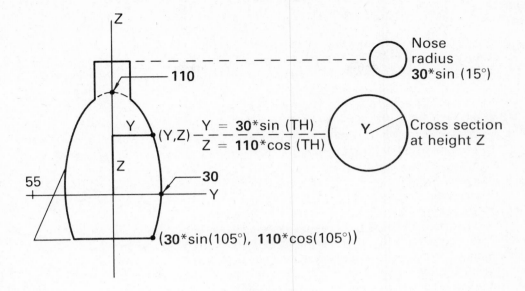

Figure 5.4.2

Through the use of Rot-Z - Rot-Y - Rot-X composite transformations, the viewer has the ability to rotate the object into any position desired. After the rotation angles are entered, a check is made to determine if the image can be contained within the screen boundaries. This is accomplished by calculating the projection coordinates of the nose and fin tips. If the difference between the maximum and minimum coordinate values of these special points is greater than the screen resolution, the user is notified and processing is terminated. For certain "overhead" views, this test is insufficient; these situations will be handled by the viewing distance limitations.

```
NEW
10  REM   ********************************
11  REM   *           CE5.4             *
12  REM   ********************************
13  REM
14  REM   ***** BRANCH AROUND SUBRTS *****
15  LOMEM: 24576: GOTO 100
16  REM
47  REM   ********************************
48  REM   * MULTIPLE ROTATION/PERSP PROJ *
49  REM   ********************************
50  TX = X * CO - Y * SO:TY = X * SO + Y * CO
52  SX = Z * S1 + TX * C1:SZ = Z * C1 - TX * S1
54  RX = SX:RY = TY * C2 - SZ * S2:RZ = TY * S2 + SZ * C2
56  A = RY / (RX - DS):B = RZ / (RX - DS)
58  PX = RY - A * RX:PY = RZ - B * RX
60  H% = OH + PX:V% = OV - PY
62  RETURN
```

```
63  REM  **    END ROTATION/PERSP PROJ  **
64  REM
67  REM  ********************************
68  REM  *    (CIRCLE) PLOTTING SUBRT    *
69  REM  ********************************
70  X = R:Y = 0: GOSUB 50
72  HPLOT H%,V%:H%(O,I) = H%:V%(O,I) = V%
74  FOR K = 1 TO 24
76  X = X(K):Y = Y(K): GOSUB 50
78  HPLOT  TO H%,V%:H%(K,I) = H%:V%(K,I) = V%
80  NEXT K
82  RETURN
83  REM  **      END PLOTTING SUBRT      **
84  REM
97  REM  ********************************
98  REM  *           MAIN PROGRAM        *
99  REM  ********************************
100  GOSUB 1000: REM  GO CALC COSINES AND SINES
110  DIM H%(24,10),V%(24,10),X(24),Y(24),HF%(3),VF%(3): REM
     H%,V% HOLD THE SCREEN COORDS FOR EACH OF THE 10+1 CIRCLES
     THAT MAKE UP CIRCULAR CROSS SECTIONS OF ROCKET.
120  TEXT : HOME
130  PRINT "ENTER YOUR VIEWING DISTANCE DS.": INPUT "SET DS
     >=  2000: ";DS
140  INPUT "ENTER ROT-Z ANGLE (IN DEG): ";DZ:DZ = DZ * FAC
150  INPUT "ENTER ROT-Y ANGLE (IN DEG): ";DY:DY = DY * FAC
160  INPUT "ENTER ROT-X ANGLE (IN DEG): ";DX:DX = DX * FAC
170  CO =  COS (DZ):SO =  SIN (DZ):C1 =  COS (DY):S1 =  SIN
     (DY):C2 =  COS (DX):S2 =  SIN (DX)
180  RA = 110:RB = 30: REM  RA = SEMI-MAJOR LENGTH OF ELLIPSE
     USED FOR ROCKET BODY; RB = SEMI-MINOR LENGTH OF SAME
     ELLIPSE.
190  GOSUB 3000: REM  GOTO ROUTINE TO DETERMINE THE PROJ COORDS
     OF SPECIAL POINTS (INITIALLY OH,OV ARE ZERO). ROUTINE
     DETERMINES THE OH,OV NECESSARY TO CENTER OBJECT ON SCREEN,
     AND TESTS TO SEE IF COMPLETE IMAGE CAN BE DISPLAYED.
200  HGR : POKE  - 16302,0: HCOLOR =  3: REM  FULL SCRN PAGE
     1.
210  HPLOT HT%,VT%: REM  PLOT TIP OF ROCKET NOSE 'SPEAR'
     CALCULATED IN SUBRT AT 3000.
220  ZC = RA * C(1): REM  ZC IS THE HEIGHT OF THE BOTTOM OF
     THE CYLINDRICALLY SHAPED SECOND STAGE OF THE ROCKET.
230  X = 0:Y = 0:Z = ZC + 35: GOSUB 50: REM  HERE X,Y,Z IS
     THE COORD OF THE BASE OF THE NOSE 'SPEAR'.
240  HPLOT  TO H%,V%:H2% = H%:V2% = V%: REM  DRAW NOSE
     'SPEAR'.
```

```
250  R = RB * S(1): GOSUB 2000: REM  R IS THE RADIUS OF THE
     CYLINDRICALLY SHAPED 2ND STAGE. GO CALC X,Y COORDS OF
     CIRCLE OF RADIUS R CENTERED AT ORIGIN. 2ND STAGE CROSS
     SECTIONS OBTAINED BY PLACING THIS CIRCLE AT DIFFERENT
     Z-HEIGHTS.
260  FOR I = 1 TO 3: REM  FOR EACH OF THREE DIFFERENT ...
270  Z = ZC + 10 * (4 - I): REM  ... HEIGHTS PLACED 10 PIXELS
     APART BEGINNING WITH ZC + 30 TO ZC + 10, ...
280  GOSUB 70: REM  ... PLOT THE PERSPECTIVE PROJECTION OF THE
     ROTATED CROSS-SECTIONAL CIRCLE.
290  NEXT I
300  FOR I = 4 TO 10: REM  FOR EACH OF THE REMAINING 7
     CROSS-SECTIONAL CIRCLES IN THE 1ST STAGE ...
310  J = I - 3
320  Z = RA * C(J): REM  ... PLACED AT A HEIGHT GIVEN BY THE
     DISPLACEMENT ALONG THE SEMI MAJOR AXIS FOR PARAMETRIC
     VALUE J*(15 DEG) ...
330  R = RB * S(J): GOSUB 2000: REM  ... USING A RADIUS
     CORRESP TO DISPLACEMENT ALONG THE SEMI-MINOR AXIS FOR
     PARAMETRIC VALUE J*(15 DEG), GO DETERM X,Y COORDS OF
     CROSS-SECTIONAL CIRCLE.
340  GOSUB 70: REM  GO ROT, PROJ AND PLOT CROSS-SECTIONAL
     CIRCLE.
350  NEXT I
360  FOR K = 0 TO 23 STEP 2: REM  FOR EACH ANGLE BETWEEN 0 AND
     23*15 = 330 DEG STEPPING BY 2*15 = 30 DEGREES, ...
370  HPLOT H2%,V2%: REM  START BY PLOTTING TOP POINT AT BASE OF
     NOSE 'SPEAR'.
380  FOR I = 1 TO 10: REM  FOR EACH OF THE TEN CROSS-SECTIONAL
     CIRCLES ...
390  HPLOT  TO H%(K,I),V%(K,I): REM  PLOT TO THE POINT ON THE
     I-TH CROSS-SECTIONAL CIRCLE CORRESP TO K*15 DEGREES.
400  NEXT I,K
410  FOR K = 0 TO 18 STEP 6: REM  AT 90 DEGREE INTERVALS
     BEGINNING WITH THE ANGLE AT 0 DEGREES, ...
420  HPLOT H%(K,8),V%(K,8): REM  ... PLOT A 'FIN' AT THE ROCKET
     BASE ...
430  HPLOT  TO HF%(K / 6),VF%(K / 6): REM  TIPS OF 'FINS' WERE
     CALCULATED IN SUBRT AT 3000.
440  HPLOT  TO H%(K,10),V%(K,10)
450  NEXT K
460  GET Q$: REM  WAIT FOR KEYPRESS ...
470  POKE  - 16301,0: HOME : VTAB 21: REM  SET MIXED MODE.
480  INPUT "TRY ANOTHER VIEW < Y,N >? ";K$
490  IF K$ = "Y" THEN 120
500  TEXT : HOME : END
501  REM  **      END MAIN PROGRAM       **
```

```
 502  REM
 997  REM  *******************************
 998  REM  * CALC COS/SIN EVERY 15 DEGS  *
 999  REM  *******************************
1000  FAC = 3.14152966 / 180
1010  DIM C(24),S(24)
1020  K = 0
1030  FOR D = 0 TO 360 STEP 15
1040  TH = D * FAC
1050  C(K) =  COS (TH):S(K) =  SIN (TH)
1060  K = K + 1
1070  NEXT D
1080  RETURN
1081  REM  **    END CALC COS/SIN SUBR  **
1082  REM
1097  REM  *******************************
1098  REM  * CALC X,Y ON CIRCLE @15 DEG *
1099  REM  *******************************
2000  FOR K = 1 TO 24
2010  X(K) = R * C(K):Y(K) = R * S(K)
2020  NEXT K
2030  RETURN
2031  REM  **    END CALC PTS ON CIRCL  **
2032  REM
2997  REM  *******************************
2998  REM  * CENTER IMAGE AND TEST SUBR *
2999  REM  *******************************
3000  OH = 0:OV = 0: REM  BEGIN WITH OH AND OV ZERO.
3010  X = 0:Y = 0:Z = 155: GOSUB 50: REM  X,Y,Z TIP OF NOSE
      'SPEAR'; GET ROT AND PROJ COORDS.
3020  HT% = H%:VT% = V%: REM  STORE IT AWAY.
3030  HO% = H%:H1% = H%:VO% = V%:V1% = V%: REM  HO%, H1%,
      VO%, V1% ARE MIN AND MAX COORDS OF SCREEN IMAGE OF NOSE
      TIP AND FIN TIPS (WHICH WILL BE FURTHER DETERMINED
      BELOW).
3040  FOR K = 0 TO 18 STEP 6
3050  X = 55 * C(K):Y = 55 * S(K):Z = RA * C(7): REM  X,Y,Z
      COORDS OF FIN TIP PTS.
3060  GOSUB 50: REM  GO CALC ROT AND PROJ COORDS OF TIPS.
3070  HF%(K / 6) = H%:VF%(K / 6) = V%: REM  STORE THEM AWAY,
      AND THEN CALC MIN AND MAX COORD VALUES (INCLUDING NOSE
      TIP PROJ COORDS).
3080  IF H% < HO% THEN HO% = H%
3090  IF H% > H1% THEN H1% = H%
3100  IF V% < V1% THEN V1% = V%
3110  IF V% > VO% THEN VO% = V%
3120  NEXT K
```

```
3130   IF (H1% - H0%) > 279 OR (V0% - V1%) > 191 THEN
       TEXT : HOME : PRINT "IMAGE OUT OF SCREEN BOUNDS.": END :
       REM IF THE DISPLACEMENTS FROM NOSE TIP TO FIN TIP ARE
       LARGER THAN SCREEN WIDTH OR HEIGHT THEN ABORT.
       OR HEIGHT THEN ABORT.
3140   OH = 140 -  INT ((H1% - H0%) / 2) - H0%:OV = 95 -
       INT ((V0% - V1%) / 2) - V1%: REM  ... OTHERWISE,
       DETERMINE SCREEN COORDS TO CENTER OBJECT.
3150   HT% = HT% + OH:VT% = OV + VT%: REM  ADJUST SCREEN
       COORDS OF NOSE 'SPEAR' TIP.
3160   FOR I = 0 TO 3
3170   HF%(I) = OH + HF%(I):VF%(I) = OV + VF%(I): REM  ...
       AND ADJUST SCREEN COORDS OF FIN TIPS.
3180   NEXT I
3190   RETURN
3191   REM  **   END OF CENTERING/TEST  **
LIST
```

When RUNning the program, you are requested to input the viewing distance DS. Your viewpoint will be from the point (DS,0,0). To view the basic cross-sectional designs of the rocket, use the following input : DS = 2000; DZ, DY, DX = 0, 0, 0; and DS = 2000; DZ, DY, DX = 0, 90, 0.

**Check Your Comprehension**
What do the variables C0,S0; C1,S1; and C2,S2 represent in the above program and what purpose do they serve? _____
When drawing the cross-sectional circles, what is the angle between the successively calculated points on the circle? _____
Where is the vanishing point for every display created by the program? _____
What input parameters are necessary to have the rocket pointed directly toward you?

_____

What do the values H0%, H1%, V1%, and V0% represent in the program? _____

**EXERCISE**   Using the wire-frame technique of the COMPREHENSIVE EXAMPLE program, exhibit a sphere. Use horizontal circle cross sections, then connect the points on the circles pole-to-pole. The horizontal circles correspond to circles of latitude, while the circles pole-to-pole are circles of longitude.

**CHALLENGE**   Create an image of Saturn with rings.

# ACTIVITY 5.5   Viewpoint & Normalized Perspective Projections

**LEARNING BY DISCOVERY**   In this activity you will learn how to obtain a normalized perspective view from any viewpoint in three-dimensional space.

**DISCUSSION**   In the previous activity you used composite rotations to rotate an object in order to see it from different views. If the viewer is positioned on the X-axis, a normalized perspective view is obtained (since the projection plane is perpendicular to your line-of-sight with the origin).

Consider the problem of obtaining a normalized perspective view from any viewpoint in three-dimensional space. There are basically two ways of accomplishing this.

(1)  Determine the plane incident with the origin and perpendicular to the view direction (or vector) (VX,VY,VZ). Establish a PX-PY coordinate system on this plane with origin coinciding with (0,0,0), and PY-axis the projection of the Z-axis. Given an arbitrary point (X,Y,Z) in three-dimensional space, determine the plane coordinates (PX,PY) of the projected point. See Figure 5.5.1. For a description of this procedure, the reader should consult the paperback MICROCOMPUTER GRAPHICS by Roy B. Meyers, Addison-Wesley Publishing Company (1982).

(2)  Rotate the object until the original view direction is equivalent to a view from a coordinate axis. The viewpoint on the coordinate axis should be positioned at the same viewing distance from the origin as the original viewpoint. The projection plane is the coordinate plane perpendicular to the (viewer's) coordinate axis. See Figure 5.5.1.

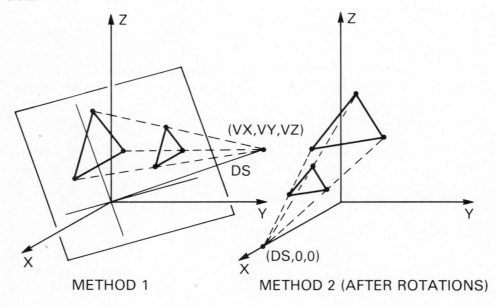

METHOD 1                                    METHOD 2 (AFTER ROTATIONS)

Figure 5.5.1

The "machinery" necessary to pursue the second option is already available.

Let's first consider the viewing position. The notion of viewpoint discussed here is not precisely the same as the interpretation used earlier. The distinction is a result of the difference in projection planes.

There are two aspects of viewing position of fundamental importance: (1) the viewing distance (distance the viewer is from the origin), and (2) the viewing direction. A popular method of describing viewing position is through spherical coordinates. In this representation, the distance from the origin and two rotation angles are used to identify a point in three-dimensional space. The distance from the origin is tradition- ally denoted by RHO. The two rotation angles are denoted by PHI and TH(eta), and their geometric interpretation is indicated in the Figure 5.5.2.

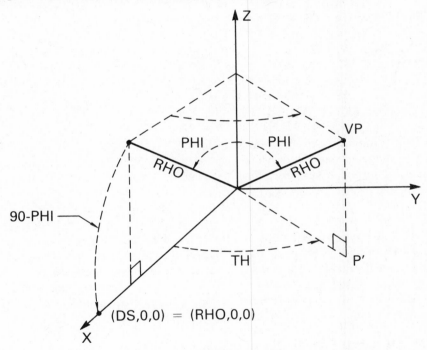

Figure 5.5.2

TH corresponds to the angle of rotation needed to rotate the positive X-axis into the line segment OP', where P' is the foot of the perpendicular of VP onto the X-Y plane. PHI is the angle needed to rotate the positive Z-axis into the line through O and VP. Observe the point VP can be obtained by rotating the point (DS,0,0) = (RHO,0,0) through an angle −(90 −PHI) degrees about the Y-axis, then followed by rotation TH degrees about the Z-axis. If the process is reversed, then VP can be rotated into (DS,0,0) via the rotation sequence: −TH degrees about the Z-axis, followed by rota- tion 90-PHI degrees about the Y-axis.

Using composite rotations, the plane perpendicular to the direction VP will be rotated into the Y-Z plane. The point VP will be rotated into the point on the X-axis RHO units from the origin. This is the solution to our problem.

Specifically, to obtain a normalized perspective view from any viewpoint in three-dimensional space, one can apply the following procedure. Identify the viewpoint in spherical coordinates, i.e., identify the distance RHO from the origin and the angles TH and PHI. Rotate the object to be observed through an angle $-$TH about the Z-axis, then rotate through an angle 90-PHI about the Y-axis. Finally, determine the perspective projection of the rotated object onto the Y-Z plane using the viewpoint at $(VX,VY,VZ) = (RHO,0,0)$.

A summary of the required transformation formulas appears below. They are adaptations of the formulas for the composite rotation, Rot-Z followed by Rot-Y, developed in Section 5.4.2.

GIVEN: RHO,
        PHI, TH (in degrees)

DEFINE: C0 = COS($-$TH * FAC) : S0 = SIN($-$TH * FAC)
        C1 = COS((90 $-$ PHI)*FAC) : S1 = SIN((90 $-$ PHI)*FAC)

FOR EACH: X, Y, Z

COMPUTE: SX = X * C0 $-$ Y * S0 : SY = X * S0 + Y * C0
        RX = Z * S1 + SX * C1 : RZ = Z * C1 $-$ SX * S1
        AB = RHO / (RHO $-$ RX)
        PX = SY * AB : PY = RZ * AB
        H% = OH + PX : V% = OV $-$ PY

In the formulas above, the expressions for AB, PX, and PY require some explanation. According to the model developed earlier (e.g., LINES 50 - 60 in Section 5.4.2), the following formulas will persist for the viewpoint $(VX,VY,VZ) = (RHO,0,0)$:

A = (SY $-$ VY) / (RX $-$ VX) = SY / (RX $-$ RHO)
B = (RZ $-$ VZ) / (RX $-$ VX) = RZ / (RX $-$ RHO)
PX = SY $-$ A * RX   :   PY = RZ $-$ B * RX

Substitute the expressions for A and B into the right-hand side of the equations for PX and PY. Factor the common terms SY and RZ, respectively, from the resulting expressions for PX and PY. The remaining factor in each expression is AB = 1 $-$ (RX/ (RX $-$ RHO)). Algebraic simplification will reduce AB to the form indicated earlier. We have made these changes primarily to reduce the number of required multiplications and additions.

**COMPREHENSIVE EXAMPLE**  In the program below you will experiment with normalized perspective projections. You will be requested to input the view distance RHO from the origin, and the viewing angles PHI and THeta. There is one added feature. The CLIPPING ALGORITHM will be used to clip portions of the display which may extend beyond the screen boundaries. Although the CLIPPING ALGORITHM will handle any problems with off-screen points, the viewer must be careful not to select a viewing point contained in the object to be displayed. What type of error may result if this circumstance should occur? The ON ERR GOTO statement could be used to control such situations and prevent early program termination; nevertheless, it will not be used here.

```
NEW
LOAD CLIPPING ALGORITHM
```

```
10   REM   *******************************
11   REM   *          CE5.5           *
12   REM   *******************************
13   REM
14   REM   ****  BRANCH AROUND SUBRTS  ****
15   LOMEM: 24576: GOTO 100
16   REM
17   REM   *******************************
18   REM   *       CLIPPING ALGORITHM      *
19   REM   *******************************
```
     < The CLIPPING ALGORITHM is inserted here. >
```
35   REM   **         END CLIPPING        **
36   REM
47   REM   *******************************
48   REM   *  NORMALIZED PERSP PROJ SUBRT *
49   REM   *******************************
50   SX = X * CO - Y * SO:SY = X * SO + Y * CO
52   RX = Z * S1 + SX * C1:RZ = Z * C1 - SX * S1
54   AB = RHO / (RHO - RX)
56   PX = SY * AB:PY = RZ * AB
58   H =  INT (OH + PX):V =  INT (OV - PY)
60   RETURN
61   REM   **      END PERSP PROJ SUBRT     **
62   REM
97   REM   *******************************
98   REM   *        MAIN PROGRAM          *
99   REM   *******************************
100  FAC = 3.14159266 / 180
110  DIM XP(1),YP(1),T%(1),B%(1),L%(1),R%(1)
120  GOSUB 5000: REM  GO READ DATA GENERATING OBJECT TO BE
     DISPLAYED.
130  HO = 0:H1 = 279:V1 = 0:VO = 191: REM  VIEWPORT
     PARAMETERS.
140  OH = 140:OV = 95: REM  CENTER SCREEN.
150  HGR : HCOLOR =  3
160  HOME : VTAB 21
170  PRINT "ENTER THE VIEWPT:": PRINT "RHO (DIST > = 85);
     PHI, TH < DEGREES >"
180  INPUT "RHO, PHI, TH(ETA): ";RHO,PHI,TH
190  CO =  COS ( - TH * FAC):SO =  SIN ( - TH * FAC): REM
     COMPUTE COS AND SIN FOR ROTATION BY -TH ABOUT Z-AXIS.
200  C1 =  COS ((90 - PHI) * FAC):S1 =  SIN ((90 - PHI) *
     FAC): REM  COMPUTE COS AND SIN FOR ROTATION BY 90-PHI
     ABOUT Y-AXIS.
210  POKE  - 16302,0: REM  SET FULL SCRN GRAPHICS.
220  NS = 0: REM  STARTING INDEX OF ARRAY CONTAINING PT DATA.
230  GOSUB 1000: REM  GOTO PLOTTING ROUTINE TO DISPLAY OBJECT.
```

```
240   GOSUB 2000: REM  GOTO SPECIAL DISPLAY.
250   HOME : VTAB 21: POKE  - 16301,0: REM  SET MIXED GRAPHICS
      MODE.
260   PRINT "TRY A NEW VIEWPT <Y,N>? ";: GET Q$
270   IF Q$ = "Y" THEN 150
280   TEXT : HOME : END
281   REM  **     END MAIN PROGRAM        **
282   REM
997   REM  ********************************
998   REM  *     PLOTTING SUBROUTINE     *
999   REM  ********************************
1000  FL = 1: REM  SET FLAG 'ON' FOR DENOTING START OF
      CONTINUOUSLY CONNECTED PTS.
1010  FOR K = NS TO NP
1020  IF Z(K) = EPL THEN FL = 1: NEXT K: REM  IF END OF PLOT
      THEN SET FLAG 'ON' AND GO BACK FOR FIRST POINT.
1030  PH = H:PV = V: REM  STORE COORDINATES OF LAST PLOTTED
      POINT.
1040  X = X(K):Y = Y(K):Z = Z(K): GOSUB 50: REM  CALCULATE
      SCREEN COORDS OF PROJECTED POINT; RETURNED IN H,V.
1050  IF FL THEN FL = 0: NEXT K: RETURN : REM  IF START FLAG
      IS 'ON' THEN ANOTHER DATA PT MUST BE READ; THE CLIPPING
      ALGRTHM NEEDS TWO PTS. 'RETURN' IS NEEDED IN CASE OF NO
      MORE POINTS.
1060  XP(0) = PH:YP(0) = PV:XP(1) = H:YP(1) = V: REM  STORE
      SCREEN COORDS IN ARRAYS FOR CLIPPING ALG.
1070  GOSUB 20: REM  GO TO CLIPPING ALGORITHM.
1080  NEXT K
1090  RETURN
1091  REM  **     END PLOTTING SUBRT     **
1092  REM
1997  REM  ********************************
1998  REM  * SPECL PG FLIPPING DISPLAY *
1999  REM  ********************************
2000  POKE 230,64: REM  SET HIRES DRAW PAGE TO PG 2.
2010  CALL 62450: REM  CLEAR HIRES PAGE 2.
2020  NS = 31: REM  INDEX OF START OF NON-LETTER POINTS.
2030  GOSUB 1000: REM  GO PLOT NON-LETTER POINTS ON HIRES PAGE
      2.
2040  POKE 230,32: REM  RESET DRAW PAGE BYTE TO PAGE ONE.
2050  POKE  - 16368,0: REM  SET KEYBOARD STROBE TO PERMIT
      READING KEYPRESS.
2060  FOR I = 0 TO 1 STEP 0: REM  REPEAT INDEFINITELY UNTIL
      ...
2070  POKE  - 16299 - SW,0: REM  FLIP HIRES PAGE DISPLAY
      SWITCH.
```

```
2080   FOR J = 1 TO 400: NEXT : REM   DELAY
2090   IF SW = 1 AND  PEEK ( - 16384) > 127 THEN  POKE  -
       16368,0: RETURN : REM  IF KEYPRESS HAS OCCURRED AND WE
       ARE ON THE PAGE 1 DISPLAY CYCLE, THEN RESET STROBE AND
       RETURN TO MAIN.
2100   SW =  NOT SW: REM  CHANGE DISPLAY SWITCH.
2110   NEXT I: REM  DISPLAY OTHER PAGE.
2111   REM
4997   REM  ********************************
4998   REM  *      READ DATA SUBROUTINE     *
4999   REM  ********************************
5000   EPL = - 99: REM  END OF PLOT VALUE.
5010   NP = 56: REM  # OF DATA POINTS.
5020   DIM X(NP),Y(NP),Z(NP)
5030   FOR K = 0 TO NP
5040   READ X(K),Y(K),Z(K)
5050   NEXT K
5060   RETURN
5061   REM  **     END READ DATA SUBRT    **
5062   REM
5997   REM  ********************************
5998   REM  *      OBJECT POINT DATA      *
5999   REM  ********************************
6000   DATA  50,-43,20, 50,-43,-20, -99,-99,-99, 50,-31,20,
       50,-31,-20, -99,-99,-99, 50,-45,0, 50,-31,0,
       -99,-99,-99 : REM  LETTER 'H'
6010   DATA  50,-13,20, 50,-25,20, 50,-25,-20, 50,-13,-20,
       -99,-99,-99, 50,-25,0, 50,-13,0, -99,-99,-99     :
       REM LETTER 'E'
6020   DATA  50,-7,20, 50,-7,-20, 50,5,-20, -99,-99,-99
       : REM  LETTER 'L'
6030   DATA  50,11,20, 50,11,-20, 50,23,-20, -99,-99,-99
       : REM  LETTER 'L'
6040   DATA  50,29,20, 50,29,-20, 50,43,-20, 50,43,20,
       50,29,20, -99,-99,-99     : REM  LETTER 'O'
6050   DATA  50,-52,27, 50,-52,-27, 50,52,-27, 50,52,27,
       50,-52,27, -99,-99,-99
       : REM  BILLBOARD BOUNDARY.
6060   DATA  50,-47,27, 60,-47,27, 65,-47,22,
       65,-43,22, 65,-51,22, -99,-99,-99    : REM  'LEFT'
       LIGHT STANDARD.
6070   DATA  50,47,27, 60,47,27, 65,47,22, 65,43,22, 65,51,22,
       -99,-99,-99     : REM  'RIGHT' LIGHT STANDARD.
6080   DATA  50,-47,-27, 50,-47,-80, -99,-99,-99,
       50,0,-27, 50,0,-80, -99,-99,-99, 50,47,-27,
       50,47,-80,  : REM  LEG SUPPORTS OF BILLBOARD.
6081   REM  **    END OF POINT DATA      **
LIST
```

RUN the program using at least the following set of input values:

| RHO | PHI | TH(ETA) |
|-----|-----|---------|
| 150 | 90 | 0 |
| 85 | 90 | 0 |
| 85 | 70 | 30 |
| 120 | 115 | 20 |
| 92 | 80 | −40 |

**Check Your Comprehension**

What parameter values must be assigned to RHO, PHI and TH(eta) to position yourself on the X-axis 200 units from the origin? _____

How is the flashing billboard effect accomplished? _____

If the values 85, 130, and 0 are input for RHO, PHI, and TH(eta), strange lines crisscross the screen. What do you think is happening? _____

What would you expect to happen with the input values 100, 270, 0? Try it! _____

---

The CLIPPING ALGORITHM can be an effective way to handle points which extend beyond the screen boundaries. The disadvantage is it further slows down program execution. In the program above, the billboard boundaries, light standards, and legs are drawn on both high resolution pages. By flipping the page display switch alternately between Page 1 and Page 2, one sees the lettering on Page 1, while on Page 2 the billboard space is blank. Because the remaining sections of the billboard are the same on both pages, there is no loss of these portions of the display.

**EXERCISE**   The COMPREHENSIVE EXAMPLE program is very inefficient in the way the display on high resolution Page 2 is created. (Points previously calculated for drawing on Page 1 are recalculated for drawing on Page 2.) Modify the program so the drawing on Page 1 and Page 2 can occur within the same loop. As each segment is calculated, alternately set the draw page byte location 230 to 32 and 64 for drawing the connecting lines. In this way, the screen coordinates only need to be calculated once.

**EXERCISE**   Alter the COMPREHENSIVE EXAMPLE program so that the display can be used for orthogonal projections; that is, an orthogonal projection is applied after the object is rotated.

**CHALLENGE**   Add a road next to the billboard. Clip the sections of the road which will cross through the billboard display, but which really lie behind the billboard.

# ACTIVITY 5.6   Scaling Projected Displays

**LEARNING BY DISCOVERY**   In this activity you will learn how to use scaling techniques in three-dimensional graphics.

1. In the previous activity, the CLIPPING ALGORITHM was used to a display a projected image when it possibly extends beyond the screen boundaries. There are

occasions when it is desirable to see the full display. This can sometimes result in considerable trial and error in selecting the view position. In other cases, it may be altogether impossible to display the image entirely within the screen. An alternative, albeit a brute force method, is to determine a suitable "enclosing" rectangle for the projected image, then use scaling techniques to obtain the final display. As you have previously seen, scaling methods have the added advantage you can display the image anywhere you want on the screen. Let's consider a few examples.

One simple way of controlling the size of the projected image is to simply scale the projected coordinates. It will not be shown here, but, geometrically, scaling is equivalent to moving the projection plane either away from the viewer (increasing the image size) or closer to the viewer (decreasing the image size). Once the projection coordinates PX and PY have been determined, they can be scaled using the following rule:

$$H = PX * XSCL : V = PY * YSCL$$

where XSCL and YSCL denote scale factors. By varying the values of the scale factors, the size of the projected image can be controlled.

2. In the program below, DATA is supplied for a pyramid in three-dimensional space. The dimensions of the pyramid are too large to display entirely on the screen, regardless of the viewing distance from the origin. The objective is to determine the minimum enclosing rectangle of the projected image, then use scaling techniques to transform the image to a predetermined viewport on the screen. If a new viewing position (viewpoint) is selected, it will be necessary to repeat the entire procedure.

Enter the following program.

```
NEW
15   GOTO 100
50   SX = X * CO - Y * SO:SY = X * SO + Y * CO
52   RX = Z * S1 + SX * C1:RZ = Z * C1 - SX * S1
54   AB = RHO / (RHO - RX)
56   PX = SY * AB:PY = RZ * AB
58   RETURN
100  H0 = 80:H1 = 200:V0 = 140:V1 = 20
110  FAC = 3.14159266 / 180:SFAC = 1.20
120  READ NP
130  DIM X(NP),Y(NP),Z(NP)
140  FOR K = 0 TO NP
150  READ X(K),Y(K),Z(K)
160  NEXT K
170  HGR : HCOLOR =  3: HOME : VTAB 21
180  INPUT "ENTER RHO, PHI, TH(ETA): ";RHO,PHI,TH
190  CO =  COS ( - TH * FAC):SO =  SIN ( - TH * FAC):C1 =
     COS ((90 - PHI) * FAC):S1 =  SIN ((90 - PHI) * FAC)
200  XL = 1E38:XR= - XL:YL = XL:YR = XR: REM   INITIALIZE
     MIN AND MAX PX & PY VALUES.
210  FOR K = 0 TO NP
220  X = X(K):Y = Y(K):Z = Z(K): GOSUB 50
```

```
230  PX(K) = PX:PY(K) = PY
240  IF PX < XL THEN XL = PX
250  IF PX > XR THEN XR = PX
260  IF PY < YL THEN YL = PY
270  IF PY > YR THEN YR = PY
280  NEXT K
290  XSCL = (H1 - HO) / (XR - XL):YSCL = (VO - V1) / (YR
     - YL)
330  OH = HO - XL * XSCL:OV = VO + YL * YSCL
340  FOR K = 0 TO NP
350  H%(K) = OH + PX(K) * XSCL:V%(K) = OV - PY(K) * YSCL
360  NEXT K
370  HPLOT H%(0),V%(0) TO H%(1),V%(1) TO H%(2),V%(2) TO
     H%(3),V%(3) TO   H%(0),V%(0) TO H%(4),V%(4) TO
     H%(1),V%(1)
380  HPLOT H%(3),V%(3) TO H%(4),V%(4) TO H%(2),V%(2)
390  PRINT "TRY ANOTHER VIEW?";: GET K$
400  IF K$ = "Y" THEN 170
410  TEXT : HOME : END
500  DATA  4
510  DATA  100,200,50, 200,200,50, 200,300,50, 100,300,50,
     150,250,150
LIST
```

RUN the program selecting a variety of different viewpoints. The viewing parameters RHO = 600, PHI = 60, TH = 30 will get you started. Although the method will permit a wide range of viewpoints to be entered, some choices will give misleading results. For example, if you select the viewpoint inside the object, very strange things will happen. Selecting RHO > = 500 will permit a normal display.

What are the viewport dimensions? _____

Which lines of the program are used to determine the minimum enclosing rectangle of the projected image? _____

Which method (normalized or not) of perspective projection is used? _____

3. Make the following modifications to the program in Section 5.6.2.

```
300 EXSCL = YSCL * SFAC
310  IF EXSCL > XSCL THEN YSCL = XSCL / SFAC:EXSCL =
     XSCL
320 XSCL = EXSCL
LIST  300,320
RUN
```

What effect do the above statements have on the final display? _____

RUN the program using a variety of different viewpoints. The view parameters RHO = 600, PHI = 60, and TH = 30 will again get you started.

4. The position of an object can have an effect on the projected display. In fact, the final image can experience some distortion similar to what was observed for parallel

projections. The distortion factor can be rectified by translating the object nearer the origin.

For example, the pyramid in the program above is a considerable distance from the origin. Let's add the lines necessary to translate the object closer to the origin. Consider the DATA points defining the pyramid. What is the mid coordinate in each coordinate direction?

Add the following line.

```
155  X(K) = X(K) - 150: Y(K) = Y(K) - 250: Z(K) = Z(K)
       -100 : REM  TRANSLATE THE MIDPOINT TO THE ORIGIN.
LIST  155
```

RUN the modified program using several different viewpoints.

**DISCUSSION**   As adapted here, scaling techniques in three-dimensional graphics are implemented in conjuction with the following sequence of events. A viewpoint is selected. The projection coordinates (PX,PY) are calculated for the points (X,Y,Z) defining the object. The minimum and maximum values of each projection coordinate are calculated; suppose they are denoted by XL, XR and YL, YR respectively. One has $XL <= PX <= XR$ and $YL <= PY <= YR$ for every PX, PY. The rectangle determined by XL, XR, YL, and YR is the minimum enclosing rectangle for the projected image. If a viewport is selected, the scale factors XSCL and YSCL can be determined following the techniques of CHAPTER 4, ACTIVITIES 4.2-4.4. It is now a routine matter to transform the projected image to the viewport.

If there is sufficient memory space, arrays should be used to store the calculated values of the projected coordinates. Since all the projection coordinates must be calculated before the scaling factors can be determined, storing the calculated values will save execution time when scaling and plotting the image points. If there is insufficient memory to save the points, then simple recalculation of projected coordinates will always work.

There is an alternative method of scaling three-dimensional displays which will not be treated here in detail. Basically, the technique involves scaling the object BEFORE the projection is obtained. In particular, scale factors XSCL, YSCL, and ZSCL are applied to the original (X,Y,Z) coordinates, then the scaled point is projected. This technique requires the object to be intially translated near the origin. Finally, there is generally considerable trial and error in selecting the scales if complete screen images are wanted.

**COMPREHENSIVE EXAMPLE**   In the program below, scaling is used to display a pyramid in a style similar to movieframe "stills." Each frame represents a perspective view of the pyramid at a fixed distance RHO from the origin. As one frame to the next is generated, one of the two viewing parameters PHI and TH(ETA) has been incremented by a fixed angular amount. As a result, it is easy to see the  effect of changing the viewing parameters.

The program is not particularly difficult, but there are a few details deserving of attention. The projected coordinates PX and PY are calculated and stored in the triple arrays PX(I,J,K) and PY(I,J,K). I and J denote the indices of the (I,J)th display frame, and K is the index of the Kth point in the DATA defining the object. As the coordinates of projected points are calculated for the (I,J)th display, the boundary values of the minimum enclosing rectangle are determined and stored in XL(I,J), XR(I,J), etc. The overall maximum width and height of the enclosing rectangles are stored in the variables WD and HT. By determining the scale factors using the values WD and HT, uniformity of the relative size of the images in all 25 frames can be maintained. Equivalent scaling is also used to prevent distortion.

The coordinates of the enclosing rectangle for the I,J-th display are redefined to permit the image to be centered in the viewport. OH and OV denote the screen coordinates of scaled image of the origin; they must be recalculated for each display frame.

Enter the program below.

```
NEW
10    REM   ********************************
11    REM   *            CE5.6             *
12    REM   ********************************
13    REM
14    REM   ***** BRANCH AROUND SUBRTS *****
15    LOMEM: 16384: GOTO 100
16    REM
47    REM   ********************************
48    REM   *   PERSPECTV PROJ SUBROUTINE  *
49    REM   ********************************
50    SX = X * CO - Y * SO:SY = X * SO + Y * CO
52    RX = Z * S1 + SX * C1:RZ = Z * C1 - SX * S1
54    AB = RHO / (RHO - RX)
56    PX = SY * AB:PY = RZ * AB
58    RETURN
59    REM   **    END PERSP PROJ SUBRT    **
97    REM   ********************************
98    REM   *            MAIN PROGRAM      *
99    REM   ********************************
100   FAC = 3.14159266 / 180:SFAC = 1.20: REM  USE YOUR SCREEN
      SCALE FACTOR FOR SFAC IF DIFFERENT.
110   READ T1,T2,P1,P2: REM  READ THE RANGE VALUES OF TH(ETA)
      AND PHI TO BE DISPLAYED.
120   NFRM = 4: REM  NFRM IS ONE LESS THAN THE NUMBER OF FRAMES
      PER ROW AND COLUMN.
130   DT = (T2 - T1) / NFRM:DP = (P2 - P1) / NFRM: REM
      COMPUTE THE INCREMENT BETWEEN SUCCESSIVE TH(ETA) AND PHI
      VALUES FOR NFRM FRAMES.
140   READ NP: REM  READ THE NUMBER OF POINTS USED IN
      DETERMINING OBJECT TO BE DISPLAYED.
150   DIM
      X(NP),Y(NP),Z(NP),PX(5,5,NP),PY(5,5,NP),XL(5,5),YL(5,5)
160   FOR K = 0 TO NP
170   READ X(K),Y(K),Z(K)
180   NEXT K
```

```
190  HGR : HCOLOR =  3: HOME : VTAB 21
200  INPUT "ENTER RHO  >  =   200: ";HO
205  VTAB 23: HTAB 6: PRINT "... JUST A FEW MOMENTS ..."
210  GOSUB 2000: REM  GOTO SUBRT TO DETERMINE ALL PROJ COORDS
     OF ALL IMAGES AND MIN AND MAX VALUES NEEDED FOR SCALING.
220  XSCL = 54 / WD:YSCL = 36 / HT: REM   54 AND 36 DENOTE THE
     COMMON WIDTH AND HEIGHT OF THE VIEWPORTS USED FOR
     DISPLAYING EACH FRAME.
230  EXSCL = YSCL * SFAC: REM  DETERMINE EQUIVALENT HORIZ AND
     EQUIVALENT SCALES IN THIS AND THE NEXT TWO LINES.
240  IF EXSCL > XSCL THEN YSCL = XSCL / SFAC:EXSCL = XSCL
250  XSCL = EXSCL
260  POKE  - 16302,0: REM  FULL SCREEN GRAPHICS.
270  HPLOT 0,0 TO 0,191 TO 279,191 TO 279,0 TO 0,0: REM  PUT
     BORDER AROUND SCREEN.
280  V1 = 1: REM  IN THE 1ST FRAME THE VERT COORD OF THE TOP
     OF 1ST VIEWPORT IS 1.
290  PHI = P1: REM  START WITH THE VIEWING ANGLE PHI AT P1.
300  FOR I = 0 TO NFRM: REM  FOR EACH FRAME ROW FROM THE 0-TH
     TO THE NFRM-TH ...
310  TH = T1:HO = 1: REM  START WITH VIEWING ANGLE TH(ETA) AT
     P1 AND LEFT HORIZ COORD OF 1ST VIEWPORT IN ROW EQUAL TO 1.
320  FOR J = 0 TO NFRM: REM  FOR EACH FRAME COLUMN FROM THE
     0-TH TO THE NFRM-TH ...
330  XL = XL(I,J):XR = XR(I,J):YL = YL(I,J):YR = YR(I,J):
     REM  GET THE COORDS OF THE MINIMUM ENCLOSING RECTANGLE FOR
     THE I,J-TH PROJECTION IMAGE.
340  XL = (XL + XR - 54 / XSCL) * .5:YL = (YL + YR - 36 /
     YSCL) * .5: REM  RECALCULATE LOWER LEFT COORDS SO THAT
     IMAGE WILL BE CENTERED IN ENCLOSING RECTANGLE.
350  VO = V1 + 36: REM  GET BOTTOM VERT COORD OF VIEWPORT.
360  OH = HO - XL * XSCL:OV = VO + YL * YSCL: REM  DETERMINE
     SCREEN COORDS (OF ORIGIN) SO THAT PROJ COORDS CAN BE
     SCALED TO SCREEN DISTANCES AND THEN TRANSLATED TO
     VIEWPORT.
370  GOSUB 1000: REM  GOTO THE PLOTTING ROUTINE FOR THIS
     OBJECT.
380  PHI = PHI + DP:HO = HO + 55: REM  INCREMENT PHI AND HO
     FOR NEXT COLUMN FRAME IN THE I-TH ROW.
390  NEXT J: REM  DO ANOTHER COLUMN FRAME ...
400  TH = TH + DT:V1 = V1 + 37: REM  INCREMENT TH AND V1 FOR
     NEXT ROW OF FRAMES.
410  NEXT I: REM  DO ANOTHER ROW OF FRAMES ...
420  GET Q$: TEXT : HOME : END
421  REM  **      END MAIN PROG       **
422  REM
997  REM  *******************************
```

```
998   REM  *  PYRAMID PLOTTING SUBROUTN  *
999   REM  *******************************
1000  FOR K = 0 TO NP: REM  FOR EACH PROJ POINT, ...
1010  H%(K) = OH + PX(I,J,K) * XSCL:V%(K) = OV - PY(I,J,K)
      * YSCL: REM  SCALE AND TRANSLATE TO SCREEN COORDS, ...
1020  NEXT K
1030  HPLOT H%(0),V%(0) TO H%(1),V%(1) TO H%(2),V%(2) TO H%(3),
      V%(3) TO H%(0),V%(0) TO H%(4),V%(4) TO H%(1),V%(1)
1040  HPLOT H%(3),V%(3) TO H%(4),V%(4) TO H%(2),V%(2)
1050  RETURN
1051  REM  **     END PYRMD PLOT SUBR    **
1052  REM
1997  REM  *******************************
1998  REM  * CALC PROJ COORDS/MIN & MAX  *
1999  REM  *******************************
2000  WD = 0:HT = 0: REM  INITIALIZE VARIABLES DENOTING THE
      MAX WIDTH AND HEIGHT OF MINIMUM ENCLOSING RECTANGLES OF
      THE NFRM*NFRM PROJ IMAGES.
2010  PHI = P1: REM  STARTING WITH VIEW ANGLE PHI AT P1, ...
2020  FOR I = 0 TO NFRM: REM  FOR EACH OF NFRM+1 DIFFERENT
      VALUES OF PHI ...
2030  C1 =  COS ((90 - PHI) * FAC):S1 =  SIN ((90 - PHI) *
      FAC): REM  GET THE COS AND SIN FOR ROTATION ABOUT THE
      Y-AXIS BY 90-PHI DEGREES.
2040  TH = T1: REM  STARTING WITH THE VIEW ANGLE TH(ETA) AT
      T1, ...
2050  FOR J = 0 TO NFRM: REM  FOR EACH OF NFRM+1 VALUES OF
      TH(ETA), DO ...
2060  CO =  COS ( - TH * FAC):SO =  SIN ( - TH * FAC): REM
      GET THE COS AND SIN VALUES FOR ROTATION ABOUT Z-AXIS BY
      -TH DEGREES.
2070  XL = 1E38:XR= - XL:YL = XL:YR = XR: REM  INITIALIZE
      MIN AND MAX PX & PY VALUES.
2080  FOR K = 0 TO NP: REM  FOR EACH OF THE NP+1 POINTS IN THE
      OBJECT ...
2090  X = X(K):Y = Y(K):Z = Z(K): GOSUB 50: REM  CALC THE
      PROJ COORDS ...
2100  PX(I,J,K) = PX:PY(I,J,K) = PY: REM  ... AND STORE THEM
      AWAY;
2110  IF PX < XL THEN XL = PX: REM  GET THE MIN PX FOR
      I,J-TH DISPLAY, ...
2120  IF PX > XR THEN XR = PX: REM  ... AND THE MAX PX, ...
2130  IF PY < YL THEN YL = PY: REM  ... AND THE MIN PY, ...
2140  IF PY > YR THEN YR = PY: REM  ... AND THE MAX PY.
2150  NEXT K
2160  XL(I,J) = XL:XR(I,J) = XR:YL(I,J) = YL:YR(I,J) = YR:
      REM  STORE AWAY THE COORDS OF THE MINIMUM ENCLOSING
      RECTANGLE.
```

```
2170   IF XR — XL > WD THEN WD = XR — XL: REM  GET THE MAX
       WIDTH OF MINIMUM ENCLOSING RECTANGLES.
2180   IF YR — YL > HT THEN HT = YR — YL: REM  GET THE MAX
       HEIGHT, TOO.
2190   TH = TH + DT: REM  INCREMENT TH(ETA) FOR NEXT DISPLAY.
2200   NEXT J
2210   PHI = PHI + DP: REM  INCREMENT PHI
2220   NEXT I
2230   RETURN
2231   REM  **     END CALC PROJ SUBRT    **
2232   REM
5997   REM  ******************************
5998   REM  *         POINT DATA          *
5999   REM  ******************************
6000   DATA  0,75,15,90      : REM  T1,T2,P1,P2
6010   DATA  4     : REM  NP
6020   DATA  0,0,0, 100,0,0, 100,100,0, 0,100,0, 50,50,100
6021   REM  **     END POINT DATA        **
LIST
```

RUN the program using a few different input values for RHO > = 200. As you will discover, considerable execution time is required to make all the calculations for all the frames and any given viewpoint.

**Check Your Comprehension**

In which rotational direction is your viewpoint changing as you look at a sequence of frames from the bottom to the top? _____ from the left to the right? _____

What changes occur in the viewing parameters in the sequence of frames from the lower left to the upper right corner? _____

What would you expect to happen if the range values of PHI, P1, and P2 were reversed? _____

Change the values of T1, T2, P1, P2 to −45, 45, 45, 135. What do you observe?

_____

**EXERCISE**   Select a different object to display on the screen using the COMPRE-HENSIVE EXAMPLE program (a box, for example). You will need to modify plotting subroutine in the program.

**EXERCISE**   Modify the COMPREHENSIVE EXAMPLE program so a general (not necessarily normalized) perspective projection can be used. The viewpoint should be entered in the form VX, VY, VZ.

**EXERCISE**   Write a global 3-D plotting program. Specifically, your program will permit the display of any three-dimensional object. This program is similar in purpose to CE4.3 for two-dimensional displays. The basic functions of the program are the following.

1. The object for display is described using DATA statements. Use end-of-plot and end-of-file signal values when designing the point data.

2. Read the DATA into arrays X(I), Y(I), Z(I). Centralize the data points about the origin.

3. Compute the projected coordinates and determine the minimum enclosing rectangle. The projected coordinates can be saved in arrays for plotting the scaled image.

4. Compute the scale factors XSCL and YSCL based upon the minimum enclosing rectangle and the viewport within the screen. Allow the user to select equivalent scales if desired; the use of equivalent scales provides the "truest" three dimensional image.

5. Plot the projected image using scaling.

**CHALLENGE**   Modify the COMPREHENSIVE EXAMPLE program so the grid size (now 5 × 5) can be selected by the user. For example, the user may wish to display a 4 × 4 grid of frames. Your program should permit the user to select from 1 to 6 frames per row and column.

# MODULE 5C   Graphing Functions

## ACTIVITY 5.7   Surface Plotting

**LEARNING BY DISCOVERY**   In this activity you will learn how to display three-dimensional surfaces generated as graphs of functions of the form Z = F(X,Y).

1. A function F of two variables X and Y is a rule by which values are assigned to a third variable Z for each pair of values (X,Y). The permissible (X,Y) values belong to a collection of points called the domain of the function. The rule for determining the Z value from X and Y is customarily determined by an algebraic expression, such as: Z = F(X,Y) = algebraic expression in X and Y. For example,

   (a)  Z = Y * Y − .2 * X
   (b)  Z = X * Y
   (c)  Z = COS (X * X + Y * Y)

   In each case, the graph of the function is obtained by plotting the points (X,Y,Z) in three-dimensional space as (X,Y) varies over the domain of the function. The Z value is determined by applying the function rule to the (X,Y) value. See Figure 5.7.1.

   For example, if the function rule is given by (b) (above) and (X,Y) = (−2,3), then the point (X,Y,Z) = (−2,3,−6) is plotted on the graph of the function; the value Z= −6 is determined from X * Y = (−2) *3=−6.

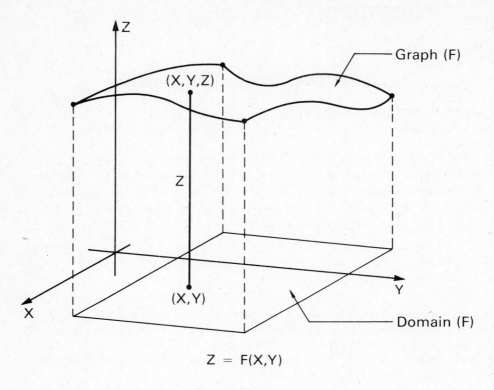

$$Z = F(X,Y)$$

Figure 5.7.1

2. Let's consider an example. Enter the following program.

```
NEW
15   GOTO 100
50   SX = X * CO - Y * SO:SY = X * SO + Y * CO
52   RX = Z * S1 + SX * C1:RZ = Z * C1 - SX * S1
54   AB = SCL * RHO / (RHO - RX)
56   H = OH + SY * AB:V = OV - RZ * AB
58   RETURN
100  HO = 0:H1 = 279:V0 = 159:V1 = 0
110  OH = 140:OV = 96
120  FAC = 3.14159266 / 180
130  READ RHO,PHI,TH,SCL
140  CO =  COS ( - TH * FAC):SO =  SIN ( - TH * FAC):C1 =
     COS ((90 - PHI) * FAC):S1 =  SIN ((90 -
     PHI) * FAC)
150  DEF  FN Z(X) = .2 * X * Y - X * Y * Y
160  HGR2 : HCOLOR =  3
170  FOR X = 1 TO  - 1 STEP  - .1
190  FOR Y= - 1 TO 1 STEP .05
```

```
200   Z =   FN Z(X): GOSUB 50
210   IF H < HO OR H > H1 OR V < V1 OR V > VO
      THEN   NEXT Y,X: GOTO 250
230   HPLOT H,V
240   NEXT Y,X
250   GET Q$: TEXT : HOME : END
300   DATA  50,70,30,70
LIST
RUN
```

Does the display remind you of a sheet of paper folded in the palm of your hand?

_____

What is the range of X and Y values over which this function is apparently defined and graphed? _____

What is the "rule" for this function and in which program line is it defined? _____

_____

Which line of the program accesses the function and assigns a value to Z for predetermined values of X and Y? _____

Compare the order in which points are plotted with the order of the X- and Y- loops in the program. What is your observation? _____

Change the value of the scale variable, SCL, to one hundred by entering the following:

```
300  DATA  10, 50, 30, 100
```

3. Make the following modifications to the program in memory.

```
LIST
180   SF = 1
210   IF H < HO OR H > H1 OR V < V1 OR V > VO THEN
      SF = 1: NEXT Y,X: GOTO 250
220   IF SF THEN  HPLOT H,V:SF = 0: NEXT Y,X: GOTO 250
230   HPLOT  TO H,V
RUN
```

What change did this produce in the screen display? _____

Change the viewing parameters to the following: RHO = 8; PHI = 50 degrees; TH = −70 degrees. What do you observe? _____

4. Change the projection subroutine to the (general) perspective projection, and also change the method of viewpoint selection.

```
DEL 50, 58
50   A = (Y − VY) / (X − VX):B = (Z − VZ) / (X − VX)
52   PX = Y − A * X:PY = Z − B * X
54   H = OH + SCL * PX:V = OV − SCL * PY
56   RETURN
130   READ VX,VY,VZ,SCL
```

```
300  DATA  40,25,15,70
LIST
RUN
```

Observe the screen display and compare it with the previous displays. Note your impressions. _____

5. Change the projection subroutine to accommodate parallel projections.

```
DEL  50, 56
50  PX = SCL * (Y − A * X):PY = SCL * (Z − B * X)
52  H = OH + PX:V = OV − PY
54  RETURN
130  READ A,B,SCL
300  DATA  .6, .4, 70
LIST
RUN
```

Does the current display differ significantly from the previous displays? _____

_____

Do you observe any increase in execution speed? _____

**DISCUSSION**    In Section 2, the program was designed to select a grid of (X,Y) points from a rectangular region of the X-Y plane ($-1 < = $ X, Y $ < = $ 1). The corresponding points (X,Y,Z) are calculated, projected, scaled, and plotted on the screen. However, as the scale is changed the point plots give rise to large gaps and the surface tends to lose its definition. If a large number of points are plotted in this fashion, very effective results can be obtained.

A popular method of displaying the graphs of functions Z = F(X,Y) is the wireframe method used in Section 3. The "wires" are called (linear) splines. Basically, each spline is representative of a cross section of the surface graph. A cross-sectional curve is obtained by graphing the function Z = F(X,Y) considered as a function of one of the variables X or Y, while holding the other variable constant. In the example program, X-splines were generated for fixed X value as the graphs of Z = .2 * X * Y − X * Y * Y, considered as functions of the single variable Y.

In the programs of Sections 2, 3, 4, and 5, the function Z = F(X,Y) was defined in a function definition statement (line 150) as follows:

```
150  DEF FN Z(X) = .2 * X * Y − X * Y * Y
```

In APPLESOFT BASIC, only one value may be passed as an argument of the function in the function definition statement. Other variables can be used in the function definition statement. This explains why one cannot use a statement such as FN Z(X,Y) = ..., and why the use of both X and Y in line 150 is an acceptable definition of the function. Since only one variable can be passed as an argument, it is extremely important the appropriate value of the second variable has been previously assigned before accessing function values.

From a technical standpoint, each spline generated is a piecewise linear approximation to the actual cross section which lies in the surface graph. Technically, only the points determined in the X and Y loops can be guaranteed to be points on the surface. The line segments joining these points are linear approximations to the actual curves between them. Obtaining images which appear smoother and less angular in appearance requires increasing the number of points used to generate the spline. This must be weighed against the increased execution time. In general, a balance between the amount of execution time and the desired smoothness of the display can be achieved to give satisfactory results.

Finally, there is no particular reason why the splines generated in the example programs are chosen to be X-cross sections. One can also consider spline generation corresponding to Y-cross sections by switching the order of the X and Y loops. This is delegated to the exercises.

**COMPREHENSIVE EXAMPLE**   The program below combines scaling methods with the basic techniques of surface generation using splines to display the graph of any function $Z = F(X,Y)$ over a rectangular domain in the X-Y plane. The user supplies the function in a function definition statement in line 100. The domain is entered using an input statement. The syntax for defining the function is the following:

```
100  DEF FN Z(X) = algebraic expression in X, Y
```

When the program is executed, the user is expected to enter the domain limits which correspond to interval [A,B] of X-values and interval [C,D] of Y-values under consideration.

The user is also requested to enter the viewpoint. Since normalized perspective projections are used, the viewpoint is entered in spherical coordinates RHO, PHI, TH(eta). Remember, choosing a viewpoint close to the X-Y plane entails selecting PHI close to 90 degrees. To obtain a more overhead view, select values of PHI closer to zero. Selecting a viewpoint near the X-Z plane requires selecting TH(eta) near zero. Increasing TH will rotate your viewpoint counterclockwise about the Z-axis.

After the X-range and Y-range have been supplied, a grid of equally spaced points is selected; the coordinates are stored in the arrays X(I) and Y(J) for $0 <= I,J <=$ NP. The $Z = FN\ Z(X,Y)$ values are computed from the $(X,Y) = (X(I),Y(J))$ values, then projected. The coordinates of the projected points are stored in the arrays PX(I,J) and PY(I,J).

As the projected points are calculated, the minimum and maximum PX and PY values are also determined. The variables XL, XR and YL, YR are used to denote the minimum and maximum values and they represent the coordinates of the minimum enclosing rectangle.

The process of actually calculating the function values, computing the projection coordinates, and determining the minimum enclosing rectangle is very time consuming when compared to most of the programs you have observed so far. It is not unusual for computations to require several minutes before the surface is ready for display. The amount of time necessary will depend on the number of points selected per spline and on the complexity of the function. Once the calculations have been performed, the plotting will proceed very rapidly.

```
NEW
10   REM   ********************************
11   REM   *            CE5.7            *
```

```
12    REM    **********************************
13    REM
14    REM    ***** BRANCH AROUND SUBRTS *****
15    LOMEM: 16384: GOTO 100
16    REM
17    REM    **********************************
18    REM    *       PERSP PROJ SUBROUTINE    *
19    REM    **********************************
20    SX = X * CO - Y * SO:SY = X * SO + Y * CO
22    RX = Z * S1 + SX * C1:RZ = Z * C1 - SX * S1
24    AB = RHO / (RHO - RX)
26    PX = SY * AB:PY = RZ * AB
28    RETURN
29    REM    **        END PERSP PROJ SUB        **
30    REM
97    REM    **********************************
98    REM    *             MAIN PROGRAM          *
99    REM    **********************************
100   DEF  FN Z(X) =   COS (X * X + Y * Y)
110   FAC = 3.14159266 / 180:SFAC = 1.20: REM  USE YOUR SCREEN
      SCALE FACTOR IF DIFFERENT.
120   HO = 1:H1 = 278:VO = 190:V1 = 1: REM  SET VIEWPORT,
      ALLOWING ROOM FOR BORDER.
130   WDSCR = H1 - HO:HTSCR = VO - V1
140   NP = 25: REM  NP+1 = NUMBER OF X PTS (Y PTS) IN X- (Y-)
      DIRECTION AT WHICH EVALUATION IS TO OCCUR.
150   DIM X(NP),Y(NP),PX(NP,NP),PY(NP,NP)
160   HOME
170   HTAB 6: PRINT "DISPLAY GRAPH OF Z = F(X,Y)"
180   VTAB 3: PRINT "CURRENTLY DEFINED FUNCTION:"
190   LIST 100: REM  DISPLAY CURRENTLY DEFINED FUNCTION.
200   INPUT "ENTER THE X-RANGE A,B: ";AA,BB
210   INPUT "ENTER THE Y-RANGE C,D: ";CC,DD
220   DX = (AA - BB) / NP:DY = (DD - CC) / NP: REM  DETERMINE
      X AND Y INCREMENTS; DX < 0 WHILE DY > 0.
230   X(0) = BB:Y(0) = CC:X(NP) = AA:Y(NP) = DD: REM  STORE
      AWAY X AND Y INPUT VALUES.
240   FOR K = 1 TO NP - 1
250   X(K) = X(K - 1) + DX:Y(K) = Y(K - 1) + DY: REM  STORE
      AWAY INTERMEDIATE VALUES.
260   NEXT K
270   PRINT "ENTER THE VIEWING PARAMETERS:"
280   INPUT "RHO,PHI,TH(ETA): ";RHO,PHI,TH
290   CO =   COS ( - TH * FAC):SO =   SIN ( - TH * FAC):C1 =
      COS ((90 - PHI) * FAC):S1 =   SIN ((90 - PHI) * FAC)
300   GOSUB 3000: REM  TOSS THIS SUBRT OUT IF YOU DON'T WANT IT.
310   XL = 1E38:XR= - XL:YL = XL:YR = XR: REM  INIT MIN AND
```

```
      MAX PX,PY VALUES.
320   FOR I = 0 TO NP: REM  FOR EACH X(I) DO ...
330   X = X(I)
340   FOR J = 0 TO NP: REM  ... AND FOR EACH Y(J) DO ...
350   Y = Y(J)
360   Z =  FN Z(X): GOSUB 20: REM   CALCULATE PROJ COORDS OF
      (X,Y,Z).
370   PX(I,J) = PX:PY(I,J) = PY: REM  STORE AWAY PROJECTION
      VALUES.
380   IF PX < XL THEN XL = PX: REM  GET MIN PX
390   IF PX > XR THEN XR = PX: REM  GET MAX PX
400   IF PY < YL THEN YL = PY: REM  GET MIN PY
410   IF PY > YR THEN YR = PY: REM  GET MAX PY
420   NEXT J,I
430   XSCL = WDSCR / (XR — XL):YSCL = HTSCR / (YR — YL)
440   OH = HO — XL * XSCL:OV = VO + YL * YSCL
450   HGR : HCOLOR =  3
460   HOME : VTAB 21
470   FOR K = 1 TO 6: PRINT  CHR$ (7): NEXT K: REM  RING BELL 6
      TIMES; MENU IS READY!
480   PRINT "SELECT: 1) SPLINES BOTH DIRECTNS"
490   PRINT "        2) X-SPLINES ONLY"
500   PRINT "        3) Y-SPLINES ONLY"
510   GET Q$:DSPLY =  VAL (Q$): REM  PROPER INPUT WILL RESULT
      IN DSPLY = 1,2, OR 3.
520   IF DSPLY < 1 OR DSPLY > 3 THEN 460: REM  IF IMPROPER
      INPUT THEN GO BACK FOR VALID RESPONSE.
530   POKE  — 16302,0: REM  FULL SCREEN GRAPHICS
540   ON DSPLY GOSUB 1000,1000,1500: REM  IF 1,2 THEN START WITH
      X-SPLINES; OTHERWISE Y-SPLINES ONLY.
550   GOSUB 2000: REM  DRAW BORDER
560   GET Q$
570   POKE  — 16301,0: REM  MIXED MODE GRAPHICS
580   HOME : VTAB 21
590   PRINT "DISPLAY GRAPH WITH EQUIVALENT SCALES?";: GET Q$
600   IF Q$ <  > "Y" THEN 700
610   CALL 62450: POKE  — 16302,0: REM  CLEAR SCREEN AND SET
      FULL SCREEN GRAPHICS.
620   EXSCL = YSCL * SFAC
630   IF EXSCL > XSCL THEN YSCL = XSCL / SFAC:EXSCL = XSCL
640   XSCL = EXSCL
650   XL = (XL + XR — WDSCR / XSCL) * .5:YL = (YL + YR —
      HTSCR / YSCL) * .5: REM  SET COORDS FOR CENTERING DISPLAY
      IN VIEWPORT.
660   OH = HO — XL * XSCL:OV = VO + YL * YSCL
670   ON DSPLY GOSUB 1000,1000,1500
680   GOSUB 2000: REM  DRAW BORDER
```

```
690    GET Q$
700    TEXT : HOME : END
701    REM   **        END MAIN PROGRAM        **
702    REM
997    REM   ******************************
998    REM   *       PLOTTING SUBROUTINE      *
999    REM   ******************************
1000   FOR I = 0 TO NP
1010   HPLOT OH + PX(I,0) * XSCL,OV - PY(I,0) * YSCL
1020   FOR J = 1 TO NP
1030   HPLOT  TO OH + PX(I,J) * XSCL,OV - PY(I,J) * YSCL
1040   NEXT J,I
1050   IF DSPLY = 2 THEN  RETURN : REM  IF ONLY X-SPLINES
       WANTED THEN RETURN; IF NOT THEN Y-SPLINES WANTED TOO
       (DSPLY = 1).
1500   FOR J = 0 TO NP
1510   HPLOT OH + PX(0,J) * XSCL,OV - PY(0,J) * YSCL
1520   FOR I = 1 TO NP
1530   HPLOT  TO OH + PX(I,J) * XSCL,OV - PY(I,J) * YSCL
1540   NEXT I,J
1550   RETURN
1551   REM   **        END PLOTTING SUBRTN    **
1552   REM
1997   REM   ******************************
1998   REM   *       PLOT BORDER SUBRT        *
1999   REM   ******************************
2000   HPLOT 0,0 TO 0,191 TO 279,191 TO 279,0 TO 0,0
2010   RETURN
2011   REM   **         END PLOT BORDER       **
2012   REM
3000   VTAB 13: HTAB 11: PRINT "...";: FLASH : PRINT
       "CALCULATING";: NORMAL : PRINT "..."
3010   VTAB 15: HTAB 2: PRINT "GET A CUP OF COFFEE, I'LL RING
       YOU!"
3020   PRINT "I HAVE TO PERFORM AT LEAST:"
3030   N2 = (NP + 1) * (NP + 1)
3040   HTAB 5: PRINT N2;" FUNCTION EVALUATIONS;"
3050   HTAB 5: PRINT N2 * 11;" MULTIPLICATIONS & DIVISIONS;"
3060   HTAB 5: PRINT N2 * 5;" ADDITIONS & SUBTRACTIONS;"
3070   HTAB 5: PRINT N2 * 6 + NP + 2;" COMPARISONS;"
3080   HTAB 5: PRINT "> =  ";N2 * 11 + NP + 9;" ASSIGNMENTS
       (MINIMUM ESTM.)"
3090   RETURN
LIST
```

When the above program is RUN, use the following input initially.
ENTER THE X-RANGE A, B: −2.5, 2.5

ENTER THE Y-RANGE A, B: −2.5, 2.5
RHO, PHI, TH (ETA): 10, 50, 30
The viewpoint must be selected so it is neither on nor inside the object to be observed. There are no other restrictions.

Some care must be taken when selecting the X-limits and Y-limits. If too large of an interval is chosen for a function possessing many "hills" or "valleys" in its graph, the final display may provide misleading results, or splines which appear very angular. The problem is each spline is generated from only a finite number of points. If the sample points are "spread" too far apart, the spline will be a poor approximation of the true cross-sectional curve.

Experiment with some other functions. Here are a few examples.

1. Z = SIN (X * Y)
   A, B=−2.5, 2.5; C, D=−2.5, 2.5
   RHO, PHI, TH = 10, 50, −20


2. Z = EXP ( − (X^2 + Y^2) / 30) * COS((X^2 + Y^2) / 5)
   A, B=−5, 5   C, D=−4, 4
   RHO, PHI, TH = 30, 60, 30


3. Z = Y * X * (X * X − Y * Y) / (X * X + Y * Y)
   A, B = −3, 3; C, D=−3, 3
   RHO, PHI, TH = 20, 30, −20


4. Z = SIN (X + Y)
   A, B=−10, 10; C, D=−10, 10
   RHO, PHI, TH = 30, 60, 30

## Check Your Comprehension

Which lines of the program calculate the coordinates of the minimum enclosing rectangle of the projected image? _____
Which lines of the program calculate the scale factors for transporting the projected image to the viewport? _____
Which lines of the program compute the grid of points in the rectangular domain of the function? _____
In which order are the X-splines generated (for increasing X values or decreasing X values)? _____

As different viewpoints are selected or as different functions are used, the projected image may become a jumble of overlapping splines. Since the images created on the screen are transparent, this can lead to confusing images and misinterpretation of the three-dimensional objects displayed. In the next activity we will consider methods for removing hidden lines from surface plots.

**EXERCISE**   Modify the program of Section 5.7.2 so Y-cross sections are generated. Perform similar modifications on the programs in Sections 5.7.3 - 5.7.5.

**CHALLENGE**   Write a program to provide four different views of a function graph on the screen, one display per screen corner. Store the points X,Y,Z in arrays (particularly, Z !) so it is not necessary to recalculate the function values for each display. On the other hand, the projected coordinates (PX,PY) will need to be calculated for each separate view.

# ACTIVITY 5.8   Hidden Line Surface Plotting

**LEARNING BY DISCOVERY**   In this section you will learn how to remove hidden lines from the graphic display of three-dimensional surfaces Z = F(X,Y). Two methods will be investigated. One approach is similar to an artist's technique of painting over those portions of a picture closer to the viewer. The second method removes the hidden segments of a wire-frame display.

1. The plotting program of ACTIVITY 5.7 will display the graph of functions Z = F(X,Y), but the transparent image can at times create considerable confusion and misinterpretation of the true display. The procedure needed to eliminate the transparency requires hiding or removing the offending portions of the surface. There are two basic methods of achieving this. One method effects the removal of hidden lines from the wire-frame plots. This will be treated in the DISCUSSION and COMPREHENSIVE EXAMPLE section of this activity. In this method, the surface is generated from front to back.

   The second method requires generation of the surface from back to front, just the opposite of the wire-frame procedure. The portions of the surface farthest from the viewer are generated first. The surface image is created one cross section at a time. As each slice is generated the section of the screen immediately below the cross section is "blacked out" or filled with a solid background color. The black out color must be different from the plot color. Let's consider an example.

2. Enter the program below. The method used for generating screen points combines scaling and parallel projection.

```
NEW
10  HS = 125:VS = 55: REM  STARTING PT ON SCREEN; IT
    CORRESPONDS TO PROJECTED IMAGE OF STARTING PT (AA,CC) IN
    FUNCTION DOMAIN.
20  HW = 80:VW = 80: REM  HORIZ WIDTH AND VERT HEIGHT OF
    (SCREEN) IMAGE OF DOMAIN.
30  DH = 2:DV = 2: REM  DH = INCRMNT OF H FROM ONE PT TO
    NEXT IN SAME SLICE; DV = INCRMNT IN V FROM SLICE TO
    SLICE.
40  HDEC= − DV: REM  AMOUNT TO DECREMENT VARIABLE HS FOR
    NEXT SLICE.
50  PC = 3:BG = 0:VO = 191: REM  PC = PLOT COLOR; BG =
    BACKGROUND COLOR; VO = BOTTOM OF SCREEN.
60  HGR2
```

```
70   DATA   -2.5,2.5   : REM   X-RANGE AA,BB
80   DATA   -2.5,2.5   : REM   Y-RANGE CC,DD
90   DATA   10         : REM   Z-SCALE (ZSC)
100  DEF  FN Z(X) =  COS (X * X + Y * Y) + 1 -  ABS (X *
     X) / 4  -  ABS (Y * Y) / 4
110  READ AA,BB,CC,DD,ZSC
120  DX = DV * (BB - AA) / VW:DY = DH * (DD - CC) / HW:
     REM  DX AND DY DENOTE AMOUNT OF X- AND Y- INCREMENTS
     CORRESPONDING SCREEN V- AND H- INCREMENTS DH AND DV.
130  X = AA
140  FOR V = VS TO VS + VW STEP DV
150  Y = CC
160  FOR HP = HS TO HS + HW STEP DH
170  VP = V -  FN Z(X) * ZSC
180  HCOLOR =  PC: HPLOT HP,VP
190  HCOLOR =  BG: HPLOT HP,VP + 1 TO HP,VO
200  Y = Y + DY
210  NEXT HP
220  HS = HS + HDEC:X = X + DX
230  NEXT V
240  GET Q$: TEXT : HOME : END
LIST
RUN
```

As you observe the display, notice some previously generated points seem to magically disappear as new cross sections are generated. This is the effect of "painting over" more distant points. The back to front generation of points guarantees more distant points are generated first.

Which lines of the program control the actual plotting of points in each cross section and then black out the region immediately below the point? _____

The rectangular domain of the function actually projects to a parallelogram region on the screen. The top left corner of this parallelogram is located at H = 125, V = 55. This point corresponds to the point X = AA, Y = BB in the domain. What are the screen coordinates and the corresponding X, Y values for the remaining three corners?

_____

Notice the variables DX and DY represent conversion factors for converting DH and DV pixel units to units along the X and Y axes. What are the formulas actually defining DX and DY? _____

Which variables denote the screen coordinates of the image point corresponding to (X,Y,0)? _____

Which variables denote the screen coordinates of the projected and scaled image of (X,Y,Z)? _____

The corners of the parallelogram, alluded to in the question above, are located at the points (135,55), (55,135), (135,135) and (215,55). These screen points correspond to the X,Y points (AA,CC), (BB,CC), (BB,DD), and (AA,DD) respectively. Since there is a horizontal and vertical difference of 80 pixels in the parallelogram, the quantities (BB

− AA)/80 and (DD − CC)/80 represent the corresponding amount of X- and Y-change per pixel unit. If DH and DV denote the increment in H and V, then the expressions DX = DV * (BB − AA)/80 and DY = DH * (DD − CC)/80 denote the corresponding changes in X and Y. The point (HP,V) denotes the screen coordinates of the image of (X,Y,0), i.e., (X,Y). The values of V are incremented by the scaled value of Z = FN Z(X) and the result is stored in VP. Therefore, the screen image point corresponding to (X,Y,Z) is given by (HP,VP).

**DISCUSSION**   The second method of "hiding" hidden portions of the surface is programmatically much more involved. The COMPREHENSIVE EXAMPLE program will demonstrate this technique. We will begin a discussion of its content.

The wire-frame display method is used. However, the splines (X-splines) are generated in primarily one direction, left to right on the screen. The cross sections closest to the viewer are generated first. This imposes a restriction on the viewpoint. At the very least, it must be chosen in the half-space determined by the positive X-axis and the YZ plane, v.z., RHO > 0 and −90 deg < = TH < = 90 deg. (Mathematically, one must have RHO * COS (TH) greater than the X-coordinate of any point on the surface.)

As each spline is generated, two arrays are constantly updated. The array BV(H) maintains a record of the bottom-most V-coordinate plotted in column H. The second array, TV(H), keeps a record of the top-most V-coordinate plotted in column H. At a specific stage of the surface generation, these arrays represent the upper and lower bounds of the vertical screen coordinates of visible points on the surface. If a point (H,V) lies between BV(H) and TV(H), that point is not visible; it represents a hidden point of the surface.

Let's take a close look at the hidden line subroutine to be used in the COMPREHENSIVE EXAMPLE.

```
37   REM   ********************************
38   REM   *       HIDDEN LINE SUBRT      *
39   REM   ********************************
40   CH = NH% − PH%: IF CH = 0 THEN CH = 1:PH% = NH% − 1
42   DH% =  SGN (CH):M = (NV% − PV%) /  ABS (CH):V = PV%
44   FOR H = PH% + DH% TO NH% STEP DH%
46   V = V + M:V% = V + P5
48   TS = V% <  = TV(H):BS = V% >  = BV(H)
50   IF  NOT (TS OR BS) THEN FL = 1: NEXT H: RETURN
52   IF TS THEN TV(H) = V%
54   IF BS THEN BV(H) = V%
56   IF FL THEN  HPLOT H,V%:FL = 0: NEXT H: RETURN
58   HPLOT  TO H,V%
60   NEXT H
62   RETURN
78   REM  **    END HIDDEN LINE SBRT     **
```

Suppose (PH%,PV%) are the screen coordinates of a grid point (X(I),Y(J−1),Z) previously considered for plotting in a spline. Let (NH%,NV%) be the screen coordinates of the next point (X(I),Y(J),Z) in the grid of points at which the function is evaluated. In the program of ACTIVITY 5.7, the line segment joining these points was drawn without consideration of visibility. The flag variable FL denotes whether or not the most recent point considered is hidden. If FL = 1, the point is hidden; otherwise the point is visible. Now, one must consider the visibility of EVERY point on the line segment joining (PH%,PV%) and (NH%,NV%); specifically, it is insufficient to consider only the visibility of the grid points.

Beginning with line 40, one must test whether or not the line segment is vertical (CH = 0?). If the segment is vertical, then variables must be redefined so the loop beginning at line 44, which decides the visibility of the segment joining (PH%,PV% +1) and (NV%,NV%), can be used. PH% must be redefined as PH%-1 since the loop begins by adding one to PH%. The value of CH is redefined to one to insure that the first and last point considered in the loop is (NH%,NV%).

Let's turn our attention to the more likely event, CH < > 0. In line 42, the quantity DH% is either +1 or −1 and represents the H-increment necessary to step from (PH%, PV%) to (NH%, NV%). There are occasions when the stepping will proceed from right to left (DH% = −1 in this case). The variable M denotes the corresponding vertical change for each increment DH of horizontal change. The variable V is used to denote the vertical coordinate of each point on the line segment being considered. We start with V = PV%.

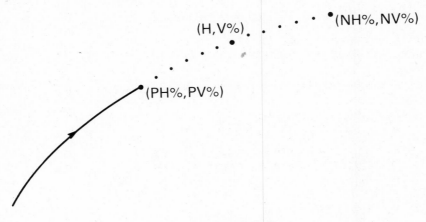

Figure 5.8.1

In lines 44-46 we consider each screen point (H,V%) on the line segment joining (PH%,PV%) and (NH%,NV%). The assignment V% = V + .5 results in rounding V to the nearest integer value; this has a smoothing effect on the segment displayed.

The visibility of the point (H,V%) is determined in line 48. The value of the logical expression V% < = TV(H) is one if true ((H,V%) is visible) or is zero if false ((H,V%) is hidden). This is assigned to the variable TS and designates whether or not the point is currently visible at the top. Similarly, BS denotes whether or not the point can be seen below the current image of the surface. If TS and BS are both zero, then the point is hidden (line 50). The hidden point flag variable FL is set to one, and the next point on the joining segment is considered. If it is the last point, the RETURN in line 50 insures a proper return to the plotting subroutine.

If the point (H,V%) is visible, then lines 52 and 54 update the arrays TV(H) and BV(H) accordingly. V% now becomes the vertical coordinate of the top-most or bottom-most visible point in column H. If the hidden point flag variable FL has a value of one, the previous point was not visible. This is a signal (line 56) that a new contiguous sequence of visible points is to be plotted. The flag variable FL is turned "off" and the next point is considered. If it is the last point in the joining segment, program control returns to the plotting subroutine. If the previous point was visible (FL = 0) and therefore plotted, an HPLOT TO this point is performed (line 58). The hidden point flag variable has a value of zero and need not be changed.

Let's incorporate this subroutine into a plotting program. To help speed execution, the variables N0, N1, and P5 will be used in the hidden-line and plotting subroutines to denote the contants 0, 1, and 0.5.

**COMPREHENSIVE EXAMPLE** Incorporating the hidden-line subroutine into the plotting program in ACTIVITY 5.7 requires a few modifications. The major differences are the following: (1) splines must be generated from front to back and generally in one direction; (2) the hidden-line subroutine is added; and (3) the plotting subroutine must be altered. For those readers who have not purchased the supplementary diskette, the simplest approach is to load the COMPREHENSIVE EXAMPLE program CE 5.7 and modify it to agree with the listing below. The only portion of the program requiring REMarks is the plotting subroutine.

```
<LOAD and modify CE5.7>
10   REM   ********************************
11   REM   *          CE5.8               *
12   REM   ********************************
13   REM
15   LOMEM: 16384: GOTO 100
17   REM   ********************************
18   REM   *        PERSP PROJ SUBRT      *
19   REM   ********************************
20   SX = X * CO - Y * SO:SY = X * SO + Y * CO
22   RX = Z * S1 + SX * C1:RZ = Z * C1 - SX * S1
24   AB = RHO / (RHO - RX)
26   PX = SY * AB:PY = RZ * AB
28   RETURN
29   REM   **        END PERSP PROJ SBRT    **
30   REM
37   REM   ********************************
38   REM   *        HIDDEN LINE SUBRT     *
39   REM   ********************************
40   CH = NH% - PH%: IF CH = NO THEN CH = N1:PH% = NH% - N1
42   DH% =  SGN (CH):M = (NV% - PV%) /  ABS (CH):V = PV%
44   FOR H = PH% + DH% TO NH% STEP DH%
46   V = V + M:V% = V + P5
48   TS = V% <  = TV(H):BS = V% >  = BV(H)
50   IF  NOT (TS OR BS) THEN FL = N1: NEXT H: RETURN
52   IF TS THEN TV(H) = V%
```

```
54   IF BS THEN BV(H) = V%
56   IF FL THEN  HPLOT H,V%:FL = NO: NEXT H: RETURN
58   HPLOT  TO H,V%
60   NEXT H
62   RETURN
78   REM  **    END HIDDEN LINE SBRT      **
79   REM
97   REM  ********************************
98   REM  *         MAIN PROGRAM         *
99   REM  ********************************
100  DEF  FN Z(X) =   COS (X * Y)
110  FAC = 3.14159266 / 180:SFAC = 1.20
120  HO = 1:H1 = 278:VO = 190:V1 = 1
130  WDSCR = H1 - HO:HTSCR = VO - V1
140  NP = 25
150  DIM X(NP),Y(NP),TV(279),BV(279),PX(NP,NP),PY(NP,NP)
160  HOME
170  HTAB 3: PRINT "HIDDEN LINE GRAPH OF Z = F(X,Y)"
180  VTAB 3: PRINT "CURRENTLY DEFINED FUNCTION:"
190  LIST 100
200  INPUT "ENTER THE X-RANGE A,B: ";AA,BB
210  INPUT "ENTER THE Y-RANGE C,D: ";CC,DD
220  DX = (AA - BB) / NP:DY = (DD - CC) / NP
230  X(0) = BB:Y(0) = CC:X(NP) = AA:Y(NP) = DD
240  FOR K = 1 TO NP - 1
250  X(K) = X(K - 1) + DX:Y(K) = Y(K - 1) + DY
260  NEXT K
270  PRINT "ENTER THE VIEWING PARAMETERS:"
280  INPUT "RHO,PHI,TH(ETA): ";RHO,PHI,TH
290  CO = COS (- TH * FAC):SO = SIN (- TH * FAC):C1 =
     COS ((90 - PHI) * FAC):S1 =  SIN ((90 - PHI) * FAC)
300  GOSUB 3000
310  XL = 1E38:XR= - XL:YL = XL:YR = XR
320  FOR I = 0 TO NP
330  X = X(I)
340  FOR J = 0 TO NP
350  Y = Y(J)
360  Z =  FN Z(X): GOSUB 20
370  PX(I,J) = PX:PY(I,J) = PY
380  IF PX < XL THEN XL = PX
390  IF PX > XR THEN XR = PX
400  IF PY < YL THEN YL = PY
410  IF PY > YR THEN YR = PY
420  NEXT J,I
430  XSCL = WDSCR / (XR - XL):YSCL = HTSCR / (YR - YL)
440  OH = HO - XL * XSCL:OV = VO + YL * YSCL
450  HGR : HCOLOR =  3
```

```
460   HOME : VTAB 21
470   FOR K = 1 TO 6: PRINT  CHR$ (7): NEXT K
480   PRINT "READY!!"
590   PRINT "DISPLAY GRAPH WITH EQUIVALENT SCALES?";: GET Q$
600   POKE  - 16302,0
610   IF Q$ < > "Y" THEN 670
620   EXSCL = YSCL * SFAC
630   IF EXSCL > XSCL THEN YSCL = XSCL / SFAC:EXSCL = XSCL
640   XSCL = EXSCL
650   XL = (XL + XR - WDSCR / XSCL) * .5:YL = (YL + YR -
      HTSCR / YSCL) * .5
660   OH = HO - XL * XSCL:OV = VO + YL * YSCL
670   GOSUB 1000
680   GOSUB 2000
690   GET Q$
700   TEXT : HOME : END
701   REM  **     END MAIN PROGRAM      **
702   REM
997   REM  *******************************
998   REM  *     PLOTTING SUBROUTINE     *
999   REM  *******************************
1000  FOR K = 0 TO 279:TV(K) = VO: NEXT : REM  INITIALIZE
      ARRAY TV(K).
1010  P5 = .5:NO = 0:N1 = 1: REM  DEFINE CONSTANTS TO HELP
      SPEED EXECUTION.
1020  PH% = OH + PX(NO,NO) * XSCL:PV% = OV - PY(NO,NO) *
      YSCL: REM  SET SCREEN COORDS OF PREV PT TO 1ST PT; THIS
      WILL REPRESENT THE 1ST PT OF PREV SPLINE.
1030  FL = N1
1040  FOR I = NO TO NP: REM  FOR EACH X(I)-SPLINE DO ...
1050  NH% = OH + PX(I,NO) * XSCL:NV% = OV - PY(I,NO) * YSCL
1060  GOSUB 40: REM  GOTO HIDDEN LINE SUBRT.
1070  SH% = NH%:SV% = NV%:SFL = FL: REM  SAVE COORDS OF
      STARTING PT OF X(I)-SPLINE AND HIDDEN FLAG VALUE.
1080  PH% = NH%:PV% = NV%: REM  REDEFINE NEWEST PT CONSIDERED
      TO PREV PT CONSIDERED.
1090  FOR J = N1 TO NP: REM  FOR EACH OF THE REMAINING Y(J)
      VALUES IN THE X(I)-SPLINE DO ...
1100  NH% = OH + PX(I,J) * XSCL:NV% = OV - PY(I,J) * YSCL:
      REM  GET A NEW SCREEN PT ... IT CORRESPS TO PT
      (X(I),Y(J),Z).
1110  GOSUB 40: REM  GOTO HIDDEN LINE SUBRT.
1120  PH% = NH%:PV% = NV%: REM  REDEFINE NEWEST PT CONSIDERED
      TO PREV PT CONSIDERED.
1130  NEXT J
1140  IF I = NP THEN  RETURN
1150  NH% = OH + PX(I + N1,NP) * XSCL:NV% = OV - PY(I +
```

```
        N1,NP) * YSCL: REM CONSIDER LAST PT IN NEXT SPLINE.
1160    GOSUB 40: REM   GOTO HIDDEN LINE SUBRT.
1170    FL = SFL: IF  NOT FL THEN  HPLOT SH%,SV%: REM   RECALL
        HIDDEN STATUS OF 1ST PT OF X(I)-SPLINE; IF NOT HIDDEN
        THEN PLOT IT.
1180    PH% = SH%:PV% = SV%
1190    NEXT I
1191    REM **      END PLOTTING SUBRT      **
1192    REM
1998    REM *         BNDRY PLOT SUBRT        *
2000    HPLOT 0,0 TO 0,191 TO 279,191 TO 279,0 TO 0,0
2010    RETURN
2998    REM *        CALC OPERATIONS SUB      *
3000    VTAB 13: HTAB 11: PRINT "...";: FLASH : PRINT
        "CALCULATING";: NORMAL : PRINT "..."
3010    VTAB 15: HTAB 2: PRINT "GET A CUP OF COFFEE, I'LL RING
        YOU!"
3020    PRINT "I HAVE TO PERFORM AT LEAST:"
3030    N2 = (NP + 1) * (NP + 1)
3040    HTAB 5: PRINT N2;" FUNCTION EVALUATIONS;"
3050    HTAB 5: PRINT N2 * 11;" MULTIPLICATIONS & DIVISIONS;"
3060    HTAB 5: PRINT N2 * 5;" ADDITIONS & SUBTRACTIONS;"
3070    HTAB 5: PRINT N2 * 6 + NP + 2;" COMPARISONS;"
3080    HTAB 5: PRINT "> =  ";N2 * 11 + NP + 9;" ASSIGNMENTS
        (MINIMUM ESTM.)"
3090    RETURN
3091    REM **      END CALC OPERTNS SBR    **
RUN
```

When RUNning the program, use the input values: A, B = −2.8, 2.8; C, D = −2.8, 2.8; and RHO, PHI, TH = 10, 50, 30. Experiment with the other example functions as well. You should even try entering a viewpoint you know will violate the front-to-back plotting requirement and observe the effect (e.g., RHO, PHI, TH = 10, −60, 20).

The plotting subroutine (lines 1000-1190) requires some explanation. The array $TV(K)$ must be initialized to show every point is initially visible. The array $BV(K)$ is initially set to zero, so no change is needed. The constants $N0$, $N1$, and $P5$ are defined in line 1010; their use will help speed execution. In line 1020 the previously considered point variables, $PH\%$ and $PV\%$, are initialized to represent the first point. The hidden point flag variable is set "ON" (line 1030).

Beginning with the loop at line 1040, each $X(I)$ spline is generated by successively considering new points $(NH\%, NV\%)$ (lines 1050 and 1100), branching to the hidden line subroutine (lines 1060 and 1110), and then resetting the previously considered point $(PH\%, PV\%)$ to $(NH\%, NV\%)$ (lines 1080 and 1120). Because the Y-splines at each end (ie., $Y = Y(0)$ and $Y = Y(NP)$) are also displayed, the segment between $(X(I), Y(NP), Z)$ and $(X(I+1), Y(NP), Z)$ is considered in lines 1150 − 60. The screen coordinates of the starting point of the $X(I)$th spline and its visibility status are retained in line 1070. It is recalled for use in lines 1170 − 80, where preparations are made for considering the segment between (X(I),Y(0),Z) and (X(I+1), Y(0),Z).

Finally, the subroutine is terminated in line 1140 when I = NP is detected. The subroutine must be terminated at this point since the Y(0)- and Y(NP)-splines terminate at X = X(NP).

There is an improvement which can be made to the hidden-line subroutine. It was omitted earlier since it will add additional execution time to an already long-running program, and the improved algorithm is more involved. Consider the situation in which transition is made from a previously hidden point to a visible point, or vice versa. The horizontal separation between such points is either zero or one.

Under the current subroutine, it is possible to have a section of visible line not plotted between such transition points.

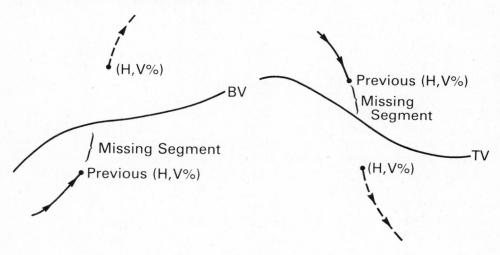

Figure 5.8.2

In the case of transition from visible-to-hidden, it is necessary to HPLOT TO either (H,BV(H)) or (H,TV(H)). However, the proper choice depends on whether the PRE-VIOUS point was visible from the top or from below. If the transition is from hidden-to-visible then we must HPLOT from either (H,BV(H)) or (H,TV(H)) to (H,V%). The proper choice depends on whether the CURRENT point is visible from the top or from below.

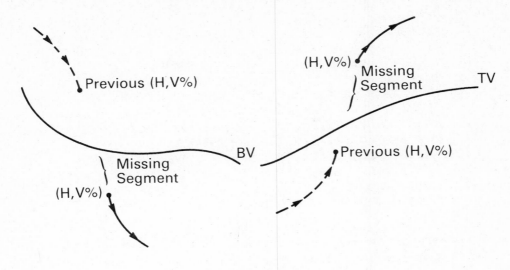

Figure 5.8.3

Since the type of visibility a point experiences is of importance, we must make provisions to remember the visibility status of the first point in the generation of each spline. This is necessary because at the completion of the X(I)th spline, the plotting routine returns to the initial point of the spline to display any visible points on the segment joining this point to the initial point of the next spline.

With these considerations in mind, make the following revisions in the hidden-line subroutine and the plotting subroutine.

<Modify CE5.8 to reflect the following changes>

```
37  REM   ********************************
38  REM   *  MODIFIED HIDDEN LINE SBRT   *
39  REM   ********************************
40  CH = NH% - PH%: IF CH = NO THEN CH = N1:PH% = NH% - N1
42  DH% =  SGN (CH):M = (NV% - PV%) /  ABS (CH):V = PV%
44  FOR H = PH% + DH% TO NH% STEP DH%
46  V = V + M:V% = V + P5
48  T% = V% > TV(H):B% = V% < BV(H)
50  IF T% AND B% THEN 70: REM  IF NOT VISIBLE THEN GOTO 70
52  TS =  NOT T%:BS =  NOT B%
54  IF TS THEN W% = TV(H):TV(H) = V%: REM  IF VISIBLE ABOVE
    THEN REMEMBER CURRENT UPPER BOUND IN W% AND RESET TO NEW
    BOUND.
56  IF BS THEN W% = BV(H):BV(H) = V%: REM  IF VISIBLE BELOW
    THEN REMEMBER CURRENT LOWER BOUND IN W% AND RESET TO NEW
    BOUND.
58  IF FL THEN  HPLOT H,W% TO H,V%:FL = NO: NEXT : RETURN: REM
    IF PREVIOUS PT WAS NOT VISIBLE THEN HPLOT FROM BOUNDARY TO
    NEW POINT. TURN NOT-VISIBLE FLAG 'OFF'.
60  HPLOT  TO H,V%: REM  PREV AND NEW PTS ARE BOTH VISIBLE.
```

```
62  NEXT
64  RETURN
70  IF FL THEN  NEXT : RETURN: REM  PREV AND NEW PTS NOT
    VISIBLE SO DO NOTHING.
72  FL = N1: REM  SET NOT-VISIBLE FLAG 'ON'.
74  IF TS THEN  HPLOT  TO H,TV(H): NEXT : RETURN: REM  IF PREV
    PT WAS VISIBLE FROM TOP THEN PLOT TO UPPER BOUNDARY.
76  HPLOT  TO H,BV(H): NEXT : RETURN: REM  PREV PT WAS VISIBLE
    FROM BELOW SO PLOT TO LOWER BOUNDARY.
1030  HPLOT PH%,PV%:FL = NO: REM  PLOT VERY FIRST POINT WHICH
      IS ALWAYS VISIBLE.
1070  SH% = NH%:SV% = NV%:SFL = FL:STS = TS:SBS = BS
1180  PH% = SH%:PV% = SV%:TS = STS:BS = SBS
RUN
```

Use the input parameters and example functions presented earlier to test this feature. Do you observe improved transition from hidden to visible points and vice versa; i.e., are the splines more complete near these points? _____

**Check Your Comprehension**
  What condition is being checked in line 50? _____
  What is the function of lines 70-76? _____
  What is the purpose of line 58? _____
  What do the variables TS and BS represent? _____
  In lines 1070 and 1180 it is necessary to remember and recall the status of TS and BS for the first point of a spline. Can you explain why? _____
  If you cannot see the purpose of changing line 1030 then experiment with using it in the original form to see what happens. Why is it needed? _____

**EXERCISE**   Modify the COMPREHENSIVE EXAMPLE program so that Y-splines are generated and hidden lines are removed. Assume the generation is from left to right. The viewpoint must be appropriately selected. Generally, one must have $0 < = $ TH $< = 180$ and RHO $> 0$.

**EXERCISE**   Include the X-splines at the endpoints $Y(0) = CC$ and $Y(NP) = DD$ in the previous exercise.

**EXERCISE**   Modify the program of Section 5.8.2 so the order of X- and Y-points considered is reversed.

**CHALLENGE**   Write a program to permit the user to select either method of principle spline generation.

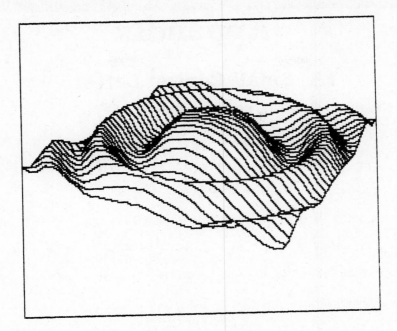

**Figure 5.8.4**

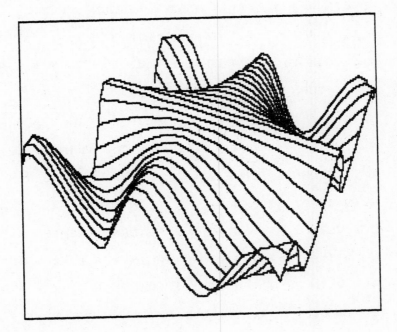

**Figure 5.8.5**

# Appendix

## 1A  Small Capital Letters

```
100   REM ALPHABET : SMALL CAPS

101   HLIN X + 1, X + 3 AT Y : HLIN X + 1, X + 3 AT Y +
      2 : VLIN Y + 1, Y + 4 AT X : VLIN Y + 1, Y + 4 AT
      X + 4 : RETURN : REM A

102   HLIN X + 1, X + 3 AT Y : HLIN X + 1, X + 3 AT Y +
      2 : HLIN X + 1, X + 3 AT Y + 4 : PLOT X + 4, Y + 1
      : PLOT X + 4, Y + 3 : VLIN Y, Y + 4 AT X : RETURN
      : REM B

103   HLIN X + 1,X + 4 AT Y : HLIN X + 1, X + 4 AT Y + 4
      : VLIN Y + 1, Y + 3 AT X : RETURN : REM C

104   HLIN X + 1, X + 3 AT Y : HLIN X + 1, X + 3 AT Y +
      4 : VLIN Y, Y + 4 AT X : VLIN Y + 1, Y + 3 AT X +
      4 : RETURN : REM D

105   HLIN X + 1, X + 4 AT Y : HLIN X + 1, X + 4 AT Y +
      4 : HLIN X + 1, X + 3 AT Y + 2 : VLIN Y, Y + 4 AT
      X : RETURN : REM E

106   HLIN X + 1, X + 4 AT Y : HLIN X + 1, X + 3 AT Y +
      2 : VLIN Y, Y + 4 AT X : RETURN : REM F

107   HLIN X + 1, X + 4 AT Y : HLIN X + 1, X + 4 AT Y +
      4 : VLIN Y, Y + 4 AT X : HLIN X + 3, X + 4 AT Y +
      2 : PLOT X + 4, Y + 3 : RETURN : REM G

108   HLIN X + 1, X + 3 AT Y + 2 : VLIN Y, Y + 4 AT X :
      VLIN Y, Y + 4 AT X + 4 : RETURN : REM H
```

```
109  HLIN X, X + 4 AT Y : HLIN X, X + 4 AT Y + 4 : VLIN
     Y + 1, Y + 3 AT X + 2 : RETURN : REM I

110  HLIN X + 1, X + 4 AT Y : HLIN X, X + 3 AT Y + 4 :
     VLIN Y + 1, Y + 3 AT X + 3 : PLOT X, Y + 3 :
     RETURN : REM J

111  VLIN Y, Y + 4 AT X : PLOT X + 4, Y : PLOT X + 3, Y
     + 1 : PLOT X + 2, Y + 2 : PLOT X + 3, Y + 3 : PLOT
     X + 4, Y + 4 : PLOT X + 1, Y + 2 : RETURN : REM K

112  VLIN Y, Y + 4 AT X : HLIN X + 1, X + 4 AT Y + 4 :
     RETURN : REM L

113  VLIN Y, Y + 4 AT X : VLIN Y, Y + 4 AT X + 4 : VLIN
     Y, Y + 1 AT X + 1 : VLIN Y, Y + 1 AT X + 3 : PLOT
     X + 2, Y + 2 : RETURN : REM M

114  VLIN Y, Y + 4 AT X : VLIN Y, Y + 4 AT X + 4 : VLIN
     Y, Y + 1 AT X + 1 : VLIN Y + 3, Y + 4 AT X + 3 :
     PLOT X + 2, Y + 2 : RETURN : REM N

115  HLIN X + 1, X + 3 AT Y : HLIN X + 1, X + 3 AT Y +
     4 : VLIN Y + 1, Y + 3 AT X : VLIN Y + 1, Y + 3 AT
     X + 4 : RETURN : REM O

116  VLIN Y, Y + 4 AT X : HLIN X + 1, X + 4 AT Y : HLIN
     X + 1, X + 4 AT Y + 2 : PLOT X + 4, Y + 1 : RETURN
     : REM P

117  HLIN X + 1, X + 3 AT Y : HLIN X + 1, X + 3 AT Y +
     4 : VLIN Y + 1, Y + 3 AT X : VLIN Y + 1, Y + 3 AT
     X + 4 : PLOT X + 2, Y + 2 : PLOT X + 3, Y + 3 :
     PLOT X + 3, Y + 5 : RETURN : REM Q
```

```
118    HLIN X + 1, X + 4 AT Y : HLIN X + 1, X + 4 AT Y +
       2 : VLIN Y, Y + 4 AT X : VLIN Y, Y + 1 AT X + 4 :
       REM R

119    HLIN X, X + 4 AT Y : HLIN X, X + 4 AT Y + 2 : HLIN
       X, X + 4 AT Y + 4 : PLOT X, Y + 1 : PLOT X + 4, Y
       + 3 : RETURN : REM S

120    HLIN X, X + 4 AT Y : VLIN Y + 1, Y + 4 AT X + 2 :
       RETURN : REM T

121    HLIN X, X + 4 AT Y + 4 : VLIN Y, Y + 3 AT X : VLIN
       Y, Y + 3 AT X + 4 : RETURN : REM U

122    VLIN Y, Y + 2 AT X : VLIN Y, Y + 2 AT X + 4 : PLOT
       X + 1, Y + 3 : PLOT X + 3, Y + 3 : PLOT X + 2, Y +
       4 : RETURN : REM V

123    PLOT X + 1, Y + 4 : PLOT X + 3, Y + 4 : VLIN Y, Y
       + 3 AT X : VLIN Y, Y + 3 AT X + 4 : VLIN Y + 2, Y
       + 3 AT X + 2 : RETURN : REM W

124    PLOT X, Y : PLOT X + 4, Y : PLOT X + 1, Y + 1 :
       PLOT X + 3, Y + 1 : PLOT X + 2, Y + 2 : PLOT X +
       1, Y + 3 : PLOT X + 3, Y + 3 : PLOT X, Y + 4 :
       PLOT X + 4, Y + 4 : RETURN : REM X

125    PLOT X, Y : PLOT X + 4, Y : PLOT X + 1, Y + 1 :
       PLOT X + 3, Y + 1 : VLIN Y + 2, Y + 4 AT X + 2 :
       RETURN : REM Y

126    HLIN X, X + 4 AT Y : HLIN X, X + 4 AT Y + 4 : PLOT
       X + 3, Y + 1 : PLOT X + 2, Y + 2 : PLOT X + 1, Y +
       3 : RETURN : REM Z
```

# 1B   Large Capital Letters

```
200   REM LARGE CAPS
201   VLIN Y + 1, Y + 8 AT X : VLIN Y + 1, Y + 8 AT X +
      6 : HLIN X + 1, X + 5 AT Y + 4 : HLIN X + 1, X + 5
      AT Y : RETURN : REM A
202   VLIN Y, Y + 8 AT X : HLIN X + 1, X + 5 AT Y : HLIN
      X + 1, X + 5 AT Y + 8 : HLIN X + 1, X + 4 AT Y + 4
      : VLIN Y + 1, Y + 2 AT X + 6 : VLIN Y + 6, Y + 7
      AT X + 6 : PLOT X + 5, Y + 3 : PLOT X + 5, Y + 5 :
      RETURN : REM B
203   VLIN Y + 1, Y + 7 AT X : HLIN X + 1, X + 5 AT Y:
      HLIN X + 1, X + 6 AT Y + 8 : RETURN : REM C
204   VLIN Y, Y + 8 AT X : VLIN Y + 2, Y + 6 AT X + 6 :
      HLIN X + 1, X + 4 AT Y : HLIN X + 1, X + 4 AT Y +
      8 : PLOT X + Y, Y + 1 : PLOT X + Y, Y + 7 : RETURN
      : REM D
205   VLIN Y, Y + 8 AT X : HLIN X + 1, X + 6 AT Y : HLIN
      X + 1, X + 6 AT Y + 8 : HLIN X + 1, X + 4 AT Y + 4
      : RETURN : REM E
206   VLIN Y, Y + 8 AT X : HLIN X + 1, X + 6 AT Y : HLIN
      X + 1, X + 4 AT Y + 4 : RETURN : REM F
207   VLIN Y, Y + 8 AT X : VLIN Y + 4, Y + 8 AT X + 6 :
      HLIN X + 1, X + 6 AT Y : HLIN X + 1, X + 6 AT Y +
      8 : HLIN X + 3, X + 5 AT Y + 4 : RETURN : REM G
208   VLIN Y, Y + 8 AT X : VLIN Y, Y + 8 AT X + 6 : HLIN
      X + 1, X + 5 AT Y + 4 : RETURN : REM H
```

```
209   HLIN X, X + 6 AT Y : HLIN X, X + 6 AT Y + 8 : VLIN
      Y + 1, Y + 7 AT X + 3 : RETURN : REM I

210   HLIN X + 1, X + 6 AT Y : VLIN Y + 1, Y + 8 AT X +
      4 : VLIN Y + 6, Y + 8 AT X : HLIN X + 1, X + 3 AT
      Y + 8 : RETURN : REM J

211   VLIN Y, Y + 8 AT X : PLOT X + 1, Y + 4 : PLOT X +
      2, Y + 4 : PLOT X + 3, Y + 5 : PLOT X + 3, Y + 3 :
      PLOT X + 4, Y + 6 : PLOT X + 4, Y + 2 : PLOT X +
      5, Y + 7 : PLOT X + 5, Y + 1 : PLOT X + 6, Y + 8 :
      PLOT X + 6, Y : RETURN : REM K

212   VLIN Y, Y + 8 AT X : HLIN X + 1, X + 6 AT Y + 8 :
      RETURN : REM L

213   VLIN Y, Y + 8 AT X : VLIN Y, Y + 8 AT X + 6 : PLOT
      X + 1, Y + 1 : PLOT X + 5, Y + 1 : PLOT X + 2, Y +
      2 : PLOT X + 4, Y + 2 : PLOT X + 3, Y + 3 : PLOT X
      + 1, Y : PLOT X + 5, Y : RETURN : REM M

214   VLIN Y, Y + 8 AT X : VLIN Y, Y + 8 AT X + 6 : VLIN
      Y, Y + 2 AT X + 1 : VLIN Y + 6, Y + 8 AT X + 5 :
      PLOT X + 2, Y + 3 : PLOT X + 3, Y + 4 : PLOT X +
      4, Y + 5 : RETURN : REM N

215   VLIN Y + 1, Y + 7 AT X : VLIN Y + 1, Y + 7 AT X +
      6 : HLIN X + 1, X + 5 AT Y : HLIN X + 1, X + 5 AT
      Y + 8 : RETURN : REM O

216   VLIN Y, Y + 8 AT X : VLIN Y, Y + 4 AT X + 6 : HLIN
      X + 1, X + 5 AT Y : HLIN X + 1, X + 5 AT Y + 4 :
      RETURN : REM P
```

```
217   VLIN Y + 1, Y + 7 AT X : VLIN Y + 1, Y + 7 AT X +
      6 : HLIN X + 1, X + 5 AT Y : HLIN X + 1, X + 5 AT
      Y + 8 : PLOT X + 3, Y + 6 : PLOT X + 4, Y + 7 :
      PLOT X + 5, Y + 9 : RETURN : REM Q
218   VLIN Y, Y + 8 AT X : VLIN Y, Y + 4 AT X + 6 : HLIN
      X + 1, X + 5 AT Y : HLIN X + 1, X + 5 AT Y + 4 :
      PLOT X + 3, Y + 5 : PLOT X + 4, Y + 6 : PLOT X +
      5, Y + 7 : PLOT X + 6, Y + 8 : RETURN : REM R
219   HLIN X, X + 6 AT Y : HLIN X, X + 6 AT Y + 4 : HLIN
      X, X + 6 AT Y + 8 : VLIN Y + 1, Y + 3 AT X : VLIN
      Y + 5, Y + 7 AT X + 6 : RETURN : REM S
220   HLIN X, X + 6 AT Y : VLIN Y + 1, Y + 8 AT X + 3 :
      RETURN : REM T
221   VLIN Y, Y + 7 AT X : VLIN Y, Y + 7 AT X + 6 : HLIN
      X + 1, X + 5 AT Y + 8 : RETURN : REM U
222   VLIN Y, Y + 5 AT X : VLIN Y, Y + 5 AT X + 6 : PLOT
      X + 1, Y + 6 : PLOT X + 5, Y + 6 : PLOT X + 2, Y +
      7 : PLOT X + 4, Y + 7 : PLOT X + 3, Y + 8 : RETURN
      : REM V
223   VLIN Y, Y + 6 AT X : VLIN Y, Y + 6 AT X + 6 : PLOT
      X + 1, Y + 7 : PLOT X + 5, Y + 7 : PLOT X + 2, Y +
      8 : PLOT X + 4, Y + 8 : VLIN Y + 6, Y + 7 AT X + 3
      : RETURN : REM W
224   VLIN Y + 3, Y + 5 AT X + 3 : PLOT X, Y : PLOT X +
      1, Y + 1 : PLOT X + 2, Y + 2 : PLOT X + 4, Y + 2 :
      PLOT X + 5, Y + 1 : PLOT X + 6, Y : PLOT X + 2, Y
```

```
    + 6 : PLOT X + 1, Y + 7 : PLOT X, Y + 8 : PLOT X +
    4, Y + 6 : PLOT X + 5, Y + 7 : PLOT X + 6, Y + 8 :
    RETURN : REM X
225 VLIN Y + 3, Y + 8 AT X + 3 : PLOT X, Y : PLOT X +
    1, Y + 1 : PLOT X + 2, Y + 2 : PLOT X + 4, Y + 2 :
    PLOT X + 5, Y + 1 : PLOT X + 6, Y : RETURN : REM Y
226 HLIN X, X + 6 AT Y : HLIN X, X + 6 AT Y + 8 : PLOT
    X, Y + 7 : PLOT X + 1, Y + 6 : PLOT X + 2, Y + 5 :
    PLOT X + 3, Y + 4 : PLOT X + 4, Y + 3 : PLOT X +
    5, Y + 2 : PLOT X + 6, Y + 1 : RETURN : REM Z
```

# 1C   Binary Alphabet

```
500   REM BINARY ALPHABET

501   A$(1) = "01110100011111110000110001"

502   A$(2) = "111101000111110100011110"

503   A$(3) = "01111100001000010000011111"

504   A$(4) = "11110100011000110001111110"

505   A$(5) = "111111000011111010000011111"

506   A$(6) = "1111110000111101000010000"

507   A$(7) = "11111100001001110001111111"

508   A$(8) = "10001100011111110000110001"

509   A$(9) = "111110010000100001001111"

510   A$(10) = "11111000100001010010111111"

511   A$(11) = "100011001011100100101010001"

512   A$(12) = "100001000010000100001111"
```

```
513   A$(13) = "110111101110101100011000110001"

514   A$(14) = "11001110011010110011100011"

515   A$(15) = "01110100011000110001000101110"

516   A$(16) = "11111100011111110000010000"

517   A$(17) = "011101000110101100110001110"

518   A$(18) = "111111000111111100101000010001"

519   A$(19) = "11111100001111100001111111"

520   A$(20) = "11111001000010000100000100"

521   A$(21) = "10001100011000110001000101110"

522   A$(22) = "100011000110001010010000100"

523   A$(23) = "100011000110101110101110001"

524   A$(24) = "100010101000100010101010001"

525   A$(25) = "1000101010001000010000100"

526   A$(26) = "1111100010001000100011111"
```

# 3A Numeration Systems

Man is accustomed to performing arithmetic operations with decimal numbers. A computer does its processing using a binary number system. The hexadecimal number system provides a convenient means by which man can communicate more easily with computers. It is necessary for the serious programmer to become proficient in converting from one number system to another.

The decimal system, or base ten (10), is so named because it has ten symbols or digits (0, 1, 2, 3, 4, 5, 6, 7, 8, 9). The binary system, or base two (2), consists of two digits (0, 1). Similarly, the hexadecimal system or base sixteen (16) has sixteen symbols (0, 1, 2, 3, 4, 5, 6, 7, 8, 9, A, B, C, D, E, F). A problem arises when denoting base 16 because there are no familiar symbols beyond 9. The standard practice for resolving this difficulty is to extend the system by using letters of the alphabet. It has become customary to equate the letter A with 10, B with 11, C with 12, D with 13, E with 14, and F with 15.

Now that the symbols used for denoting each numeration system are established, it is time to learn how to count. With no intent toward insulting your intelligence, base 10 will be considered first, not because you do not understand the system, but to establish the pattern which pervades all numeration systems.

Counting is the operation of adding one (1) to some previous number. This procedure usually presents no difficulty until the last digit in a particular base system is encountered. For example, when counting in base 10, what happens when (9 + 1) is to be performed? You have learned the answer is 10. But it is important to this discussion to understand how 10 is obtained.

If 9 were to be written as a two-digit number, it would be represented as 09. When 1 is added to 09 (since 9 is the last digit in the system) the cycle begins again. The digit in the next position to the left is increased by 1. Thus, (9 + 1) is equivalent to (09 + 1) which becomes 10. Similarly, (19 + 1) becomes 20, (29 + 1) becomes 30 until (99 + 1) is encountered. Thinking of 99 as the three-digit number, 099, and following the previously illustrated pattern, (099 + 1) becomes 100. Extending the counting, (999 + 1) = 1000, (9999 + 1) = 10000, and so on.

Following the same pattern, when counting in base 16,

F + 1 = 10 (0F + 1 = 10),

1F + 1 = 20,

2F + 1 = 30,

AF + 1 = BF, and

FF + 1 = 100 (0FF + 1 = 100).

Counting in base 2 occurs in a similar manner, but it appears more complicated because there are only two digits. Except for the first two counting numbers, binary numbers will always require more digits. Some examples are:

1 + 1 = 10 (01 + 1 = 10),

11 + 1 = 100 (011 + 1 = 100), and

101 + 1 = 110

Table 3A1 illustrates counting within these three numeration systems, with numerals appearing on the same line being equivalent to each other. For example, 18 (base 10), 12 (base 16), and 10010 (base 2), all represent the same quantity. To explain this phenomenon, an understanding of place value is required.

| Decimal | Binary | Hexadecimal |
|---|---|---|
| 0 | 0 | 0 |
| 1 | 1 | 1 |
| 2 | 10 | 2 |
| 3 | 11 | 3 |
| 4 | 100 | 4 |
| 5 | 101 | 5 |
| 6 | 110 | 6 |
| 7 | 111 | 7 |
| 8 | 1000 | 8 |
| 9 | 1001 | 9 |
| 10 | 1010 | A |
| 11 | 1011 | B |
| 12 | 1100 | C |
| 13 | 1101 | D |
| 14 | 1110 | E |
| 15 | 1111 | F |
| 16 | 10000 | 10 |
| 17 | 10001 | 11 |
| 18 | 10010 | 12 |
| 19 | 10011 | 13 |
| 20 | 10100 | 14 |
| 21 | 10101 | 15 |
| 22 | 10110 | 16 |
| 23 | 10111 | 17 |
| 24 | 11000 | 18 |
| . | . | . |
| . | . | . |
| 32 | 100000 | 20 |
| 79 | 1001111 | 4F |
| 255 | 11111111 | FF |
| 256 | 100000000 | 100 |

Table 3.A.1

The decimal number,

247 means $2 * 100 + 4 * 10 + 7 * 1$

The hexadecimal number,

A3F means $A * 256 + 3 * 16 + F * 1 =$

$10 * 256 + 3 * 16 + 15 * 1$

and the binary number,

101101 means $1 * 32 + 0 * 16 + 1 * 8 + 1 * 4 + 0 * 2 + 1 * 1$

Moving from right to left, notice each new place value is a multiple of the particular base with the previous place value. Table 3A2 shows the place values associated with each of the numeration systems.

Place Values

| Numeration Systems | Decimal | $100000 = 10^5$ | $10000 = 10^4$ | $1000 = 10^3$ | $100 = 10^2$ | $10 = 10^1$ | $1 = 10^0$ |
|---|---|---|---|---|---|---|---|
| | Hexadecimal | $1048576 = 16^5$ | $65536 = 16^4$ | $4096 = 16^3$ | $256 = 16^2$ | $16 = 16^1$ | $1 = 16^0$ |
| | Binary | $32 = 2^5$ | $16 = 2^4$ | $8 = 2^3$ | $4 = 2^2$ | $2 = 2^1$ | $1 = 2^0$ |

Table 3.A.2

Now, using Table 3A2 to verify the equivalencies mentioned above

18 (base 10) means $1 * 10 + 8 * 1 = 18$,
10010 (base 2) means $1 * 16 + 0 * 8 + 0 * 4 + 1 * 2 + 0 * 1 = 18$,
12 (base 16) means $1 * 16 + 2 * 1 = 18$.
As another example,
79 (base 10) $= 7 * 10 + 9 * 1 = 79$
1001111 (base 2) $= 1 * 64 + 0 * 32 + 0 * 16 + 1 * 8 + 1 * 4 + 1 * 2 + 1 * 1 = 79$
4F (base 16) $= 4 * 16 + F * 1 = 4 * 16 + 15 * 1 = 79$

The reader should verify the other equivalencies indicated in Table 3A1 to assure an understanding of the conversion process.

Now, how is binary arithmetic associated with electronic computers? Very simplistically, a computer consists of a series of integrated circuits and other electronic components which behave like switches. A switch is either OFF (denoted by 0) or ON (denoted by 1). Counting in binary arithmetic is related to changing the status of these switches. The operations $0 + 0$, $0 + 1$, $1 + 0$, and $1 + 1$ define the four possible changes which can occur. These operations are described in Figure 3A1.

Note the only time the status of the left switch is changed is when the right switch is ON and receives a change of status. The operation, $1 + 1 = 10$, is what connects two switches. Similarly, $011 + 1 = 100$ is the symbolic representation of a status change which involves three connected switches.

| Case | Binary Operation | Status of Adjacent Switches |
|---|---|---|
| 1 | $\begin{array}{r} 1 \\ +\ 0 \\ \hline 1 \end{array}$ or $\begin{array}{r} 01 \\ +\ 0 \\ \hline 01 \end{array}$ | ⊕ ⊕ right switch on / left switch off / do not change status of right switch — ⊕ ⊕ right switch on / left switch off |
| 2 | $\begin{array}{r} 0 \\ +\ 1 \\ \hline 1 \end{array}$ $\begin{array}{r} 00 \\ +\ 1 \\ \hline 01 \end{array}$ | ⊕ ⊕ right switch off / left switch off / change status of right switch — ⊕ ⊕ right switch on / left switch off |
| 3 | $\begin{array}{r} 0 \\ +\ 0 \\ \hline 0 \end{array}$ $\begin{array}{r} 00 \\ +\ 0 \\ \hline 0 \end{array}$ | ⊕ ⊕ right switch off / left switch off / do not change status of right switch — ⊕ ⊕ right switch off / left switch off |
| 4 | $\begin{array}{r} 1 \\ +\ 1 \\ \hline 10 \end{array}$ $\begin{array}{r} 01 \\ +\ 1 \\ \hline 10 \end{array}$ | ⊕ ⊕ right switch on / left switch off / change status of right switch — ⊕ ⊕ right switch off / left switch on |

Figure 3.A.1

Consider the internal memory of the microcomputer as a very lengthy series of these binary digits, which are more frequently called bits. On the Apple II Plus and IIe computer systems, four bits are grouped together to form a nybble. Two nybbles, or eight bits, then form a byte. Two adjacent bytes might appear as illustrated in Figure 3A2.

Because it is difficult to remember strings of 0's and 1's, the hexadecimal number system makes it easier to remember the contents of a nybble or byte. A simple way to convert binary to hexadecimal is to consider the binary string as a sequence of nybbles. Table 3A3 demonstrates there are sixteen possible four-bit arrangements, which suggests the binary contents of any nybble can be described as a hexadecimal number.

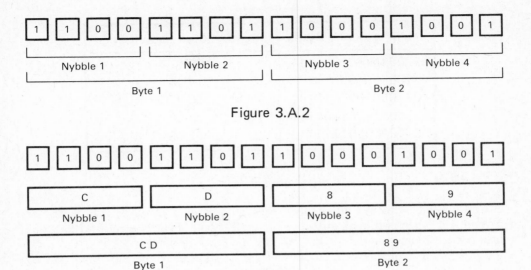

Figure 3.A.2

Figure 3.A.3

| Binary Representation of a Nybble | Decimal Equivalent | Hexadecimal Equivalent |
|---|---|---|
| 0000 | 0 | 0 |
| 0001 | 1 | 1 |
| 0010 | 2 | 2 |
| 0011 | 3 | 3 |
| 0100 | 4 | 4 |
| 0101 | 5 | 5 |
| 0110 | 6 | 6 |
| 0111 | 7 | 7 |
| 1000 | 8 | 8 |
| 1001 | 9 | 9 |
| 1010 | 10 | A |
| 1011 | 11 | B |
| 1100 | 12 | C |
| 1101 | 13 | D |
| 1110 | 14 | E |
| 1111 | 15 | F |

Table 3.A.3

Reconsidering the two adjacent bytes from Figure 3A2, the hexadecimal equivalents for each nybble and byte are translated in Figure 3A3. Other equivalencies are provided in Table 3A4 for you to verify.

When two nybbles are adjacent, it is common to refer to the left nybble as the "high order nybble" and the right nybble as the "low order nybble." For example, in Figure 3A2, nybble 1 is the high order nybble of byte 1; nybble 2 is low order nybble

| Two Adjacent Bytes | Hexadecimal Equivalence |
|---|---|
| 1000101100001111 | 8B0F |
| 1100100100010100 | C914 |
| 0110001000110101 | A235 |
| 0100111101001111 | 4F4F |
| 0110110101111110 | 6D7E |

Table 3.A.4

of byte 1. Nybbles 3 and 4 are, respectively, high order and low order nybbles of byte 2. Similarly, when two bytes are adjacent, the left byte (byte 1) is referred to as the high order byte and the right byte (byte 2) is the low order byte.

Each byte represents a memory location or address. Numerical values can be placed in memory location through a POKE command, but only decimal numbers are allowed to be POKEd. Thus, POKE 230, 32 assigns the decimal number 32 to reside in address 230.

But how does one assign an address for numbers in hexadecimal form? The obvious answer is to convert the hexadecimal number to its decimal equivalent. For example, suppose one wants to place the hexadecimal number \$4001 (rather than writing base 16 each time, the \$ prefix is commonly used to denote hexadecimal numbers) into memory. Since only two hexadecimal numbers can "fit" into one byte, two adjacent bytes are required, a high order byte and a low order byte. Assuming memory addresses 104 and 103 are, respectively, the high order and low order bytes, Figure 3A4 illustrates that \$40 is to reside in high order address 104 and \$01 in low order address 103. Since only decimal numbers can be POKEd into memory addresses, \$40 converts to decimal number 64 ($4 * 16 + 0 * 1$) and \$01 converts to decimal number 1 ($0 * 16 + 1 * 1$). Hence POKE 104, 64: POKE 103, 1 accomplishes the task.

| high order byte 104 | | low order byte 103 | |
|---|---|---|---|
| 2 | 0 | 0 | 0 |

Figure 3.A.4

As you progress through the book, you will discover this example was not arbitrarily selected, but actually has a very useful purpose.

# Index

# Index